THE AMERICAN NEGRO
HIS HISTORY AND LITERATURE

THE
AFRO-AMERICAN PRESS
AND
ITS EDITORS

I. Garland Penn

AYER COMPANY, PUBLISHERS, INC.
SALEM, NEW HAMPSHIRE 03079

Reprint Edition, 1988
Ayer Company, Publishers, Inc.
382 Main Street
Salem, New Hampshire 03079
All rights reserved

*

Library of Congress Catalog Card No. 69–18574

*

Reprinted from a copy in the collection of
Harvard College Library

*

Manufactured in the United States of America

ISBN 0-4050-1887-9

General Editor
WILLIAM LOREN KATZ

I. GARLAND PENN WAS BORN OCTOBER 7, 1867, IN New Glasgow, Virginia. Educated at the Lynchburg, Virginia, high school and at the Rust, Mississippi, and Wiley, Texas colleges for Negroes, he was a principal in the public school system of Lynchburg, an editor of the short-lived Negro newspaper, *The Lynchburg Virginia Laborer,* and a correspondent for several newspapers, including *The New York Age.* He was also National Commissioner of Negro Exhibits at the 1895 Atlanta Exposition, where he received a Gold Medal for his excellent exhibits. He married in 1889 and had seven children.

Later making his home in Cincinnati, Ohio, Penn was a prominent public speaker, a business man, a Republican, a trustee of several Negro colleges, an officer of the Cincinnati Board of Education for Negroes, and a long-time activist in the Colored Methodist Episcopal Church. He served as Corresponding Secretary of both the Freedmen's Aid Society and the Negro Young People's Christian and Educational Congress and was Assistant General Secretary of the Epworth League—all in the C.M.E.

Church. With J. W. E. Bowen, he coedited *The United Negro: His Problems and His Progress* (a six-hundred-page compilation of the addresses and proceedings of the 1902 Negro Young People's Christian and Educational Congress) and edited the *Souvenir Official Program And Music* of the 1906 Christian and Educational Congress. He also coauthored *Seven Graded Sunday School* (1893) and authored *The College of Life or Self-Educator* (1896).

Penn was only twenty-four when he published *The Afro-American Press and Its Editors* (1891), an ambitious book. The book is divided into two parts. The first part takes up all of the Afro-American newspapers and magazines, from *Freedom's Journal* (1827) to 1891. The second part, which is very long, consists of many sketches of editors and correspondents (men and women) of Afro-American newspapers, plus opinions of eminent Negro men on the Afro-American press, its editors' mission, and other chapters on the relation of the Negro press to the white press (including Negroes who write for white newspapers and magazines), the Afro-American League and the Associated Correspondents of Race Newspapers. There are scores of photographs throughout the book.

There have been later, somewhat different, sometimes better, critical studies of the Afro-American press by Frederick G. Detweiler, Elizabeth D. Johns (unpublished manuscript), G. James Fleming (A.B. thesis and manuscript for Gunnar Myrdal's *An*

American Dilemma, both unpublished, the latter on microfilm), Vishnu V. Oak, Maxwell R. Brooks, Roy L. Hill, and Armistead S. Pride (unpublished doctoral dissertation on microfilm). But *The Afro-American Press And Its Editors* stands as a landmark for its period.

Ernest Kaiser
SCHOMBURG COLLECTION
NEW YORK PUBLIC LIBRARY

THE

AFRO-AMERICAN PRESS,

AND

ITS EDITORS

Yours fraternally,
I. Garland Penn.

THE

AFRO-AMERICAN PRESS,

AND

ITS EDITORS

By I. GARLAND PENN,

PRINCIPAL IN LYNCHBURG, VA., SCHOOLS, AND EX-EDITOR LYNCH-
BURG, VA., LABORER, WITH CONTRIBUTIONS BY

Hon. Frederick Douglass, Hon. John R. Lynch, Hon. J. T. Settle, Hon. D. A.
Straker. Hon. Jere A. Brown, Hon. T. Thomas Fortune. Hon John Mercer
Langston, Hon. P. B. S. Pinchback. Prof. W. S. Scarborough, Prof.
J. H. Lawson, Prof. Booker T. Washington, Prof. George E.
Stephens. Prof. Frank Trigg, Bishop B W. Arnett,
D. D., Rev. J C Price. D. D., Rev. T. G. Stewart,
D. D., Rev. A A Burleigh Rev. L. J.
Coppin. D. D . James T Still. M. D.,
William H. Johnson. M D.,
and Mrs. N. F Mossell.

Souls dwell in printer's type.—*Joseph Ames.*

Ink is the blood of the printing Press.—*Milton.*

Hostile newspapers are more to be feared than bayonets.—*Napoleon.*

I am myself a gentleman of the press and need no other escutcheon.
—*Beaconsfield.*

In the long fierce struggle for freedom the press, like the church,
counted its martyrs by thousands.—*President Garfield.*

SPRINGFIELD, MASS.
WILLEY & CO., PUBLISHERS.
1891.

CLARK W. BRYAN & CO., PRINTERS,
SPRINGFIELD, MASS
CHARLES VAN VLACK, ELECTROTYPER.

TO
THE UNCONQUERABLE HOST OF
AFRO-AMERICANS
WHO ARE LAYING THEIR SACRIFICES
UPON THE EDITORIAL ALTAR
FOR THEIR RACE,
THIS VOLUME IS RESPECTFULLY
DEDICATED.

INTRODUCTION.

" We live in deeds, not years ; in thoughts, not breaths ;
In feelings, not in figures on a dial ;
We should count time by heart throbs ; he most lives
Who thinks most, feels the noblest, acts the best."

Having been requested by Mr. Penn to write a brief introduction to his book, I cheerfully consented to do so from several considerations. In the first place, I admire the manly energy, venture, and intellectual power displayed by him in undertaking to chronicle facts concerning Colored American journalism. Then again, I heartily love to encourage intellectual and moral efforts of young Colored American men and women. For the last ten years, I have endeavored to do this as a teacher, associate, and friend. Suidas relates that Thucydides, when a boy, listened with delight to Herodotus as he recited publicly his famous history at the great Olympic festival, and that he was so deeply moved that he shed tears. Thucydides was so inspired by the occasion that he finally became a more distinguished historian than Herodotus himself. It is possible that a perusal of this unpretentious sketch may so energize and inspire some boy or girl, young man or woman, that he or she will determine to perform for the race a greater service than Mr. Penn has rendered.

I. HIS BIRTH AND EARLY TRAINING.

Irvine Garland Penn was born in the year 1867, in New Glasgow, a small village in Amherst County, Virginia. His father and mother, Isham Penn and Mariah Penn, were fully aware of the superior advantages of a public school training to their children, and moved to the city of Lynchburg when Irvine was five years old. He passed with success through the primary and grammar grades of the schools, and in 1882 entered the junior class of the high school. Circumstances, over which he had no control, prevented him from attending school during the

INTRODUCTION.

succeeding school year, and, in consequence, he taught a school
in Bedford County, Virginia. After teaching for one school year,
he decided to re-enter the high school, from which he graduated
in 1886. Before he graduated, he accepted a position on the
editorial staff of *The Lynchburg Laborer*.

II. AS AN EDUCATOR.

The subject of our sketch has had almost five years experience
as a teacher, and has successfully managed county and city
schools. During 1883-4, he taught with credit to himself, and
satisfaction to his superintendent and patrons, a school in Bedford
County, Virginia. During the school year 1886-7, he superin-
tended a school in Amherst County, Virginia. In 1887 he was
elected as a teacher in the public schools of Lynchburg, and, in a
short time, arose to the position of principal. Though he is
young, his executive ability enables him to discharge well the
duties of his responsible post.

Mr. Penn seeks to inform himself on the principles and
methods of education. He aims to keep abreast of the times by
purchasing and studying the works of leading writers on educational methods. He is in deep sympathy with The New Education, which has so materially changed in the last eight years our
educational modes and systems. Nor is he insensible to the
merits and excellencies of leading Colored American educators,
but aims to learn from all that he may make his own school the
more excellent. He has attended several institutes for teachers,
and exhibited earnestness and industry in class recitations. As
an educator, he takes as his motto—"Labor et perseverentia
omnia vincunt." (Labor and perseverance conquer all things.)

III. AS AN EDITOR AND WRITER.

The subject of our sketch accepted a position upon the editorial
staff of *The Lynchburg Laborer* before his graduation. In 1886
Messrs. Penn and Johnson purchased it, and Mr. Penn took
control of the editorial department. The paper was not properly
supported, and its publication was suspended. As editor of this
paper, Mr. Penn proved himself a skilled and forcible writer.
Though he was only about twenty years of age, he evinced a good
acquaintance with practical life and the needs of the race. He
freely and frequently discussed questions relating to the material,

intellectual, moral, and religious welfare of his people and state. The unusual ability displayed by this youthful editor won for him laudable encomiums, even from several white editors in Virginia. *The Spirit of the Valley*, edited by D. Sheffey Lewis, said: "We have received *The Lynchburg Virginia Laborer*, edited by I. Garland Penn. It is edited with dignity and ability. *The Lynchburg Daily Advance* gave this testimony: "We most cheerfully commend *The Lynchburg Virginia Laborer* to all the sons of toil."

Our subject ardently loves newspaper work. He was once a pleasing and trenchant writer for *The Richmond Planet* and *The Virginia Lancet*. He is at present a correspondent for *The Knoxville Negro World* and *The New York Age*. He seems to observe closely, and he expresses his ideas with great clearness and strength. No one needs to read a sentence of Addison or Washington Irving twice to understand it. This may with truth be said of the young man whose life we are now considering.

IV. AS A SPEAKER.

Mr. Penn is an easy, fluent speaker. Though he has on several occasions been requested to make political speeches in the Old Dominion, he prefers to confine his speech-making to educational subjects. He has frequently delivered discourses to Sunday-Schools, and has been, in several instances, invited to speak on prominent public occasions. At the annual conference of the Colored M. E. Church which met in Charlottesville in July, 1889, Mr. Penn delivered a convincing address, advocating the establishment of a Theological and Normal School within Virginia.

V. HIS REPUTATION.

It may be readily affirmed from what has been said, that Mr. Penn is one of the few young men of our state who enjoys national recognition. He has on several occasions been honored by some of our leading men. On March 16, 1889, a fine cut and well-written sketch of him appeared in *The Freeman* of Indianapolis. Creditable sketches of him have also adorned the brilliant columns of *The Cleveland Gazette* and *The Negro World* of Knoxville. His publication of his intention to write a history of Colored American journalism has brought him into closer contact with the foremost men of our race, and caused him to receive numerous complimentary notices.

INTRODUCTION.

He has been repeatedly honored, too, by the people of his own state. He was twice appointed commissioner at Lynchburg for the Petersburg Industrial Association. He is Recording Steward of the Jackson Street M. E. Church and Superintendent of the Sunday-School. The business tact of our subject was fully recognized in his election as Secretary of the Board of Directors of the Lynchburg Real Estate Loan and Trust Company.

Mr. Penn is a member of the Colored M. E. Church, and a man of good moral character. He respects himself, and is respected by his friends and acquaintances.

VI. HIS PRESENT WORK.

The work for which this introduction is prepared will be of no little benefit to the race. It will serve as a cyclopædia of information on a power which has exerted an untold influence on our progress. "Afro-American Journalism and its editors" must of necessity cover a broad field. Its conception is grand, and the labor and culture essential to its accomplishment are great and varied. It may be thought by some that Mr. Penn is too young for the undertaking. The fallacy of such an idea is apparent from the fact, that the world's literature is greatly indebted to young men and women.

Thomas Sackville wrote, at the age of twenty-three, "A Mirror for Magistrates," and "Rare Ben Johnson," at the same age, produced "Every Man in his Humor." "The Fall of Robespierre" was finished by Samuel Taylor Coleridge before he was twenty-two, and "Hours of Idleness" was completed by Lord Byron, at the age of twenty. Amelie Rives conceived and brought forth "The Quick and the Dead," before she was twenty-one, and Phillis Wheatley issued a volume of poems before she was twenty. "Pleasures of Hope," "Essay on Criticism," "As a Man and Not a Man," were produced, respectively, by Thomas Campbell, Alexander Pope, and A. A. Whitman, when each was about twenty. How remarkable it is that Euripides penned a laudable tragedy and William Cullen Bryant wrote "Thanatopsis," when they were each eighteen; that Aristophanes, at the age of seventeen, exhibited his first comedy; and that Robert Burns and Hannah More produced, respectively, "Handsome Nell" and "The Search after Happiness," when each was about sixteen.

INTRODUCTION.

And what shall we say of that wonderful instance of precocious mentality, Thomas Chatterton, who, at the age of eleven, wrote excellent verses, and who, before he was eighteen, successfully forged descriptions, names, and poems from the antiquated coffer of Canynge, in the church at Bristol?

An investigation of Colored American literature reveals the fact, that most of our literature was produced before our authors were thirty-five years of age. This is certainly true of the works of B. T. Tanner; W. S. Scarborough; R. C. O. Benjamin; Phillis Wheatley; A. A. Whitman; T. T. Fortune; E. A. Randolph; J. J. Coles; C. W. B. Gordon; and others whom I might mention. It may not be inappropriate for me to state, at this juncture, that "The Negro Race, a Pioneer in Civilization," was penned when I was almost twenty-two; "The Life and Times of Paul," at twenty-four; "Science, Art, and Methods of Teaching," at twenty-six; and "Freedom and Progress" is now ready for press.

In the light of these historic facts, let no one think or say that Mr. Penn is too young and inexperienced for the compilation of his valuable work. Let us be thankful that among us are young men and women who are able to think and pen thoughts worthy of themselves and race. Let us encourage, by word and deed, every intellectual and moral effort put forth by our young men and women for the enlightenment and advancement of our people.

This grand work should illumine with its light every home of our beloved state, and every fireside of the Colored Americans of our country. Its many principles and precepts; its record of struggles and conflicts, born of contending forces; its narration of the lives and deeds of energetic, intelligent men and women are well calculated to impart useful knowledge, beget lofty aspirations, and direct the life to high, manly, womanly achievements. Its every sentence is pregnant with wholesome instruction, and its every page admonishes us to exert our best endeavors to prevent and allay racial antagonism and estrangement, and to labor for the time when white and colored citizens alike will vie with each other in making Virginia the foremost state in the Nation.

DANIEL B. WILLIAMS.

Professor of Ancient Languages, and Instructor in Methods of Teaching in the V. N. & C. I., Ettrick P. O., Va., November 7, 1889.

PREFACE.

In preparing this work on the Afro-American Press, I am not unmindful of the fact, that while I pursue somewhat of a beaten road I deal with a work which has proven a power in the promotion of truth, justice and equal rights for an oppressed people. The reader cannot fail to recognize some achievement won by that people, the measure of whose rights is yet being questioned, and will readily see that the social, moral, political and educational ills of the Afro-American have been fittingly championed by these Afro-American journals and their editors. Certainly, the importance and magnitude of the work done by the Afro-American Press, the scope of its influence, and the beneficent results accruing from its labors, cannot fail of appreciation.

In seeking the information contained in this volume, great pains have been taken, and expense incurred to insure its truth and accuracy. The aid of those of experienced years, of both races, has been secured. The information has been carefully given and the facts culled and put together with the utmost care and thought.

Believing that credit is at all times due those who merit it, I am pleased to announce the names of some friends to whom I shall be ever grateful, and for whose kindness I shall always be ready to say words expressive of my thankfulness:

Mr. Jno. J. Zuille, an Afro-American printer of abolition times; P. W. Ray, M. D.; Prof. R. T. Greener; Miss Florence Ray; Mr. Robert H. Hamilton; Editors: A. M. Hodges, T. Thos. Fortune; R. H. Hamilton; Dr. Alex. Crummell; Hon. Frederick Douglass; Dr. William H. Johnson; Mr. John H. Deyo; Prof. Joseph E. Jones, D. D.; Bishop Benj. W. Arnett; Hon. J. J. Spellman, and others. These gentlemen and ladies I greatly thank for the loan of books, papers, periodicals, and for their kindness for gratuitous information. I also remember the aid of Hon. E. E. Cooper, editor of *The Freeman*, for the loan of some cuts, and the *New South*, at Beaufort, S. C., and other papers, for gratuitous editorial mention. Above all, I can not forget the aid of friendly interest as well as the great honor my

PREFACE.

distinguished friend and brother, Prof. D. B. Williams, A. M., of the Virginia Normal and Collegiate Institute does me in the association of his name with this poor effort. As the reader will note, Prof. Williams has written the introductory sketch, for which I am under great obligations to him.

The object in putting forth this feeble effort is not for the praise of men or for the reaping of money, but to promote the future welfare of Afro-American journalism by telling to its constituents the story of its heroic labors in their behalf. As I have said in my circular to editors, January 1st, 1890, so say I now: "I believe that the greatest reason why our papers are not better supported is because the Afro-Americans do not sufficiently comprehend the responsibilities and magnitude of the work."

If the eyes of my people shall be opened to see the Afro-American Press as it is, and as it labors with the greatest sacrifice, I shall feel that Providence has blessed my work and that I have been amply rewarded. This volume may find its way to the cottage of the lowly and humble, the home of the scholar and the hands of the critic. I would invite its earnest perusal by each and all, and, at the same time, pray your most lenient criticism of its make-up, construction and thought. I would ask you to speak a good word for it, not in the hope of placing honor upon my head or the dime in my pocket, but in the hope of forming a favorable sentiment and creating an able and constant support for the Afro-American editor whose labor unites with all in building up and furthering the interest of our common country.

Lynchburg, Va., 1890.

P. S. To the hundreds of men and women laboring in journalism, the author owes an apology for not making personal mention of all of our papers now published, and their editors; also, the numerous correspondents and great phalanx of our brave and ambitious women who have espoused the cause. Many of you are able and efficient, and all of you deserve particular mention, but you will agree that it would take ten volumes, yea, more, to make satisfactory personal mention in this work of the many laboring for the race and for humanity.

CONTENTS.

PART I.

CHAPTER I.

PART II.

CHAPTER XVIII.

CHAPTER XIX.

CHAPTER XX.

CHAPTER XXI.

CHAPTER XXII.

CHAPTER XXVI.

CHAPTER XXVII

CHAPTER XXVIII.

JOHN B. RUSSWURM.

CHAPTER I.

THE FIRST AFRO-AMERICAN NEWSPAPERS.

FROM the very first time the Afro-American had a right to exercise his freedom in this country, his course with regard to church, state and society, has been followed with more than ordinary zeal, and his progress in the various pursuits undertaken by him have been noted with an exacting eye, characteristic of the most watchful. Why he has been watched in this peculiar way is not hard to be seen when the circumstances surrounding his life has been taken into consideration. When one remembers that he was brought from Africa only two centuries ago, an uncivilized and barbarous creature, and settled in a country where he was deprived the privileges of becoming even properly civilized; when one remembers that during this aforesaid period he had not one iota of opportunity to understand the most unpretentious business act in state or church; when one remembers that he was not allowed, (if he desired,) to think of a business transaction in any of its ramifications, were they ever so small; when it is remembered that the whole world was closed against him for centuries, save that of labor in the field of his owner; and when it is remembered that he faced the world as freeman, laborer, mechanic, student, scholar, lawyer, doctor, engineer, business man, journalist, etc., under the most embarrassing circumstances, the desire of mind and heart for a complete knowledge of his development grows into a mountain of curiosity. Thus it can be said that he is to-day the cynosure of all nations.

If the above be true, (which every one in fairness will admit,) the next thought that would likely present itself is: Has the Afro-American made any commendable progress amid the multiplicity of disadvantages which have beset him? We freely assert that he has; and it is with this thought in mind that we propose to deal with the facts of his journalistic career of sixty-three years, dating from the first paper published in New York City, March 30, 1827, to the present auspicious year of 1890. And from our observations we predict that the Nineteenth Century will close with a halo of journalistic sunshine about his head, and the Twentieth Century open with succeeding new events indicative of his triumphant success.

Between the years of 1827 and 1830, there were published in New York City by an Afro-American two papers known as *Freedom's Journal* and *Rights of All*. These two papers were both edited by Mr. John B. Russwurm. They both seem to have been one and the same paper, only during publication the names were changed; thus the two names. There is some conflict of opinion among those few who now live and remember anything about the matter, as to whether *The Freedom's Journal* or *The Rights of All* was the name of Mr. Russwurm's paper. Be this as it may, the decision of those who were most intimately acquainted with Mr. Rossoworm, and upon whose breadth of intelligence and scope of memory we feel safely secure, is that *The Freedom's Journal* was the first publication by Afro-Americans. It was issued, Vol. I, No. 1, March 30, 1827. Of course, any paper established by Afro-Americans at that time and for the succeeding forty years, would have fought absolutely in the interest of abolition of slavery. As a matter of fact, this publication by Mr. Russwurm met with more and greater obstacles than did any other paper ever published upon the continent. Besides having to fight for a cause which then had but few advocates, it could see in the popular mind no indication of support.

The Afro-Americans in the North that would patronize the journal were few, while the Abolitionists numbered no great throng at that time.

The Journal was a medium-sized weekly, presenting a very neat appearance, while the composition was as good as some journals of to-day. Mr. Russwurm had a most excellent estimate as to how an Afro-American journal should be conducted, particularly at that time, and for the people in whose interests it was published. There are few men who have lived who knew more about the business, or whose editorial pen could battle with such force against a volcano of sin and oppression, like unto that of American slavery. It devolved upon him and his journal to create sentiment, and to prove the interest which the free Afro-American of the North had in his oppressed brethren in the South.

At this time there appeared a mighty question involving life, the chastity of our women, the property, home and happiness of the freedmen of the South, to which the best efforts of Afro-American journalism must be directed yet it was not half so great as that of American slavery. Now the journalist contends for our rights as citizens; then he contended for our freedom from bondage, or our deliverance from a human curse which then seemed riveted about us with a most tenacious grip. It was for this, Mr. Russwurm caused *The Journal* to open its way and contend through discouragement and embarrassment for rights.

He was a man of positive journalistic ability, singleness of purpose and strong character. It is said he entered the forum of debate for the Abolition cause doing what he could with a heartiness and zeal only equalled by the martyrs of abolition. The North had not fully waked up to the abolition cause. Many, who hated the Afro-American, published papers attacking the free Afro-American as well as the poor slave. It was on this account, too, that the leading Afro-Americans of New York City met, formulated plans and encouraged, to the best of their ability, the efforts of Mr. Russwurm.

There was a local paper published in New York City in 1827 and 1828 by an Afro-American-hating Jew, which made the vilest attacks upon the Afro-Americans. It encouraged slavery and deplored the thought of freedom for the slave. It seems to have been a power in that direction. Against this *The. Journal* was directed, and it did heavy cannonading against this perpetrator of evil.

Mr. Russwurm had associated with him in the publication of *The Journal* Rev. Samuel E. Cornish, and possibly others whose names are not editorially mentioned, since the inception of *The Journal* was the result of a meeting of Messrs. Russwurm, Cornish and others at the house of M. Bostin Crummell (Rev. Dr. Crummell's father,) in New York, called to consider the attacks of the local paper mentioned above.

Rev. Cornish also did editorial work upon *The Journal.* He was a man of wonderful intellectual parts, having keen perception and a mind full of thought and judgment. He was very probably the most thoughtful and reliable, certainly the most popular and conversant, editor of his time. This is seen in the fact that in all his succeeding journalistic efforts, ranging through a course of twenty years, he was actively connected with some paper as editor or associate editor. A gentleman writing to the author says: "He was a most successful journalist." Another, writing about Rev. Cornish, says: "He was an old and indefatigable journalist." Another says: "Undoubtedly he was the greatest wielder of the pen in a quarter of a century of Afro-American journalism."

The following editorial which appeared in the *Colored American*, a paper since edited by him, will serve, we are sure, to justify the reader in accepting the above comments.

THE IMPORTANCE OF AGRICULTURAL PURSUITS.

America in many respects is a glorious country. She rivals boasted England in the excellence of her agriculture. The whole length and breadth of her land might, by proper culture, be converted into one universal and fertile garden, pouring forth her riches in exuberant abundance. Thus, blessed by the smiles, and watered by the showers of a bountiful Heaven, she may well and justly call forth loud and hearty praises of her sons. In a land then, like this, characterized by its geniality of climate, and great fertility of soil, many are the inducements held out to the sober and industrious; and morally culpable is he who can "eat the bread of idleness," or who can, with health and strength, sit down surrounded by pinching misery and want.

On the subject of agricultural pursuits, our people are too indifferent. It is a subject, however, of immense importance to colored interest, both individual and general, and cannot be treated of too frequently or earnestly, by journals which advocate our cause.

If we would have more men among us in comfortable circumstances, we must turn our attention to farming. If we would have men who might exert a powerful influence in different communities, we must have the sturdy cultivators of the soil.

It is beyond a doubt, that the influence which our farmers exert is great and extensive; and it is evident, that wherever there may be located respectable, intelligent, and wealthy colored agriculturists, there they will be respected, and soon rise into power and influence.

Want of necessary capital may be urged by many, as the great difficulty in the way of our people on this subject. One might venture to say that the great portion of our most able farmers commenced their labors with far less capital than many of our colored citizens can lay claim to. Many have risen to their present affluence, who had at first scarcely as much money as would enable them to till a garden of cabbages. They struggled with difficulties apparently insuperable; but by their fixed determination and firm resolves, they removed all barriers, overcame all obstacles, conquered the soil, and finally became the independent masters of it. If we would be the "lords of the soil" we must go and do likewise,

There is too great a disposition among our men of capital to congregate in large cities, where their influence is, in a measure, entirely lost. To be sure, the advantages accruing to some, from a city settlement, are infinitely greater than a country one; but in many cases the individual, and the community at large, would be vastly benefited by the residence of our capitalists in different parts of our country.

It is highly important, therefore, I conceive, that this subject be duly and attentively considered by our people generally. We must gain some influence in our own country. At present, we have none. In our large cities, we are passed by as not at all incorporated in the body politic. Let us then resort to those measures, and pursue that course, which will be of the most advantage to us and will cause a colored American's influence to be weighed and valued.

Rev. Cornish retired from the publication of *The Freedom's Journal*, Mr. Russwurm assuming sole editorial control, with the issue of September 4, 1827, Vol. I, No. 27. *The Journal* was continued the year out. With the issue of March 21, 1828, the name of the paper was changed to *Rights of All*. Mr. Russwurm continued to follow, with unabating interest, the line of policy prescribed by *The Freedom's Journal*. It fought for Afro-American freedom and Afro-American citizenship. Mr. Russwurm's two publications were made more powerful, and the sentiment of the two more respected, because of its large list of agents and contributors, who were remarkable men, either for their work in behalf of the Afro-American or as the fathers of public-spirited descendants.

The following are some of them as found upon the paper: David Walker, (Author of Walker's Appeal) Reuben ———, Portland, Me; Rev. Thomas Paul, Boston; Francis Webb, Boston; Stephen Smith, Columbia, Penn.; John Lemond, Salem, Mass.; Hezekiah Grice, Baltimore, Md.; Rev. Nathaniel Paul, Albany, N. Y.; Rev. Theodore S. Wright, Princeton, N. Y.; M. De Baptist, Fredericksburg, Va.; B. F. Hughes, Newark, N. J.; John W. Print, Washington, D. C.; Austin Stewart, Rochester, N. Y.; Rev. R. Vaughn, Richmond, Va.; George De Grave, Brooklyn, N. Y.; Seth Henhaws, Post-Master, New Salem; John C. Stanley, New Berne; Lewis Sheridan, Elizabethtown, N. C.; Joseph Hughes, Richmond, Va.; and others.

The *Rights of All* suspended publication in 1830, it having been conducted under more opposing circumstances than *The Freedom's Journal*, owing, possibly, to the great amount of good it was doing for the cause of Abolition. The exact date of its suspension it seems impossible to ascertain.

Mr. Russwurm's career as an Afro American journalist, was soon cut short after the suspension of his paper. He was captured by the Colonization Society and sent to Africa. Many notices and comments on Mr. Russwurm's work and upon him as a man, appeared in *The Colonization Journal* of 1839.

CHAPTER II.

THE WEEKLY ADVOCATE.

A FRO-AMERICANS North began now to feel the need of an exponent of sentiment and thought. The road had been opened, if any one by dint of sacrifice and strength of effort would lay all on the altar in the publication of another journal.

Phillip A. Bell, the Nestor of Afro-American journalism, came forward and put upon the uncertain wings of journalistic time a paper, which battled with unrelenting vigor for the right.

In January, 1837, appeared the first issue of the second journal edited by Afro-Americans under the name of *The Weekly Advocate*, the editor being Rev. Samuel E. Cornish, and the proprietor Mr. Phillip A. Bell. It was published by Mr. Robert Sears, of Toronto, Canada, a warm friend to the race. "After two months it was thought best," so informs Mr. Sears, to change the name of this paper to the *Colored American*; therefore March 4, 1837, it appeared under the last mentioned name.

The means to aid in its publication were largely contributed by Anti-Slavery Advocates, prominent among whom must be noticed that fearless and generous defender, Mr. Tappan. In "The Life of Mr. Tappan" occurs this passage·" The paper was intended to be the organ of the colored Americans.' Its columns were filled with excellently selected and original matter It ably advocated the emancipation of the enslaved and the elevation of the free colored people; and to this end it urged on the whites the abolition of caste and on their own people a thorough education.

Gifted men among the people of New York and elsewhere, (and there were not a few of them,) had an opportunity that was well worth improving of addressing their people and the public at large, through the columns of this excellent paper.

The proprietor, Mr. Bell, was known and respected for the work he did for the race in the newspaper field. He was one of those men who not only gave his literary ability to the cause but his money also, and died in destitute circumstances, after fifty years of earnest and persistent work for his race.

At the time of his death he was more experienced, older, and abler, than any of his associates. He longed to see Afro-American journalism a fixed thing in this country, and he did not die without the sight.

Wm. Welles Brown, in his "Rising Sun," says, "Mr. Bell's enthusiastic admirers regarded him as the Napoleon of the Afro-American Press. The person of Mr. Bell, as described by Mr. Brown in his volume, is as follows: "He is medium in size, dark complexion, pleasing countenance, and very gentlemanly in his manners."

After the retirement of Mr. Cornish, Mr. Bell had as co· editor, Dr. James McCune Smith, of whom much has been said as a writer and contributor. Wm. Welles Brown, in chronicling the success of Dr. Smith as a writer, says: "The Doctor has contributed many papers to different journals published by colored men in the last quarter of the century. The New

3

York dailies have also received aid from him during the same period.   History, antiquity, biography, translation, criticism, political economy, statistics, and almost every department of knowledge, received attention from his able, ready, versatile and unwearied pen.

The emancipator of the slave, and of the elevation of the free colored people, has been the greatest slave of his time as a writer.

Dr. Smith was born and raised in New York City, but educated at Edinburgh.   During the years 1838-49, he had some memorable newspaper controversies; prominent among them was the fight with Bishop Hughes and, later on, with one Grant.

A lecture of his on the "Destiny of the People of Color," delivered before the Philomathean Society and the Hamilton Society in January, 1841, and published by request, received flattering comments.   He was one of the most logical and scientific writers the world ever knew.

Besides this eminent gentleman, Mr. Bell had an able corps of correspondents, which made *The Colored American* felt as a power in the land.   Mr. Bell severed his connection with *The American* in 1839; but did not leave the work, for which it seems the Maker had intended him.   We shall have cause to notice him later on in this volume.

CHAPTER III.

THE COLORED AMERICAN.

IN April, 1837, while Mr. Bell was yet proprietor and editorial writer of the *American*, Mr. Charles Bennett Ray became associated with *The Colored American*, as general agent. In this capacity, he travelled extensively, writing letters to the paper which embodied the result of his labors and reflections on the progress of the race in different parts of the country. He also lectured successfully in many cities, East and West, to bring before the people the interests of the paper and the noble aims to which it was devoted, never neglecting, meanwhile, to speak in behalf of the slave, whose welfare lay always near his heart.

In 1838, he became one of the proprietors of the paper; and in 1839, on the retirement of Mr. Bell, he assumed the position of editor. Under his charge, as before, *The Colored American* continued to be ably conducted, and strong in its advocacy of the principles underlying humanity and justice. He retained the editorial management until 1842, when the paper was discontinued. Rev. C. B. Ray was born in Falmouth, Mass., on Christmas-day, 1807. He was the son of Joseph Aspinwall Ray and Annie Harrington. His early

education was received at the schools and academy of his
native town. His theological training was obtained at the
Wesleyan Academy at Wilbraham, Mass. Later on, he
studied at the Wesleyan University, Middletown, Conn.

In addition to his life as a useful journalist, should be
recorded his life as a minister. He served as pastor of the
Bethesda Congregational church in New York, and was its
faithful shepherd for twenty years or more.

During the greater part of Mr. Ray's activity, slavery was
at its highest state of agitation. The times were perilous,
great deeds being enacted everywhere by noble champions of
freedom, roused to action by an unquenchable love of justice
and the resolve that all men should be free. He entered
with eager earnestness into the contest to secure freedom for
a down-trodden race, and proved his fidelity to the sacred
cause of liberty, and his zeal in furthering the overthrow of
slavery, by rendering practical aid. It often became necessary, therefore, to interest those whose hearts not only beat
in unison with the movement but whose means could be made
available. In co-operation with Lewis Tappan, and others
whose purse-strings were wont to be loosed at the call of
humanity, he assisted in enabling many a slave to see the
light of freedom.

Mr. Ray always manifested a keen interest in the affairs of
the government, and was a staunch republican, entering
heartily into all things affecting the welfare of the government. When the great right of suffrage was accorded to his
race, none rejoiced more than he that now the Afro-American
citizen was truly a man, under the law; and, thenceforth, he
uniformly endeavored to impart the knowledge of an intelligent use of the franchise to those whose limited experience in
such matters might cause them to err in judgment.

He never ceased to give earnest support to any great
measure designed to elevate his race; and not only in this

way did he serve the people, but private matters were often brought to him for adjustment,—his natural grasp of the legal points of the subject enabling him to reach the solution of many a seemingly entangled situation.

He lived to see his race enjoying the blessings of that freedom to which he had consecrated his best days, and passed to the blessed fulfillment of a better world, on Sunday morning, August 15, 1886.

A general idea of *The Colored American,* which was Mr. Ray's greatest work for the race, issued, as it was, a half a century ago, in the interests of the Afro-American, under the editorial management of one of the race, will be obtained through the following extracts, embodying the plan and scope of the paper, and showing the rank it held among the leading journals of that time. It cannot fail of proper interest. They are taken from "In Memoriam," compiled by the family of the late Rev. Chas. B. Ray, March 7, 1840.

"Terms of the paper:

The Colored American is published weekly by Charles B. Ray, at No. 9 Spruce Street, New York, at two dollars per annum, in advance, excepting where a local agent will be responsible to collect the balance, when one-half may be received in advance.

No subscription received for a less term than six months.

No paper will be considered discontinued until arrearages are paid, except at the discretion of the publisher.

Four copies will be sent to one address for six dollars,— *i. e.* a person wishing the paper, by obtaining three subscribers, with the money in full, shall have his own paper.

Local agents shall be allowed one-fourth, in all cases,.on all money raised from subscribers.

Traveling agents shall be allowed one-third on all new subscribers, and one-fourth for collecting from old ones.

Postmasters, and all ministers of the gospel, friendly to our object, are requested to act as agents for us; also, students in seminaries.

Addresses, in all cases, (post paid), on all business pertaining to the paper: "Charles B. Ray, Publisher of *The Colored American.*"

Philadelphia depositories, where this paper can be had: 136 Lombard Sreet, and No. 2 Acorn Alley. S. H. Gloucester and J. J. G. Bias, Agents.

Prospectus of *The Colored American,* Volume II:

The Second Volume, New Series, of *The Colored American,* will be issued on the first Saturday in March, 1841.

This is the only paper in the United States, published and edited by a colored man, and expressly for the colored people.

Its objects are, more directly, the *moral, social* and *political* elevation and improvement of the free colored people; and the peaceful emancipation of the enslaved.

It will, therefore, advocate all lawful, as well as moral measures, to accomplish those objects.

The editor being a colored man, necessarily feels an interest in the welfare of the colored people, wherever found.

The paper, therefore, will not be regardless of the welfare of the colored people of other countries.

The editor, also being a Man, "whatever interests man, interests him." The paper, therefore, will not pass by, in silence, the reforms of the age, and whatever relates to our common humanity.

As the paper is devoted primarily to the interests of the colored population, and ought to be in every family, the editor intends to make it a first-rate family paper, devoting a column to the instruction of children, giving the general news of the day, as far as practicable, etc.; and nothing of an immoral tendency can find a place in its columns.

The paper ought to be patronized by the white community, to aid them in becoming better acquainted with the condition and claims of their fellow-citizens, and on account of the influence it will exert among the latter, and in their behalf. The colored population ought to patronize it, because it belongs to them, and for the sake of its success.

Price, Two Dollars per annum, always in advance. No subscription received for a less term than six months.

CHARLES B. RAY, Editor and Proprietor, No. 9 Spruce Street, New York.

The sentiments of the press are here given concerning the re-appearance of *The Colored American*, after a short term of suspension. Says *The American*,—"We insert, once. for all, the sentiments of the press in relation to our re-appearance among them; and our readers must not attribute to us motives of vanity in doing so,—for better things move us than a vain show. We intend to keep self where it should be, out of sight.

In combating the prejudices of the strong, on the one hand, and in defending the character of the weak, on the other; in advocating an unpopular cause, and coming in contact with such a variety of mind and of taste, and in bearing up under our present duties and responsibilities, in such times as these, such sentiments from an enlightened and judicious corps-editorial are encouraging, and furnish us with additional testimony that we are not ill-timed and out of place but needful, and deserve a place among the mouth-pieces of different sects, parties and classes now existing.

We presume our readers, who do not see these expressions of opinion as we do, will be glad to know what the press has said about us; and we think such sentiments will both encourage and stimulate them to be vigilant in giving us aid as they incite us to labor to show ourselves worthy to be sustained."

" *The Colored American*, we are glad to see, has re-appeared in the field, under the conduct of our enterprising and talented Brother Ray. It will maintain a very handsome rank among the anti-slavery periodicals, and we hope will be well sustained and kept up by both colored and uncolored patronage.

It must be a matter of pride to our colored friends, as it is to us, that they are already able to vindicate the claims our enterprise has always made in their behalf,—to an equal intellectual rank in this heterogeneous, (but "homogeneous") community.

It is no longer necessary for abolitionists to contend against the blunder of pro-slavery,—that the colored people are inferior to the whites; for these people are practically demonstrating its falseness. They have men enough in action now, to maintain the anti-slavery enterprise, and to win their liberty, and that of their enslaved brethren,—if every white abolitionist were drawn from the field: McCune Smith, and Cornish, and Wright, and Ray, and a host of others,—not to mention our eloquent brother, Remond, of Maine, and Brother Lewis who is the stay and staff of field anti-slavery in New Hampshire.

The people of such men as these cannot be held in slavery. They have got their pens drawn, and tried their voices, and and they are seen to be the pens and voices of human genius; and they will neither lay down the one, nor will they hush the other, till their brethren are free.

The Calhouns and Clays may display their vain oratory and metaphysics, but they tremble when they behold the colored man is in the intellectual field. The time is at hand, when this terrible denunciation shall thunder in their own race.—*Herald of Freedom*, Concord, N. H."

The Colored American.

The Colored American after a suspension of three months has started afresh, under the charge of our friend, Charles B. Ray, as sole editor and proprietor. If among the four hundred thousand free colored people in this country,—to say nothing of the white population from whom it ought to receive a strong support, a living patronage for this paper can not be obtained, it will be greatly to their reproach.

In their present condition, a special organ of their own conducted by one of their own number, ought to be regarded by them as an object of great importance. True, it does not follow that because the paper is called *The Colored American*, and is edited by a colored man, therefore the colored population are under obligation to support it; for if it be not in itself a faithful and useful journal, it cannot claim support, on any other grounds. But we have confidence in the ability, perseverance, and integrity of Mr. Ray, and we doubt not that he will make *The American* an interesting sheet.

If any persons, white or colored, in this city, desire to become subscribers to it, we will forward their names with great pleasure.

The names of several persons are published who have severally pledged five, ten, twenty, and twenty-five dollars, in aid of *The American*. This looks like being in earnest.

In the midst of the present unhappy divisions in our ranks, we trust our friend Ray will be enabled to distinguish by intuition the true from the spurious, the right from the wrong, and to utter his convictions in a true and fearless spirit."— *Liberator.*

" *The Colored American.* Returning from the country, we are glad to find upon our table several copies of this excellent paper, which has waked up with renewed strength and beauty. It is now under the exclusive control of Charles B. Ray, a gentleman in every manner competent to the duties devolving upon him in the station he occupies. Our colored friends generally, and all those who can do so, would bestow their patronage worthily by giving it to *The Colored American.*"—*Christian Witness.*

"In the days when *The Colored American* found its way into many homes, bearing the weight of influence ever exerted by the press, some of the vital questions claiming public attention did not differ materially from those that serve to interest the thinking community of to-day, as will be evidenced by the following editorials:

Prejudice.

"Prejudice," said a noble man, "is an aristocratic hatred of humble life."

Prejudice, of every character, and existing against whom it may, is hatred. It is a fruit of our corrupt nature, and has its being in the depravity of the human heart. It is sin.

To hate a man, for any consideration whatever, is murderous; and to hate him, in any degree, is, in the same degree murderous; and to hate a man for no cause whatever, magnifies the evil. "Whosoever hateth his brother is a murderer," says Holy Writ.

There is a kind of aristocracy in our country, as in nearly all others,—a looking down with disdain upon humble life and a disregard of it. Still, we hear little about prejudice against any class among us, excepting against color, or against the colored population of this Union, which so monopolizes this state of feeling in our country that we hear less of it in its operations upon others, than in other countries. It is the only sense in which there is equality; here, the democratic principle is adopted, and all come together as equals, and unite the rich and the poor, the high and the low, in an equal right to hate the colored man; and its operations upon the mind and character are cruel and disastrous, as it is murderous and wicked in itself. One needs to feel it, and to wither under its effects, to know it; and the colored men of the United States, wherever found, and in whatever circumstances, are living epistles, which may be read by all men in proof of all that is· paralyzing to enterprise, destructive to ambition, ruinous to character, crushing to mind, and painful to the soul, in the monster, Prejudice. For it is found equally malignant, active, and strong,—associated with the mechanical arts, in the work-shop, in the mercantile house, in the commercial affairs of the country, in the halls of learning in the temple of God, and in the highways and hedges. It almost possesses ubiquity; it is everywhere, doing its deleterious work wherever one of the proscribed class lives and moves.

Yet prejudice against color, prevalent as it is in the minds of one class of our community against another, is unnatural, though habitual. If it were natural, children would manifest it with the first signs of consciousness; but with them, all are alike affectionate and beloved. They have not the feeling, because it is a creature of education and habit.

While we write, there are now playing at our right, a few steps away, a colored and a white child, with all the affection and harmony of feeling, as though prejudice had always been unknown.

Prejudice overlooks all that is noble and grand in man's being. It forgets that, housed in a dark complexion is, equally and alike, with the white, all that is lofty in mind and noble in soul; that there lies an equal immortality. It teaches to grade mind and soul, either by the texture of the hair, or the form of the features, or the color of the skin. This is an education fostered by prejudice; consequently, an education almost universally prevalent in our country; an education, too, subverting the principles of our humanity, and turning away the dictates of our noble being from what is important, to meaner things."

This Country, our only Home.

"When we say, "our home," we refer to the colored community. When we say, "our only home," we speak in a general sense, and do not suppose but in individual cases some may, and will, take up a residence under another government, and perhaps in some other quarter of the globe. We are disposed to say something upon this subject now, in refutation of certain positions that have been assumed by a class of men, as the American people are too well aware, and to the reproach of the Christian church and the Christian religion, too, viz.: that we never can rise here, and that no power whatsoever is sufficient to correct the American spirit, and equalize the laws in reference to our people, so as to give them power and influence in this country.

If we cannot be an elevated people here, in a country the resort of almost all nations to improve their condition; a country of which we are native, constituent members; our native home, (as we shall attempt to show) and where there are more means available to bring people into power and influence, and more territory to extend to them than in any other country; also the spirit and genius of whose institution we so well understand, being completely 'Americanized, as it will be found most of our people are,—we say, if we can not be raised up in this country, we are at great loss to know where, all things considered, we can be.

If the Colored Americans are citizens of this country, it follows, of course, that, in the broadest sense, this country is our home. If we are not citizens of this country, then we cannot see of what country we are, or can be, citizens; for Blackstone, who is quoted, we believe, as the standard of civil law, tells us that the strongest claim to citizenship is birthplace. We understand him to say, that in whatever country or place you may be born, of that country or place you are, in the highest sense, a citizen; in fine, this appears to us to be too self-evident to require argument to prove it.

Now, probably three-fourths of the present colored people are American born, and therefore American citizens.

Suppose we should remove to some other country, and claim a foothold there, could we not be rejected on the ground that we were not of them, because not born among them? Even in Africa, identity of complexion would be nothing, neither would it weigh anything because our ancestry were of that country; the fact of our not having been born there would be sufficient ground for any civil power to refuse us citizenship. If this principle were carried out, it would be seen that we could not be even a cosmopolite, but must be of nowhere, and of no section of the globe. This is so absurd, that it is as clear as day that we must revert to the country which gave us birth, as being, in the highest sense, citizens of it.

These points, it appears to us, are true, indisputably true. We are satisfied as to our claims as citizens here, and as to this being the virtual and destined home of colored Americans.

We reflect upon this subject now, on account of the frequent agitations, introduced among us, in reference to our emigrating to some other country, each of which embodies more or less of the colonizing principle, and all of which are of bad tendency, thowing our people into an unsettled state; and turning away our attention from vital matters which involve our attention in this country, to uncertain things under another government, and evidently putting us back. All such agitations introduced among us, with a view to our emigrating, ought to be frowned upon by us, and we ought to teach the people that they may as well come here and agitate the emigration of the Jays, the Rings, the Adamses, the Otises, the Hancocks, et al, as to agitate our removal. We are all alike constituents of the same government, and members of the same rising family. Although we come up much more slowly, our rise is to be none the less sure. This subject is pressed upon us, because we not unfrequently meet some of our brethren in this unsettled state of mind, who, though by no means colonizationists, yet adopt the colonization motto, and say they can not see how or when we are going to rise here. Perhaps, if we looked only to the selfishness of man, and to him as absolute, we should think so, too. But while we know that God lives and governs, and always will; that He is just, and has declared that righteousness shall prevail; and that one day with Him is as a thousand years, and a thousand years as one day; we believe that, despite all corruption and caste, we shall yet be elevated with the American people here.

It appears to us most conclusive, that our destinies in this country are for the better, not for the worse, in view of the many schemes introduced to our notice for emigrating to other countries having failed; thus teaching us that our rights, hopes, and prospects, are in this country; and it is a waste of time and of power to look for them under another government; and also, that God, in His providence, is instructing us to remain at home, where are all our interests and claims, and to adopt proper measures and pursue them, and we yet shall participate in all the immunities and privileges the American nation holds out to her citizens, and be happy. We are also strongly American in our character and disposition.

We believe, therefore, in view of all the facts, that it is our duty and privilege to claim an equal place among the American people; to identify ourselves with American interests, and to exert all the power and influence we have, to break down all the disabilities under which we labor, and thus look to become a happy people in this extensive country."

Thus Editor Ray was no dupe in the editorial fight that he made for his race. He successfully made *The American* a paper that will be known for ages as a bold and uncompromising fighter for freedom.

We will not invite the reader to any comment of ours upon the character and ability of Mr. Ray as a journalist, or upon the influence and magnitude of the work done by his paper. Any remarks would be lost in the ocean of comments by others, some of which are here quoted. We give what recognized historians say of Mr. Ray: "In the year of 1839, he became the editor of *The Colored American*, a paper which he conducted with signal ability. *The Colored American* was well conducted, had the confidence of the public, and was distinguished for the ability shown in its editorials, as well as in its correspondence."

In another place Mr. Brown says: "All, however, who remember as far back as thirty-five years, will bear testimony to the efficient work done by *The Colored American*, and to the honor that is due to its noble founder." He is an original and subtile writer, having fine powers to analyze, and often flings the sparkling rays of a vivid imagination over the productions of his pen. His articles are usually of a practical nature, always trying to remove evils, working for the moral, social, and political elevation of his race. He was always true to the cause of the Southern slave, and the elevation of the black man, everywhere."

Another writer says: "Dr. Ray is a terse and vigorous writer, well informed upon all subjects of the day."

The American suspended publication in the early part of 1842, having made a brilliant record and opened a comparatively easy road for future efforts in Afro-American journalism.

CHAPTER IV.

THE ELEVATOR.

THE time for decisive, urgent, and unceasing fight for freedom and citizenship, from 1838 on, seems to have taken firm root in the mind and heart of every leading Afro-American, whose intelligence and practical knowledge enabled him to engage in the contest in anything like an effectual way.

This is seen in the ways and means established, through which they could express themselves. New York state appears to have been the great fighting-ground of the Afro-American abolitionists. Not only in New York, but throughout the whole section of New York state, papers were established, here and there, for the purpose of agitating Afro-American freedom and citizenship.

A small but bright and newsy sheet, under the title of *The Elevator*, was established at Albany, N. Y., in 1842. This journal, as were the others, was devoted to the Anti-Slavery cause and to the interests and progress of the Afro-Americans. It was published by Stephen Myers, whose efforts made it a strong advocate of everything looking to the advancement and up-building of the Afro-American.

Mr. Myers was born at Hoosic Four Corners, Rensselaer County, N. Y., in 1800. He was a slave of Gen. Warren, of Revolutionary fame, and made free by him, in the city of Albany, at the age of eighteen. He was a man of very limited education, but of great natural gifts. He was both an orator and a writer.

In the publication of his paper and the make-up of subject-matter, he was greatly aided by his wife, who was a lady of education and refinement. Before marriage, she was a Miss Harriet Johnson, the daughter of Capt. Abram Johnson. She aided her husband in the preparation of all his editorials, she, too, having caught the Abolition spirit. In the publication of his journal, Mr. Myers was backed by Horace Greeley, Gerrit Smith, Erastus Corning of Albany, N. Y., Henry J. Raymond, Hugh Hastings, Thurlow Weed, William Cassidy, and Peter Cagger.

Mr. Myers conducted his paper purely in the interest of the abolition of slavery and in the interest of his race, and never for the purpose of making money. The above-named gentlemen, and many others, aided him with contributions from time to time; and they were largely instrumental in enabling him to circulate his journal throughout the country. Although it did not appear regularly, nevertheless it was a potent factor in aiding him to make his work effective.

The cause of Abolition was supported by many able men and influential newspapers; but by none with more earnestness and self-sacrificing devotion than that which characterized the life of Stephen Myers. *The Elevator*, like many other journals of its class, proved a powerful lever in diverting public opinion, public sympathy, and public support, towards the liberation of the slave. It seems almost incredible that Mr. Myers, with no education, could have accomplished so great a work. Nothing but unceasing labor and unwavering vigilance could have made him so

4

successful. Impressed by these qualifications, those at whose hands he sought and obtained assistance were ever ready to respond to his appeals. True, there were many other men like Mr. Myers engaged in the same glorious work; but he seems to have had more than ordinary success in accomplishing anything he attempted, to strengthen the mission to which he consecrated his life.

Wherever and whenever he attended Anti-slavery gatherings, he was an effective and even powerful speaker; and no one could listen to him without becoming a warm supporter of his cause.

Meanwhile, *The Elevator* found its way into the homes of several thousands of patriotic citizens of all races, molding Anti-slavery sentiments in its ceaseless efforts to arouse the American people to a sense of their duty to exterminate from our land a condition of affairs wholly inconsistent with the sublime principles of a republican form of government.

Happily, Mr. Myers lived to see slavery abolished, the Union restored, the Fifteenth Amendment attached to the Constitution of the Nation, and, best of all, the barriers of prejudice gradually weaken their hold upon commercial and professional circles.

He was also permitted to see the Afro-American, the shackled and despised being whom "man's inhumanity to man" had made a chattel, take his initial step in the pathway of ideal American citizenship, unfettered and free; while the cloud of darkness which had enveloped him for two centuries, gave way to the sunshine of education, with opportunities to reach any point in the path of success which nature intended for him.

The last days of Mr. Myers were a fitting end to a life that future generations can but be pleased to admit was crowned with glory and splendor, by his magnificent achievements in behalf of his fellow-men; and connected with his name will

always be a lustre and a sanctity, which is the certain reward
of an honorable, upright life.

> "Press on! press on! nor doubt nor fear,
> From age to age this voice shall cheer—
> Whate'er may die, and be forgot,
> Work done for Freedom dieth not."

CHAPTER V.

THE NATIONAL WATCHMAN AND CLARION.

T HE state of New York still gave evidence of her Afro-American sons' interest in the Abolition cause.

Still another messenger of warfare was issued from another portion of the state, under the title of *The National Watchman*. This paper was first published in Troy, in the latter part of 1842, having as its publisher and editor, Mr. William G. Allen, assisted by Henry Highland Garnett. His paper had but a very brief existence; however, it contended manfully for what its projectors hoped to see, and for what their soulsdesired.

Mr. Allen was among the few men of his time who could be looked upon as a highly educated gentleman. Into his paper he put all the intellectual strength his mighty brain could master, which made it no less able as an advocate than any of its contemporaries. In this brief period, he conducted his publication with journalistic tact and energy. In his editorial work he was assisted by one of the brainiest and most successful black men in the country.

Mr. Garnett, after his connection with the *Watchman*, and while he was pastor of the Liberty-Street Presbyterian Church

HENRY HIGHLAND GARNETT.

of Troy, published *The Clarion.* This paper, while not failing to treat the most momentous of questions—American Slavery—with weighty argument and skillful debate, was run, we are informed, mostly in the interest of the religious and moral improvement of his race, to whose wellfare he was wedded.

As one puts it,—" Mr. Garnett was a remarkable man." He was as telling a speaker, as he was a writer. A gentleman of ability and worth sums him up in the following manner: "He has gained the reputation of being a courteous and accomplished man, an able and eloquent debater, and a good writer."

CHAPTER VI.

THE PEOPLE'S PRESS AND THE MYSTERY.

THE *Clarion* was followed next by an effort at journalism in the p iblication of *The People's Press*, by Thomas Hamilton and John Dias, about 1843. This publication, like many succeeding ones, lasted only a few months.

Mr. Hamilton was book-keeper in the office of *The Evangelist*, at the time when a desire to be an editor first took control of him, which desire resulted in the publication of *The Press*.

There is a belief among some that this paper, for a while before its suspension, was known as *The Anglo-African*, but this must not in any way be connected with the later publication of "Hamilton's Magazine," and a paper known also as *Anglo-African*. Further mention will be made of Mr. Hamilton in a succeeding chapter.

The Afro-Americans, at this stage, evidently caught inspiration, wherever settled in the North, as to the duty of the hour. Those who were able, intellectually, found it their imperative duty to agitate through the medium of the Press, for but little could be accomplished by means of speech; even at the North.

Not only was New York the garden-spot for journalistic fruit, but Pennsylvania also occupies a place on that record. In 1843, when the interest of every man at the North had been stirred up on the slave question, the Afro-Americans of Pittsburgh, not unlike their friends in New York, desired and sought to publish letters in their behalf, but could find no means of expression. Their pleas to the white publishers of papers were not heeded. This prompted Major Martin R. Delaney to publish a weekly sheet in the early part of the year, under the title of *The Mystery*, which was devoted solely to the interest of his race.

As we have seen in preceding chapters, and as is generally the case at this writing, Afro-American papers were always lacking support. The most pretentious newspapers, run strictly on business principles, would be hardly able to live upon the support the race offers.

While Mr. Delaney put ability, money and business spirit into his paper, yet it survived as personal property only nine months, when it was transferred to a joint-stock company of six gentlemen, he being retained as editor.

Mr. Delaney was an editor of attractive power. His friends who now live are loud in their praises of his editorial ability. A writer says—"The editorials of his journal elicited praises from even his enemies, and were frequently transferred to their columns."

To his editorial influence is due the originating of the Avery fund. He was the only editor from 1827 to '70, to our knowledge, who was ever arrested for what his enemies would term libel; certainly he was the first. A verdict of guilty was rendered in the suit for libel, and he was fined. Mr. Delaney stood well with his newspaper friends. They were loud in praises of him and his editorial work; and upon the occasion of the suit for libel, this was fully exemplified; for as soon as they found out the court had fined him, they proceeded immediately to start a subscription paper to pay the fine. Happily, it had been remitted and the money was not needed.

Mr. Delaney was a physician of great skill. He was among the first Afro-Americans to graduate from Harvard College. He championed the cause of the Afro-Americans for four years through *The Mystery*, which suspended publication in 1847. This connection with *The Mystery*, was his first appearance in public life.

Mr. Brown, in his "Lives of Representative Men and Women," says—"His journal was faithful in its advocacy of the rights of man, and had the reputation of being a well-conducted sheet."

Dr. Delaney died January 24, 1885, after living a useful life seventy odd years.

CHAPTER VII.

THE GENIUS OF FREEDOM.

S HORTLY after this, another effort at Afro-American
journalism was made in the publication of *The Genius
of Freedom*, issued some time between 1845 and 1847,
with Mr. David Ruggles as editor and publisher. The exact
date of the commencement of this paper is not known, the
writer having exhausted all resources to find out.

Ruggles also published contemporaneously with *The Colored
American* a quarterly magazine, under the style and title of
"The Mirror of Liberty," which we shall notice in another
chapter.

It is safe to conclude that *The Genius of Freedom* was not
published until after the suspension of Mr. Ruggles' Magazine in 1841, and prior to the establishment of *The North
Star*, at Rochester, N. Y., in 1847. This paper, while edited
for the interest of the Afro-American, did not survive a long
life. It was soon gathered into its projectors' arms, however,
with the knowledge of its having done something for an oppressed people. Thus, little is known of it by any one save
the most careful observer of men, times and events.

Mr. Ruggles was a highly educated gentleman, refined in

manners. He was one of the first promoters of the Under-
ground Railroad, and was one who stood by it in times of
peril. He was a terror to the Southern er; but a friend to his
brethren in the South. He labored for his people with unfal-
tering trust.

He was the most logical writer of his time; indeed, there
are few now of the craft who can excel our subject in the
editorial field where logic and argument have most power.
He was a quick and ready writer, his articles being of that
nature befitting the time and occasion.

Wm. Welles Brown, in his "Rising Sun," says,—"The first
thing ever read, coming from the pen of a colored man, was
D. M. Reese, M. D., used up by David Ruggles, a man of color.
Dr. Reese was a noted colonizationist, and had written a work,
in which he advocated the expatriation of the blacks from the
American continent. Mr. Ruggles' work was a reply to it.
In this argument, the Afro-American proved too much for the
Anglo-Saxon, and exhibited in Mr. Ruggles those qualities of
keen perception, deep thought, and originality, that mark the
critic and the man of letters.

Mr. Ruggles was an editor of the indomitable stamp. He
was respected by all of his constituents, as an able and fearless advocate.

Hon. Frederick Douglass says of Mr. Ruggles,—"He was
not only an intelligent man, but one of the bravest and bold-
est spirits of the times. John J. Zuille of New York, says,
—"He was a man of profound ability and force of character.
During most of his active public life, he was the soul of the
Under-ground Railroad in New York City, respected as an
editor, and in the courts of New York for his intimate knowledge of law in slave cases." Another says,—"He was a keen
and witty writer, sending his arrows directly at his opponent."

The most striking characteristic of Mr. Ruggles, with regard to his work and his time, is that he was of unmixed

blood, which clearly showed the possibilities of a race of people, some of whom were slaves and others free but without the right of franchisement, and with no means of elevation.

The Genius of Freedom, as has been said, was short-lived. However, Mr. Ruggles' journalistic career numbered through several years, the rest of which will be noted in a succeeding chapter.

It is highly probable that his life, in this respect, would have been longer, had he not been overtaken with blindness. He died in 1849, highly respected and esteemed and with a popularity which not many of his race enjoy to-day.

CHAPTER VIII.

THE RAM'S HORN.

IN New York, before the war, there was embodied in the Constitution of that state a clause relating to the voting qualifications of the Afro-American, which was called the "Colored Clause." It was to the effect, that no Afro-American could have the right of suffrage who was not actually worth two hundred and fifty dollars of real estate, accurately rated and taxes paid thereon; while any white man of twenty years, without a foot of land, could vote. The fact of such a law existing, many intelligent and level-headed Afro-Americans were deprived of a just right; while his white brother, in many cases not so capable as the other, was allowed it.

As the Afro-Americans became more and more intelligent and able to see and discern events of a public nature, and capable to sit in judgment upon matters of public concern to them, sentiment among their fellows with regard to this injustice arose to such a height, that the more thoughtful and efficient of the race met in New York city, sometime between 1845 and '47, to take into consideration this special feature of injustice. The result was a unanimous decision to petition the legislature to eliminate the word "color," and

61

have every man to vote on the same terms and conditions. The legislature, after some fighting, decided to leave the matter with the voters, who were to vote Yes or No, on the question. Now was the most favorable opportunity for the publication of an Afro-American journal; but there was not one then issued in the land.

About this time, Mr. Willis A. Hodges, a man full of zeal and devotion for his race, enthused by utterances from the editorial columns of *The New York Sun* calling on the voters to vote "No," prepared an article in answer to these utterances, and sought space for the same in *The Sun's* columns.

Mr. Hodges' article was published for a fifteen-dollar consideration; but its sentiment was modified, and it was published in the advertising columns. Mr. Hodges upon inquiry relative to the alteration of his article and the manner of its publication, was told—" *The Sun* shines for all white men, and not for colored men." He was also told if he wished the Afro-American cause advocated, he would have to publish a paper himself for the purpose.

Right here, Mr. Hodges, as was the case of all his friends with whom he consulted, saw the irreparable loss his people had sustained by the suspension of Afro-American newspapers, formerly published in New York.

As has been said, there was not a paper published by an Afro-American, at this time, in the Union. Mr. Hodges, being a man of energy, public-spirited and to the manor born, hastily came to the conclusion that one should be published in New York city by Afro-Americans. He consulted with leading Afro-Americans who had been interested in former publications, only to be discouraged. All seemed to be seeking personal ends, and not what, at this time, demanded the closest attention of their leading minds.

Finally, Mr. Hodges met with an old friend, Thomas Van

Rensselaer, with whom he formed a co-partnership. This was done in October, 1840, at which meeting they also decided upon *The Ram's Horn*, as a title for the paper.

There was no money in hand to make the first issue It was agreed that Mr. Hodges should furnish the finances and contribute editorially, while Mr. Van Rensselaer was to be the business manager.

It is amusing, as well as interesting, to recall what Mr. Hodges himself has to say about it: "I had not one dollar of my own for the paper; but as white-washing was a good business in New York, I went to work at it, and in two months I had nearly all the money that was necessary to get out the first number; and I can truly say that I furnished every dollar that started *The Ram's Horn*, and wrote the first article that was published in its columns."

To the surprise of many, on the first day of January, 1847, three thousand copies of *The Ram's Horn* were gotten out, with the significant motto,—"We are men, and therefore interested in whatever concerns men."

It was published in the second story of 141 Fulton Street, the price of subscription being $1.50 to persons living in New York, and $1.00 to those who received it by mail.

The paper was well received, though it met with some opposition on the part of Afro-Americans in the Metropolis, and was published until dissension arose among its projectors.

It was edited by Messrs. Hodges and Van Rensselaer, assisted by Frederick Douglass. Mr. Douglass, while he did little writing for *The Ram's Horn*, was then so highly popular, that no paper was considered of much importance without the name of Douglass connected with it. He was probably to Afro-American journalism of that day, what Bill Nye and Bret Harte are to the journalism of their day. *The Ram's Horn* was well distributed. At one time it had upon its books two thousand five hundred subscribers. Of course, these were enough to support several journals of its size, but few of them represented fully paid subscriptions.

The Ram's Horn was greatly aided in living by such men as John Brown, who was a supporter and contributor, and whose sympathy was gained by the publication of Mr. Hodges treatment in Virginia.

The Ram's Horn was as neatly printed, and presented as pleasing a journalistic look, as any paper published at that time. It was a five-column folio, printed on both sides with original matter, and was full in every issue with anti-slavery sentiment from the editors, as well as from able contributors.

The writer of this, especially, was attracted by the clean-cut logic of an editorial, written by Mr. Hodges on one occasion, entitled,—" The South Land Again."

We put Mr. Hodges down as a man of prolific brain, good practical sense, and sound reasoning faculties. In fact, the articles of *The Ram's Horn*, in general, were noted for their readableness and force of character.

Vol. I, No. 43, November 5, 1847, which we have before us, contains a reply of a correspondent to the following clause of a circular sent out by Rev. Alexander Crummell, dated April 19, 1846:

"The rising anti-slavery feeling of the North confines itself almost entirely to the interests and rights of the white race, with an almost utter disregard of the Afro-Americans; which tendency is dangerous to us and should be changed."

It also contained other interesting articles, which space forbids us to mention here.

After *The Ram's Horn* had been published eighteen months, a dissension arose which resulted in Mr. Hodges retiring from the paper, leaving Mr. Van Rensselaer as editor and owner. It is due Mr. Hodges to say he left *The Ram's Horn* free of debt.

Hodges, while crude in his English, was one of the most

sagacious and practical men of his time. He was the soul of *The Ram's Horn*, though little credit has been given him by some who comment on Afro-American journalism. He now resides at Norfolk, Va., a trusted citizen.

The Ram's Horn appeared only once with Mr. Van Rensselaer as editor and owner, when it fell asleep in June, 1848. It, however, had done good work for the race, in whose special interests it was run.

Mr. Van Rensselaer, while a very indiscreet man, was a brave and undaunted advocate of the equal rights of the Afro-American in the United States. T. T. Fortune, in writing an article on Afro-American journalism for the holiday number of *The New York Journalist*, takes his subject "From *The Ram's Horn*." He comments on *The Ram's Horn* as follows: "Before the war, few newspapers were published by Afro-Americans. Here and there, a man more intelligent, more venturesome, more affluent than his fellows, turned to journalism as the most effective means of pleading for the abolition of slavery; but his funds would be soon wasted and the issue of his paper would be stopped."

It was thus with *The Ram's Horn*, and its service must not be forgotten.

DR. JAMES McCUNE SMITH.

CHAPTER IX.

THE NORTH STAR.

THE suspension of *The Ram's Horn* did not leave the Afro-Americans entirely without an organ. Vol. I, No. 43, of *The Ram's Horn* contained the following prospectus for an anti-slavery organ at Rochester, N. Y.: "Prospectus for an Anti-slavery paper, to be entitled—" *The North Star*:

Frederick Douglass proposes to publish in Rochester, New York, a weekly anti-slavery paper with the above title. The object of *The North Star* will be to attack slavery in all its forms and aspects; advocate Universal Emancipation; exact the standard of public morality; promote the moral and intellectual improvement of the colored people; and to hasten the day of freedom to our three million enslaved fellow-countrymen.

The paper will be printed on a double medium sheet, at $2.00 per annum, if paid in advance, and $2.50 if payment be delayed over six months.

The names of subscribers can be sent to the following persons, and should be forwarded, as far as practicable, by the first of November, proximo.

The following are the agents: Frederick Douglass, Lynn, Mass,; Samuel B. ————, Salem, Ohio; M. R. Delaney, Pittsburgh, Pa.; Val Nicholson, Harrisburg, Ohio; Mr. Walcott, Boston, Mass.; J. P. Davis, Economy, Indiana; Christian Donaldson, Cincinnati, Ohio; J. M. M. Rinn, Philadelphia, Pa.; Amaraney Paine, Providence, R. I.; Mr. Gay, New York."

The North Star was issued the first day of November, 1847. It and *The Ram's Horn* were contemporaries.

The editor of *The Star* being head and shoulders above many of his colleagues, his paper was readily accepted as one of the most formidable enemies to American Slavery. Its aims and purposes, as set forth in the prospectus, drew to it good support from those of the whites who favored Abolition.

The North Star was conducted on a much higher plane than any of the preceding publications. Mr. Douglass had, by his eloquent appeals in behalf of the Abolition cause, created a wide-spread sentiment, and he was known as an orator. While much of his time was spent on the rostrum in behalf of Abolition, yet many say his best and most effective work for freedom was as editor, in the publication of *The Star* at Rochester, New York.

Mr. Douglass was what is hard to find in any one man,—a good speaker, as well as an effective, able, and logical writer. There is no man to-day who is a Douglass with the quill and upon the rostrum.

Previous to this publication, Mr. Douglass was not known as a writer; but he was afterward recognized as a great man in more than one sphere.

No writer ever expressed truth in better and more fitting language than did the man who said—"His (Mr. Douglass') boldness and superior journalistic ability won for him a world-wide reputation."

His power as a writer was large, while his ready and

vigorous use of the English language was always effective and good.

We clip the following from *The Rising Sun* : " Frederick Douglass' ability as an editor and publisher has done more for the freedom and elevation of his race than all his platform appeals."

The commencement of the publication of *The North Star* was the beginning of a new era in the black-man's literature. Mr. Douglass' great fame gave his paper at once a place among the first journals of the country ; and he drew around him a corps of contributors and correspondents from Europe, as well as from all parts of America and the West Indies, that made his columns rich with the current literature of the world.

While *The North Star* became a welcome visitor to the homes of the whites who had never before read a paper edited by an Afro-American, its proprietor became still more popular as a speaker in every state in the Union where Abolitionism was tolerated.

Of all his labors, we regard Mr. Douglass' efforts as publisher and editor the most useful to his race.

For sixteen years, against much opposition. single-handed and alone, he demonstrated the fact that the Afro-American was equal to the white man in conducting a useful and popular journal.

The paper was continued under the title of *The North Star* until, in 1850, its name was changed, and it was afterwards known as " *Frederick Douglass' Paper.*"

But there was only a change in name ; for the same principles, the same ability, and fight for Abolition, characterized its every movement.

In the publication and work incident to the paper, Mr. Douglass was assisted by his sons. This accounts, in a great measure, for their love of newspapers at this writing, and their connection, from time to time, with many different journals. *Fred Douglass' Paper* continued to be published until it was able to chronicle the emancipation of the slaves. It was then gathered into the arms of its promoters, having triumphed in the cause for which it so vigorously fought.

CHAPTER X.

CONTEMPORARIES OF THE NORTH STAR.

BEGINNING with *The North Star*, journalism among Afro-Americans took a higher stand, and was of a more elevated plane than that previous to 1847.

About this time, the Abolition cause began to wax warm, and the fight was a vigorous one. In this condition of affairs the Afro-American could not have less interest than those among the other race who made many sacrifices for the sake of Abolition.

Upon the rostrum could be heard, all over the North, the voices of the abolitionists for the emancipation of the slave.

In this, the Afro-Americans enlisted. The matchless oratory of Frederick Douglass, John Remond, and others, was listened to in almost every section of the North, pleading for their brethren's freedom from oppression. This was seen to have been a necessary means of agitation.

It was also necessary that the press should be conducted by able and fearless advocates. It is true, Douglass had his *Star*, at Rochester; but other papers were needed to make the press heard in the hum of battle, in union with the musical voice of the orator; therefore, the *Star* should have its contemporaries.

71

Of these, some were of short and others were of long duration. The first of them was *The Impartial Citizen*, at Syracuse, N. Y., in 1848, published by Samuel Ward. Mr. Ward was a very intelligent and sober man, and conducted his journal on a very lofty plane. He was as able as any other journalist since that time, and his publication was managed with as much shrewdness and practical ability as any of his day. By many he was regarded as an abler speaker than writer.

The principles for which the paper fought are indicated by its name. It clamored particularly for Afro-American citizenship at the North, and the freedom of the slave at the South. Mr. Douglass, an able man himself, says—" To my mind, Mr. Ward was the ablest black man the country has ever produced." It follows that Mr. Ward must have been an able man.

The Citizen advocated, with convincing logic, political action against slavery. Though the paper had unfortunately but a brief existence, it gained for itself the reputation of being a spirited sheet. The editor of *The North Star*, which was a contemporary of *The Citizen*, says—"Mr. Ward was an educated man, and his paper was ably edited." This was an excellent effort at journalism.

There was now no Afro-American journal published in New York City. *The Ram's Horn* having been suspended in 1848, left the Afro-Americans in that city without any organ.

While journals, backed by men of brains, were springing up in other parts of the North, New York City contained, probably, a greater number of able black men, both speakers and writers than could be found elsewhere.

Mr. Louis H. Putman, a man identified with all the Afro-American interests, began the publication of *The Colored Man's Journal*, in New York City. It was backed by a man of some financial strength, and therefore survived many a

Saml Ringgold Ward

shock to which it must otherwise have succumbed. It was issued in 1851, and continued to be published during a period of ten years of stormy agitation, until the outbreak of the civil war.

As a writer, Mr. Putman was known very well. He, however, did little work as a speaker, save in his native town on matters of local interest. His main efforts were made through his paper. He was what might be termed a practical man, full of common sense, which he used abundantly in conducting his journal. No paper up to this time, save *The Star*, survived the existence of *The Journal*.

There is one feature about Mr. Putman's life as a writer which is very flattering. He never fought for anything he did not conceive to be right. He had his faults, as all men have; but he looked far and thought soberly before acting. A friend speaks thus of him: "Mr. Putman was a man full of historical facts, and possessed keen perceptive powers; and he was a good writer." His paper was neat in appearance, and exhibited, in its mechanical make-up, a knowledge of the higher order of journalism.

The next effort at journalism among the early contemporaries of *The North Star* was *The Alienated American*, edited by Prof. W. H. H. Day, which he published at Cleveland, Ohio, in 1852, in the interest of Abolition, immediately after he graduated from Oberlin, in 1847. *The American* was decidedly one of the best journals ever published, supported by a well-trained man, as well as of recognized ability. This paper was wholly devoted to the cause for which it was every Afro-American's pleasure to fight,—that of freedom. A man eminently able and thoughtful, says—"It rendered timely and efficient service in the cause of freedom and the elevation of the colored people in the state."

Mr. Day was a scholarly writer, of as much ability as any of that day; and since he still lives, with years of experience upon his head, it is safe to say there are very few now who are his equals at the editorial desk. To judge from historical accounts of Mr. Day and his journalistic life, it is indeed safe to say that then there were only a few in that department of life's work who could attain to his measure.

He is spoken of in *The Rising Sun*, as follows : " As a writer, Mr. Day is far above newspaper editors generally, exhibiting much care and thought in many of his articles. As a speaker and writer, he has done much for his race."

He is admitted to be among the few who, with Douglass, may justly claim the distinction of being a prolific writer.

The great secret of Mr. Day's success and triumphant ability as a writer is, that he had a finely stored memory, from which he could draw at will. *The American* was a paper that could be regarded as a creditable publication, and it realized a good support. It was the first paper that had ever been published in Ohio by an Afro-American for his race ; and it is a matter of fact that an enthusiastic and hearty support was at once created for it.

The American suspended publication, for a while, before Mr. Day sailed for England, in 1856 and '57. There, he was recognized for his worth and scholarly training, his manner of deportment, and for his genuine eloquence in his preaching and lecturing. Some time after he returned, he embarked again in journalism, which we shall have occasion to refer to later on.

Mr. Day lives at Harrisburg, Pa., where he is yet engaged in toiling for his people. He is a preacher in the A. M. E. Zion church, and one of its best and brainiest men.

In 1887, Livingstone College, Rev. J. C. Price, President, gave him the degree of " D. D." The honor has never been conferred on one more worthy.

Truly he has helped to make the history of journalism bright and shining by his having been in it.

It must seem to the reader that now the Afro-Americans were of some consequence, for we see them rising on all sides, whenever allowed any freedom at all, aiming at the one great evil of slavery.

The work, as the reader will note, was not now confined to the state of New York or Pennsylvania, but was reaching into the far West and there getting foothold for a crusade for the right.

Another contemporary of *The North Star* was *The Mirror of the Times*, of which Hon. Mifflin W. Gibbs was one of the proprietors and editors. It was published in San Francisco, Cal., in 1855.

That *The Mirror of the Times* did much good work can not be denied by any one. It could not have been otherwise with the name of Judge Gibbs attached to it.

This journal was published for seven years, and nobly defended the race and fought for the common cause of Abolition, until, in 1862, it was merged into *The Pacific Appeal*.

The Times did excellent work, and the Afro-Americans of to-day feel proud of its efforts.

Judge Gibbs is at present Receiver of Public Moneys, at Little Rock, Ark.

Another excellent contemporary of *The North Star* was *The Herald of Freedom*, published in 1855 by Mr. Peter H. Clark. It was one of the best advocates of Abolition among the Afro-Americans, for the reason that it had an editor of good sense and vast knowledge, both natural and acquired. Mr. Clark was born in 1827.

There are possibly few men of our race who have lived, and now live, better known as of literary and intelligent worth than Mr. Clark, every person of importance giving him the credit of being an acute thinker.

His journal had a very short existence, but it, no doubt,

PETER H. CLARK.

helped on the fight for a just principle, which was afterwards maintained.

Its name indicated a long-looked-for desire. It joined in the fight with a vim, and went to rest, doubtless, with the feeling that it had accomplished something.

After the suspension of *The Herald of Freedom*, in Ohio, Mr. Clark was associated with Mr. Douglass in the publication of *The North Star*. Upon the editorial staff of this paper he labored zealously.

The Star had already been actively battling for Abolition for some years, and with Mr. Clark's vigorous and pricking pen, its aims and purposes for triumph were greatly strengthened.

Respecting his contributions to *The Star*, a writer to the author quotes William Welles Brown as expressing his sentiment: "His articles were fresh, vigorous and telling."

Mr. Clark is one of the bright Afro-American minds, and the world has been made brighter and more attractive for his having lived in it.

Up to this time there had been no part taken by the Afro-American churches in the interest of Abolition, save, here and there, a few individual attempts. There seems to have been no organized effort among the churches; and nothing of a tangible nature was done to battle against the wrong.

This the members saw; and the A. M. E. Church, having had some years of existence, now made a very interesting and permanent stand in the North. The principles of the church, as taught by Richard Allen, were laid down with much power and strength.

The Press, an indispensable factor, was seen to be necessary here; and it was about this time (1856) that *The Christian Recorder* was established in Philadelphia, with Rev. Jabez Campbell, now Bishop Campbell, as editor.

It is hardly necessary for us to comment here upon the

work of *The Recorder*, or to attempt to tell its history; for
to every churchman *The Christian Recorder* is a familiar
periodical.

It was established as the official organ of the A. M. E.
Church, and has manfully fought the fight.   Its heroic efforts

REV. RICHARD ALLEN,
First Bishop of The African M. E. Church.

in the days of slavery for Abolition, are well known to the
Afro-American student of times and events.

Rev. Campbell brought its editorial work to a high standard, which was carried even higher by succeeding editors.

Rev. Campbell resigned his position after a few years'
service, and was succeeded by Rev. John M. Brown, who
afterward became Bishop.

Mr. Brown kept up the high order of editorial work attained by Mr. Campbell. By these two gentlemen the standard was fixed, and the foundation laid for a more glorious service in the time of absolute freedom.

This brings us to 1868, when Rev. Benjamin T. Tanner took the editorial chair, which he occupied for sixteen years, during which time he made *The Recorder* an assured publication, giving it that distinction and prominence which it well deserved under his management.

In 1870, after Rev. Tanner had had control of *The Recorder* only two years, a man of eminence and high intellectual ability speaks thus of him and his paper: " As editor of *The Recorder*, he has written many witty, pithy, and brilliant sentiments. There is a tinge of opulent fancy running through his editorials, which always refreshes one. The wide reputation of his journal, outside of his own denomination, is probably the best test of his ability as a newspaper conductor." This can be said of his whole career.

Upon the establishment of a church magazine in 1884, Rev. Tanner was chosen editor, whereupon he resigned the editorship of *The Recorder*, when Rev. Dr. Lee was chosen as his successor.

As is known, Dr. Lee is one of the greatest Afro-American writers upon the continent of America, and with entire satisfaction to his race and his church he fills the responsible editorial chair of *The Recorder*. He is one of those who had to toil by the sweat of his brow for an education.

It is highly interesting to think of Dr. Lee as once having been the stable-man upon the Wilberforce University grounds, and of his return, after a few years, to be its President. The divine injunction that the first shall be last and the last shall be first, is fully illustrated in this case.

There is nothing harsh about Editor Lee's productions. He is rather an easy, mellifluous writer, and fully conversant with his church polity. It may safely be said that he is one of the most distinguished men of his race and church.

BLACK HARRY—"The Preacher."
Bishop Coke's servant, and said by Dr. Rush, Bishop Asbury and others, to have been the greatest orator in America.

STEPHEN MYERS.

WILLIS A. HODGES.

82

CHAPTER XI.

THE ANGLO-AFRICAN.

THE next marked effort in this field was in New York City, and was opportunely made.

Mr. Thomas Hamilton, of *The People's Press* fame, again dares to brave the storm in another publication, This time it was a decided success, reflecting credit upon his journalistic experience and his active brain. It was called *The Anglo-African*, and was one of the most powerful journals, irrespective of the color of the publisher, in the Abolition cause.

Published a few years before the war, it entered upon a heated period, which demanded fight,—fight to the bitter end.

Mr. Hamilton put every thing serviceable into his paper. He decided it should be a creditable and effective sheet, and to accomplish this he made many sacrifices, and flung to the breeze the first number of *The African*, (Vol. 1., No. 1.) July 23, 1859. It started with a high order of journalism, and occupied that elevated plane of Afro-American press work, inaugurated by *The North Star*.

Mr. Hamilton was, at this time, sole owner of the paper; but his brother Robert was associated with him in the editorial department. *The Anglo-African* was a most worthy paper. The publishers were men of great intellectual, as well as journalistic ability. The opinion of Mr. Douglass is—" It had more promise, and more journalistic ability about it, than any of the other papers."

It was a large sheet of four pages, with seven columns to a page. These were larger than ordinary newspaper columns.

It had at their head the following :

The Weekly Anglo-African is published every Saturday by Thomas Hamilton, 43 Beekman Street, New York.

Terms of subscription : Two dollars per year, or four cents per copy. Thus it went forth, and made a noble fight for the Abolition cause.

Papers published at this time were watched with a criticising eye by almost every man among the white people. The editorial backing was closely observed, as well as the journalistic look of the paper.

This ordeal *The Anglo-African* was able to meet. Whenever weighed in the journalistic balances, it was not found wanting.

Mr. Thomas Hamilton, like his brother, was a man of superior ability, and of much experience in his profession. He was on *The Evangelist* for a long while, and had been one of the proprietors of *The People's Press.* Many are of the opinion that *The Anglo-African* was the better publication of the two. We will not venture the opinion that it was the best paper published, but we will say it was the largest.

The great feature of *The Anglo-African* was, that it did not seek to make itself a paper whose matter should originate in the Hamilton family alone; and some of its contributors were known to embrace the best Afro-American talent of those days; the result being a genuine Afro-American newspaper.

M. R. DeLANEY.

Hamilton was devoted to journalistic efforts, and proved eminently successful therein.

The motto of *The Anglo-African* was as significant as that of any paper ever published. It was—"Man must be free; if not through the law, then above the law." With this motto, it manfully contended for Afro-American freedom and citizenship.

Mr. Thomas Hamilton continued to be the owner and editor of *The Anglo-African* until it was bought by Mr. James Redpath, one of the old and substantial Abolitionists,—the object of his purchase being the advocating of the Haytian Emigration Movement; a project that seemed then to be the only hope for the Afro-Americans. This occurred in the early part of 1860.

After its purchase by Mr. Redpath, the paper was known as *The Weekly Anglo-African*, for a short time, when the following notice appeared in Vol. II, No. 13, May 11, 1861: *The Anglo-African* will appear next week under a new name —*The Pine and Palm*.

What does it mean? Wait and you will see."

GEORGE LAWRENCE, JR., Publisher.

While Mr. Redpath was owner, Mr. Lawrence seems to have done the work for him, and carried out his wishes with respect to the Haytian Emigration Movement. This Movement was pressed with earnestness by Mr. Redpath and by his representative, Mr. Lawrence, through *The African*, as well as *The Pine and Palm*.

The Anglo-African of March 23, 1861, Vol. II, No. 36, contained a full outline of the Movement, and some very pertinent and interesting articles on the feasibility of it.

Mr. Redpath, the General Agent, resided in Boston, and used *The African*, afterwards *The Pine and Palm*, as the surest medium through which the Afro-American could be reached.

The issue spoken of above also contained circulars setting forth the advantages of the Movement, signed by Mr. Redpath. We would insert them *verbatim et literatim*, as they appear in *The African*, but for the great consumption of space it would require. It kept up to the old landmark of journalistic enterprise, during the year it was published.

About August or Septembur of 1861, Mr. Redpath having resigned the position of Emigration Agent of the Haytian Movement, the paper reverted to the hands of one of the Hamiltons, this time being owned and edited by Mr. Robert Hamilton, Mr. Thomas Hamilton having died. It also resumed its original name, *Anglo-African*.

Mr. Hamilton was assisted in the editorial work by Rev. Henry Highland Garnett, who appears in the paper as "Editor of the Southern Department;" and who was interested in every good enterprise started during this perilous time in the interest of American Slavery   Under Mr. Robert Hamilton's management the paper increased in size, and the editorial dash of its columns was perceptibly quickened.

Mr. Garnett was a man of affairs, and contributed in a magnificent way to the brilliancy of the paper.

It was published at 50 Beekman Street, a part of the time, and then at 184 Church Street, New York City.

Much of the services of *The Anglo-African*, in these later days of its publication, was due to Mr. William G. Hamilton, son of the former owner and editor, who acted in the capacity of business manager.

Mr. Robert Hamilton was known throughout New York state, and, in fact, the Union, as an able writer; and his paper was recognized as an unflinching advocate of Republicanism, which he regarded the best friend of the slave. While an untiring advocate of Republican principles, he watched party actions with a vigilant eye, in order to detect any traitorous measure it might attempt to support.

The African also looked with a piercing eye to the educational interests of the freedmen in the South.—Vol, V, No. 5, September 9th, 1865, immediately after the Surrender, contains a most potent and well-timed article on the kind of education the freedmen should have, and the way in which he should be taught. The editorial was headed: "The Southern Field and the proper agents."

The following are the introductory words of the article:

"We notice an increasing solicitude among the whites, as to the influence likely to be exerted upon the freed brethren of those talented colored men who are now going South. This is quite natural, The whites are conscious of the fact that heretofore they have had the field all to themselves; that for patronage and perquisites they have taught what and how they pleased."

"It is reasonable and proper that colored men should feel that it is their mission now to enter this field and educate and elevate their freed brethren. This field is naturally ours, and is the only fair one we ever had for usefulness before. Moreover, the race to be educated and elevated is ours; therefore we are deeply interested in the kind of education it receives, etc."

The Anglo-African lived to see the Afro-American a freedman, and to enjoy the awarded—"Well done, good and faithful servant," in the Abolition fight.

It lived to see the Afro-American on the march to an intellectual position and to civil citizenship; and with this consciousness it died peacefully in the arms of its promoters.

The Hamiltons will be known as long as the cause for which men fought, mentally and physically, is remembered by their countrymen. Their names will be treasured in the archives of history in connection with that of Phillips, Garrison, and a phalanx of others, whose arms are stacked by the Jordan of eternal rest.

REV. J. P. SAMPSON, D. D.

CHAPTER XII.

CONTEMPORARIES OF THE ANGLO-AFRICAN.

THE only paper we have heard of that was published by one of our race during the war, or that began publication during that period, was *The Colored Citizen*, at Cincinnati, by Mr. John P. Sampson. It was issued in the interest of the black soldiers, then fighting in the Civil War.

The Citizen was the only Afro-American war-policy paper published. It was generally known as the "Soldiers' Organ."

Many humane Christians at the North aided in the publication of this paper, and circulated thousands of copies of it among the Afro-American soldiers.

It was a successfully conducted sheet, having the tone of a journal whose mission was a high and lofty one.

Mr. Sampson was a man of eminent learning, having been sent North from his home in North Carolina to obtain an education, which he received in the schools of Boston.

He began work as a teacher in the public schools of New York, and so endeared himself to the hearts of his people and won the esteem of the nation, that when he entered upon this mission he gave a prestige to his paper which made it an ever-welcome visitor to many homes.

Mr. Welles Brown, who possibly knew more about the ability and work of the men of his times than most people, says—"Mr. Sampson was an able writer, etc.," which compliment speaks well for him.

John P. Sampson was as well known for his good deeds, and for his arduous work as editor in war and reconstruction times, as any man who ever espoused the Abolition cause.

He was an enterprising editor; which is much to say of a colored man of his profession at that time, for, usually, those so disposed were not suffered to exercise their ability in that direction.

His journal was an authority, owing to the fact that Mr, Sampson was a reliable man. He might be termed an impressive writer,—one whose thoughts in print would leave their lessons deeply stamped upon the reader's mind. His services as an editor and correspondent were largely sought. In addition to his duties in connection with *The Citizen*, he edited, through the mail, for a brief period, a paper at Louisville, Ky., which was owned by a joint-stock company. We have been unable to find out the name of this paper. *The Citizen* suspended publication in the latter part of 1865, having done great service in the West for the colored people.

The year 1862 brings us to the period when *The Mirror of the Times*, previously spoken of, changed hands, and was published as *The Pacific Appeal*, the proprietor being Mr. William H. Carter. It was because of this paper that Mr. Philip A. Bell left for the Pacific Coast to become its associate editor. *The Appeal* was also one of *The Anglo-African's* contemporaries. It was regarded as the official organ of the Afro-Americans on the Pacific Slope, at this time.

The following, which was found weekly in its columns as an advertisement of its aims and purposes, as well as a delineation of the principles for which it fought, will doubtless enlighten the reader as to its stand:

" *The Pacific Appeal*, established in 1862, is the immediate successor of *The Mirror of the Times*, which was established by colored men in San Francisco, in 1855.

The Pacific Appeal has always been regarded on the Pacific Coast, also in the Eastern states, as a reliable index of the doings of the colored citizens of the Pacific states and adjacent territories. Every important political, or other movement, made by the citizens of the Pacific coast, is promptly detailed by correspondents.

The Pacific Appeal is independent in thought and in action. Its columns are open to all parties for the logical discussion of every question pertaining to the welfare and progress of the people, without regard to race, color, or condition, etc."

With these characteristics, viz.: its political attitude, extensive influence, and wide circulation, it was regarded by the intelligent of all classes as the most desirable and readable newspaper ever published by Afro-Americans on the Pacific Slope; and as the equal of any by Afro-Americans in the Atlantic States.

During Mr. Bell's connection with this paper, he exercised all of his journalistic zeal, for which he was so well and favorably known, and this, as a matter of fact, did its part towards enabling it to stand. It was a sprightly-looking sheet, a six-column folio, and attractively printed. Its editorials were of a sober and sound character, which always indicated the power and make-up of the paper.

As was the practice of every Afro-American journal, *The Pacific Appeal* had a motto: " He who would be free, himself must strike the blow ;" which it adhered to as best it could, under existing circumstances. This, it would seem, was the vital principle underlying the contest this paper intended to make, in view of what was a common fight,—that of Abolition, or freedom to the enslaved.

PHILLIP A. BELL.

The Appeal was permitted to witness the accomplishment of this, and the bondman become a freeman and a citizen; and lived for several years afterwards to see him develop his citizenship.

Mr. Philip A. Bell, one of the very earliest editors of which mention was made in a preceding chapter, having moved to the Pacific Slope with the desire to continue the good work of editorial fighting for his race, began, April 18, 1865, to issue *The Elevator.* The following is the prospectus, as it appeared in *The Anglo-African:*

" Prospectus:—*The Elevator*,—a weekly journal of progress, published every Friday.

Office, Phoenix Building, corner of Sampson and Jackson Streets, San Francisco, Cal., Room No. 9.   Terms:—Per year, $5.00; six months, $2.50; three months, $1.25; one month, 50 cents; single copies, 15 cents.

This paper is the organ of the Executive Committee, and will advocate the largest political and civil liberty to all American citizens, irrespective of creed or color.

Such are our general principles and objects; but we shall have, in addition thereto, a special mission to fulfill: We shall labor for the civil and political enfranchisement of the colored people,—not as a distinct and separate race, but as American citizens.

We solicit the patronage of all classes, as we intend to make *The Elevator* a *real*, *live* paper, and an evidence of the progress of the age.

As an advertising column for retail business, we offer peculiar advantages, as our circulation will principally be among persons who patronize such establishments.

To make our advertising columns accessible to all, we have established the following low rates of advertising :—One square, six lines or less, one insertion, 60 cents; each subsequent insertion, 25 cents.

A liberal discount will be made to those who wish to contract for advertising quarterly or by the year.

P. A. BELL, Editor.

Publishing Committee: William H. Yates, James R. Starkey, R. A. Hall, James P. Dyer and F. G. Barbadoes."

Mr. Bell, having had up to this time twenty-five years of experience in editorial work, of course started *The Elevator* without any trouble whatever, either as to journalistic finish or business enterprise. It was a neatly printed paper, of four pages, with seven columns to a page. Its motto was "Equality before the law;" for which it fought with might and main. It was devoted to the literary culture of his race on the Pacific Slope, and though a contemporary of *The Pacific Appeal*, it claimed to be the organ of the Afro-Americans in California. The place of publication was 615 Battery Street, San Francisco, Cal.

While an earnest and efficient writer himself, in these his last days of journalism, he had an able corresponding editor in the person of Mr. William J. Powell.

The Elevator was known as a journal of progress, devoted to Science, Art and Literature, and also to the Drama.

As in the other publications of Mr. Bell, he had about him an able class of correspondents, and a willing force of agents.

Very often, during the publication of *The Elevator*, Mr. Bell was in very straitened circumstances, but he managed to continue the publication of his journal, and it was always readable. Unfortunately, he died April 24, 1889, in destitute circumstances, but his paper still lives, Mr. Bell having given it an impetus that will make it flourish for a long time.

How he was estimated as a journalist can best be told by those who knew him, and loved him for his noble deeds and generosity of heart. The following is the tribute from *The Gate City Press*, of Kansas City, Mo.:

"Philip A. Bell, the octogenarian journalist is dead. In

his death the Negro race loses the oldest and one of the ablest of American editors. Fifty-two years ago, in New York, he flung to the breeze as a menace to the slave owner and slave hunter, *The Colored American*. A quarter of a century ago, he removed to San Francisco, where *The Pacific Appeal* was started. In 1865 Mr. Bell launched *The Elevator*, a spicy weekly, which continues to this day the oldest secular Negro newspaper. Educated, original, capable of fine powers of analysis, he flung tne sparkling rays of his imagination over the productions of his pen, and came to be regarded as the Napoleon of the Colored press. For some years he had been too feeble to engage in newspaper work. Wednesday, April 24, at the age of 81, his spirit fled to his Maker. He died in the poor-house. And this is the end of a great historic character. Peace to his ashes!"

Below is the tribute paid to him by a writer in *The New York Age*:

"Philip Alexander Bell has closed his eyes in death, in his 81st year. To all New Yorkers the fact opens a history of the past that is not only interesting but profitable to consider. It brings up precious names; it calls to mind when New York City would call her roll of fifty and more of big-hearted, self-sacrificing men who publicly distinguished themselves and served the cause of their race not selfishly but for justice sake; men upon whom each other could safely rely; sensible, considerate men; stirring, energetic men; who were not simply active in efforts to free and enfranchise their brethren in bonds, but who were actively interested to forward the cause of morality generally, of education, of refinement and of the general weal. They were men of inflexible character when a principle was at stake."

*　　*　　*　　*　　*　　*　　*　　*　　*

"All of these, and more besides, are worthy of a place in the heart of every lover of liberty, and especially in the

Yours truly,
Charles B. Ray.

memory of the colored race. It is but seldom we hear mentioned the name of any of the above, though they all labored faithfully to bring about what is to-day enjoyed throughout the land by millions of their race. They were giants in efforts; they were heroes in devotion and in sacrifice.

If you would be informed of the labors of Philip A. Bell, seek the files of *The Colored American*, the Negro's pioneer paper. He started this journal in 1837, in New York City. There was associated with him the Rev. Samuel E. Cornish, one of the ablest colored men of his day, ranking with Hamilton, Simpkins and Williams. At a later date Dr. James McCune Smith was one of its editors. Dr. Smith, it will be remembered, graduated with high honors from Glasgow University, Scotland. About 1857 Mr. Bell went to California, where he wrote vigorously as an associate editor for *The Pacific Appeal*. He, with Frederick G. Barbadoes, did nobly in manufacturing a liberal sentiment in California, favorable to the colored people. In 1865 he gave to San Francisco and to the country *The Elevator*, which paper had his name at its head as editor and proprietor until his spirit from bondage was set free on the 25th ult.

Mr. Bell was a strong, vigorous but chaste writer, quite poetic; in fact he was fond of the poets, many of whom he could quote readily. He was well versed in history and belles-lettres and was a fine dramatic critic. He wrote several articles for the California daily papers, criticising Keene, Macready, Forrest and others.

*   *   *   *   *   *   *   *   *

" To be restless and aggressive, is the lesson his life presents to the individuals of this day; to those who have the manliness to feel that their talents, character, and citizenship are not properly respected. He was tall and prepossessing in appearance and manners; he had a fine address, was quick, impulsive and brave, with a keen sensibility as to honor and those other amenities that mark a gentleman and refined society. He was open-hearted and generous. Philip A. Bell has left behind but a very few of those old New Yorkers who labored with him nearly a half-century ago."

CHAPTER XIII.

THE COLORED AMERICAN.

———

THE close of the war, and an epoch of freedom for the Afro-American, mark an entirely new phase in journalistic pursuit, as in all other interests.

The South, the main place of abode for our people, is vastly in need of a press, not only as a defender of our rights but as a popular educator; for as one of eminence has said of the Afro-American journals—"They would be, for a long time, the popular educator of the masses."

Afro-American papers educate the masses of the Afro-American people. These papers would seem to be not so much a defender as teachers of the masses, leading them to see the course they should pursue as freedmen in educating and elevating themselves as a people.

The keenest and most far-seeing Afro-Americans were the ones, too, whose labors were in demand.

With these facts in view, the Afro-Americans were not long in stretching themselves out. becoming editors and putting their thoughts, well mapped out and carefully arranged, on the printed page, before the public.

The prospectus of the first paper published in the South,

appeared in *The Anglo-African*, Vol. 5, No. 6.   The following is the prospectus, as it appeared:

The Colored American Prospectus ·

"The undersigned propose to establish in Georgia, in Augusta, a Weekly Newspaper, to be entitled *The Colored American.*

It is designed to be a vehicle for the diffusion of *Religious, Political* and *General Intelligence.* It will be devoted to the promotion of harmony and good-will between the whites and colored people of the South, and untiring in its advocacy of Industry and Education among all classes; but particularly the class most in need of our agency.   It will steadfastly oppose all forms of vice that prey upon society, and give that counsel that tends to virtue, peace, prosperity and happiness.

Accepting, at all times, the decision of the public sentiment and Legislative Assemblies, and bowing to the majesty of law, it will fearlessly remonstrate against legal and constitutional proscription by appeal to the public sense of justice.

This paper will be conducted in a kind, conciliatory, and candid spirit, never countenancing that which serves to engender hostility.   Its greatest aims shall be to keep before the minds of our race the duties and responsibilities of freedom; and to call attention to the wants and grievances of the colored people.

We earnestly ask the patronage of the colored people of Georgia, who must see the importance of such an organ.

We earnestly ask the cordial support of our white friends at the South, who are striving to bring about an "era of good feeling" and prosperity, and who believe that the colored race can materially aid in developing the resources of this section.   We earnestly ask aid from our Northern friends, of all classes, who can be kept posted on all the affairs of the colored people, through our journal.

The Colored American will be issued in the latter part of October next. It will be of medium size, good type, and in all respects a good journal, and a very live one.

Terms $4.00 per annum, in advance.

Send in donations or subscriptions to Rev. James Lynch, 34 Edward Street, Baltimore, Md., or to J. T. Shuften, Augusta, Ga.

Before proceding to comment respecting the work of *The Colored American*, it may be interesting to know the cause of the establishment of *The American* by the two gentlemen who signed the Prospectus:

In May, 1865, when the United States Commissioner was sent South to the freedmen, Mr. Shuften, then a very young man, was chosen to deliver the address of welcome. He did so and acquitted himself nicely. He was followed by Rev. Dr. Lynch of Baltimore, one of the leading lights of the Afro-American race.

Mr. Shuften saw the necessity of newspapers as the herald and sentiment of the Afro-American, in connection with the work of elevating his people. Being a young man of no great influence,—certainly not enough to give that prestige to a publication necessary to draw about it a support, he succeeded in securing the aid of Dr. Lynch. In September, 1865, he purchased type from a Mr. Singer and issued the above Prospectus for a publication in October. The first week of that month marked the issue of *The American*, the first Afro-American newspaper published in the South, after the war. It was received with great favor, by both white and black citizens; and heartily endorsed by the people of Augusta for its good and timely counsels, under the new order of things.

It had no politics to advocate at that time; for its advent was before the enfranchisement of the Afro-American, or the ratification of the Fifteenth Amendment. It therefore had nothing to promote but the intellectual and moral advance-

J. T. SHUFTEN.

ment of its constituents, which it did to no little extent. *The American* had but one exchange upon its file,—that of *The Colored Citizen*, published at Cincinnati, O.

The American had but a brief existence. Mr. Shuften having consented to form a joint-stock company for the purpose of placing the paper upon a more permanent basis, he was forced, in February, 1866, through the bad faith of the stockholders, to abandon the enterprise to its creditors. It was purchased by Mr. J. E. Bryant and afterwards appeared under the name of *The Loyal Georgian*.

The American, during its career, received valuable support and encouragement from Bishop H. M. Turner and Rev. Dr. James Lynch. In fact, Mr. Lynch did a vast deal of good by writing for the paper, which made it a journal of interesting matter. He was not only a man of great experience but of vast learning, and was a ready writer.

Says an eminent man : "Lynch's articles were always carefully prepared, thoughtful, argumentative, and convincing; and they performed a good work wherever read." Another says : "Mr. Shuften was a writer of natural ability."

He has issued several pamphlets, and, at present, has a work of fiction prepared for the press, which is entirely original. *The New York World* and *Churchman* credits Mr. Shuften as the author of the best article yet published on the "Negro Question."

He was born in 1840, in Augusta, Ga., and at present is a successful, practicing lawyer, at the bar of Orlando, Florida.

CHAPTER XIV.

CONTEMPORARIES OF THE COLORED AMERICAN.

CONTEMPORANEOUS with *The American* was published *The Colored Tenneseean*, in the state of Tennessee, (the second Afro-American journal published in the South) and *The True Communicator*, at Baltimore, Md.

These were journals of much ability and influence. Though all were of very brief existence, they aided *The American* in its great work of advising the race.

The Anglo-African of Nov. 11, 1865, says of these papers: " *The True Communicator* is edited with much spirit, and shows that the gentlemen having it in charge fully comprehend their duties, and are thoroughly alive on all the questions of the hour. We hope that great success will attend the efforts of the publishers.

In speaking of *The Tenneseean*, the same paper says:—

"This paper, which we have heretofore mentioned with much pleasure, has been enlarged, and our friend Waring of Ohio has joined the editorial corps. The people of Tennessee and the adjoining states appear to be coming up to the support of this sterling paper; and we hope that the publishers are meeting a just reward for their zeal and faithfulness in our cause.

Thus we see that these two papers, published in '65 and '66, did excellent work as contemporaries of *The Colored American.*

CHAPTER XV.

GENERAL IDEA OF AFRO-AMERICAN JOURNALISM.

THE establishment of *The Communicator* and *The Tenneseean* opened the way for the introduction of like papers all over the South.

From the year 1866 on, Afro-American newspapers were being founded in almost every state, some of which died an early death, while others survived many years. Some dropped their original name, and, under another, exist to-day.

These papers were started by some of the ablest men of the race at that time. They were men whose loyalty to their people could not be questioned, and whose efforts for race development could not fail to win appreciation. They labored at a time when the Afro-American, just out of slavery, did not engage to any great extent in literary efforts; and consequently a support for their journals was obtained by the hardest efforts only.

While the South did not accept defeat with any great magnanimity of soul, and consequently was not interested in the Afro-American's development,—in fact, did not, as a whole, wish to see it, yet there were a few whose love of principles and a desire to do what is right in the sight of

God led them to receive properly the great result of the war, and at once unite with the Christian people of the North in helping the freedmen.

Wherever an Afro-American was found with brain sufficient to establish a literary effort, he was aided by these people. These journals were, in many respects, of more importance as advocates than we find the average Afro-American journals now. Why? The answer is plain, when we remember that only the ablest men of the race engaged in these undertakings then. In 1866 *The American* was a thing of the past, yet *The Loyal Georgian* was, in a measure, doing its work.

The Sunbeam, at Brooklyn, edited by Rev. Rufus L. Perry, (now D. D. and Ph. D.), and *The Zion Standard* and *Weekly Review*, edited by Rev. S. T. Jones, (now Bishop Jones) assisted by Prof. W. Howard Day, (now a D. D.,) were all marching to the front and early demonstrating the capabilities of this people, once oppressed.

These were supplemented in their efforts by neater and more substantial publications. In 1868, Rev. R. H. Cain, later a member of Congress, and Bishop in the A. M. E. Church, established *The Charleston Leader*, at Charleston, S. C. He afterwards made it the organ of his church, when it was known as *The Missionary Record*.

Rev. Mr. Cain, as is known, is a very able man, and of course much of his brilliancy was manifest in his paper. It was continued many years under the editorial management of Hon. R. Brown Elliott; but when he was elected a member of Congress, it suspended.

There were still papers rising here and there, advocating Afro-American advancement. The year 1870 opened gloriously for the Afro-Americans, in the field of journalism. *The People's Journal*, a juvenile paper, (which had 10,000 subscribers) was now being issued by Dr. R. L. Perry, as was also *The National Monitor*.

BISHOP RICHARD HARVEY CAIN, D. D.

Not one among the many Afro-American journalists has been more progressive and aggressive in journalistic work than Rev. Dr. R. L. Perry.

Rev. Perry was born in Smith County, Tenn. He is a highly educated man, having, as has been previously stated, two honorary degrees at the present time. He has an excellent idea of journalism, as one may see by a glance at *The Monitor*. He is a writer of vast learning and experience. *The Monitor* has survived many shocks in these twenty years of labor.

A writer says of our subject: "His pen has never in all these years failed to warn the race of dangers ahead. He always puts God first, and the race next."

Concerning the first paper he edited, in 1866, *The Brooklyn Daily Union* says: "It is edited by an intelligent, active, clear-headed colored man. It is temperate, sensible, and manly." This is the true estimate of his *Monitor*, to this day.

Mr. Jas. J. Spellman, now Special U. S. Lumber Agent, and Mr. John R. Lynch, now Fourth Auditor U. S. Treasury, began in this year, *The Colored Citizen*, in Mississippi. They were among the few able leaders in Mississippi, and their journal was creditably gotten up.

December 25th of that year, Mr. P. B. S. Pinchback started *The New Orleans Louisianian*, which was the first semi-weekly paper published by Afro-Americans. It was published in this way for three years, when it was issued weekly. This paper was a noteworthy effort, and a champion of the race. Its editor put into it all of the zeal and fire for which he is noted.

In this year W. Howard Day also published at Wilmington, Del., *Our National Progress*, which he edited with his accustomed vigor. It was a very good effort in this line, but eked out only a short existence. All during this time the intellectual state of the Afro-American was being improved, and his love for newspapers was daily increasing.

In August, 1861, John J. Freeman issued *The Progressive American*, in New York City, which ran from August 15, 1871, to February, 1887. It would not then have been suspended, but for the failing health of Mr. Freeman, who was advised by his physician to retire from the business.

No publication, save *The Recorder*, *Elevator*, and *North Star*, had so long an existence as this paper; and there is no exaggeration when the assertion is made, that none did more good. There was bitter prejudice to Afro-American journals, when *The American* made its appearance in New York; but it successfully combated every obstacle, and came out conqueror.

Many things profitable to the race that *The American* fought for were gained. Notably among these was the fight made for Afro-American teachers in the public schools of New York, the result being there are now twenty-three such teachers in said schools. *The American* also fought many an evil of the race, while advocating many good measures.

Mr. Freeman was a man of good journalistic ability, and excelled in press work. In journalism his was a rough road to travel; but all was laid upon the altar as his contribution to elevate the race. His editorials exhibited more than ordinary tact and talent, and were always on the side of right, morality, and the elevation of man.

William Welles Brown, in writing on the merits of *The American*, says: "That spicy and spirited weekly, *The Progressive American*, is edited by the gentleman whose name heads this sketch. By his natural genius, untiring industry, and scholarly attainments, he has created, and kept alive, a newspaper that is a welcome guest in New York and the county around."

Mr. Freeman is worthy of a more extended notice, but it must be withheld for want of space. The author would like to mention many things which he succeeded in obtaining through his editorial efforts, but must forbear.

The Progressive American was followed by *The Commoner,* and others equally as prominent. Prof. P. H. Murray published *The Colored Citizen,* at Washington, D. C. Mr. Murray is the present editor of *The St. Louis Advance,* and his editorials are always fresh, vigorous, far-seeing, and bristling with argument backed with facts.

From this time to 1880, journals were continually being started, which would require several volumes to mention. Many of them survived but a short time.

This period was one of great political excitement for the Afro-American. The ballot had just been given to him, with which it became possible to place his brother in the Congressional Halls. Publications were started in various localities for the achievement of a certain political end, which having been accomplished, their career would then terminate. This decade was, however, a successful period for Afro-American journalism, which made a great stride, though not equal to that from 1880 to 1890.

In 1870 there were but ten journals published by Afro-Americans in the United States, and in 1880 there were thirty; therefore we perceive there was a gain of twenty in ten years,—the most of these having been started after 1875. This is a good and notable increase, when we remember the lack of literary culture of the Afro-American, his limited knowledge of newspapers, and his want of desire for enlightenment then, and his support of newspapers now.

The following list does not, by any means, comprise the exact number of newspapers published by our people, for some were known only in the immediate vicinity of their publication.

The following is a complete list of Afro-American journals that were published when the year 1880 was ushered in:

Leader, ...	Indianapolis, Ind.
Christian Recorder, . .	Philadelphia, Pa.
Conservator, ...	Chicago, Ill.
Louisianian, . . .	New Orleans, La.
National Tribune, . . .	St. Louis, Mo.
Progressive American, .	New York City.
Virginia Star, . . .	Richmond, Va.
People's Advocate, . .	Washington, D. C.
Co-Operator, ...	. Boston, Mass.
Western Sentinel, . .	Kansas City, Mo.
National Monitor, . .	Brooklyn, N. Y.
Freeman's Journal, . .	St. Louis, Mo.
Advance, ...	Montgomery, Ala.
People's Journal, . .	Jackson, Miss.
Spectator, ...	Galveston, Tex.
Journal of Industry, . .	Raleigh, N. C.
Observer, ...	New Orleans, La.
Concordia Eagle, . .	Vidalia, La.
Colored Citizen, . . .	Topeka, Kan.
Golden Enterprise, . .	Baltimore, Md.
Eastern Review, . .	Providence, R. I.
Elevator, ...	San Francisco, Cal.
Afro-American Presbyterian,	Wilmington, N. C.
Independent Pilot, . .	Concord, N. C.
African Expositor, . .	Raleigh, N. C.
Star of Zion, . . .	New Berne, N. C.
Educator and Reformer, .	Nashville, Tenn.
People's Journal, . .	New Orleans, La.
People's Watchman, . .	Charleston, S. C.
The Argus, . . .	Washington, D. C.

These papers were held in high regard for their journalistic tact and worth, and for their national reputation as reliable journals. To our mind, the greatest stride made in Afro-American journalism, was in the decade which ends with the present year, 1890. Let us note the advance in the comparative estimates of 1880 and 1890. For convenience, we will do so by states:

STATES.	1880.	1890.	GAIN.
Texas,	1	16	15
Pennsylvania,	1	10	9
Virginia,	1	10	9
Tennessee,	1	9	8
Ohio,		6	6
Arkansas,		7	7
Louisiana,	4	7	3
Georgia,		10	10
Illinois,	1	6	5
Missouri,	3	6	3
Kentucky,		5	5
Alabama,	1	10	9
Dist. of Columbia,	2	4	2
New York,	2	4	2
South Carolina,	1	4	3
Indiana,	1	2	1
Maryland,	1	5	4
Mississippi,	1	4	3
Florida,		3	3
Colorado,		2	2
North Carolina,	5	11	6
California,	2	3	1
Kansas,	1	2	1
Michigan,		1	1
Minnesota,		1	1
West Virginia,		2	2
New Jersey,		2	2
Massachusetts,	1	1	
Connecticut,		1	1
Rhode Island,	1		
Total,	31	154	123

This period begins with a year when the Afro-American is seeking to advance in the educational field, and to be thirsting for knowledge.   It begins with a time when Afro-American journalism is deeply interwoven in the fabric of the nation, and is seen to be an indispensable factor in the improvement of our race.

Some of the states not mentioned have had Afro-American papers, but they were short-lived. This increase of journalism in these last years indicates as plainly as anything can the triumphant progress of the race. Since the beginning of 1890, there has been a marked gain in Afro-American journals over the last decade. The typographical appearance and the editorial standard of these papers are their noticeable characteristics. They assume greater proportions, and seem more comprehensive in their editorial dealings. In summing up this chapter, we can readily conclude that the increase in our journalistic efforts is a fair measure of our literary ability, which has been so developed within a quarter of a century. Onward! fellow-craftsmen, is the watchword.

CHAPTER XVI.

AFRO-AMERICAN MAGAZINES.

———

THAT the measure of a people's literary qualifications is its press facilities has been accepted, we think, as a fact; yet a people's literary worth is not to be estimated solely by the number of its newspapers, magazines and periodicals; for a hundred of them united may not possess as much merit as one other journal in point of editorial excellence. Therefore, we deduce this from careful study: that press facilities may be a measure of a people's literary worth, only insomuch as the press is able, practical, and efficient; and so far as it expresses itself clearly and produces sentiment in accordance with the principles of right, truth and justice.

What kind of press work goes to make up this measure, is the question for each of us to consider. What kind of press work has aided in demonstrating the Afro-American's literary worth, is another question for solution.

We believe all nations consider the magazine the best exponent of its literary worth. This being so, it is fair to conclude that such is the case with the Afro-American.

There is found in the magazine not only the purest and best thought of the editor but also the richest and best thought of the leaders and representatives of his race; made so by culture, experience, and pure Christian character.

If, then, a race possess any number of these magazines, which are well contributed to and sustained by its own people, it becomes a self-evident fact that they are growing in literary merit.

The Afro-Americans early began this work. Those at the North, even while their brethren were enslaved in the South, and they themselves were not enjoying many of the blessings of freedom, and while their elevation was retarded, saw in this branch of journalism a timely and effective means of advocacy for the abolition of slavery in the South, and the improvement of the black man at the North. As early as the 30's an Afro-American was at the head of a popular monthly magazine, Mr. William Whipper having editorial control of *The National Reformer* in 1833, which was the property of the American Moral Reform Society.

This magazine was exceedingly popular, and was, as a matter of fact, read by more whites than blacks. It was published in the interest of the Abolition Movement, and of the moral, educational, and social reform of the people, irrespective of color. It therefore occupied a position, in which the Afro-American editor had to strive bravely to reach a high standard.

Mr. Whipper was a man of fine editorial powers; and the magazine under his control was, in most respects, the equal of its former literary managers. A leader of the race, familiar with Mr. Whipper's editorial work for reform, pays him this tribute: " Mr. Whipper's editorials were couched in chaste and plain language; but they were bold and out-spoken in the advocacy of truth."

It was in 1833 that Mr. Whipper sent to the world these favorable and suggestive words through *The Reformer*, relative to moral reform. Said he: " Our country is rich with means for resuscitating her from moral degeneracy. She possesses all the elements for her redemption. She has but to will it, and she is free." If '33 presented this glorious aspect for moral reform, how much greater should this day offer!

This magazine we have just been considering, while in every respect Afro-American by having an Afro-American as editor, was not owned by a black man. It, however, demonstrated the Afro-American's capacity for the editorial work of a magazine.

But it was not long before the Afro-American was sole owner of a magazine, as well as editor of it. With the year 1837 came the publication of *The Mirror of Liberty*, a quarterly magazine, (taking William Welles Brown as authority), published by David Ruggles, whom we have noticed in a preceding chapter. Mr. Ruggles was much interested in the moral, social, and political elevation of the free Afro-Americans in the North, and for this he labored zealously through the columns of his magazine for many years. He was not so interested in the Abolition Movement. when editing *The Mirror of Liberty*. The magazine had an able corps of writers and was a credit to the race.

Between the years 1840 and 1850, there is no record that tells us of any publication of the nature we have been considering. Not until '59 do we hear of another Afro-American magazine. True to the spirit of the Afro-American, unhindered, this time his effort for a magazine was greater than ever, resulting in one the journalistic neatness of which was worthy of that of the most pretentious. It was called *The Anglo-African Magazine*, and was an outcome of *The Anglo-African* paper, both being owned and edited by Mr. Hamilton. Vol. 1, No. 1, appeared January, 1859. It was a monthly magazine of thirty-two pages. The title page had the following: "Et nigri Memnonis arma." January 1st,

1856. Published by Thomas Hamilton, 48 Beekman Street, New York.

This magazine adhered closely to the outline of policy given in the prospectus, it being devoted to Literature, Science, Statistics, and the advancement of the cause of human freedom. The name of Thomas Hamilton as editor was a guarantee for its editorial matter. Its contributors, who were men of unimpeachable character and ability, kept its columns constantly teeming with light. They always presented a clear and concise statement of the race's condition at that time, both free and enslaved.

The objects mentioned below, set forth in the prospectus, were faithfully adhered to and worked for. They were as follows: "To chronicle the population and movements of the colored people.

To present reliable statements of their religious, as well as their moral and economic standing.

To present statements of their educational condition and movements, and of their legal status in the several states.

To examine the basis on which rest their claims for citizenship in the several states and of the United States.

To give an elaborate account of the various books, pamphlets, and newspapers, written or edited by colored men.

To present the biographies of noteworthy colored men throughout the world."

The price of subscription to this magazine was $1.00. It had fifty correspondents. Upon the death of Mr. Hamliton, in 1861, its publication was suspended; but it was resurrected in 1864 by his son, William G. Hamilton, then bookkeeper in the office of *The Weekly Anglo-African*, published by his uncle; it lived, however, but a short time, to serve as a reminder of what had been.

The period intervening before we hear of another magazine, is a very long one,—freedom and citizenship having come to the Afro-American, meanwhile. True, there were magazines and periodicals published in the Afro-American schools; but we speak of such as were for the Afro-American people at large.

The *A. M. E. Church Review*, an organ of the General Conference of the A. M. E. Church at Baltimore, next claims our attention. The first number appeared in July, 1884. It was a quarterly of never less than one hundred and twenty-five pages. Its journalistic finish is pleasing to the eye, while its literary contributions are of high order. In the beginning it was edited by Rev. B. T. Tanner, now Bishop Tanner; but at present its editorial head is Dr. L. J. Coppin, a writer of acknowledged ability.

The Review has a circulation of 1500, which is daily increasing. It goes to all points of the United States, Africa, Europe, Hayti, etc. As a writer says: "It is an example of race enterprise and superior ability." The price of subscription is $1.50, and it is fully worth it."

After *The A. M. E. Church Review*, came the magazine published at Louisville, Ky., known as "*Our Women and Children,*" with Dr. William J. Simmons, editor. This magazine was established in 1888. Its purpose was the uplifting of the race, particularly our Afro-American women and children. Being devoted to this kind of work, it has done more than all the Afro-American papers together in bringing to the front the latent talent of our lady writers. Its columns have been open, from time to time, to all our women, for articles on the particular questions which affect home, the mother and children. By the efforts of its editor it has thus given to the world a bright array of female writers, upon different questions hitherto unknown to the literary world.

Its editor, Rev. William J. Simmons, D. D., is recognized by the nation as an educator, both with respect to the

BENJAMIN T. TANNER.

WILLIAM WHIPPER.

121

school-room and the newspaper. He occupies a prominent place in the affairs of his church and his people. At present he is the honored Secretary of the Southern District of the American Baptist Home Mission Society, President of the National Press Convention, and President of the State University, Louisville, Ky. He has edited, in his time, several newspapers,—a prominent one being *The American Baptist.*

Dr. Simmons' capacity for thought is an unusual one. His literary efforts are such, we feel that the world of journalism is becoming so great a power through him, that men yet unborn will regard him as of superior mind.

We clip two tributes to Dr. Simmons as a writer, and leave the reader to think about the man: "As an editorial writer he has obtained a national reputation for a pungent and aggressive style. He is an unremitting champion of right as against wrong of any kind, and has a bluff straightforward way of expressing himself on all occasions, that is as refreshing as it is startling at times."—*Ind. Freeman.*

A writer in the North pays the following: "Rev. Wm. J. Simmons, D. D., President of the State University of Louisville, Ky., and the chief Baptist scholar on this continent, is one of the race's big coming men. He has seen much of the world and men, and is a versatile, luminous thinker and writer. His chief work, 'Men of Mark,' brought him into immediate and famous notice, and is a book of priceless value to all who desire to know and learn of the magnates, 'chief scribes' and orators of the Negro race. He is President of the Colored Press Association and has always been looked upon as a Nestor in its different councils."

Howard's Negro American, published at Harrisburg, Pa., is another creditable feature of magazine literature among the Afro-Americans. It is an octavo of at least sixty pages of reading matter of the best kind. The first number was issued by its proprietor, Jas. H. W. Howard, July 1st, 1889. It

REV. W. J. SIMMONS, D. D.,
President of State University, Louisville, Ky.

is neat and tasty in its typographical arrangement, and has, at this writing, an excellent circulation. Its editor, Mr. Howard, is a man of thrift, born, in 1856, at Hamilton, and was educated in the schools of Buffalo, N. Y. He is a writer of ability and long experience, having edited the State Journal from 1881 to '86, in Harrisburg, Pa.

The next magazine we find is farther west, and is called *The Afro-American Budget.* It is published monthly at Evanston, Ill., with Rev. J. S. Woods as editor and proprietor, and Rev. W. H. Twiggs as Corresponding Editor. This magazine, in many respects, is a very praiseworthy production, particularly because of its bright journalistic touch. Its editor, a man highly educated in letters and in theology, and with natural editorial capacity, makes *The Budget* a gem, editorially. It is devoted to the practical problems of the Afro-American race, and always contains contributions from many of the excellent writers among our people. It is of thirty-two pages, carefully arranged, and is sold at the low price of seventy-five cents per year.

As we conclude this chapter we are greeted by the finest and fairest publication yet, *The Southland,* a monthly magazine, founded by Rev. J. C. Price, D. D., of Livingstone College, Salisbury, N. C., and edited by Prof. S. G. Atkins of that school. It is truly the Forum of the Afro-American press. Words too commendable of *The Southland* cannot be said. The high mission it comes to fulfill must indeed be carried out to the letter; and in order to do this it demands the support of the race. There is no more worthy magazine than this. The first number was issued in February, 1890, and received great encomiums from the press generally.

The founder, as well as the editor, needs no introduction at our hands: one, the leading educator of our race; the other, a writer of supreme excellence.

The Southland is the fac-simile of *The Forum* in its

REV. J. C. PRICE, D. D.

typographical arrangement. It is published more particularly as an exponent of the leaders' opinions of the situation in the South, It is bound to "hoe its row" through the intellectual field.

There are other magazines and periodicals published in the Afro-American educational institutions South, but they are issued more with reference to these institutions than to the broad discussion of the race question.

CHAPTER XVII.

THE DAILY AFRO-AMERICAN JOURNALS.

THE Afro-American has not lost any time in learning the advantage of a daily paper, with respect to the good it may do in a community. He has made efforts in this line that have been somewhat successful.

But there are many obstacles attending publications of this sort among the Afro-Americans. The prejudices existing prevent his connection with any united or Associated Press organization; which debars him from the privilege of receiving telegraphic communications at the cheap rates accorded the members of such a body. Then it is our opinion that while the race is prepared for daily papers, yet the support now given our weeklies argues that no great number of dailies among us would be supported. The history of Afro-American dailies thus far, proves to us that where they have been published the patronage was, in the main, white; and in order to obtain and hold this, it would not answer to have the papers too deeply "colored;" but if regard were paid to this, it would offend the Afro-American. These are only a few of the many reasons for the lack of daily Afro-American journals.

But, for all this, it is our pleasure to record some efforts in this line which have met, and now seem to be meeting, with success, though attended with many difficulties.

The first attempt made to establish a daily publication was at Cairo, Ill., where Hon. W. S. Scott, then publishing a weekly, started a daily in connection with it. It was known as *The Cairo Gazette*, Mr. Scott being owner and editor. He bought a complete outfit, at a cost of $2000, which enabled him very successfully to put his paper into operation. Vol.

B. T. HARVEY.

1, No. 1, of the daily issue, came out April 23, 1882, as an independent publication, in the interest of the race. Mr. Scott was a prominent man, and as popular with the whites as with the blacks; a proof of the fact being that his job office did all the city's printing. Four-fifths of the circulation of his paper was among the whites. It was a readable sheet, all original matter, and had a good force of reporters. Mr. Scott's politics do not meet the approval of many; but his ability is never questioned. *The Daily Gazette* was issued six months, when it was destroyed by fire.

The next effort at a daily issue was *The Columbus Messenger*, at Columbus, Ga. It was started June 20, 1887, as a weekly paper, and published for a year and a half as such, when it became a semi-weekly, and finally a daily. It was edited with much spirit and fitness by Mr. B. T. Harvey, a

HON. W. S. SCOTT.

graduate of the Tuskeegee Normal School. We have his word for the fact that, as a daily, it had a good circulation, or, in other words, a paying circulation, and its receipts were clearly satisfactory to him. Its size was 12 by 20 inches, and full of reading matter.

The Daily Messenger would not have suspended publication, but the editor having accepted a position in the Railway Mail Service, he was necessarily compelled to close up his business enterprise for a time.

As we have said, the paper, as a daily, met with the success Mr. Harvey anticipated, which will be seen in a part of a personal letter to us, which we insert: "Let me add, that, with my experience in newspaper work, I am confident the colored press could be made more confidential and powerful, if more would attempt daily issues. They can be made a success."

The Knoxville Negro World, Patteson Bros. & Co., publishers, Knoxville, Tenn., was issued daily for two weeks, but more as an advertiser than a regular daily medium of news.

As we close this chapter we learn of a daily publication in Baltimore, known as *The Public Ledger*. It is edited by Mr. Wesley Adams. *The Public Ledger* is having great success, we are informed, and our wish is that its efforts may be so appreciated as to warrant its continued publication.

PART SECOND.

MARSHALL W. TAYLOR.

CHAPTER XVIII.

SKETCHES AND PORTRAITS OF AFRO-AMERICAN EDITORS.

TIMOTHY THOMAS FORTUNE, EDITOR NEW YORK AGE,

THE most noted man in Afro-American journalism is T. Thomas Fortune of New York. He was born of slave parents in the town of Marianna, Jackson County, Florida, October 3, 1856. His parents were Sarah Jane and Emanuel Fortune,—the former of whom died in 1869; the latter, who was a conspicuous character in the Reconstruction period of Florida politics, is now a well-to-do and respected citizen of Jacksonville.

It is evident that young Fortune was destined to be a power in journalism. While a mere lad he haunted newspaper offices, soon after the war, making himself useful around the office of *The Marianna Courier*; and later, when his parents moved to East Florida, he entered, first the composing room of *The Jacksonville Courier*, then *The Union*, where he gathered a fair knowledge of the "art preservative." He then attended the Stanton school at Jacksonville for a while, and afterward entered the Jacksonville post-office as office-boy. He was soon promoted to the position of letter stamper and paper clerk. The Postmaster and he failing to agree in a small matter, Mr. Fortune threw up his position and returned to the "case."

While "sticking type" he received an appointment in 1874 as mail-route agent between Jacksonville and Chattahoochee. He resigned this position in 1875, and was appointed Special Inspector of Customs for the Eastern District of Delaware by Sec. B. H. Bristow, at the instance of his unwavering friend, Congressman William J. Purnam of the First Congressional District of Florida. He resigned this position in the fall of 1875 and entered the Normal Department of Howard University at Washington, where he remained two school years. He then entered the composing-room of *The People's Advocate*, at Washington, and while there he was married to Miss Carrie C. Smiley. Soon after this he returned to Florida, and spent a year teaching county schools. In 1879 Mr. Fortune went to New York City, and entered the composing-room of *The Weekly Witness.* In 1880 he made his bow as a journalist, as editor of *The Rumor*, Geo. Parker and William Walter Sampson being partners in the publication, the name of which was soon changed to *The New York Globe.*

The Globe wielded a powerful influence for the right. The author well remembers the frequent references made to *The Globe* and its editor. At that time few Afro-American journals were published whose columns were as reliable and newsy as those of *The Globe.* Owing to a disagreement in the partnership, *The Globe* suspended in November, 1884.

In speaking of our subject, at the time of the suspension of *The Globe*, a writer in Dr. Simmons' "Men of Mark" has the following to say : " The suspension of *The Globe* did not discourage its editor. He had commenced his work with a well-defined plan in view, and he was determined to continue it. He felt the need of a journal to contend for the just rights of his race, and thought that much good might be done

T. THOMAS FORTUNE.

through such an agency. He maintained that for a paper to be a power for good among his people, it must be fearless in its tone; that its editor should not fail to speak his just convictions; that he should hold himself aloof from parties, and maintain his position untrammelled by parties and party bosses."

Adhering to the principles in the above he re-entered his chosen field as publisher of *The New York Freeman*, November 22, 1884. This was only a week after the suspension of *The Globe*, of which Mr. Fortune was editor and proprietor.

The Freeman was decidedly the most popular paper published among Afro-American journals, for several reasons, the most prominent being these: In typographical make-up it resembled the best journals of the whites, and contained all the most important news about the Afro-American, sent by trustworthy and brilliant correspondents. Having such a corps of writers the paper contained such news, and carried with it such influence, as did no other. In this respect it pleased the masses.

Another good reason for its success was Mr. Fortune's ability as an editorial writer. He declares himself boldly, and by many is regarded as the ablest among the many Afro-Americans who wield the "goose quill." W. Allison Sweeney, a reputable writer, speaks of him in *The Indianapolis Freeman*, as follows: "T. Thomas Fortune, the well-known newspaper man, although, comparatively speaking, a young man, came near going to the front amongst the big literary men of the race, at one jump. Coming into notice first, a few years since, as editor of *The Globe*, published in New York City, he has since then, through his editorship of *The Freeman*, published in the same city, made his name nearly a household word throughout the land. As a brilliant, pointed, aggressive editorial writer, Mr. Fortune deserves all the fame he has garnered to himself. It is not indulging the least in hyperbole to say that he is considered by many the leading editorial writer and all-around newspaper man of his race, He also ranks as an essayist of no mean order, and in the language of Pollok, occasionally 'touches his harp'; and if 'nations' do not 'hear entranced,' they may some day, for the 'fine frenzy' of the poet is largely developed in his mental organism. Seriously, Mr. Fortune has given fugitive verses to the world, at different times, that burned and sparkled with true poetic fire."

The Freeman had a most encouraging career, and Mr. Fortune, no doubt, would have remained its editor, had he not accepted a position upon the editorial staff of *The New York Evening Sun*, one of the wealthiest papers in the Metropolis. He is one of the few young men who have held a position upon the editorial staff of a leading white daily.

The Freeman having been transferred to Messrs. Fortune and Peterson, its name was changed to *The New York Age*, under which caption it is now published. Our subject is an editorial contributor to *The Age*, at present. Frequent references are made to his articles, which are always able and forcible. Hon. Jno. C. Dancy, in *The Star of Zion*, speaks of him, in reference to his contributions to *The Age*, as the "watchful paragrapher."

One thing about Fortune's articles is, that he never writes unless he makes somebody wince. When he goes for a thing in his editorials, he generally comes back victorious. He is an adherent to the idea of industrial and elementary education for the Afro-Americans of the South, since, in his judgment, they stand most in need of that kind of an education.

In politics Mr. Fortune has maintained a stand in his writings that few Afro-Americans can afford to take. He has been fierce in his condemnation of corrupting principles, in both the Democratic and Republican parties, but a pleasing and earnest advocate of every good principle in each. In other words, Mr. Fortune stands as an independent thinker in politics, as in other matters of public interest. His political writings as editor of *The Freeman*, during President Cleveland's Administration, were watched with interest by thousands of intelligent Afro-Americans, and by a large portion of whites, who were constant readers of his paper.

As an editor of *The Freeman*, he was the first to suggest and further the National League idea, to prevent mob violence and intimidation of his people at the South.

Mr. Fortune's book, entitled "Black and White," is a credit to him and the race. It is generally looked upon as being a fine work. He is also author of "The Negro in Politics." It can be truly said that Mr. Fortune is an excellent specimen of what the Afro-American may do in journalism, and what he will do. He is surely the "Prince of Journalists," and his writings have won for him a life-long reputation as "editor, author, pamphleteer and agitator." For a man so young, who has already climbed so many rounds in the hard ladder of journalism and authorship, who will say he may not reach the top before the allotted years of man have run into the minutes and seconds of a ripe and honored old age?

Col. William Murrell, Editor New Jersey Trumpet.

Colonel William Murrell, whose life is full of interesting events, and whose labor in journalism has been of a lengthy period, was born a slave in the state of Georgia. He was in the war as valet to Confederate General Longstreet, and after the latter's death he enlisted as a soldier in the 44th Regiment Virginia and South Carolina troops. After the war he moved to Louisiana, where he served in the State Legislature either as door-keeper or representative for nine

COL. WILLIAM MURRELL.

years. He was on the staff of Gov. W. P. Kellogg, with the rank of major, and was afterward promoted to be colonel, and was assigned to the command of the Louisiana State National Guards. He now occupies an important position in the Interior Department, to which he was appointed by Secretary Noble.

His life as an Afro-American journalist began while residing in Louisiana, where he edited at Delta, Madison Parish, *The Madison Vindicator.* Upon going to Washington, D. C., he edited *The Baltimore Vindicator*, then published at Baltimore, Md. He went to New Jersey in 1883, and established *The Trumpet*, of which he is now editor and proprietor. The Colonel is ably assisted in the management of his paper by his amiable wife, Mrs. Louisiana Murrell. His past success but predicts what a future there is in store for him, in regard to the ennobling work of journalism.

REV. J. ALEXANDER HOLMES, EX-EDITOR CENTRAL METHODIST.

The life of Mr. Holmes began in the city of Lexington, Va., December 11, 1848. Having some love for books and letters, he took advantage of the early school training which was offered the negro; after which he matriculated at the Storer College, Harper's Ferry, where he graduated in 1872. For a while he taught school, subsequently entering the ministry in March, 1874. He steadily pursued his studies during his ministerial connection with the Washington Annual Conference of the M. E. Church, which seems to have been a course marked out with a successful end in view.

He has lived conspicuously, having held some of the best charges in that Conference, and has several times represented it in the General Conference. His editorial life of two years' duration began in 1887, when appointed editor of *The*

Central Methodist. It did a multiplicity of good works in religious and educational fields. He is quiet and unassuming, has the affection and respect of all who know him, and particularly of those privileged to an intimate acquaintance with him. His writings speak effectively for the welfare of the race.

MESSRS. S. N. HILL AND WILLIAM H. DEWEY, EDITORS, RESPECTIVELY, OF THE PEOPLE'S ADVOCATE AND THE GOLDEN RULE.

Mr. Hill first saw the light in New Berne, in 1859, and settled at 14 years of age in Wilson, N. C., where he graduated from the St. Augustine Normal and Collegiate Institute, in 1880. He at once began the newspaper business, in connection with Prof. E. Moore, in the publication of *The Wilson News.* This was a strong paper, and was the staunchest advocate for the calling of a convention of Afro-Americans in North Carolina, with the view of having their people recognized on the juries of the courts of that state.

Mr. Hill was next upon *The Banner*, at Raleigh, N. C., the organ of the Industrial Association of that state. Upon retiring from *The Banner*, he returned home and began the publication of *The People's Advocate*, which he moved to Wilmington. While published at this place, it became one of the leading journals of the state, being frequently referred to by the local white papers, and by the leading New York dailies. He returned home with *The Advocate*, prior to this last campaign, as the organ of the Republican party of the 22d Congressional district. It did remarkable service for the party.

As a writer, Mr. Hill is bold, fearless and consistent. We are prepared to say his future will be bright as the leading editor of the free press.

Mr. Dewey, like Mr. Hill, was born at New Berne, N. C., September 13, 1858. Having to earn his own living, his means for the acquisition of books were very limited. He is prominently connected with the G. U. O. O. F., in the state of North Carolina. He owned and edited *The People's Advocate*, in 1886, which did good work in the interest of the Republican party. In 1887, this paper was merged into *The Golden Rule*, through which the solidity and harmony of the party in Craven County has more than once been accomplished. *The Golden Rule* is well edited, having for its object the amelioration of the race, and the advancement of the Afro-American, financially, educationally and morally.

REV. G. W. GAYLES, EDITOR BAPTIST SIGNAL.

Possibly no man connected with Afro-American journalism has had a brighter and more honored career than the above subject. He was born in the county of Wilkinson, Miss., January 29, 1844, of slave parents, Perry and Rebecca Gayles.

Young Gayles, being one of his master's house-servants enjoyed a privilege that was accorded only those who were similarly situated at that time. As house-servant, he was taught the alphabet by a lady who was employed as private tutor in Mrs. Nancy Barron's family. This was done on account of his diligence. He soon became able to read the Bible and his hymn book, which he gave his greatest attention. Though so interested in these, he earnestly pursued the studies requisite for a good education, until he finally became well adapted intellectually for the duties of life which lay so brilliantly before him.

Called to the ministry in November, 1867, he has since, by vigorous work, been of great credit to his race as an "expounder of the Word." Shortly after he was ordained

REV. G W. GAYLES.

minister, came his appointments to some of the most prominent places in Mississippi. Before pointing the reader to his career in journalism, we will name these positions: In 1869, he was appointed by Geo. A. Ames of the United States Army a member of the board of police for the Third District of Bolivar County. In 1870, he became a Justice of Peace for the Fifth District of Bolivar County, through Gov. J. L. Alcom. In August, 1870, he was appointed supervisor for the Fifth District. He was also elected to the State Legislature for four consecutive years, and was returned in 1877 as State Senator for the Twenty-eighth Senatorial District. He has since held the position by re-election. He was Corresponding Secretary for the Missionary State Convention, and has since been unanimously elected and re-elected to the position of president. Thus we see that his wide experience in religious, political and general affairs, has served to make him a grand force in journalism. The Convention of which he was president founded *The Baptist Signal* in 1880, and elected our subject to be its editor.

As an editorial writer, Rev..Mr. Gayles ranks high among those of the "pencil-shoving" class. He is a dignified and practical writer, believing in laying before his readers that which will be of solid benefit to them in their progress through life.

The Signal, a six-column paper, issues monthly one thousand copies, and always contains matter of a helpful nature. As a religious journal and an exponent of religious ideas, it ranks among the first. Through his great personal influence and that of his paper, the Baptist State Convention feels proud to own a college in Natchez, Miss., costing six thousand dollars.

In presenting Mr. Gayles in this work, we score another success in the pioneer labors of Afro-American journalism, for it must be conceded he has achieved much with his pen.

MR. CHRISTOPHER J. PERRY, EDITOR WEEKLY TRIBUNE.

In noting the journalistic efforts of the Afro-American, *The Philadelphia Tribune*, of which the above subject is editor, falls into the category of the most conspicuous. *The Tribune* began publication in 1884, with Mr. Perry as proprietor and editor.

Perry's life in the journalistic work had been of some duration before this effort. Born at Baltimore, Md., of free parents, September 11, 1854, he availed himself of the school facilities provided for the colored children of that city, which were very meager. Going to Philadelphia, his present home, quite young, and having the desire to be educationally a free man, he diligently applied himself to books, attending the night schools of that city. He earned his support by work in private houses, and could be often seen examining the volumes in the libraries of these homes.

As early as 1867, he began writing for newspapers, his letters being always newsy and pleasing. He has an excellent style, and prominent men complimented him highly for his letters at this early period in his journalistic life. In November, 1881, he began writing for a Northern daily, and later on became the editor of the Colored Department in *The Sunday Mercury* This led to the establishment of *The Tribune*, in 1884, which he has conducted since with editorial skill and newspaper tact. A writer says: "*The Tribune*, under his guidance, has become one of the leading Afro-American journals of this country." The same paper says: "It is a staunch advocate of the rights of the negro, and is a credit to Editor Perry's managing skill."

Mr. Perry has an excellent idea of his mission as an Afro-American editor, as will be seen from the following editorial, published when *The Tribune* began its fourth year. That the reader may rightly estimate

CHRISTOPHER J. PERRY.

the independent, energetic spirit of the man, we insert it
entire:

Our Fourth Anniversary.

"So busy were we fighting in our earnest though humble
way for Harrison and protection, that we actually forgot our
birthday. It is a fact of which we are truly proud, that *The
Tribune* is the only colored journal north of Mason and
Dixon's line, which has never wavered in its fidelity to
Republicanism. In the face of very appealing temptations
from our friends, the enemy, we have been true and steadfast.
It was this party enthusiasm which led us to forget that on
Saturday last we were just four years old.

"The retrospect is very gratifying. No other venture of
this kind ever started in the face of more appalling difficulties; but from the beginning our progress has been
persistent and steady. Envy has raised its foul-tongued
voice against us. Self-satisfied, self-constituted Phariseeism
has persistently criticised us. But onward we have steadily
pursued our way, supported and encouraged by the growing
confidence of our patrons. Our circulation has increased
every week, our advertising columns crowd out news every
issue, and they stand—as compared with those of other
colored journals throughout the country—a weekly tribute
to our facilities for reaching the eyes of purchasers.

"The reason for this is simple. *The Tribune* is a paper of
the people and for the people. It is the organ of no clique
or class. As its name indicates, its purpose is to lead the
masses to appreciate their best interests and to suggest the
best means for attaining deserved ends. We have no sympathy with the spirit of many colored editors, who complain
that their race does not support their ventures. We have
been admirably supported. Our past year has been a
complete success. We believe that it has been due to our
effort to please our patrons and to be worthy of their

confidence. It shall be our purpose in the future, as it has been in the past, to maintain *The Tribune's* reputation for consistency, reliability and news enterprise."

Noticing the past career of *The Tribune*, we can readily account for the success attending its efforts.

REVS. R. C. RANSOM, W. S. LOWRY, DANIEL S. BENTLEY, WILLIAM F. BROOKS: ASSOCIATE EDITOR, BUSINESS MANAGER, PRESIDENT AND TREASURER, RESPECTIVELY, OF THE AFRO-AMERICAN SPOKESMAN.

These men compose the back-bone of *The Afro-American Spokesman*. If brains and money will push *The Spokesman* to success, we can look confidently to the accomplishment of it, with such men at its head.

Rev. Mr. Ransom was born at Flushing, Ohio, January 4, 1861,—the only child of George and Hattie Ransom. He graduated from the Wilberforce University in 1886, with the degree of Bachelor of Divinity. As a writer, he is vigorous, possessing a somewhat caustic style. Aside from the associate editorship of *The Spokesman*, he is a large contributor to various publications on quite a variety of themes.

Rev. W. S. Lowry, the business manager, was born in Allegheny County, Pa., December 5, 1848. Having served in the war, his opportunities for early education were considerably limited. He felt deeply moved to enter the ministry in 1868, and in 1870 attended the Wilberforce University for three terms, in order to prepare himself for his life-work. Since commencing it, he has held responsible positions, now being pastor of one of the best churches in the Pittsburg Conference, viz.: that of Brown Chapel, Allegheny City, Pa.

Conceiving the idea of the need of such an organ as *The*

REV. W. S. LOWRY.

Spokesman, Rev. Mr. Lowry, with Rev. R. C. Ransom and D. S. Bentley, decided upon a way by which such a paper could be established, and accordingly pushed it to success. Through his skilful financiering he is putting the paper in every home, and making for it a sure support. As a writer, his style is graceful, rich and pure. He is an occasional contributor to the city papers.

Rev. Daniel S. Bentley, president of the company, and pastor of the Wylie Ave. A. M. E. church, was born in Madison county, Ky., and is now thirty-eight years old. His fitness for his life-work was acquired in Berea College. He is a trusted leader in the A. M. E. church, and a man highly esteemed by the Bishopric of his church. His first writings gave descriptive accounts of his people's religious and general improvement, in the early part of his ministry. Most of his productions have found ready entrance to *The Christian Recorder.* Upon the organization of the Spokesman Stock Company, he was unanimously elected its president.

Rev. Wm. F. Brooks, the treasurer, and the pastor of the Grace Memorial Presbyterian church, is a man of most excellent parts, intellectually and otherwise. He is a graduate of the famous Lincoln University, and may yet occupy a professor's chair in that institution. He is doing good work for *The Spokesman.*

MAGNUS L. ROBINSON, EDITOR NATIONAL LEADER.

Magnus L. Robinson, the managing editor and one of the proprietors of *The Washington National Leader,* was born at Alexandria, Va., November 21, 1852. His parents gave him a good private school education. Being naturally of an industrious mind, he served an apprenticeship for four years in a bakery, and for several years thereafter followed the vocation of a baker. In 1868, he entered the

REV. DANIEL S. BENTLEY.

law department of the Howard University, at Washington,
D. C., from which he earnestly endeavored to graduate, but
was forced to give up his studies on account of ill health.
He next turned his attention to teaching, and passed an
examination for a position in the public schools of his native
state.   In due time he procured a school and taught successfully for nine months, beginning in 1879.

Before recounting Mr. Robinson's journalistic career, we
would call the attention of the reader to his popularity in the
community where he lives, and to his circumstances.   He is
a bright mulatto, rather diminutive in size, with extremely

affable manners.   He owns the property
in Alexandria where he resides.   He
married young and is blessed with a
devoted wife, loving children, and a host
of friends by whom he is highly respected.
He stands high in society, and is president
of the Frederick Douglass Library Association, the most prominent literary and
social organization at his home.   He is a
true and faithful friend; and being a
shrewd politician, is easily the leader of

M. L. ROBINSON.

the Afro-American people of Alexan-
dria, who always consult him on questions of public moment
and general welfare.   He is a member of the Executive
Committee of the Colored National Press Convention, and
delivered an address at the National Press Convention which
met in the Metropolitan A. M. E. church, Washington, D. C.,
March 5, 1889, his subject being "Representative Negroes."

During the time he taught school he became interested in
journalism and politics, to which he has given much study
and attention.   Being a close student of human nature and a
good judge of men and measures, he has contributed to
the press many thoughtful, able, and logical articles upon

important and current topics of the day, which were highly acceptable to such papers as *The Baltimore Sun*, *Baltimore American*, and *The Lynchburg Daily News*.

The subject-matter of these productions was always highly appreciated by the reading public. He did such good work in the journalistic line, as to give him a considerable reputation among the professionals, and he was the first Afro-American to be regularly employed on a white journal in Baltimore, Md., having been assigned to duty as reporter on *The Baltimore Daily Bee*, which was re-established in 1876. He subsequently removed to Harrisonburg, Va., and with his brother, Robert B. Robinson, he established *The Virginia Post*, which he ably edited for three years at that place.

During this time, he was steadily growing into popular favor, and was chosen to fill many political offices, which he graced with signal ability. Among his honors may be mentioned the fact that he was the first Afro-American to hold the office of secretary of the Republican Committee of Rockingham County, Va., to which he was chosen in 1880. He was also elected secretary of the Charlottesville, Va., Congressional Convention, which nominated Hon. John Paul for Congress in 1880. In 1881, he represented Rockingham County, in the Colored State Convention, held at Petersburg; and in the same year, having removed to his native home at Alexandria, he was nominated for magistrate in that city, and received a very flattering vote. Afterward, his time was devoted to teaching, and holding other positions of trust and honor in his state.

On January 12, 1888, he established *The National Leader* at Washington, D. C., and hoisted the name of James G. Blaine for president, in his first publication. His was the first negro journal to raise the Harrison and Morton ensign at the National Capital. His paper met with phenomenal success, and did great service for the Republican party in

New York among the Afro-Americans, where it had a circulation of over 5000 copies during the campaign of 1888. It is very radical in its policy, and is endorsed by the Hon. Fred Douglass as the most staunch Republican journal now published in this country.

On the 26th of April, 1890, Mr. Robinson removed his paper to Alexandria, his native city, since when it has been regularly issued every Saturday as *The Weekly Leader*. Mr. Robinson is the oldest editor in the state, in point of service, having entered upon the work of journalism in 1880 as editor of *The Virginia Post*.

In conclusion, it is well to refer to some of the later honors conferred upon Mr. Robinson. On the 16th of October, 1889, he was chief marshal of the largest and most imposing Odd Fellows' parade that ever marched through the streets of Washington, D. C. He was the Republican candidate for alderman in his city in 1889, but was defeated. He was also a prominent candidate for the legislature that year. He was president of the 8th Virginia District convention of colored men, held in Alexandria, May 15, 1890, at Odd Fellows' hall, which was called for the betterment of the intellectual and industrial interests of the race.

Thus, as is seen, when his people desire a leader they turn instinctively to him to represent them; and if his days are prolonged, his future career, it is safe to predict, will be of greater distinction than that of the past.

HON. JNO. W. CROMWELL, EDITOR PEOPLE'S ADVOCATE.

Mr. Cromwell, the well-known editor of *The People's Advocate*, was born in Portsmouth, Va., September 5, 1845, being the youngest child of Willis and Elizabeth Carney Cromwell. When but a few years old his parents moved to Philadelphia, and he was sent to the public schools, after

HON. JNO. W. CROMWELL.

which he was admitted to the institute for colored youth,
whose principal was the learned Prof. E. D. Bassett.
Our subject graduated in 1864, after which he began what
proved to be a most successful career as a pedagogue. He is
regarded as one of the finest English scholars in the Union.
He was an active worker in the Reconstruction period, laboring for his people at the risk of his own life. He has held
excellent government positions, some of them highly honorary, to which we cannot further refer, as we desire to dwell
more particularly upon his journalistic career.

He graduated from the Law Department of Howard University in 1874, and was admitted to the bar. He has not
done much as a lawyer, though he has been almost invariably
successful in the few cases intrusted to him. His success as
senior counsel in the cases against the Georgia Railroad, under
the Inter-State Commerce Act, is very flattering to his ability.
He and his associate, Mr. W. C. Martin, are the only Afro-
American lawyers that have appeared before that Commission.
When Hon. Grover Cleveland assumed the Chief Magistracy
of the nation, he was removed from the government service
for " offensive partisanship," which consisted in the publication of a Republican newspaper, *The People's Advocate*,
which, by the way, is Mr. Cromwell's most conspicuous public
service.

The Advocate was first thrown to the breeze at Alexandria,
Virginia, April 16, 1876. After a spirited fight against it
during Mr. Cromwell's absence, it received the commendation
and endorsement of the Republican Convention, assembled at
Lynchburg to select delegates to the Chicago Convention.
T. B. Pinn was publisher, R. D. Beckley business manager,
and John W. Cromwell editor. A few weeks after its
publication, it absorbed *The Sumner Tribune*, irregularly
published at Culpepper Court House, and afterwards at
Alexandria, by Hon. A. W. Harris. The connection of

Messrs. Pinn and Beckley with *The Advocate* was brief, and so was that of Mr. Harris, leaving Mr. Cromwell the sole proprietor before it had been in existence more than three months.

Then came the question: What shall be done with it? which was solved by a determination to continue it as a permanent enterprise, though the month of December showed receipts amounting to but sixty-six cents. The persistent advice of his wife Lucy not to give up, proved the turning point. In June, 1887, he bought a second-hand outfit, and published his first "all-at-home" sheet June 29, in the city of Washington, Mr. T. T. Fortune supervising its mechanical work. *The Advocate* has been published ever since, with varying fortunes ; and it has never missed but one issue.

Among its editors at different times, besides its proprietor, may be named the late Charles N. Otey, George H. Richardson, and Rev. S. P. Smith, who were its regular contributors and correspondents at different periods, as were also well-known journalists, now in other fields of labor. Young men who learned to stick type on *The Advocate* have found employment at the government printing-office, and with *The Christian Recorder*, *The New York Age*, *The Conservator*, and doubtless other journals.

Mr. Cromwell's specialty is in the collection of facts, which he presents with such clearness and force as to command universal attention. His "Negro in Business," prepared for a syndicate of Northern newspapers, received editorial notice in *The Forum*, and in one form and another was published widely throughout the country. Having had several years of experience as a teacher, his editorials on educational topics, race organizations, etc., reveal his trained bent of mind and unselfish ambitions. A writer in Dr. William J. Simmons' "Men of Mark," speaks gloriously of our subject's work in this field. He says: "All praise and honor should be

given him. None have worked more faithfully or unremit-
tingly in this field than Mr. Cromwell, and none is held
higher in the esteem of the colored press. * * * * *
Mr. Cromwell has kept his paper going through these trying
years, and has succeeded in business, laying by some money
for a rainy day.

As a writer, Cromwell is specific, close, logical and comprehensive. His paper is pure, and is of the sort that can be
put into the hands of the virtuous, and will rather lead them
to a higher life, than in any way degrade them. As would
be expected, his English is plain and forcible and his style
not at all bombastic."

Concerning the make-up and appearance of the paper, the
same writer says: "Its weekly issue is looked for with
considerable interest, as it discusses thoroughly all questions
which may arise in the District of Columbia, and concerning
which he expresses himself. The paper is especially notable
for its typographical make-up and its excellent proof-reading."
We can not say more of *The Advocate* and its learned editor
than is here quoted.

MESSRS. WILLIAM H. ANDERSON, BENJAMIN B. PELHAM,
W. H. STOWERS, AND R. PELHAM, JR., EDITORS
AND PROPRIETORS PLAINDEALER.

Afro-American journalism is attended with many difficulties
in the way to success, that are not met by other people in the
same kind of work; yet there are journals published by the
members of the race to-day, which show that with the proper
business capacity and editorial ability, the work can be made
most emphatically a success.

Such a paper is *The Detroit Plaindealer*, with the gentlemen as editors and proprietors whose names appear at the
head of this article. The origin of this now-famed news-

W. H. ANDERSON.

WALTER H. STOWERS.

ROB'T. PELHAM JR.

B. B. PELHAM.

paper was under very adverse circumstances. Its first number, (May 19, 1883,) was a seven-column folio, with three columns of advertising matter. At its anniversary issue, May, 1888, it had twenty pages, with fifty-four columns of advertising matter. In reading the history of *The Plaindealer*, as found in the anniversary issue of May, 1888, one can see that the glorious achievements which have attended the efforts of this ideal newspaper were due to its lofty conception of such work. *The Plaindealer* saw, at the very beginning, that there was more in Afro-American journalism than the desire for financial success, for it says:

"But Afro-American newspapers have for their *raison d'etre* other motives higher than money-making or notoriety, seeking which make their success or failure of more moment and of much more interest to those who appreciate their necessity. The failure of an Afro-American journal, *i. e.*, a good one, means not simply that the people are supporting some other in its place, but that they are not inclined to support any. It does not mean simply a transfer of patronage, but a lack of it. It does not mean that the desire is elsewhere gratified, but that there is no desire. It is an index of the tendencies of a people and, to a certain extent, a measure of their progress." After citing this, *The Plaindealer* then says its mission was and is "To overcome distrust; to demonstrate that *The Plaindealer* is an impartial advocate of everything for the welfare of Afro-Americans; to set an example that there is no field of labor which cannot be successfully explored and cultivated by the Afro-American who is energetic and painstaking; to provide a medium for the encouragement of literary work, for the creation of a distinctive and favorable Afro-American sentiment, for the dislodgment of prejudice and for the encouragement of patriotism."

These objects, it must be admitted, *The Plaindealer* has

endeavored, with all the life and power of the free press, to demonstrate and carry out; and it may be added that the right conception of its mission among a class of emancipated freemen has been the secret of its success. Its history has been made eventful, useful and authoritative, by its numerous representative and versatile contributors. The leading men of the race, as Douglass, Lynch, Bruce, and others, have been upon its staff of contributors. Its editors and proprietors, men of push and men of the hour, are Messrs. William H. Anderson, Benjamin B. Pelham, William H. Stowers, and Robert Pelham, Jr., a brief sketch of whom we now give.

William H. Anderson, one of the four original members of The Plaindealer Company, first saw the light in Sandusky, O., August 13th, 1857. He attended the common schools there until he came to Detroit with his parents at 16. On graduating from the High School in '75, he commenced as parcel boy with Newcomb, Endicott & Company, and steadily rose to the position of bookkeeper. He is now one of their most trusted employes, beside doing his editorial work upon *The Plaindealer*. His first newspaper experience was with *The Detroit Free Press*. He then corresponded with *The New York Globe*, and since his connection with *The Plaindealer* conducted the series of articles that attracted such wide mention, "Our Relation to Labor."

Benjamin B. Pelham was born in Detroit, February 7, 1862. He began his school life at the age of nine years at the Everett School, and was a member of the first class which graduated from that school to the Detroit High School. At the termination of his course in the High School, he accepted a position with the Detroit Post and Tribune Company. His first experience in journalism began with the publication of *The Venture*, an amateur paper, which he edited three years. He has been connected with *The Tribune* in various capacities for fifteen years, during a portion of which time he also held a clerkship in the Revenue Office under Collector Stone, but was decapitated because Cleveland believed a public office a public trust and correctly surmised that dyed-in-the-wool Republicans could not be depended on to do Democratic missionary work. His early connection with *The Venture* was an excellent school of preparation for his after labors on *The Plaindealer*, and much of the early success of the paper is due to his terse, witty and well-written articles.

William H. Stowers was born February 7th, 1859, in Canada, where his parents had fled to escape the persecution of slavery. His parents returned to Michigan when he was seven years of age. He attended the county schools until 17; then came to the city to attend the High School, which he did under difficulties, having to walk eight miles each way in hot and cold, wet and dry weather. He graduated in '79. He then became Receiving Clerk for Root, Stone & Co., which position he held for seven years. Mr. Stowers has had some experience in amateur journalism, having been associated with Mr. B. B. Pelham in issuing *The Venture*, an amateur sheet. He has a practical knowledge of stenography, having taken a course at the Detroit Business College. He has been Deputy Sheriff since '86. With all his other duties he has ably held up his end as one of *The Plaindealer* editors. It is safe to add that there is no more able or forcible writer in Afro-American journalism than he.

Robert Pelham, Jr.,—our hustler—was born January 4th, 1859, in Petersburg, Va. At an early age his parents came to Detroit. He attended the public schools, graduating from the High School in '77. He commenced his labors with *The Detroit Tribune* at 10 years of age, as carrier boy. By faithful, energetic service he has risen in their employ, and now has control of its mailing and subscription department and gives employment to a number of Afro-American youths. Last year he was made Deputy Oil Inspector. Ever since its inception he has been business manager of *The Plaindealer*, and much of its success has been due to his untiring zeal and labors in its behalf.

The crowning results of their efforts is seen in every issue of *The Plaindealer*. Full of news, and its columns teeming with bright editorials, it will always be a welcome visitor to the home of every Afro-American. A writer in *The Beaumont* (Texas) *Recorder* expresses our sentiment in the following lines:

"Another good paper is *The Detroit Plaindealer*. This paper is just what its name indicates. It does not mince matters, but it calls a spade a spade every time. And what is most interesting about it is, it is making money and enjoys a good circulation throughout the country. The Messrs. Pelham seem to know what they are about."

The exact truth as to the consistency of Southern editors found in the editorial columns of *The Plaindealer* cannot fail to command attention, as well as prove true all that has been said of them respecting their editorial capacity. Says *The Plaindealer*:

"Consistency is a jewel little prized by Southern editors. One issue of their papers teems with tirades against Northern agents who entice Afro-American labor from the South, and the next declares 'the negro a detriment' rather than aid to that section, and clamors for his speedy departure or annihilation. He is said at one time to be utterly devoid of ambition, contented and happy in the state which Southern brutality has placed him, and at another berated because he aspires to social equality with his former master. He is regarded as an arrant coward; but one single specimen, unarmed and alone, is sufficient to cause a 'Negro riot' and warrant the calling out of the 'militia.' He is said to be utterly devoid of moral sense, yet is expected to display qualities of forbearance, patience and generosity, which are only possible to types of humanity, inherently pertaining to the whites. * * * * * * If St. Peter springs the 'Negro' question on the average American at the gates of Paradise, the a. A. will be in a trying position, for he will find in Heaven a numerous host of black men who have come up 'through tribulation;' and if he elects to try the warmer climes of Hades to escape contamination, it is reasonably sure that he'll find a few there."

Thus we close the career of a representative newspaper, with the Afro-American as its trustworthy and faithful promoter.

PROF. J. E. JONES, EDITOR AFRICAN MISSIONS.

Among Virginia's proud and noble Afro-American sons, there is none more worthy than the above subject, who was born in the Rome of Virginia, October 15th, 1850, of slave parents, and was himself a slave until the Surrender.

During the war our subject's mother was impressed with the idea that her son should possess, at least, the ability to read and write, and she accordingly sought the aid of a fellow-slave to instruct her boy several nights in the week. This was continued until 1864, when matters became quite heated, and the teacher began to doubt whether he could continue the instruction of this youth. However, after some consideration it was decided that he should be taught between the hours of ten and twelve, on Sunday mornings, during the absence of the people, who were at that time attending divine services. The master, discovering that the tutor of young Jones could read and write, sold him; but the mother was so moved to have her son educated, she secured the services of a sick Confederate soldier, which were soon terminated by the surrender of Lee. A private school was opened soon after the war, the lamented R. A. Perkins of

PROF. J. E. JONES.

Lynchburg being teacher. To this our subject was sent. Not having considered, heretofore, the advantages a good education would afford, he was now led to see how unsatisfactory his present attainments were, and became eager to improve. Afterward, on entering the school of James M. Gregory, now dean of the College Department of Howard University, he began to recognize more fully what it was to be learned in the science of letters; therefore he made rapid progress, and was regarded as one of the best pupils in the school.

In the spring of 1868 he was baptized, and connected himself with the Court Street Baptist church of his city. In October of '68 he entered the Richmond Institute, at Richmond, Va., for the purpose of pursuing a theological course, having a desire to propagate Scriptural truth. He completed the academic and theological course in three years; after which, he left Virginia, and entered the Madison University at Hamilton, New York, in 1871. In 1876 he graduated from the collegiate department. The same year he was appointed by the American Baptist Home Missionary Society to a professorship in the Richmond Institute, now Richmond Theological Seminary, which position he still holds, filling the chairs of Homiletics and Greek. The degrees of A. M. and D. D. have been conferred upon him by his Alma Mater, and by Selma (Ala.) University, respectively. It can thus be readily seen, that as a student of theology and science he is eminently qualified for the trusts committed to him.

No one has been more active in securing for his people, by word and pen, their rights, than Prof. Jones. While his journalistic life has not been as extensive as that of training the Afro-American for " Theologs," he has had a wonderful career in this field, which should by no means be overlooked. His career in newspaperdom begins with his editorial work as a member upon the staff of *The Baptist Companion.* This journal, the organ of the Virginia Baptists, was conspicuous for its many brilliant editions; and as for the subsequent writings of Prof. Jones, we know that not one upon the staff contributed more to *The Companion's* high reputation than he.

In 1883 he was elected corresponding secretary of the Baptist Foreign Mission Convention of the United States, and by virtue of this position he edits the organ of the Convention, known as *African Missions.*

To deviate a little from his journalistic career, we wish to call the reader's attention to what *The Religious Herald,* organ of the white Baptists of Virginia, said about him when elected to this responsible position :

" Prof. Jones is one of the most gifted colored men in America. Besides being a Professor in Richmond Theological Seminary, he is corresponding secretary of the Baptist Foreign Mission Convention. He has the ear and heart of his people, and fills with distinction the high position to which his brethren, North and South, have called him."

Now let us return to Prof. Jones' journalistic life, inasmuch as this work should especially inform the reader upon that. Though *The Companion* suspended publication, Prof. Jones continued his labors as a writer. He is known over the country for possessing a quick and ready pen. He once held a newspaper controversy with the learned Roman Catholic Bishop Keane of Richmond, Va., which created widespread interest. Dr. Cathcart, in the Baptist Encyclopedia, speaks of the controversy thus : " Prof. Jones is an efficient teacher and a forcible writer. In 1878, he held a controversy with Bishop Keane, in which, according to the decision of many of the most competent judges, the bishop was *worsted."* If we said no more, this Afro-American's ability as a writer must be fully demonstrated. As a " pusher of the pen," he never fails to elicit the interest of all,

Our subject, in writing the Introductory Sketch of Rev. A.

Binga, Jr., D. D., in "Binga's Sermons," discusses, in his preliminary to the life of Dr. Binga, the progress of the Afro-American, in a most pleasing and soul-cheering manner. Says he: "At the end of every revolution in a country, there can be observed an effort to throw off the old and take on a newer and higher civilization. This has been peculiarly true of the negro race. The race is moving forward in the face of great obstacles, and is rising from the low and depressing depths of degradation, to which the system of American slavery has reduced it. If the character of this progress be scrutinized, it will be found that the forces which propel in the direction of improvement. and the ideas we form of the nature of that improvement will be the same forces and ideas that propel other races and society in general. Improvement in a race is an indication that the race is alive; for progress is but the movements of life to attain worthy and noble objects. The manhood and ability of a race command the attention of the public. Attention is commanded wherever power is possessed. Power is possessed by a race when it makes progress along those lines that indicate general development, etc." Thus our subject proceeds until he shows the Afro-American to actually be on the progressive.

Prof. Jones, in his writings, editorially or otherwise, is known for the calm, deliberate and conservative way in which he deals with things, as will be seen in an editorial in the April issue of *The African Missions*. After having been invited into a religious meeting of white Baptists to take a seat on the main floor, one Sunday night, he was approached by an usher who requested him to repair to the gallery. He quietly left the house, and later on, in a cool and most deliberate manner, writes editorially about the affair:

" We went into a meeting, in this city, last Sunday night, to hear a sermon from a gentleman who is conducting a revival. The meeting was had for men exclusively. The usher invited us to walk in and take a seat. We did so, but pretty soon he came to us and said: 'You will have to go to the gallery. I made a mistake; you cannot remain here.' We were puzzled. We could not see the reason for such conduct upon the part of those having the meeting in hand.

"We have attended the political meetings held at different times, in different parts of the city, by the respective parties, but have never had any one invite us to the gallery. Why such a thing should be done in a religious meeting, we cannot understand. It does seem to us that there should be as much charity in a meeting of this character as there is in a political meeting, but there was not. It was exceedingly painful to us to receive such unchristian-like treatment from our denomination. We fail to see the relation between this sort of treatment and religion. There may be some practical morality in it, but according to our judgment it does not harmonize with the teaching of the New Testament. The Negro may be wrong, in many respects, as to what constitutes the ideal Christian, but he certainly will not get much light on the subject from the men who cannot keep their prejudice in abeyance through one religious service. We suggest that our white friends write over the doors of the places in which they hold religious services, *No negroes need apply. We wish only white persons to be saved.* If it were a fact that the Negro had no better conceptions of the religious life than stated by his critics, it would be in keeping with his early training, both from precept and example."

With this manner of dealing with religious and social ostracism, the recognition of the Afro-American is an assured fact. The Caucasian must be reasoned with, not bulldozed. This Prof. Jones understands, as is evident by the way he has expressed himself above, and which no fair-minded white man can read without emphatic approval.

Hon. M. M. Lewey, Editor Florida Sentinel.

Matthew M. Lewey, son of John W. and Eliza Lewey, was born in Baltimore, Maryland, 1845. Up to the age of fifteen he had received no schooling, except the little that was afforded by the private schools of that slave state. At sixteen his parents sent him to New York, where his aunt, Mrs. Emeline Carter, and grandfather, Rev. William McFarlin, lived. There he attended the well-known school on Mulberry street, Rev. John Petterson, principal. When Governor John A. Andrew of Massachusetts was about to organize the colored 54th and 55th regiments of volunteers, the subject of this sketch dropped his school books and joined the 55th regiment, although but eighteen years of age. He had fully caught and recognized the sentiment of President Lincoln's proclamation.

His regiment took part in several hard-fought engagements, among which were the siege of Fort Wagner, the battle of James Island, and the fearful, horrible slaughter of Honey Hill, S. C. In this latter engagement he was shot three times while bearing the colors of his regiment, and finally fell badly wounded. After a period of several months in the hospital at David's Island, New York, being totally disabled, he was honorably discharged in the summer of 1865.

In the fall and winter of that year, he pursued his studies under the instruction of Rev. William T. Carr, then pastor of the Madison Street Presbyterian church, Baltimore. In the fall of 1867 he entered the preparatory department of Lincoln University at Oxford, and graduated from the collegiate department with full honors in the spring of '72. The following year he entered the law department of Howard University, under the deanship of Hon. John M. Langston, in the class with Josiah Settle, H. B. Fry, Robert Peel Brooks, and others. Before completing the full course he removed to Florida and began teaching school at Newmansville. In '74, Governor M. L. Sterns commissioned him justice of the peace for his county. From this time till '77 he held the offices of mayor of Newmansville and postmaster of the town. In 1878, after admission to the bar, he began the practice of law in the 5th Judicial circuit of his adopted state. In '82, he was elected to the legislature, in which capacity he accomplished some good work in the interest of education, among his race. In the same year he was married to Miss Bessie H. Chestnut, of Gainesville, Florida, where he has lived ever since, pursuing the practice of his profession.

In 1887 he founded *The Florida Sentinel*, a weekly journal published at Gainesville, Florida, in the interest of his people. Before the close of the year the paper grew to exceptional popularity throughout the state. *The Sentinel* is warmly Republican in politics, but not so hide-bound in partisan proclivities that it forgets to resent an insult to the race from a Republican, whether black or white.

The Sentinel has developed within two years to an extent that will compare favorably with any negro journal of the South. M. M. Lewey is sole editor and proprietor, and owns an outfit worth $3000, all new material. He runs a No. 2 Campbell's improved power-press, capable of 800 impressions per hour. His job department is complete with a quarter medium favorite job press, and is doing his full share of work among all classes of people, notwithstanding there are two daily papers in the city, with job offices connected.

Filling the columns of *The Sentinel* with news is not all of Mr. Lewey's ambition in the field of journalistic pursuits, for when the reader scans the editorials of that paper, he is at once struck with the ability displayed, and the very practical way in which the editor deals with questions affecting the educational and political interests of his race. The author was never more fired to a realization of the political condition of the colored men under the present administration, than was he while reading an editorial in *The Sentinel*, under the caption of "Colored Men, Don't." After citing many reasons for the Afro-American's failure to attain influential offices under the Republican administration commensurate with his numerical strength, the editor cites as another reason the following, which in its entirety is the most telling reason we have yet seen given:

"Another trouble negro Republicans get into, which appears almost like premeditated design to commit political death, is that they go into convention, and permit a few men, with no political influence at home, to get control of the party organization, carry it to Washington City, and have their men appointed to office, with the negro left out. Worse still ; after experiencing these sad disappointments some colored men will cringe and apologize for having aspired to positions of influence and trust, for the purpose of securing a subordinate place. This is political cowardice, and unmanly in the extreme."

Not only is Mr. Lewey level-headed in this, but as editor of *The Sentinel*, we find him, in a most considerate manner, endeavoring to inspire the race with a desire to be a self-respecting and a self-assisting people—not content to live in the atmosphere of dependency. In an editorial, "Brains will Tell," Mr. Lewey clearly proves the Afro-American press responsible for an abstract mixture of the so-called race problem, which has led our people, says he, "into a wonder of mysteries as to their relationship to this government, and what must be done to command personal respect and civil recognition from the white men, not only in the South but the North, likewise." The plucky editor then says :

"Douglass, Langston and Bruce, have obtained recognition among white men, Democrats as well as Republicans, North

and South, by reason of their indomitable self-perseverance
in their peculiar field of labor; and other colored men,
through pluck and energy, will obtain similar respect and
recognition in their peculiar fields of labor, no matter what
this labor is, whether it be in the cotton fields, work-shop,
school-room, or the grocery store. The sooner we rely
entirely upon ourselves in the development of manly character, aspire to excel in everything, work hard day and night,
get money, educate our children, don't beg but depend upon
our own brain and muscles,—in the very nature of things,
white men will soon recognize seven millions of Douglasses,
Langdons and Bruces." He then backs his assertions by
that of *The New York Herald*, whose stand, in this instance,
is to be commended. Says *The Herald*: "But the patent
facts are that it is not, and never can be, exclusively a white
man's government. The seven millions of negroes constitute
one-ninth of our population. They have the same rights, the
same privileges, that the rest of us enjoy.

"As for putting negroes into office, why that depends on the
negroes, not on us. If a black man shows the ability to use
power, he will probably acquire it. He must make himself,
and we cannot unmake him. If he is satisfied to always
remain a field-hand, that is his business; and the race
question settles itself. But if he develops executive talent,
business capacity, political astuteness and skill, he will
gravitate to his place, whether it is the counting-room or the
rostrum. This is not, after all, a question of prejudice, but a
question of brains. Brains will solve the problem."

If *The Sentinel* continues to grow in the future, as it has in
the past, Florida can well afford to claim, in this journal,
one of the best colored newspapers published in the South.
With such dignified utterances as are found in his quoted
editorial, his influence over the race to which he belongs can
but be uplifting, and of the most helpful nature.

COL. JOSEPH T. WILSON, EDITOR INDUSTRIAL DAY.

Amid the roar of cannon and in the smoke of battle, the first Republican newspaper published in Virginia made its appearance in the little town of Hampton, in March, 1865. Its editor, Col. D. B. White, had served as colonel of the 88th Regiment New York Volunteers, then serving before Richmond, in Gen. Butler's army of the James. At that time Hampton contained among its ruins and ashes about 5000 people,—contrabands, refugees and soldiers, nearly all of whom were negroes.

The advent of *The True Southerner* (the name of the new venture) was attended with great success. The names of more than three thousand persons, paying ten dollars in advance, made up its list of subscribers; and Colonel White's pen enlightened them on the movements of Grant's and Lee's armies, as they advanced upon or retreated from the beleaguered city, Richmond, the rebel's capital. It was published weekly, printed on a Franklin hand-press in a building often rocked by the heavy ordnance at Fortress Monroe, three miles away.

In 1855, Col. Joseph T. Wilson, the subject of this sketch, whose connection with *The True Southerner* we shall hereafter mention, was graduated from the schools of New Bedford, Mass. After graduating, he went in August of the same year, as steersman on board the ship Seconet, of Mattapoisett, for a three year's whaling voyage in the Pacific Ocean. His stay was prolonged, and mixed with thrilling events until 1862.

While building a trestle on the Valparaiso and Santiago railroad, he heard of the Rebellion, and immediately took passage on the Bio-Bio, arriving in New York the following August, and sailed thence in the bark Indian Belle for New Orleans, La., with government stores. At New Orleans he

COL. JOSEPH T. WILSON.

175

joined the army, entering the Second Regiment Louisiana
Native Guard Volunteers as a private. He served in several
positions in this regiment, which so distinguished itself during
the siege of Port Hudson, in 1863. He continued in the
army until 1864, when he was furloughed from the Hilton
Head South Carolina hospital. After spending a few weeks
with friends in New Bedford, he entered the Massachusetts
General Hospital at Boston, from which he was discharged
from the army.

He returned to Norfolk, Virginia, in September, and
entered the secret service of the Government, operating with
his squad on the Elizabeth and James rivers, and in front
of Richmond with the army of the James. In December of
the same year he took part in the battles of Fort Fisher and
Petersburg, becoming so disabled by wounds as to leave the
service entirely. In March of the following year he had
charge of the Government supply store, at Norfolk, Va.

After the Surrender he began the mercantile business, and
managed a large fruit store. In the meantime, with the fall
of Richmond and the disbanding of the Army of the James,
The True Southerner was moved to Norfolk, where the local
columns of the paper were placed under the editorship of Col.
Wilson, through whose energy the paper acquired a large
circulation. The following September, Col. White, its publisher, gave him full charge of the journal, with its six
thousand and two hundred subscribers, which he continued
to edit until a mob, in 1866, broke in and destroyed the office
and its contents. In August, 1867, he was placed in charge
of *The Union Republican* office at Petersburg. These papers
were owned entirely by white men, many of whom became
prominent office holders in the State and Federal Govern-
ments.

Wilson had assumed a very important position in 1867, in
the organization of the Republican party, and is remembered

now for his speeches in favor of confiscation, in the conventions of those days. He entered the Internal Revenue Service in 1869 as the first gauger in the state. In 1870, he was transferred to the Customs Department as an Inspector at Norfolk. In 1880 he established *The American Sentinel,* and supported Garfield and Arthur. He was a warm and enthusiastic admirer of General Grant; was in attendance at the convention when he was defeated for the third term. He was presidential elector in 1876, on the Hayes and Wheeler ticket, and was defeated in the convention by Hon. Joseph Segar the same year when candidate for Congress.

The American Sentinel was a strong Republican weekly, to whose influence Mr. John Goode attributed his defeat when candidate for Congress on the Democratic ticket, and the Hon. John F. Dezendorf was elected. Mr. Goode had held the position for four years, having defeated Hon. James H. Platt, Jr. *The American Sentinel* ceased to appear in the latter part of 1881, Wilson being unable to attend to it on account of his business as Inspector.

In 1882 Wilson led the Republicans against the Mahone Re-adjuster party, in the colored convention at Petersburg, and was elected chairman of the convention. A struggle ensued for the mastery of the proceedings, which lasted for hours. The mayor, W. E. Cameron, afterwards re-adjuster governor of the state, with his police took charge, and seated the re-adjuster Afro-Americans.

In August of the same year, he attended as a delegate the state Republican convention, at Lynchburg. It was at this convention that a number of Republicans sided with the re-adjusters, and held an opposing convention at the same time, in the same city. Wilson remained with the Republicans, was elected chairman of the convention and conducted its proceedings so satisfactorily, that he was nominated by acclamation as its candidate for governor, the motion having

been made by Rev. M. C. Young, and the vote declared by
Hon. John F. Dezendorf. He declined the nomination,
however, on account of the division in the party ranks and
retired from active service in politics until the next fall,
when, by his influence, Judge Spaulding was nominated for
Congress, in the Second District. Spaulding withdrew before
the election, and Harry Libby was nominated. Wilson can-
vased the district with Mr. Libby, and was credited with
having saved it to the Republicans.

In March, 1883, he was appointed one of a corps of
thirty-five Special Internal Revenue agents, and was stationed
at Cincinnati, Ohio. At his request, he was transferred to
Virginia in July, with headquarters at Richmond. In July,
1884, Congress reduced the number of agents one-half, and
Wilson was one of those retired.

In March, 1885, he began the publication of *The Right
Way*, at Norfolk. In a few months, however, his terse
articles caused him to incur the hatred of William Lamb,
mayor of the city, and the enmity of George E. Bowden,
then Collector of the port, and since the representative in
Congress from that district. By questionable legal proceedings these men got control of the printing material, and in
order to stop the publication of the paper, gave it away.
Thus *The Right Way* ceased to appear, expiring in September
of that year.

Wilson removed to Richmond in 1885, and organized the
Galilean Fisherman's Insurance Company, which he managed
with sagacity and success. In 1888, he was elected a
member of the colored committee of the Virginia Agricultural, Mechanical and Tobacco Exposition, and subsequently
became its secretary. He met with great success in securing
exhibits for the Colored department.

In October, under the auspices of the Fisherman's organization, he began the publication of *The Industrial Day*, a

thirty-two page monthly; and in January, 1889, commenced to issue it weekly. This publication he devoted to the industrial idea, as a means of assisting to solve what is termed the race problem.

In 1881, Col. Wilson published a volume of his poems, the entire edition of which (1000) was sold in sixty days, and the proceeds devoted to his post of the Grand Army of the Republic at Norfolk. In 1882, his work on Emancipation was published at the Hampton Normal and Agricultural Institute. In 1888, "The Black Phalanx," written by him, was published by the American Publishing Company, of Hartford, Conn. This work needs no commendation here. Its sale surpasses that of any other work written by an Afro-American. Wilson has contributed to the press constantly, and there are few papers published by Afro-Americans whose pages have not been adorned and its readers enlightened by his articles upon the living issues and questions of the hour.

He has written several articles concerning the work and duties of the Afro-American press. We reproduce a portion of one of these written by Wilson for *The Planet.* After citing the pioneer work of the Caucasian press, and what it had to do in reaching its present position, this veteran says: "What was true of the whites is now true of the negro race. Twenty-five years ago you could count on the fingers of one hand all the newspapers published by negroes in the United States, and as easily count the books written by negro men and women; but to-day more than one hundred and thirty-five newspapers are printed every week, and not less than twenty-five issued monthly, not including two or three magazines. These, like the white press of fifty years ago, are the pioneers of the race's literature, and are read by two hundred thousand negroes who accept their teaching as readily as does a school child that of the teacher, with, perhaps, one exception." We see that he has the right conception of the relation of our press to the people.

Col. Wilson is the oldest Afro-American newspaper man now living in Virginia, and his writings, full of sound judgment and precious experience, ought to be well accepted by the youth of our race. Our subject makes use of the following words in *The Day*, which plainly show the severe troubles the Afro-American press has been, and is now, subjected to. "The Negro press, with a few exceptions, has for quite a period been under fire—a galling fire, such as no press, not excepting the press of Old Ireland, has had to confront."

The Colonel is active and aggressive, a bold writer, an astute thinker, and an ornament to Virginia's journalism.

HON. JOHN H. WILLIAMSON, EDITOR NORTH CAROLINA GAZETTE.

John H. Williamson first saw the light of day, October 3, 1844, at Covington, Ga., his parents being James and —————— Williamson, the property of Gen. John N. Williamson. Upon the death of their master, his parents moved with their mistress to Louisburg, N. C., this now being the home of our subject.

At an early period he longed to be able to read, and so began to study. To prevent him from learning, his mistress hired him out. The white people said in those days, as they say now, sometimes—"It is a dangerous thing for a negro to read." He succeeded, however, in his effort.

He held responsible positions during the Reconstruction period. He has spent most of his time in legislative halls and at the editorial desk, contributing to the success of the race, both by word and pen. In 1867 he was appointed register for Franklin County by Gen. Sickles, and was elected

HON. JOHN H. WILLIAMSON.

181

the same year to the Constitutional convention to frame a
new constitution, under an act of Congress. His legislative
career begins with 1866—'68. He has since served in that
capacity from '68 to '72,' 76 to '78, and '86 to '88. He was
defeated in '74 and '78, and '88, owing to party differences
each time. He was a justice of the peace in his state for
years, a position of considerable responsibility in North
Carolina. For ten years he was a member of the county
board of education, and a school committeeman of his school
district. He was also a delegate to the National Republican
conventions of '72, '84, and '88. In 1881, he was elected
secretary of the North Carolina Industrial Association, holding
that position for seven years, managing its affairs with
ability and success.

His course in journalism has been of an extensive nature,
and is worthy of mention. It begins with the founding of
The Banner, April 14, 1881,—of which he was editor and
proprietor. It was the organ of the Industrial Association,
and as such it was devoted mainly to educational and
industrial pursuits. *The Banner* met with great favor
throughout the state, its circulation running up in a brief
period to two thousand, the majority of subscribers being
laborers. While the paper was devoted mainly to the
industrial interests of the race, it did not fail to speak boldly
upon all questions where the rights of the Afro-American
were involved.

In 1883, to promote its interests and accomplish more
good, believing in the maxim—"In union is strength,"—*The
Banner* united with *The Goldsboro Enterprise*, controlled by
George A. Mebane, and E. E. Smith, now minister to Liberia.
This paper assumed the name of *The Banner Enterprise*, and
was published at Raleigh, N. C. It was devoted to politics,
and other matters pertaining to the race, and had a most
successful career for quite a while, a powerful influence being

exerted by the efforts of George A. Mebane, and E. E. Smith and John H. Williamson, who were well known as editors. When a difference of opinion arose upon the matter of publication, Mr. Williamson sold his interest to George A. Mebane, and retired from the paper, leaving Mr. Mebane sole editor and proprietor, Mr Smith having also retired.

Mr. Williamson's journalistic career did not end here. In August, 1884, he commenced the publication of *The North Carolina Gazette*, a weekly paper, which was devoted, in accordance with his bent of mind, to education, industry and politics, among the Afro-Americans. As with his former papers, so with *The Gazette*, a large circulation was secured, it reaching two thousand or more. Many of the able lady writers of the old North State contributed to its columns, among whom were Misses L. T. Jackson, Annie C. Mitchell, and Jane E. Thomas. These made the paper very popular with their own sex, and it was eagerly sought for. The advertisements came largely from the white business men of Raleigh. *The Gazette* truly did much good, and we regret, with scores of Afro-Americans of the state, that the editor's other duties prevented his continuing the publication of his paper.

JOHN MITCHELL, JR., EDITOR RICHMOND PLANET.

The New York World, in its issue of February 22, 1887, said: "One of the most daring and vigorous negro editors is John Mitchell, Jr., editor of *The Richmond Planet*. The fact that he is a negro, and lives in Richmond, does not prevent him from being courageous, almost to a fault."

Without one more word, these lines from the greatest daily of the nation set forth the character and aim of the man and paper who heads this sketch. He entered into life July 11, 1863, amid the roar of cannon and the smoke of battle, in Henrico County, where his parents lived, his father being a coachman and his mother a seamstress. In Richmond, Va., he first attended school, through the push of his mother, his instructor being Rev. A. Binga, D. D., now pastor of the First Baptist church of Manchester. Under this teacher he advanced rapidly, until in 1876 he entered the Richmond normal school, graduating from the same some years afterward. He is regarded as a natural born artist. His work has been highly commended by Senator William Mahone, Hon. B. K. Bruce, Senator John A. Logan and Hon. Frederick Douglass.

His desire for the newspaper life, which has been his most prominent public service, seems to have begun when he cried *The State Journal* upon the streets of Richmond as a newsboy. In 1883 he was the Richmond correspondent of *The New York Freeman*, and December 5th, 1884, *The Planet* was placed under his editorial survey, which he has kept revolving until this day.

The Planet was in a very precarious condition when Mr. Mitchell took charge. Since that time he has made it an indispensable possession to the people of Virginia. He has so perfected his plans, that *The Planet* may continue its revolutions without undue shock or disturbance. Since he has had control he has put in a Campbell cylinder press, which is run by an electric motor; also job presses, and the office is lighted by electricity. This is all due to Mr. Mitchell's energy and power to manage.

He has the reputation of being the gamest Afro-American editor upon the continent. His forte as an editor is to battle against the outrages perpetrated upon his people in the South. In doing this he has encountered many dangerous obstacles and undergone many daring risks. His efforts as a newspaper man caused his election to the Richmond city council in May, 1888. He is also vice-president of the

JOHN MITCHELL, JR.

National Press Association. He secured the pardon of
Thomas Hewlett, and the reprieve of Simon Walker, who
was sentenced to be hung. At this writing he is working
for a commutation of his sentence.

As a writer, "Men of Mark" says: "Mr. Mitchell is a
bold and fearless writer, carrying out to the letter all he says
he will." *The Afro-American Presbyterian*, published at Wilmington, N. C., says the following of *The Planet*: "Some of
our secular exchanges, as *The Freeman* of Indianapolis, and
The Planet of Richmond, are doing some splendid work, in
the interest of the negro race. Their urgent advocacy of the
right is bound to create a stronger sentiment against the
oppressor." At the National Press Convention in Washington, March 5, 1888, Editor Mitchell addressed the convention
upon "Southern Outrages." "Iola," the great lady writer
and secretary of the convention, writes to *The Detroit Plaindealer* the following complimentary remarks of our subject:

"Any one listening to the burning words and earnest
delivery of John Mitchell, Jr., the man who has devoted
himself to this particular phase of the "Negro Question,"
must feel some throes of indignation and bitter feeling rise
within him. My eyes filled with tears and my heart with
unspeakable pity, as I thought of *The Richmond Planet's* list
of unfortunates who had met such a fearful fate. No
requiem, save the night wind, had been sung over their dead
bodies; no memorial service to bemoan their sad and horrible
fate had before been held in their memory, and no record of
the time and place of their taking off, save this, is extant;
and like many a brave Union soldier their bodies lie in many
an unknown and unhonored spot."

"All honor, then, to John Mitchell for his memorial service
—for his record, if only to the few! May his life be spared
to continue the great work he has set for himself. May his
personal bravery and courage be an incentive to others!"

As to the mission of *The Planet*, "Bert Islew," in *The Boston Advocate*, clearly enunciates it when she says: "*The Planet* dovotoo its spaoo in oondumnulion of the wrongs and atrocities committed upon the colored men and women, in the section of the country from which it is issued."

The future is bright before Mr. Mitchell. He enjoys the confidence, esteem and support of his fellow-citizens, which bespeak for *The Planet* undisturbed revolutions.

HON. C. H. J. TAYLOR, ED. THE AMERICAN CITIZEN.

By virtue of his political life, the Hon. Mr. Taylor is known far and near as an Afro-American editor of daring traits and excellent ability. He first saw the light in a town of Alabama, the 21st of April, 1856. At an early age he began to fit himself for what afterwards proved to be a brilliant career in law, politics, and journalism. His taste for newspapers was seen early in his efforts as a newsboy about Savannah, Georgia. His training was had under a private tutor, at his home at Beach Institute, one of the American missionary schools, and at Ann Arbor college, where he finished a literary and legal course of study. He immediately began the practice of law, and in various places he held eminent positions. He is now located at Atlanta, Georgia, where he enjoys a lucrative practice, his fees amounting to four or five thousand dollars a year.

His political life has been a most popular one, in that he had the courage and manhood to espouse the cause of Democracy and work as speaker and editor for the perpetuity of a Democratic form of government. As a recognition of his services along this line, he was remembered by President Cleveland in the portfolio of Minister Resident and Consul General to the Republic of Liberia.

His editorial life was brilliant and fittingly serviceable to the party with which he claims identity. He was publisher and editor, previous to his departure to Liberia, of *The World*, published at Kansas City. After his return to America, he edited *The Public Educator*, which was in the interest of the Democrats in the national contest of 1888. His paper did great service, and the party will yet recognize Mr. Taylor's labors. We cannot say more of him as an editor than Prof. L. M. Hershaw, principal of a school in Gate City, Atlanta, Georgia, says:

"Mr. Taylor is also very well known as an editor. His efforts in this line of work are characterized by his usual energy, enthusiasm and ability. His editorials are strong, pointed and forcible. In replying to an adversary, he is cutting and caustic. However, as the law is Mr. Taylor's first love, no other pursuit has been able to lure him for any considerable time from its practice. Therefore, his history as an editor is short, but exceedingly interesting."

While in his law practice at Atlanta, his time is limited for newspaper work; yet he finds time to write as a special correspondent to *The Kansas City Times*. While the majority of Afro-American editors do not indorse or countenance Mr. Taylor's editorial fight for Democratic supremacy, yet they all vie in recognizing his ability and worth, in what some may regard as a peculiar field for the Afro-American editor. Mr. Taylor is regular correspondent of the *Atlanta Constitution*, *Nashville American*, *Chattanooga Times and Birmingham Age-Herald*.

HON. JOHN L. WALLER, EX-EDITOR WESTERN RECORDER, AND AMERICAN CITIZEN.

The life of this eminent young man is fraught with achievements as a lawyer, politician and journalist. He was a slave, having been born of slave parents in New Madrid County, Missouri, January 12, 1850. Entering his first

HON. JOHN L. WALLER.

school in 1863, he diligently studied until he graduated from the Toledo, Iowa, high school.

Concerning his first intimation of the study of law, *The Capital Commonwealth*, (white) of Topeka, Kansas, says: "In 1874, Judge N. M. Hubbard, who had been watching the career of young Waller, and who sympathized with a plucky, struggling youth, sent for John, who had no acquaintance with him, to come to his office. John was astonished, for he could not conceive what so eminent a man and jurist as Judge Hubbard wanted with him; but he called as requested. After being closely interrogated by the judge on several important literary subjects, he threw back the large folding-doors of his commodious office and pointed John to his immense legal library and offered him its free use, of which he availed himself for three years, when he was admitted to the bar in October, 1877.

"Mr. Waller came to Kansas May 1, 1878, and was admitted to practice in Judge Robert Crozier's court in the First judicial district in September, 1878, since which time the people of Kansas have known him."

Mr. Waller is an acknowledged leader in the Republican party and has held many prominent positions in that party. He was placed at the head of the Republican electoral ticket in Kansas, at the last presidential election,—an honor never before accorded an Afro-American in this country. Suffice to say, there were numbers of whites who were crazy for the honor. At the election Mr. Waller carried every county, save two, in his state. During the campaign there was a greater demand for his services than for those of any other man in the state, as the fact that he delivered fifty-one speeches for the state and national ticket will demonstrate.

Mr. Waller established *The Western Recorder*, March 10, 1882, and published it for three years. The first few issues were but a little larger than a sheet of foolscap; but before the paper had been published three months, the editor, Mr. Waller, enlarged it to six columns, and in August, 1883, it became a seven-column folio. *The Recorder* soon took rank among many of the leading weekly journals of the state, and had a large circulation all over the South-west. In many of the Southern states this paper could be found. It was republican in politics, and was bold and outspoken upon all public questions.

Mr. Waller and his wife labored hard, night and day, to make *The Recorder* a success. Upon one occasion, the day before the issue of his paper, the typos, who were white, struck for higher wages. The editor, hard pressed, was about to succumb to the demand of his workmen, when Mrs. Waller said: "No, my husband, we cannot afford it. I will get the paper out. Let the typos go." Mr. Waller took her at her word. She seized a stick, mounted the printer's stool, and got the paper out only two days behind time. She continued to "set up" the paper more than five months, and until the typos, who sought to take advantage of them in their weakness, were almost on the verge of begging bread in the streets.

During the three years' existence of *The Recorder*, Mr. Waller was both traveling agent and editor, while Mrs. Waller was typo and local editor; but the unceasing labor incident to the successful operation of a negro journal at that time, soon wore the editor out, and on account of ill-health, he was compelled to sell *The Western Recorder* to Mr. H. H. Johnson of Kansas City, Mo., in February, 1885. As editor of *The Recorder*, Mr. Waller attended the Press Convention at St. Louis, in 1883, and took an active part in its deliberations.

As early as 1883, Mr. Waller placed at the mast-head of *The Recorder* the following national ticket: For President,

Hon. John A. Logan of Illinois; for Vice-President, Hon. John M. Langston. This ticket drew fire from the opponents of the two men named, from all over the country; but Mr. Waller gallantly supported these candidates, so eminent as statesmen, until the result of the Chicago Convention, in 1884, when he hoisted the names of Blaine and Logan.

It has been alleged that Mr. Waller's first venture in Afro-American journalism came out of the unlawful hanging of a colored man at Lawrence, Kansas. The man in question was one Peter Vinegar, who was suspected as being "particeps criminis" to a crime committed by two Afro-Americans, King and Robinson. Vinegar was out of the city when the crime was committed; therefore could have had nothing to do with it, but was hanged, nevertheless. Our subject was employed in the defence of Vinegar, which shortly resulted in the launching of *The Western Recorder*. It was called by many "the *fearless* and *staunch friend* of the *Afro-American* and the *paralyzer* of *mob violence.*"

In February, 1888, Mr. Waller, in company with his cousin, Anthony Morton, established *The American Citizen*, at Topeka, Mr. Waller being editor and remaining at the head of the paper until July, 1888, at which time, he sold his interest to Mr. Morton. Those who read *The Citizen* during the canvass for the nomination of president, are familiar with the fact that Mr. Waller hoisted the name of John Sherman of Ohio, for the presidency, early in March, 1888, and kept it flying there until the nomination of Gen. Benjamin Harrison, when he substituted his name.

As a journalist, Mr. Waller is fearless, yet courteous, and earnest and decided. As a faithful exponent and defender of his race, the columns of the two papers to which he devoted so much time and hard labor, speak volumes, and clearly show the earnest and anxious solicitude with which the editor labored for the advancement of the people. His editorial, after the defeat of the Republican party in Ohio, in 1883, and his warning concerning the probable defeat of the national ticket, (which proved to be a defeat,) proves that our subject is a far-seeing journalist. He says: "For Ohio to go Democratic upon the eve of a great national election, is fraught with much cause for alarm on the part of Republicans. It strikes us that the leaders of the party will be compelled to change their base of operation, and in the future look carefully to the men who are to be nominated.

"It is an undeniable fact, that the majority of the colored men in the Buckeye State supported the Democratic ticket. *The Afro-American,* the most influential colored paper in the state, gave all its support to the Democratic ticket. The Republican nominee for governor, a few years since, reflected upon the character of a very worthy colored woman, against whom he was prosecuting a "civil rights" case in court; and more—it is alleged that Mr. Foraker abused the colored race shamefully in his argument before the jury and the court, and that he was nominated over the protest of the colored people of Ohio, who loudly clamored for the nomination of Senator Sherman, who would, as a matter of course, have swept the state.

"There are eighteen thousand colored voters in Ohio, and it is to be regretted that their admonition was not heeded. We very much regret the result in Ohio, but it need not become general,—the defeat there need not become a rout. If the Republicans of the country will be cautious and discreet in their future nominations, the broken places in our ranks will receive the necessary reinforcements to save us from defeat in 1884. The colored men of Ohio are *not Democrats;* they only meant to chastise Judge Foraker for the insult offered the race in a court of justice. The Germans or Irish would have done a similar thing. The colored men who are to the front in political affairs now, are they who were children during the late war, and thousands of them have been born since 1861. These men view politics as do white men. We desire to see Ohio reclaimed, and in our next issue we will try to set forth *how we think it can be reclaimed.* It must be borne in mind, that this is the second sweeping defeat the Republicans have suffered there inside of two years. The reasons for alarm for Republican success in 1884 are well founded."

Such is Mr. Waller as a man and a journalist.

REV. CHARLES B. W. GORDON, EDITOR NATIONAL PILOT.

The mills of the theological schools grind slowly with us as a race, yet when they turn out men, in most instances they are highly capable, and have always made their mark in the religious world. Such was the case with our subject. There is probably no young man irrespective of color, whose success in ministering to the saints and wielding the editorial pen has been greater than Rev. Mr. Gordon's.

Born of humble parentage, in the state of North Carolina, November 1, 1861, he has, by prayerful attention to word and deed, made his influence felt all over the country, being familiarly known as "the young eloquent divine." His early life in school was spent under the guidance of Mr. Thomas Mixon, on Roanoke Island. From a boy, he has been known as a good declaimer. A writer, speaking of his early career in this respect, says: "Friday afternoon being set apart by the teacher for "piece speaking," or speech making, the first time that Charles appeared on the programme was an event in the history of the school and an epoch in his life.

"He grew so exceedingly eloquent, that he held his audience charmed and spell-bound. From that day it became known that he possessed great oratorical powers." From this, he made rapid progress as an orator.

Tours for heaven,
Chas., B. W. Gordon.

Having professed faith in Christ, he determined to enter the Richmond theological seminary, at Richmond, Va., in 1881. Completing a course of three years, he was, to his surprise, called to the pastorate of a large church in Petersburg, Va. His labors at this church have been highly successful. He published, in 1884, a book of sermons, preached at various times. It is a volume of four hundred and twenty pages, and is replete with evidence of his ability as a theologian.

His journalistic career began with the launching of *The Pilot*, a monthly religious sheet, May 16, 1888, of which he was the founder, proprietor and editor. It was at once made the organ of the Virginia Baptist State Convention. After the suspension of *The Baptist Companion*, at Portsmouth, the Baptists had no organ through which they could speak, until the founding of *The Pilot*, which afforded them a mouth-piece.

The Pilot became popular at once, and in demand. After having experienced the "troubles" of journalistic life one year, Mr. Gordon became so pleased with its success that in May, 1889, it was issued weekly. It can be said of this weekly sheet, as can be said of few others, that it is sustained by the Baptists of the state. Virginia is proud of *The National Pilot*, and proud of this young divine.

In closing this sketch of Rev. Mr. Gordon, we could not say more of his present and future career than is said by a writer in *The Indianapolis Freeman* of March 30, 1889, which we here quote:

"To write a full and elaborate estimate of the brilliant and growing subject of this sketch, would be impossible in an ordinary newspaper article; therefore, suffice it to say, that as an author, orator, poet, essayist and divine, the negro race in this country has hardly produced his equal, at his age, 28."

HON. JOHN C. DANCY. EDITOR STAR OF ZION

The Star of Zion, published at Salisbury, N. C., is one of the ablest church organs the Afro-American can claim. Its editor, John C. Dancy, was born in slavery at Tarboro, N. C., May 8, 1857. He early exhibited a thirst for knowledge, and accordingly was put into school after the Surrender, and kept there until 1873. He then entered the printing-office of *The Tarboro Southerner*, where he first learned the printer's trade, and afterward became very proficient as a typo. Upon leaving the office of *The Southerner*, he entered Howard University, and while there was afflicted by the death of his mother.

He has held many positions of public trust. He was clerk in the Treasury Department in Washington; also Register of Deeds for Edgecombe County. Being prominent in politics, he has held the most conspicuous places in his party's organization. He was delegate to the Republican National Convention in 1884 and 1888. At the Convention in 1884, he attracted wide attention by a speech he made, in seconding the nomination of Hon. John A. Logan. Dr. William J. Simmons' "Men of Mark," says: "His eloquent and capital effort was greeted with a volley of hand-claps, and round after round of applause" He was secretary of the convention of Afro-Americans at Raleigh, N. C., in 1887; and president of the one at Goldsboro in 1881. He went abroad as a delegate of the Right Worthy Grand Lodge of Good Templars, in 1879. Concerning his efforts upon this occasion and his actions abroad, *The Indianapolis Freeman* says:

"He spoke at the great Hengle's Cirque in Liverpool, with Joseph Malins, the well-known temperance advocate, and Rev. George Gladstone, of Scotland, nephew of the great English statesman, to about 5,000 people, and at Crystal

Palace in London to about 40,000. He lectured extensively in England, Ireland, Scotland and Wales.

As a political speaker he is widely known, having taken an active part in National and State campaigns, under the direction of the National Committee. Mr. Dancy delivered an Emancipation address at New Bedford, Mass. The speech was published entire in *The Daily Mercury* of New Bedford. *The Virginia Lancet*, commenting on the speech and the man, says:

"Hon. John C. Dancy, of Salisbury, N. C., editor of *The Star of Zion*, delivered the oration at the Emancipation celebration at New Bedford, Mass., on August 1st. We have read the report of the oration, as published in *The New Bedford Daily Mercury*, and feel justified in pronouncing it a splendid, scholarly effort. His magnificent periods, excellent rhetoric and practical illustrations, were truly wonderful. He is one of the best thinkers of the race, and his progressiveness and intelligence will surely bring him to the top."

His brilliant career as a journalist begins with the editorship of *The North Carolina Sentinel*, at Tarboro, N. C., which he managed and edited for three years. This was only a forecast of what his journalistic career has since been.

Being a prominent layman in the A. M. E. Z. church, he was chosen by the Board of Bishops, in 1885, as editor of their organ, *The Star of Zion*. This paper, under the management of Dancy, has become a powerful and self-sustaining light in the Convention. The office is well equipped; so also is the man; hence nothing can be expected but a well-prepared paper.

"Men of Mark" says of it: "Under his management, the paper has increased wonderfully in subscription and circulation, and is now considered the equal, in ability and news, of any religious paper published by the race in America."

HON. JOHN C. DANCY.

Our subject is a reader, and, it follows, can be nothing less than a writer. He reads the best literature and newspapers. *The Star of Zion* is authority for any news it publishes concerning the race. It is frequently quoted by our leading papers, as well as by those of the whites. As a popular educator in the religious and moral sphere of our people, it has successfully served as leaven, and will continue to until we shall rise in light and power.

The Freeman of August 17, 1889, said: "*The Star of Zion* is one of the most liberal and progressive denominational colored newspapers in the country. It has a good word for every creed, and its editorials are alway spicy and pointed." We welcome *The Star* as one, bright and fixed in the planetary system of Afro-American journalism.

WILLIAM E. KING, EDITOR FAIR PLAY.

This brilliant young man, the editor of a paper whose name indicates its purpose, was born in Noxumbee County, Mississippi, June 7th, 1865, his parents being Richmond and Margaret King. Though he was free-born, his parents had been slaves.

Young King was very studious in his youth, and received a good English education in the public schools of his county, and also acquired considerable knowledge of Latin. He engaged in teaching from 1881 to 1888, when he began what has been his most conspicuous public service, journalism. In 1888, Mr. King, at the earnest request of the managers, went to Helena, Arkansas, and became business manager and contributing editor of the *Jacob's Friend*, which position he filled with satisfaction to his employes, and with much credit to himself.

In February, 1889, in company with Mr. S. S. Jones, a prominent young man of Enterprise, Mississippi, Mr. King began the publication of a paper bearing the significant name of *Fair Play*, which he himself selected. It was printed upon the press of *The Meridian* (Miss.) *Daily News.* For certain reasons, *The News* failed to continue printing the paper, when Mr. King showed a most heroic spirit in cutting the paper from a six-column folio, to one of four columns, and printed it upon his job press. The trouble between the two papers was, however, amicably settled, and *The News* resumed the printing. *The Fair Play* is now an eight-column folio. Their job outfit is worth over five hundred dollars, and they do a large job business.

Mr. King is a fluent and fearless writer. Whatever he conceives to be right, he gives utterance to, regardless of the opinions or wishes of others. This is an essential characteristic of a good editor. His chief object in life is the elevation of his race, and he delights to write and converse on that subject. He is wedded to his people, and is an example for young men in morals and religion, being a consistent member of the Baptist church.

REV. W. H. MIXON, EX-EDITOR DALLAS POST.

Rev. Mr. Mixon, who was born in Dallas County, near Selma, April 25th, 1859, (his parents being Andrew J. and Maria A. Mixon,) was one of the first men to engage in Afro-American journalism in Alabama. His education, which is, by the way, a good one, was acquired in his state, of private tutors, to whom his father constantly sent him. His theological training was greatly supplemented by a course he took in the Selma University.

He is now a conspicuous clergyman in the A. M. E. church, having joined the Alabama Conference, under Bishop J. Campbell, in 1879, and ordained deacon and elder by Bishop A. W. Wayman, before he was twenty-one years of age. He has been a pedagogue in Alabama, having last served as principal of the high school at Decatur, with the irrepressible R. C. O. Benjamin as his assistant.

With credit to himself, he has served several churches of the Alabama Conference, now being Presiding Elder of the Selma District, comprising a field four hundred miles in length. To him is accredited the completion of the Payne University, at Selma, Ala. As a journalist, he did much to foster and encourage the work in his state. He is a strong supporter of *The Southern Christian Recorder*, by pen and word. He is the author of "The Moth of Ignorance Must be Destroyed."

His associates on *The Dallas Post* are well-known gentlemen, now active members of the craft, viz.: Mr. Jno. M. Gee and Rev. M. E. Bryant. They attest that he is a sharp-pointed and ready writer. Our subject loves his God first, then his people. Such a man is bound to be of service to the country.

THOMAS T. HENRY, ESQ., EX-EDITOR HALIFAX ENTERPRISE.

In the early part of October of 1886 a conference, composed of gentlemen representing the Banister Baptist Association and the Sunday School Union of Halifax County, met at the First Baptist church of South Boston, for the purpose of considering the advisability of establishing a newspaper. It was decided it should be done; whereupon Mr. Henry was chosen as editor, and Rev. J. Russell, Jr., business manager, with instructions to prepare a prospectus, at the earliest day, setting forth the moral, educational and financial necessities of the race, and the line of policy the paper should pursue. It was also decided that it should be known as *The Halifax Enterprise*, and that it should be published in the town of South Boston.

Ignorance must die.

203

The prospectus was well received, and was closely followed by 500 copies of *The Enterprise*, which greeted an anxious public with the characteristic motto: "We will from no duty shrink." On its list of subscribers were soon some of the most prominent whites, as well as colored men, of the county, with some of the best business houses of Danville, North Carolina, and of Richmond, as advertisers. Many complimentary and substantial messages of appreciation poured into the editor's sanctum. We here insert one from T. E. Barksdale, the very efficient superintendent of schools of Halifax: "Upon my return home I found the first and second numbers of your paper. This commendable effort speaks well for the advance of your people in the last fifteen years. A strict adherence to the design of the paper, as set forth in your prospectus—the educational and religious improvement of your race—will, in my humble judgment, crown *The Enterprise* with success. Please find enclosed subscription for one year."

Mr. Henry, who was born in Richmond in 1852, received his education in the public schools of that city, including the high school. He afterwards read law, and was admitted to the bar in 1882, having as his associate in the practice the lamented R. Peel Brooks.

As a keen and magnificent writer, he proved himself equal to the task in the editorship of *The Enterprise*. For six months he stuck in a most tenacious manner to the following text, which stood at the head of its editorial columns. It bespeaks volumes for its mission. We here present it: "Educate your children; economize your earnings; acquire property; become part owners of the soil of your country. We have nailed our flag to this mast, and he who would attempt to haul it down, is an enemy to the best interests of the negro."

Mr. Henry resigned the editorship when an attempt was

made to make it a political paper, whereupon Mr. J. C. Carter assumed the position. Under Mr. Carter's management it survived four weeks, when a suspension became necessary.

Hon. S. J. Bampfield, G. W. Anderson, and I. Randall Reid: Managing Editor, and Associate Editors, Respectively, of The New South.

The above gentlemen compose the staff of *The New South*, a journal of high repute, published at Beaufort, S. C. The managing editor was born in Charleston, the fifth day of September, 1849, and is now clerk of the Court of Common Pleas and General Sessions for the county of Beaufort. Mr. Anderson, the senior associate editor, was born in New London, Pa., December 2, 1856; while Mr. Reid, the junior member of the staff, was born in Beaufort, during the latter part of the Rebellion. Mr. Anderson is at present a teacher in the Beaufort Normal and Industrial Academy; and Mr. Reid, Deputy Sheriff of Beaufort.

The early training of these gentlemen was acquired in their respective localities; later on, at different periods, they entered Lincoln University, where each graduated with honors. Mr. Bampfield pursued a course of law, until the law department of Lincoln University was abolished; after which he continued to study law under the lamented Judge Pierce L. Wiggan, and was admitted to practice by the Supreme Court of South Carolina, in 1874. They wield considerable influence in the community in which they live.

The New South, of which these gentlemen compose the staff, is a Republican journal, devoted to education, politics, literature and religion, and published weekly at Beaufort, Beaufort County, S. C., by the New South Publishing Company, composed solely of colored young men of that county.

It is issued, primarily, in the interest of the negro race, but as well for the vital principles of the Republican party and the work of building up and strengthening the material resources of its town and section. It is also an advocate of the rights of all races smarting under the rod of oppression.

The absence of a journal in Beaufort, owned and controlled by an Afro-American, and conducted with these purposes in view, brought *The New South* into the field. Its editors and publishers realize that it has met a long-felt want, and in that view they are strengthened by a liberal support from the better element of their people, and that growing class of whites who sincerely desire to see the Afro-American rise in the scale of humanity, and show himself worthy of the great boon of freedom that has been conferred upon him by the recent amendments to the Constitution.

The paper is published from its own plant, at its office on Port Republic street, Beaufort, S. C. This plant is valued at $1500, and is entirely free from debt and all encumbrances of every character whatever. It includes a complete job outfit, and the company is prepared to do neat job work at short notice. The foreman of the office, and all the help, are Afro-Americans. The type and press are of the best quality, and capable of doing first-class work. It is a seven-column weekly, 24 by 36 inches, issued every Thursday morning, at two dollars a year or one dollar for six months.

Its motto is in the words of the martyred Lincoln—"With malice toward none; with charity for all." It is in this spirit that it has entered the field of journalism, to labor unselfishly for the object stated above, and it is upon that line it proposes to fight it out, "if it takes all summer." It recognizes honest differences of opinion, in all fields of labor and among all classes of laborers, and therefore regards it the duty of the true laborers to lay aside all malice and exercise charity in all things.

G. W. ANDERSON.

The future of the Afro-American in this country will depend infinitely more upon his own exertions than upon any other agency now at work in his behalf. The real and substantial work, therefore, must be done among the race, and by members of it, and the true Afro-American journalist will play no unimportant part in that work. The deeper and more intensely that impresses itself upon his mind, the better will he be prepared for the work and the more marked and certain will be the results in the near future.

The first issue of *The New South* appeared on the 23d of May, and it has been issued regularly each week since, gradually improving alike in mechanical extension and editorial management, and with a constantly increasing subscription list.

The appearance of *The New South* created no little amount of comment. Its salutatory was telegraphed to *The New York Herald*, and published by that great paper under the caption—"The Negro must Help Himself." In that article the following sensible words appeared. After citing the fact of Afro-American advancement, it says : "These are familiar truths ; and yet it is a fact too well known to him, that he is denied the actual enjoyment of many rights under the Constitution and laws that are accorded to others. Indeed, under the laws of certain sections of the country, he is almost anything but a free man,—a pariah in his own country. Whatever else may have conspired to produce such a condition of things, every intelligent, self-respecting negro knows, and freely admits, that the main cause is as an unfortunate moral, material, and intellectual condition,—a legacy of more than two hundred and fifty years of slavery. Until that condition is materially changed, no proper recognition of the race can reasonably be expected, etc."

This but serves to show the spirit of the editor in his editorial advice to his race constituents. *The South* believes

L RANDALL REID.

in a peaceable way to settle the negro problem. The idea advanced by many of the North, in advocacy of racial protection by an organized force system, is dealt a blow by *The South* in a scathing editorial on—" Who will Bell the Cat?" These are the closing lines of the editorial, which will commend itself to all intelligent and sober-thinking people: " It seems to us that the history of every effort on the part of the colored people of the South to organize for self-protection, is of itself sufficient to satisfy every intelligent mind of the utter helplessness of such an undertaking. It has never yet proved effective, and, so far as we can see, never will be effective for such a purpose. If for these troubles there can be no other remedy suggested by these gentlemen, then we are of all races the most miserable, indeed."

These extracts prove the editorial ability of *The New South*. Its managing editor, with but little previous journalistic training, is a good writer.

PROF. E, H. LIPSCOMBE, EX-EDITOR MOUNTAIN GLEANER.

This cultured gentleman and well-known writer was born in the famous tobacco town, Durham, N. C., September 29, 1858. His editorial career began while he was a student at Shaw University, of which he is a graduate. He became associated with Dr. H. M. Tupper (president of that institution) and Prof. N. F. Roberts, in the publication of *The African Expositor*, which was then the organ of the North Carolina Baptists, as well as that of the University.

Though the junior member of the staff, he is accredited with having been the most classic writer upon *The Expositor*. The secret of his success with the paper was due to the fact that all of his articles upon religion, education, temperance, and, occasionally, politics, were prepared with the utmost care and study, and were said to be of a nervous, concise and

PROF. E. H. LIPSCOMBE.

lucid style, which fact always insured him many admiring readers. Those of *The Expositor* always wanted to see what Lipscombe had to say; this being especially true of the younger class of men, who admired him for the fearless, fiery dash, the convincing logic and the captivating rhetoric of his writings. His contributions to *The Expositor* were certainly of that nature that furthered its prospects for a successful existence. At one time he had special charge of the temperance department, and being a hearty worker for prohibition, he threw many hot shots into the camp of the anti-prohibitionists.

In 1882, he was elected by the North Carolina Baptist State Convention as one of the editors of *The Baptist Standard*. In company with other gentlemen he established *The Light House*, in 1884, being its editor-in-chief. In 1885, the paper was moved to Asheville, when it became *The Mountain Gleaner*, he still remaining editor-in-chief, in which position he greatly distinguished himself. The paper ranked among the ablest edited of the country, though by no means the largest.

The Gleaner worked zealously for the betterment of the Afro-American's condition, and likewise took a part in everything looking to the development of North Carolina, particularly the city in which it was published. Editor Lipscombe was always invited to the public meetings, regardless of the color of those who called them, and freely expressed his sentiments upon the matters at issue. These invitations were the result of the ability and influence of his paper. Though editor of a publication whose voice was never smothered in political battle, or silent when matters of public interest were discussed, he was elected to his present position, that of principal of the graded school No. 1, in Asheville.

In his work as publisher and journalist, he owes a debt of gratitude to his white brethren of the journalistic turn, whose kindness can never be forgotten by him. The principal of these are the Rev. Dr. C. J. Bailey of *The Biblical Recorder*, Raleigh, N C , Mr Theodore Hobgood of *The Asheville Advance*, and Mr. R. M. Furman of *The Asheville Citizen*. These gentlemen, while fully according him the right to hold opinions different from their own, notably in politics, have nevertheless aided him in standing upon his feet, when, without the assistance of strong men, he could not have done so. Though holding a situation under a Democratic school board, his fair and conservative expressions of opinion have given him a right to declare himself upon the stump, as to his political preferences.

In his paper, *The Gleaner*, he made a manly fight for J. C. Matthews as Recorder of Deeds, whose appointment was made by President Cleveland, and was pending confirmation in a Republican Senate. His editorials upon the subject were read far and wide, and clipped by Washington papers. A republican, on reading one of his editorials, is said to have remarked: This is fair and manly, and should remind us that however good republicans the colored men may naturally be, no policy of political coercion can be applied to them with success."

MESSRS. WILLIAM F. SIMPSON, SECRET SOCIETY EDITOR,
AND ABEL P. CALDWELL, BUSINESS MANAGER,
OF THE MONTHLY ECHO.

Mr. Simpson was born March 15, 1842, in Philadelphia, Pa., his parents being Charles and Delphine Simpson. He is the Secret Society editor of *The Monthly Echo*. He was sent to the public schools of Philadelphia until the Friends opened a school called The Institute for Colored Youths, under the principalship of Prof. E. D. Bassett, where he was then placed. He here continued his studies with a view to graduation in 1858, but for some cause he was not permitted to do so.

While in school he acquired the trade of boot and shoe maker, also that of a barber, in which he is now engaged. He is a great Society promoter. His career as editor of the Secret Society department of *The Echo* dates from 1883, which he has filled with credit and ability. He has proved a most valuable accession to the editorial staff of *The Echo*, and being well informed as to the workings of various secret orders, he is good authority in matters of that kind. *The Echo* regards him as essential to its existence.

Abel P. Caldwell, the business manager of *The Echo*, was born in Chapel Hill, N. C., January 1, 1865. His training was had through many difficulties, at the North, as well as South. He is a young man of fine sense and business ability. While managing editor of *The Echo*, he was selected by the U. S. Director General of the American Exhibition, held in London, England, to represent the young Afro-Americans, which he did with credit.

Responding to an inclination to do something to his liking, with three others, he began the publication of *The Echo* in 1882. It was then a small quarter-sheet, with Charles W. Simpson as editor, while Mr. Caldwell became business manager. Thus *The Echo* commenced what has proved, after more than seven years' experience, a staunch champion of the rights and privileges of the Afro-Americans. Mr. Caldwell assumed control as editor and proprietor, with his brother, in 1884.

Dr. B. T. Tanner, formerly editor of *The Christian Recorder*, and now Bishop Tanner, says: "In more ways than one, *The Echo* is a model which larger and more pretentious journals of our people could imitate to their advantage. With the motto—'To preserve an equable mind,'—it pursues the even tenor of its ways, as though it came to stay."

ABEL P. CALDWELL.

The National Baptist said of *The Echo*,—" It is evidently well edited for an amateur paper, and we are glad to see that it contains nothing trashy and sensational."

The Echo warmly endorsed the Industrial School project of Mrs. F. M. Coppin. In recognition of *The Echo's* services in behalf of this institution, Mrs. Coppin addressed a letter to the editors, thanking them for the interest taken in the enterprise. It reads as follows: " I am very much obliged to you for your excellent editorial on Industrial Education, in your last issue. It is impossible to calculate how much good is done by a newspaper, in enlightening the minds of the people upon great subjects, and, surely, an education in the use of tools is of first importance in a civilized country. Virgil says: 'I sing arms and the hero.' Carlyle says: 'Tools and the man are a far wider kind of epic.'

" Young men, like yourselves, Messrs. Editors, are just the ones to speak upon this subject. The man that the shoe pinches is the one to hollow. The mechanical toe of ours is very decidedly cramped and pinched by lack of opportunities for growth and improvement."

With a view to enlarging the influence and scope of *The Echo*, the editors constituted themselves a stock company in 1888, with Dr. L. J. Coppin and William F. Simpson editors, and Abel P. Caldwell business manager. This led to an increase in the size of the paper, and also in the circulation, and to-day, under the management of an able corps of editors, it enjoys a rapidly increasing subscription list.

REV. W. J. WHITE, EDITOR GEORGIA BAPTIST.

At a meeting of the Missionary Baptist Convention of Georgia, in May, 1880, at Macon, Ga., it was decided that the Convention should establish a newspaper, and it

REV. L. J. COPPIN.

accordingly appointed a committee of three to perfect the requisite arrangements. These decided that the publication should be known as *The Georgia Baptist*, and designated Rev. W. J. White as corresponding secretary and general manager, with power to issue the paper.

The Convention having appropriated nothing for the venture, Mr. White organized a stock company, and bought an outfit for the paper and job office, at an expenditure of $2000. Soon he became proprietor and editor, which positions he still holds. The religious conventions, associations, etc., adopted it as their organ, and for nine years it has defended them in their creed and doctrine.

The first issue, October 28, 1880, consisted of one thousand copies, which have gradually increased until the average for the succeeding three months, ending January 1, 1889, was three thousand two hundred and forty. This paper goes all over the country and is circulated more extensively in remote sections of the state than any other journal. It goes also to England and Africa.

The Baptist is not, like some other Afro-American journals, a tri-weekly, but a weekly, and has not missed an issue from the beginning. It has never used a patent outside, nor does it use any plate matter. This is of course due to Mr. White's exalted idea of journalism. The paper has never changed hands, he having been editor and business manager nine years.

Mr. White was born in Elbert county, Ga., December 25, 1831, and is accordingly, at this writing, fifty-seven years old. His education in the schools was acquired when he was quite young, but he is ever a constant student of men and measures.

He served as an apprentice under W. H. Goodrich, an extensive house builder, and he worked at the carpenter's trade for seven years, after which he learned cabinet making under the Platt Brothers, for whom he worked until January, 1867.

In the early part of 1866 the Republicans of Augusta started a newspaper called *The Colored American*, which was the first colored paper ever published in Georgia. John T. Shuften was its editor and proprietor, but W. J. White assisted him in getting it out. After a few issues were published, a stock company was organized and the name of the paper changed to *The Loyal Georgian*. W. J. White was elected secretary of this company, and took active part in the publication of this paper for about two years, the time it was published.

Another company was now organized and *The Loyal Georgian* merged into *The Georgia Republican*. W. J. White was its correspondent and canvasser as long as published. After the suspension of *The Loyal Georgian* he acted as correspondent for *The Atlanta Republican* and occasionally for other papers. Since *The Georgia Baptist* has been in existence he has confined himself solely to its publication, the editorials being written exclusively by him.

Mr. White is pastor of Harmony Baptist church, Augusta, Ga., and treasurer of the Shiloh Baptist Association. His pastorate of this church has been continuous since May 10, 1868, when the church was organized. He is trustee of the Atlanta University, at Atlanta, Ga., and for eighteen years has taken an active part in its management. He is trustee for the Atlanta Baptist Seminary, a theological school for young men of Atlanta, Ga. He is a trustee of Spelman Seminary and vice-president of the board. This is a school for the training of young ladies at Atlanta, Ga.

Mr. White is a strong prohibitionist and has taken an active part in the prohibition contests that have arisen in his own and adjoining states. From January, 1867, to January, 1869, he was an agent for the Freedmen's Bureau and was assigned to the duty of organizing schools in all parts of Georgia for the colored children. He encountered many dangers in the prosecution of the duties pertaining to this office.

In the spring of 1869 Mr. White was appointed assistant assessor in the Internal Revenue service by Captain Edwin Belcher, the first Afro-American assessor appointed by President Grant. When the assessors' and collectors' offices were united by a change in the law, Mr. White was appointed by Col. Isham S. Farnin deputy collector, with headquarters at the collector's office, a position that gave him charge of all revenue matters connected with distilleries and tobacco factories. For three years he had charge of a large division, with headquarters at Milledgeville, Ga. He served under Col. Farnin, Col. E. C. Wade and Col. W. H. Johnson, as deputy collector, and resigned voluntarily, January 1st, 1880. He has taken an active part in public affairs and has been closely identified with the Republican party ever since the war.

The Afro-Americans of Georgia have, during the last ten years, held conventions that were intended solely for the advancement of their interests in state affairs. The first of these met at Macon, Ga., the second at Atlanta, and the third at Macon. These conventions have been productive of much good to the Afro-Americans of Georgia. Mr. White was president of them all. The last convention met January 25, 1888, and among other things of importance done was the organization of the Union Brotherhood for the unifying of the Afro-American voters of Georgia for better state government. He is president of this organization.

He was chosen by the Republicans of his state as delegate from the state at large to the last National Republican Convention, and was the only delegate-at-large from Georgia that went over to Benjamin Harrison before his nomination.

Coming back to our subject's journalistic life, we ascertain that nothing was more lucrative and more helpful to him in the business than a job office, in connection with the publica tion of *The Baptist.* Mr. White saw this at the very beginning, and determined that it should be a first-class one. He also determined to employ colored printers, as far as possible. This was a hard task, because of the scarcity of such. He was fortunate enough to secure the services of Mr. George W. Gardner, now editor of *The Philadelphia Sentinel,* whom he made foreman of the office. Prof. A. R. Johnson, one of Georgia's best young men, to whom he was deeply devoted, rendered him invaluable aid in keeping his books. John T., George D., Lucian H., and W. J. White, Jr., four sons of W. J. White, were put in the office to learn type-setting. John L. Blocker, Esq., who has since moved to Texas and engaged in the newspaper business, was also employed by Mr. White as canvasser and general helper. Gabriel B. Maddox, Esq., who has since been foreman of the printing department at the Tuskegee Normal and Industrial school, Tuskegee, Ala., and, later, associate editor of *The Columbus* (Ga.) *Messenger,* was first devil, with W. J. White, Jr., as a good second.

Overcoming many difficulties Mr. White has persevered until *The Georgia Baptist* job office has taken a place in the front rank. A large amount of pamphlet work is turned out; and in addition to the force of eight to ten men in the building, four to six ladies are employed at Mr. White's house, of whom Mrs. White has the oversight. Three of his daughters, Mary B., Claudia T., and Emily Josephine, have learned to bind and stitch pamphlets.

The entire plant has cost about three thousand dollars, and the capital employed in the business is about six thousand. Thus it is seen that *The Georgia Baptist* and its editor have had a most prosperous career.

The Indianapolis Freeman says, in regard to *The Baptist*: "From ten to fifteen hands are employed upon it continually, the pay-roll reaching from one hundred to one hundred and fifty dollars a week. Take it for all in all, *The Georgia Baptist* is one of the positively successful newspaper properties in the country, owned by colored men."

LEVI E. CHRISTY, EDITOR INDIANAPOLIS WORLD.

One of the leading spirits of Indiana journalism is Levi E. Christy, editor and senior proprietor of *The Indianapolis World.* He was born at Salem, Ind., 1851, but became a resident of Xenia, O., in 1865, leaving Salem on account of the gross mistreatment by the whites of the colored people there.

After spending some time in the public schools of Xenia, he went to Indianapolis, when he immediately entered the employ of General, now President Harrison. Young Christy, knowing fully the value of an education, attended a night school, and afterwards took private lessons, paying as high as $1 per lesson.

His industry and perseverance were not without reward, for so well had he advanced that in 1870 he was appointed principal of one of the leading public schools in Indianapolis. After teaching some years at this place, he accepted a good school in Arkansas, intending to complete a special line of study to which he had devoted himself. He finally returned to Ohio and became a student at Wilberforce University.

In 1872, Mr. Christy was married to Miss Ella M. Roberts, a cultured and handsome young lady of Xenia, O., and again he went to Arkansas and began teaching. He took an active part in Grant's second campaign, and evinced considerable talent as a speaker. Returning to Indianapolis, he was appointed principal of a school, and held the position until 1885, when he retired from that profession, and has since given his entire time to *The World*, which passed to his control five years ago.

After fifteen years in the confines of a school-room, the active and invigorating life of a newspaper · man was a welcome change. At that time Afro-American journalism, was, to a great extent, an experiment; but Mr. Christy had unbounded faith in its ultimate success, and devoted himself to his new labor with all the zest of his enthusiastic nature.

Under his guidance, though at the cost of many sacrifices and much personal discomfort, *The World* has become a firmly established enterprise, and ranks with the best in the land. All its mechanical work is done by Afro-American hands, and besides being a leader in the intellectual arena, it furnishes an avenue for the employment and training of colored men and women as printers. It has introduced more new Afro-American writers to the reading public than any other journal published by our people.

As an editor, Mr. Christy is cool and conservative, and demands for the Afro-American the same chances and opportunities accorded to other American citizens. He appeals to the reason and better judgment, rather than to the passions or emotions.

The World is enjoying a season of unprecedented success, and is an illustration of what can be accomplished by patience and industry, supplemented by confidence and a strict adherence to the best business principles.

REV. A. E. P. ALBERT, D. D., EDITOR SOUTH-WESTERN CHRISTIAN ADVOCATE.

Rev. Dr. A. E. P. Albert, the subject of this sketch, a writer of national reputation upon religious subjects, is of French descent, his father being Pierre Albert, of Bordeaux, France, and his mother a slave, the property of a Frenchman. When the Union army captured New Orleans, our subject ran away from home, reaching the Union lines safely. He was then but poorly able to speak English; so he entered a private school, taught by Mr. William Barner. After gaining some knowledge of English, he attended the Freedman's Bureau school, the public schools of Atlanta, the Congregational Theological school, and Clark University.

Entering the Straight Congregational University at New Orleans, he graduated as Bachelor of Divinity in 1881. Four years afterwards the honorary title of D. D. was conferred upon him by the alma mater, and by the Rust Methodist Episcopal University of Holly Springs, Miss. At present, Dr. Albert is president of the board of trustees of New Orleans University, chairman of the executive committee, and lecturer on theology in the same institution. He is also secretary of the Louisiana Conference Board of Church Extension and statistical secretary of the Louisiana Conference. He was for a number of years District Dept. Worthy Grand Templar for Louisiana, I. O. G. T.; was a member of the book committee of the M. E. Church; secretary for Eastern Section for four years; a member of the General Conference and secretary of committee on the state of the church, at the General Conference held in Philadelphia in 1884, and also chairman of the colored delegation to the same body.

After Dr. Taylor's declination, he was desired by the majority of the board of bishops to go as bishop to Africa. At the last meeting of the bishops, he was appointed fraternal delegate to the General Conference of the A. M. E. Zion Church.

Like many other subjects treated in this work, his life in journalism has not been as extensive as in that of the ministry. It begins with an appointment as assistant editor to Drs. Hartzell and Cushman, from 1882 to 1884. At the

REV. A. E. P. ALBERT, D. D.

General Conference in 1884 he received one hundred and seventeen votes for the position of editor. Upon the death of Dr. Marshall W. Taylor, Dr. Albert was chosen to fill the unexpired term. This he did with so much credit, that at the General Conference in 1888 he was elected editor without an opposing vote.

Concerning the power and force of *The South-Western Advocate, The Freeman* says: " *The South-Western Christian Advocate*, of which Dr. Albert is now editor, is a great and powerful church organ, having the largest circulation of any paper in New Orleans." The honor of being editor of such a powerful religious journal, owned by the General Conference of the M. E. Church, is one that no other Afro-American has the pleasure to possess; and no one is more able than he to wear the honor befittingly.

Dr. Albert is a reliable, pointed, and pleasing writer. The editorial columns of *The Advocate* are always bright and cogent. His ready acquaintance with all questions makes him able to write in the most inviting way upon any subject he may see fit to tackle. The best thing about his success in life is, that, personally, he had to earn everything with which to educate and make himself a man. Learned in the Bible, as the lawyer is in the law, he is able to present Scripture truths unto a dying generation, with that ready vehemence and force that none could do who were less well informed. With his practical knowledge and the memory of the treatment he was subjected to in his onward march to success, he can, in a most prepossessing manner, advise his fellow-men what to do in meeting the difficulties incident to their religious, moral and social life. Since his journal represents thousands of white Methodists, as well as thousands of Afro-American Methodists, it is read by the whites more than is any other Afro-American journal in the Union. While he is ready, at all times, to picture the Afro-American's success in the most vivid and enchanting manner, yet he points out the many snares and dangers along the paths of life, which, if a race fall into, proves fatal to its existence.

In every way Dr. Albert has proven himself duly qualified to honor the race as a knight of the quill, and his journal deserves the most hearty support at the hands of a liberty-loving and free people.

In noticing *The South-Western Christian Advocate* and its present editor, its history would be manifestly incomplete if we failed to allude to Rev. Marshall W. Taylor, D. D., a former editor, who is acknowledged to have been one of the most gifted writers and eloquent speakers the race has yet produced, especially in the M. E Church. Dr. Taylor has been connected with some journalistic work ever since his service as a preacher began. In 1872, while pastor of Coke Chapel, Louisville, Ky., he edited *The Kentucky Methodist*, which was looked upon as an able sheet. He was honored with the degree of D. D. by the Central Tennessee College. In 1879 and in 1880 he was elected editor of *The South-Western Christian Advocate*, a position never before held by an Afro-American. He is author of several works, viz.: "Universal Reign of Jesus," "Life of Donney," "The Negro Evangelist," "Plantation Melodies," and "Life of Mrs. Amanda Smith, the Missionary." As one says: "He was famous as an eloquent preacher, a safe teacher, ready speaker, and an earnest writer; and we will add, a polished writer. Few, if any, can peruse his books without being impressed with the deep earnestness of the man, and his evident desire to lift his readers to a higher plane. He presents his matter in such a way, that none can lay his books aside without the consciousness of having been helped by them. Previous to his death at Indianapolis, in June, 1888, he was mentioned for the bishopric of the M. E. Church. Dr. Albert justly holds high the mark set by this worthy man.

MESSRS. R. D. LITTLEJOHN AND D. A. WILLIAMS, EDITORS
OF THE NEW LIGHT.

In Warren County, North Carolina, July, 1855, was born
Richard D. Littlejohn, whose work in Afro-American journalism has been marked by many sacrifices, and much diligent
application. He is well educated, having spent considerable
time in these universities: Lincoln, in Oxford, Pa.; Fisk, in
Nashville, Tenn.; and Oberlin, in Ohio. He has since taught
in Mississippi. For eight years he has been a member of the
teachers' examining board for his county. He is also prominent in society circles, particularly among the Odd Fellows
and Free Masons. Mr. Littlejohn has often made use of the
expression: "The destiny of the negro race in the South
rests in secrecy and brotherly love."

When Messrs. Littlejohn and Williams began the publication of *The New Light* in 1886, the community said that it
could not continue longer than two or three months, the
assertion being based on the fact that so many papers had
been commenced by our people, which seemed to flourish a
short while, only to die. Many, who really sympathized with
the new and enterprising project, subscribed for only three
or four months.

The paper proved to be a burden to the publishers for
two years, their disbursements for that time reaching $1160,
and the receipts $489. But things have changed since, and
now the monthly receipts exceed the expenditures. *The New
Light* has passed its crisis, and the dawn of a prosperous day
has come.

During all its trying and perplexing times, when it seemed
that both courage and perseverance would inevitably fail,
Mr. Littlejohn held up the flag with untiring fortitude. All
the responsibility rested upon him, but he never shrank from
duty, nor did he labor in suspense; for, encouraged by the

R. D. LITTLEJOHN.

maxim that temperance, justice, and fortitude conquer all things, he fought to the end.

The New Light is now three years old, and is a noble reflector of Afro-American sentiments, being the only paper published in Mississippi in an office the outfit of which is owned by Afro-Americans.

Mr. Littlejohn was associated with the lamented Rev. Dr. Williams in the editorship of *The New Light*, to whose popularity and influence the success of the paper is greatly due.

Dr. Williams was born in Virginia, February 3, 1839, and lived until a few months since, when he fell triumphant in the arms of the blessed Savior, having fought in war and in peace, first for God and then for his race.

He published and edited *The People's Adviser*, in Jackson, Miss., which was a religious and an educational journal. It was a strong advocate of temperance and prohibition.

In 1885 he and Editor Littlejohn associated themselves together in the publication of *The New Light*, to the success of which Dr. Williams never failed to contribute, until called from labor to reward. He was widely known in the M. E. church, to which he belonged.

J. DALLAS BOWSER, EDITOR GATE CITY PRESS.

Among the many weekly journals published in the West, none carries with it such great influence, and none is so powerful in the maintenance of right principles, as *The Gate City Press*, published at Kansas City, Mo. It is one of the largest sheets published by the Afro-American, and one of the most substantial. Papers may come and go, but *The Gate City Press* seems "to have come to stay."

Its editor is J. Dallas Bowser, who was born in the Tar Heel State, (North Carolina,) at Weldon, February 15, 1846.

His career as a good citizen, educator, and particularly as a journalist, has been marvelous. He early enjoyed the benefits of an excellent public school training, which his parents were enabled to afford him by moving to Ohio. Remaining there in the schools, he grew up well-educated and well-fitted for practical life, and as an upright citizen.

He moved to Kansas City when quite young, possibly 22, succeeding Hon. J. Milton Turner as principal of the largest school in that city. He held this position for ten years, until 1881 finds him a mail-route agent, which place he filled until President Cleveland's policy "to turn the rascals out" reached him, and out he went. In 1887 he was sealer of weights and measures for Kansas City. These positions he filled with credit.

Mr. Bowser is now a journalist. He has been successful in all of his journalistic work, and can be relied upon as being the hardest newspaper worker in Missouri, among the Afro-Americans. He has been constantly engaged thus for nine years, contributing largely to the success which now attends Afro-American journalism.

In 1880 H. H. Johnson founded *The Free Press* in Kansas City. Before the second number was issued, Mr. Johnson came to Mr. Bowser, whom he knew to be a wide-awake, vigilant writer and business man, and stated that he was in lack of means to continue the publication of *The Press*. Mr. Bowser, disliking to see the effort fail, immediately took hold, and in a few weeks he had organized a substantial stock company, which took control of the paper, changing it to its present name, *The Gate City Press*. This paper, under Mr. Bowser's editorial management, has become a household word in the West, and its columns are quoted from by the leading journals of the land.

Mr. Bowser is an editor whose writings command the most careful consideration. He is a fierce antagonist of quacks, humbugs, and political mountebanks. A writer, speaking of *The Press*, says: "*The Gate City Press* is one of the strongest papers in the United States." The same writer, in referring to its editor, says: "His paper thoroughly reflects the man."

Mr. Bowser pursues a line of duty in his writings as editor which he regards as right, without fear or favor.

Another thing that has tended to make his paper a successful sheet is, the polished writers and astute thinkers who are with him upon its staff. Such men as Profs. W. W. Yates and G. N. Gresham, so well known in the literary world, are his associate editors.

Mr. Bowser's editorials always betray him as a defender of true Republican principles. The author regards his paper as one of the most successful efforts in the pioneer work of Afro-American journalism. Having amassed a little fortune, he is enabled to "soap" his *Press*, which is a mighty lever in the work.

Not only is Mr. Bowser an able writer, but he is an orator as well. In addition to his journalistic business, he is a large coal and grain dealer.

HON. JAMES J. SPELMAN, EDITOR BAPTIST MESSENGER.

Mr. Spelman was born in Norwich, Conn., January 18, 1841, and was educated in the public schools of Connecticut. He entered upon newspaper work in 1858, in New York City, by opening a newspaper depot on Thompson street, near Amity, now West Third street. A year later he became a contributor to *The Anglo-African*, published by the Hamilton Brothers, and afterwards to *The Pine and Palm*, its successor, edited by James Redpath. He was a frequent contributor to the New York daily press, through the influence of Horace Greeley, George Alfred Townsend, Charles Fulton, Charles G. Halpin, William Caldwell, and his partner, Mr. Whitney.

HON. JAMES J. SPELMAN.

During this time, he was also a regular correspondent of *The Elevator* of San Francisco, over the *nom de plume* of Private L. Overture; of *The Colored Citizen* of Cincinnati, edited by Prof. John Corbin, now of Arkansas; and of *The Zion's Standard and Weekly Review* of New York, edited by Prof. Howard Day, having with the last-mentioned paper the *nom de plume* of Paul Pickwick.

On going to Mississippi in 1868, he became the special correspondent of *The New York Tribune*, and wrote to other papers in the North during the period of Reconstruction. His letters to *The Tribune* afterwards attracted considerable attention, and were frequently copied into the columns of other papers. Mr. Greeley, on his way to Texas, stopped over at Canton, Miss., especially to pay Mr. Spelman a visit; but, unfortunately, he was not at home, and he never afterwards saw his benefactor alive.

In 1870, he was elected vice-president of the Republican Press Association, the only colored man who was a member; and subsequently he became its president. He has been connected, as editor and proprietor, with the following papers in Mississippi: *People's Journal*, *The Messenger* and *The Mississippi Republican*. He was associated with the late Hon. James Lynch in the publication of *The Colored Citizen* and *The Jackson Tribune*; and with the Baptist denomination in the publishing of *The Baptist Signal* and *The Baptist Messenger*, of which papers he was editor.

At the National Republican Convention of 1884, Mr. Spelman was the special correspondent of *The Evening Post*, a Democratic daily paper published in Vicksburg, Miss. He is still a frequent telegraph contributor to the press, for which he is daily compensated. He contributes an occasional letter to the Afro-American press, on matters pertaining to the race in the South.

Mr. Spelman's connection with the press has been of a

nature to secure compensation rather than to gain prominence, and in this he has succeeded admirably. His work
has been constant, unceasing, and quietly done. He has
brought dignity and position to Afro-American journalism by
his efforts.

He has occupied excellent political positions, being now
in the service of the government as special Lumber Agent of
the General Land Office.

REV. WM. B. JOHNSON, D. D., EDITOR WAYLAND ALUMNI JOURNAL.

Dr. William B. Johnson, the editor of *The Wayland
Alumni Journal*, was born in the city of Toronto, December
11, 1856. He spent the major portion of his youthful days
in the schools of Buffalo, New York, and in the city of his
birth, subsequently attending Wayland Seminary, where he
graduated with honors in the class of 1879.

In 1872 he was converted, and was baptized by the Rev.
J. W. Mitchell, pastor of the Queen Street Baptist church,
Toronto. In 1875, fired by a desire to work for God, he
entered the ministry, choosing the South as his place of
labor. Upon graduating from the Wayland Seminary, fully
equipped as an expounder of divine truth, he was called to
the pastorate of the First Baptist church of Frederick, Md.
After serving the church successfully, and building a fine
edifice, he left it, beloved by all who knew him, especially by
this congregation. Immediately, he was appointed by the
American Baptist Home Mission Society to be general missionary for the states of Maryland, Virginia, West Virginia,
and the District of Columbia.

While young Johnson had a very good education on
leaving the seminary, his ambition led him to continue his
studies, and to a special course in mathematics, metaphysics,

and the languages, under Prof. Rhoan of the Columbian University, which resulted in his election to the chair of mathematics and science of government in Wayland Seminary, where he now is, having the esteem of the faculty and the students for his ability and worth. Thus, he stands as a remarkable pillar in the Baptist Convention.

Dr. Johnson has, in his time, read some of the ablest papers before deliberative bodies it has been our pleasure to hear. When the Baptist State Convention was in session at Lynchburg, Va., in 1887, we heard with untiring interest his paper on the "Religious Status of the Negro," which so forcibly impressed the convention that it was ordered to be published. The paper proved his high qualifications and and worth as a journalist, and his ready ability to present matters as they are,—to condemn or defend the race as circumstances might require.

In 1889, upon the retirement of the editor of *The Baptist Companion,* the organ of the Afro-American Baptists in Virginia, he was chosen as his successor. His management of *The Companion* showed considerate tact and newspapaper strategy, and undoubtedly he would have made that journal one of the best religious newspapers, had it not been destroyed by fire. This was his first experience as a writer, which was acknowledged by the fraternity to have been productive of good fruit.

Recognizing his merit as a "quill man," Dr. Johnson was chosen by the alumni of Wayland Seminary editor of their journal, which was known as *The Wayland Alumni Journal,* which, under his editorial survey, has done much for the seminary.

The State University of Kentucky has conferred upon him the honorary degree of D. D., making him the youngest man in our country with such a title.

As a preacher, student and writer, "he is able, diligent and forcible." Says *The American Baptist:* "His services are in constant demand at home, in the interest of every good work."

The Journal and its editor have done much in battling for the race, and will continue to supply the yearning of many a thirsty mind for editorial literature.

JOHN Q. ADAMS, ESQ., EDITOR WESTERN APPEAL.

Louisville, blessed in its many worthy sons, is the birthplace of a man whose prominence in Afro-American journalism is familiar to all,—John Q. Adams, who has stood through the blasts of forty winters and the heat of as many summers. He acquired an early training in the private schools of Fon-du-lac, Wis., and Yellow Springs, O., finishing at Oberlin.

Not unlike many Afro-American graduates, he entered the pedagogic profession, remaining in it until 1873, when he was elected engrossing clerk of the Arkansas Senate, and, later on, assistant superintendent of Public Instruction. Shortly after this he served as deputy commissioner of Public Works. So great has been the journalistic career of this gentleman, and so eager are we to direct the attention of the reader to it, that we will make no further comment on the success attending his service in these positions than to say it was great.

In 1879, he and his younger brother launched *The Bulletin,* a weekly paper, to battle on the sea of journalism with the turbulent waves that might come against it. *The Bulletin* continued to sail, making a successful run until 1885, when it was disposed of to *The American Baptist.*

Our subject was wielding the political ax in the quiet during the life of *The Bulletin,* resulting in the occupancy of a responsible position under the Garfield-Arthur administration,—that of United States storekeeper.

Upon going to St. Paul, Minn., in 1886, Mr. Adams accepted the position of editor of *The Western Appeal*, which was then in a very weak condition. A writer says this of *The Appeal:* " Under his management the paper has thrived, and has become a power in the country." In 1888, Mr. Adams moved the headquarters of *The Appeal* to Chicago, where, as one says, it has had "phenomenal success." *The Indianapolis Freeman* says this of *The Appeal*, which expresses our own sentiment, and cannot be bettered: " From a circulation of thirty-eight copies, it has, in twelve months, increased to over two thousand." *The Appeal* is published simultaneously in Chicago, St. Paul, Minneapolis and Louisville. Mr. Adams has been continuously engaged in journalism since 1879, and unless lightning should strike him under the present Republican administration, he will, in all probability, for years to come, be counted among the ' pencil pushers' of the country."

Mr. Adams's journalistic turn of mind led to the calling of the first Colored National Press Convention, and he was honored as its first president.

But what of his reputation as a writer? The success which has attended his efforts would very probably suggest this inquiry. By way of reply, we produce a clipping from the editorial columns of *The Appeal*, which, while it shows his style, manifests, also, his spirit in defence of the race. He refutes, in no uncertain tones, the insult daily put upon the colored people in classifying them with the vile and degraded. " If a colored man steals a hog, commits a rape or murder, or engages in a riot, he at once takes a conspicuous position in the eyes of the white community and is regarded with great interest. The court house is thronged when he is tried, and even when he passes along the street in custody of an officer, there is great curiosity to know what he has been doing. Thus the white community is constantly

JOHN Q. ADAMS.

being brought in contact with offcasts and outcasts of the colored people, and, naturally enough, forms its conceptions of all from the bad conduct of a few. But the refined and pleasant homes, the thousands of benevolent and Christian enterprises that are in constant operation among colored people, the well-conducted churches, schools, colleges, societies, and other civilizing and humanizing instrumentalities, attract almost no attention from the whites, and, consequently, exert almost no influence upon their idea of their progress. It is a misfortune to both races, that the white people are so constantly forced to witness and learn of the bad conduct of the saloon-loafers and criminals of the colored race, and that they take such pains to keep themselves from witnessing the decent and creditable performances of the intelligent, virtuous. and industrious ones."

The truth of the above is unmistakable; and with such presentation of facts, the Afro-American editor may live to do great good, and the world will be the better for the influence he exerts.

PROF. JULIAN TALBOT BAILEY, EDITOR LITTLE ROCK SUN.

Prof. Julian T. Bailey, widely known as a journalist, was born March 22, 1859, in Warren County, Georgia. His parents were Pierce and Adeline Bailey of Georgia and Virginia, respectively. His sister and father having died when he was a lad, he was left with his mother alone, who, knowing Julian's desire for an education, promptly resolved that she would do what she could to enable him to obtain it.

In due time he was placed in the common schools of his county, and having completed the prescribed courses in these, he was sent to the Atlanta University, and entering the college preparatory class, he graduated from the institution with first honors, at the age of seventeen. He then went

PROF. JULIAN TALBOT BAILEY.

to Howard University, where he completed the college course.

Since leaving school, he has been an earnest student, and few can equal him in the sciences, mathematics, and languages. He is known as a scholar and teacher of the ablest kind. He never fails to instill into his pupils the highest principles, with pureness of character. He has been actively engaged in the school-room during his career. He has had the degree of Master of Arts conferred upon him by Howard University.

Soon after leaving college, he accepted the principalship of the Roanoke Normal and Collegiate Institute, in North Carolina. He has since been professor of natural sciences and belles-lettres in the Philander Smith University of Little Rock. He has been professor of higher mathematics and astronomy in the Mississippi State Normal College and president of Bethel University of Little Rock.

In speaking of his political life, a writer in *The New York Freeman* had the following to say : "In politics he is an independent thinker and actor, and as such holds a free, strong, and independent political position. He has always labored to make apparent the folly of the present inclination in politics, and has advocated free, independent, thoughtful action. He bends to no party, and bows to no apparent kindness; but stands concientiously upon principle and fitness to accomplish the highest good.

" Prof. Bailey has always taken an active part in the politics of his adopted states. As a speaker, he is pleasing, interesting, and eloquent. He is a man of strong convictions, tender sympathies, great firmness and decision of purpose, with high personal character. He possesses severe earnestness, pluck, manly courage; aims high, is ambitious and far-reaching, with great self-reliance and self-respect."

Since leaving the school-room, Prof. Bailey has been actively engaged in the practice of law, in addition to his

editorial duties. He is one of the few of his race who have
boon admitted to practice before the Supreme and United
States Courts in his state. He has a large and growing
practice.

While Prof. Bailey has been wonderfully successful as a
lawyer, yet his career and experience have been so large
and varied in the journalistic field, one might think, to look
at his work in this direction, that he had no time for any
other. He has been marvelously progressive in journalism.
Certainly, few writers have been associated with as many
papers, at different intervals, as Mr. Bailey, and filled such
positions so acceptably.

As to his course in journalism before the publication of
The Sun, we call attention to a clipping from *The Indianapolis Freeman* of February 2d, 1889: "Soon after leaving
college he went to North Carolina, where he was principal,
for some time, of a school known as the Roanoke Normal
and Collegiate Institute. He also published and edited *The
National Enquirer,* in the same state, until the spring of
1884, when he was offered the editorial chair of *The Arkansas
Herald.* Considering Arkansas a more inviting field, he
accepted the offer. His editorial management of *The Herald*
was marked by signal ability and success, in consequence
of which he at once received encomiums from the leading
men and papers, both white and colored, throughout the
state. Such was the effect of his ability upon Arkansas as a
journalist, that scarcely had he edited *The Herald* a month
before it was decided by the members of the Arkansas Herald
and Mansion publishing companies, to consolidate the papers.
He was then elected editor of the consolidated paper, which
was at once regarded as one of the leading negro journals
of the country. He continued to edit *The Herald-Mansion*
until the fall of 1884, when he was elected professor of
natural science and belles-lettres in the Philander Smith

University of Little Rock. This position he fills with great credit to himself, as well as to the institution employing him.

As expressed by the author, as well as by our most eminent men in their opinions in this work, there is little pecuniary benefit to be reaped from Afro-American journals, in the earlier stage of their existence. This Prof. Bailey knew, and so he accepted a professorship in a college, in addition to his labors as editor of *The Little Rock Sun.* Thus he is enabled to support himself comfortably, and have at his command increased means for the publication of his journal.

The Sun began publication in 1885, an independent paper, with Prof. Bailey as editor. This independent stand it has since maintained, and it is noted for its out-spoken sentiments in advocacy of the rights of the race. On January 1st, 1889, it entered upon its fifth volume.

Since September 1st, 1888, Prof. Bailey has published two other papers, *The Hot Springs Sun* and *The Texarkana Sun*, (Texas,) three separate and distinct papers, the combined weekly "bona fide" circulation of which is over six thousand. *The Little Rock Sun* has as large a circulation as any other Afro-American journal in the country, and it is doubtless safe to assert that it outranks all others in the number of its readers and the weight of its influence.

Prof. Bailey is a newspaper man, "to the manor born." His success in the work is due, first, to his ability, and, second, to his energy and great zeal. As a journalist, a writer sums him up thus: "He has shown from childhood an insatiable thirst for knowledge and an immeasurable ability for grasping and retaining the most profound truths. While at college he distinguished himself as a linguist and mathematician. As a literary man, many know him. His clear, logical, conclusive, unique, though graceful style, is well known to most publishers and readers of the leading.

papers of the day. His articles are sought eagerly, and are published and read with both pleasure and benefit." The question with the fraternity is now—"Where can another Bailey be found?"

DAVID C. CARTER, EX-EDITOR VIRGINIA CRITIC.

The Critic wielded such an influence, and strove so hard to extend justice and fair play to both the people it represented and to others, that we would not fail to give it space in this volume.

The subject of this article was born in Staunton, October 25, 1862, and was educated in the public and private schools of that city, and is to-day a trusted teacher in one of the Staunton public schools.

His connection with *The Critic* began in 1884, and was continued for four years as managing editor. His paper was regarded as one of the most telling sheets ever published in Virginia by the Afro-American. Since its suspension, he has been writing constantly for Anglo-Saxon papers, as well as for various Afro-American journals.

His articles, and especially his editorials, were often found in the columns of other journals, either quoted in full or in part. Mr. Fortune, in his "Negro in Politics," clips from the editorial columns of *The Critic*. The people of Virginia lost an able and progressive medium, when *The Critic* failed to criticise the faults of the Afro-American or laud his good deeds.

WILLIAM BUFORD, EDITOR ARKANSAS DISPATCH.

The editor of *The Dispatch* dates his entrance into the world September 10, 1855, his parents being George and Clara A. Buford of Pulaski County, Arkansas.

When he was eight years old, his father died, leaving him

dependent upon a poor mother. They, however, survived the hardships to which they were subject, and William received a good, practical education in the schools of Arkansas. He taught in the public schools of the state for years, always meeting with marked success, as shown at the examinations.

Retiring from the service of a pedagogue in 1884, he became editor of *The Herald-Mansion,* published in Little Rock. This is known to have been the first Afro-American journal published in Arkansas; which makes him a pioneer in the newspaper field, in that state. He served as editor of that journal for two years, when a dissolution of *The Herald and Mansion* was effected, the paper, though, continuing, under the name and style of *The Mansion,* and he as its editor and manager.

The company publishing *The Mansion* sold, in 1887, all the good will and material to Editor Buford, and he then launched upon the journalistic sea *The Arkansas Dispatch.* In politics, *The Dispatch* is Republican. It is a six-column folio, with the motto: "Hew to the line, let the chips fall where they may."

REV. W. H. ANDERSON, D. D., EX-EDITOR BAPTIST WATCH-
TOWER.

The race, the pulpit, and the press, vie in their respect for the above gentleman, who was born in Lash Creek Settlement, Vigo County, Indiana, May 8, 1848.

His life, which has reached forty-one years, has been marked with hardships and achievements, which occur in the experience of every one who attains to any degree of eminence in the world. He is the possessor of a good English education, obtained by persistent attention to books without the aid of an instructor, the foundation having been laid in a

REV. W. H. ANDERSON, D. D.

school which he attended in his own state. He is now pastor of McFarland Chapel, of Evansville, Ind.

His prominence in political circles has won for him world-renowned fame. The press, both white and black, have given him the palm for his speeches in behalf of the greenback party, whose cause he espoused. He was several times delegate to the convention of that party. Relative to an address delivered at Kansas City once, in the interest of his party, the press of that city said: "He handled his subject in a calm, dignified, and logical manner. Keep him on the stump; he will do good." *The Standard* of Leavenworth, Kan., says: "He is a man of considerable ability, and a fluent talker." Concerning his ability as a preacher, *The Terra Haute Express* says: "His delivery is good, his pronunciation is distinct, and remarkably accurate." "He is also a writer," says one. This fact was evinced by his editorship of the Indiana Baptist *Watch-Tower*, published at Evansville, Ind., under the auspices of the Baptist Association. This paper, being well edited, took high rank among the best journals of the race. The faculty of the State University of Louisville, Ky., gave him the degree of D. D., at its commencement in 1889. Both in speaking and in writing, Dr. Anderson is seen as a man of quick, keen perceptions, and broad views. He is deeply concerned in all movements having for their object the development of a higher and a nobler civilization among his people.

REV. C. C. STUMM, EDITOR PHILADELPHIA DEPARTMENT OF THE BROOKLYN NATIONAL MONITOR.

The subject of this sketch was born at Airdrie, near Paradise, on Green River, Muhlenburg County, Ky., April 11, 1848. His early life was spent in Ohio County, on a farm, where the only education one could get was what he

REV. C. C. STUMM, D. D.

learned on rainy days and winter evenings, and in what was called a subscription school.

After the training as such facilities afforded he entered school at Grenville, where he spent three terms. He then went to a white school. This aroused such bitter opposition, he soon had to withdraw from the school, and receive private instruction. After this he entered Berea College, Madison County, Ky., in the spring of 1871, where he continued but one year, when he went to the Baptist Theological Institute, Nashville, Tenn.; but ill-health compelled him to leave school for a few years. In the meantime, however, he continued to study under private instruction.

After his health was restored he returned to Nashville, Tenn. The Baptist Theological Institute had undergone a change in the interval of his absence and was now called the Roger Williams University. Things were all new when he re-entered the university, but he was soon installed again in his classes, with the expectation of completing the regular course. Other hindrances, however, unfortunately arose to prevent this, though he was in the higher classes, and making rapid progress. Again was he compelled to avail himself of private instruction, receiving lessons in Latin, Greek and Hebrew, which were given by some of the best teachers of Boston, such as Profs. Perkins, Mitchell and Harper.

Mr. Stumm assumed charge of his first school in the spring of 1869, at the age of 20, in Christian County, Ky. He continued to teach, at intervals, for fifteen years, in private and public schools in Tennessee and Kentucky. The people of Hartsville and Lebanon, Tenn., knew him well as a teacher. The superintendent of schools of Trousdale County, Tenn., had such confidence in Mr. Stumm, he looked to him to furnish teachers for the colored schools of the county, and received much valuable aid from him by so doing.

A school was successfully taught by Mr. Stumm at Chaplaintown, Ky., in the fall and winter of 1870. He and his wife conducted a successful school at Elizabethtown, Hardin County, Ky., in the fall and winter of 1877 and 1878. In January, 1881, he was selected as president of the Bowling Green academy, with Prof. C. R. McDowell, Miss M. V. Cook, Miss A. M. Stepp, and Mrs. C. C. Stumm, as assistants. Prof. C. R. McDowell has since entered the ministry, and is the successful pastor of a Baptist church at Hartford, Ky. Miss M. V. Cook is now Prof. Mary V. Cook, at the State University at Louisville, Ky. Mrs. C. C. Stumm has since taught, and has been the matron, at the Hearne academy, Hearne, Texas, and is at present connected with *The National Monitor* of Brooklyn, N. Y., having the management of its business at Philadelphia. This closes Mr. Stumm's career as a teacher, with the exception of his instructing a few young men privately, who are preparing for the ministry, whom he attends to each winter.

While we are directing our readers more particularly to Rev. Mr. Stumm's journalistic career, we would not omit mention of his experience as a pastor. His success in this useful department of life's work has been glorious and grand. Beginning with the care of small churches, he worked untiringly for the Master, until October 4, 1885. He then became pastor of the Union Baptist church at Philadelphia, one of the largest churches in the city.

To show how the people looked upon him as a preacher, we reproduce a portion of an article concerning him which we have clipped, calling the attention of our readers more particularly to what Dr. H. L. Wayland, editor of *The National Baptist*, says of him: "The ability and high standing of Rev. C. C. Stumm caused him to be selected to preach a sermon to the Odd Fellows of this city, which elicited much favorable comment both from the press and from prominent individuals. He preached one of the re-opening sermons at Shiloh, and also at the First African Baptist church. He has frequently spoken at the Baptist Ministers' Conference, which is composed of the leading white ministers of the denomination. The paper he read before this body, entitled ' The Mission of the Negro Baptists,' received the highest praise from the Conference and the press. On May 10, 1889, Dr. H. L. Wayland, editor of *The National Baptist*, says: ' I take great pleasure in introducing to all members of the Baptist denomination, and to other friends of a good cause, the Rev. C. C. Stumm, pastor of the Union Baptist church in this city. Mr. Stumm studied at Roger Williams University, at Nashville, and, more recently, at Boston, Mass. He is a highly esteemed member of the Baptist Ministers' Conference, and is a faithful and wise pastor and a good preacher of the Word. The Conference has commended him and his church, in their present enterprise of building, to all our brethren. I sincerely hope that his appeal for aid will meet with a favorable response.' " He was several times president of Baptist conventions and associations, and has always acted promptly and well on these occasions.

Mr. Stumm's success in the ministry has not interfered at all with his progress in the glorious work of journalism, as will be seen in the following account we give of it: His career as an editor was begun in 1873, while he was a student at Nashville, Tenn. Pursuant to an adjournment, the Baptist Convention met with the First Baptist church of that city, and an editor of one of the papers asked the pastor, Rev. N. G. Merry, to have some one appointed as reporter, and the choice fell on Mr. Stumm, who accepted the position with some diffidence, but succeeded in reporting the proceedings of the meeting, though not in the most satisfactory way to all.

Subsequently, he became a writer for *The Standard*, a

HON. C. H. J. TAYLOR.

paper published by Elder N. G. Merry; for *The Baptist Herald*, published at Paducah, Ky., by Rev. G. W. Dupee; *The Pilot*, published at Nashville, Tenn.; *The American Baptist*, Louisville, Ky.; *The Tribune*, a Republican paper, published at Danville, Ky.; and for *The Baptist Companion*, published, at first, at Knoxville, Tenn., by Rev. J. M. Armstead, and then moved to Portsmouth, Va.

The children's column of *The American Baptist* was edited by him for a while, in which he was known as "Uncle Charles." A column for the colored people was conducted by him in *The Bowling-Green Democrat*, until some of the Bourbons got behind the editor and caused him to discontinue it. *The Bowling-Green Watchman* was originated by Messrs. Stumm and C. R. McDowell, and successfully published by them for a few years.

In June, 1887, he was engaged by the board of managers of the New England Convention as editor-in-chief of *The Baptist Monitor*, and held the place until the paper was sold to Dr. R. L. Perry., after which he became associate editor, a position he still occupies.

As a matter-of-fact writer, Mr. Stumm ranks high. He has, with hundreds of others, endeavored in every possible way to prevent the banner of Afro-American journalism from trailing. He is an earnest pastor and teacher, and a vigorous wielder of the pen, in any one of which positions he exerts a commanding influence.

The Christian Banner, a four-column, eight-page, religious home journal, was commenced by Rev. and Mrs. C. C. Stumm, January 2, 1890, the former being editor and the latter its business manager.

The degree of Doctor of Divinity was conferred upon Mr. Stumm May 13, 1890, by the State University of Louisville, Ky., Rev. Wm. J. Simmons, A. M., D. D., LL. D., president.

Rev. E. W. S. Peck, D. D., Ex-Editor Conference
Journal and Contributor to Prominent Journals.

Dr. Peck, a Christian minister of high repute, and a
writer of good standing, was born of devout parents, Rev.
Nathaniel and Lydia Peck, in Baltimore, October 31, 1843.

He received his educational training in the public schools
of Baltimore, Ashmore Institute, (now Lincoln University)
and under the private tuition of Rev. B. F. Crary, D. D., in
St. Louis. He puts his intellectual training to excellent use,
and is to-day one of the foremost scholars in the land. New
Orleans University conferred the honorary title of D. D. upon
this worthy divine.

From 1865, he served some of the most learned and
conspicuous congregations of the M. E. Church in the
Missouri and Washington Conferences. At this writing, he
leads the Washington Conference in point of popularity,
intellectual ability, and knowledge of Christian ethics. He
has been secretary of the same Conference for five years; was
its representative in several General Conferences, and went
abroad as its delegate to the Ecumenical Conference, which
met in London, in 1881. During his stay in the Old World,
he traveled extensively in England, France and Ireland. In
all the walks of life, he has rendered invaluable service to
his church and race.

In journalism he has been a success. While in St. Louis
filling a pastorate in 1870, he edited a local paper called *The
Welcome Friend*, in behalf of the religious and educational
interests of his people. It had a good circulation and was
warmly received. The Washington Annual Conference
having established an organ in 1886, unanimously elected
him editor, with Revs. Benj. Brown and Griffin, associates.
The organ was known as *The Washington Conference Journal*.
Its columns, week after week, teemed with live, original, and

instructive articles; while its editorials were apt, able, progressive, and full of the mind and heart of its editors. *The Journal* is no more, but its editor, whose work still goes on, reminds us that a serviceable publication was gathered into the arms of its projectors.

MR. S. B. TURNER, EDITOR STATE CAPITAL.

The Capital has become one of the most reliable papers edited by the Afro-American, which is largely due, financially and editorially, to the management of him whose career we now present. Adhering to the motto—"We advocate justice to all; On this principle we stand or fall," it has been successful in being a welcome visitor to the homes of the masses of Afro-American citizens in and around the capital of Illinois.

The editor, Mr. S. B. Turner, was born July 12, 1854, at West Feliciana, La. At the age of fourteen, he was master of the rudimentary English branches, having given close and diligent study to his books. He worked as an apprentice in a confectionery shop at the age of which we speak, but afterward became a baker, and a very excellent one. He has worked at his trade with considerable success.

For years he conducted a wood and coal yard, as well as being a trusted worker in the office of the secretary of state, Hon. H. D. Dement, at Chicago. At this place he entered a business college, completing the course of study, which has led to his financial success in journalism. Few men make journalism a success, financially.

When at Springfield he took an active part in politics, and received recognition at the hands of his party for faithful service. It was on this account he was induced to enter the journalistic field, and in 1886, though under adverse circumstances, to establish *The State Capital*, said to be the leading

REV. E. W. S. PECK, D. D.

organ of the race, west of the Ohio river. It is the recognized organ of the Afro-Americans of Illinois, and wields a potent influence in politics.

Three Afro-American journals have been started at Springfield, but with ill success. Mr. Turner has succeeded, because, as he himself states: "Energy, perseverance and individual attention to the enterprise, will eventuate in success. Any man with good business habits, a fair education, and pleasing address, who will not subordinate his advertising columns to trashy local news, can bring to his support a reasonable share of business patronage, which always pays well. Short editorials, brief correspondence from other cities and towns, a high moral tone, condemning wrong, defending right, urging the payment of subscriptions due, dropping from the list the always-promising and never-paying subscribers, will insure success."

Mr. Turner resides with his family at Springfield, where he is known for his strict business integrity; the best evidence of which is, his word commands any sum of money desired in the management of his business enterprise. About the Afro-American in politics and in business, Editor Turner says truthfully: "When the negro in America begins business for himself, and accumulates wealth and intelligence, the race problem then will be solved. Business must be first and politics last."

REV. JOSEPH A. BOOKER, A. B., EDITOR BAPTIST VANGUARD.

The subject of this sketch was born near the little hamlet of Portland, Ashley County, Arkansas, December 26, 1859. His mother died when he was only one year old. Two years afterward, his father, having some knowledge of books, was whipped to death for teaching and "spoiling the good niggers."

S. B. TURNER.

Upon the death of his father, he was placed in the hands of his maternal grandmother, who carefully nurtured him and looked after his educational interests with true motherly zeal. When the free school system was inaugurated, she saw that Joseph was one of the first pupils to be enrolled. Remaining at school until seventeen, he then became a teacher, afterward entering the branch Normal School of the University at Pine Bluff, Ark., under Prof. J. C. Corbin, the linguist. He also attended Roger Williams University. Having been licensed to preach, he here attempted a theological course, but relinquished it after one year, and continued the regular college course until graduation, which occurred May 26, 1886, when he received the degree of A. B.

On returning home from school, he was appointed state missionary of Arkansas, under the joint commission of the State Mission Board and the Executive Board of the American Baptist Home Mission Society. He was engaged in this only twelve months before he was appointed president of Arkansas Baptist College. As the Convention Board had already decided to have a denominational organ in the school, (which would be an advantage to the paper and the school alike) this brought Mr. Booker in direct connection with the paper, in the fall of 1887. He was at once made its managing editor. This position he filled creditably, and with profit to the paper, notwithstanding the overburden of work the young school necessitated, with its very small corps of teachers.

The paper was at first known as *The Arkansas Baptist*; but the white Baptists of the state presuming to name their paper *The Arkansas Baptist*, brought on a business collision between the two, and in March, 1889, *The Arkansas Baptist* (colored) changed its name to *The Baptist Vanguard*. Under this new title it continued to advance and flourish, gaining in popularity and material work.

Yours very truly,
Jos. A. Booker

The Vanguard is issued bi-weekly, first as a general religious journal, and then as a denominational organ; but, at the same time, it is a strong advocate of education, Christian, industrial, and general. Notwithstanding its religious character, it does not scruple to discuss such political issues as are likely to enhance the welfare of its race or the general progress of the country. It has a large circulation, there being no other paper of its kind in the state to compete with it. It gives special attention to inquiries made for lost kinsfolk, separated from their families in slavery days. It is the highest ambition of Rev. Joseph A. Booker to make *The Vanguard* one of the best papers in the South-west.

Rev. Richard De Baptiste, Ex-Editor Conservator and Corresponding Editor Brooklyn Monitor.

The Conservator, now published at Chicago, with Mr. Barnett as editor, began its existence the first of 1878. It changed hands about the latter part of that year, when Rev. R. De Baptiste assumed editorial control, being then pastor of the Mt. Olivet church. Rev. Mr. Boothe was associate editor. It was at that time one of the representative journals edited by the Afro-American, both for news and editorial ability.

Mr. De Baptiste is from Old Virginia stock, born and educated in the Old Dominion, and has proved a valuable acquisition to the paper in pushing it into the houses of the masses and in satisfying the thirsty intellects of the intelligent Afro-Americans.

When he assumed control of *The Conservator*, he said of the paper: " It will discuss in a fair and liberal spirit those questions that agitate and cause an honest difference of opinion among citizens, whose aims are alike patriotic; but will give special prominence to such matters as appertain

REV. RICHARD DE BAPTISTE.

to the intellectual, moral, and social development and business prosperity of the colored people, and, at the same time, keep its columns open to a fair and courteous discussion of all important subjects. 'Progress in all right directions,' shall be its motto." With this in view, Rev. De Baptiste labored zealously for the principles he had enunciated.

As pastor, editor and citizen, he did a work in Chicago that will long be felt. He has now the pastoral charge of the church at Galesburg. He is also statistical secretary of the National Baptist Association. The State University conferred " D. D." upon him at its commencement, 1887.

Some of his best editorials while editor of *The Conservator* are : " The Negro in Debt; but who owes him?" " Colored voters and the Republican Party ;" " The Emigration Question ;" and " Social Equality." Upon these questions, he wrote in that style peculiar to the true, able and vigorous writer.

After withdrawing from *The Conservator*, September, 1884, he began the publication of *The Western Herald*, a religious journal, which ran until December, 1885. After this he was for several years upon the editorial staff of *The Brooklyn Monitor* with Dr. R. L. Perry.

Among the ablest articles appearing in *The Monitor* from his pen, are : " Are we Doing our Duty?" having reference to Christians; and " Christian Co-operation." He is a journalist whom the race admire and love. The influence he has been able to exert through the medium of his pen has been uplifting and highly spiritual. The inspiration to a better life has been imparted to many a soul by a perusal of his writings, and many a one cheered and comforted thereby. His work in this direction is missed. Unlike many, Rev. Dr. De Baptiste possesses the power to write and talk.

He has three children, one of whom partakes of the father's journalistic nature.

REV. T. W. COFFEE.

Rev. T. W. Coffee, Editor Vindicator.

The subject of this sketch first saw the light on the 4th day of July, 1853, in Lauderdale County, Alabama. His mother was a slave, and the fetters of bondage held him during the first eleven years of his life; but so great was his horror of servitude, that he ran away twice before he attained the age of twelve. Cruel treatment and his extreme hatred of slavery caused him to renew his efforts to obtain freedom, and in 1864 he succeeded in finding refuge with his father and mother.

At the age of thirteen he became an orphan, and grew up under the most adverse circumstances, with few advantages, being in one of the most benighted regions of the state. At the age of twenty this child of misfortune was unable to write his name; but, with the strong determination "to find a way or make one," he, by the assistance of a paid instructor, soon learned to write legibly.

In course of time he entered Le Moyne Institute, at Memphis, Tenn., and by close application was, in a short time, enabled to pass a creditable examination. He began teaching, which calling he followed for several years, with great benefit to his pupils, as well as credit to himself and to his profession. In 1878, he joined the A. M. E. Conference, and has had some of the best appointments in Alabama.

His first journalistic effort was as editor of *The Christian Era*, in 1887. Though occupying the position of associate editor of the paper, he was regarded by many as being the actual editor-in-chief. *The Era* was first published exclusively as a religious journal; but owing to the failure of other Afro-American papers to discuss boldly the issues of the day, Mr. Coffee entered the arena of controversy, and his keen and polished shafts of logic and sarcasm arrested the attention of the leading dailies of the state. After a time the name of his paper was changed from *The Christian Era* to *The Birmingham Era*.

In 1888, Mr. Coffee was appointed pastor of a church in Mobile, where he commenced the publication of a sheet known as *The Methodist Vindicator*, which, as the name indicated, was a religious paper, but it did not fail, on occasion, to give voice to those great race issues which were and are now agitating the public mind. The publication of this paper was suspended on account of the great demand upon the editor's time by urgent church business, and by his subsequent removal to Eufala. As soon as he became settled in the latter city, he commenced the publication of a sheet known as *The Vindicator*, an unsectarian paper devoted to news and the general interests of the Afro-American race.

As a writer, Mr. Coffee is caustic and fearless, though discreet. He knows the right, and dares to maintain it. He is destined to become one of the most brilliant journalistic lights of the country, and is a man of whom his race has reason to be proud, especially in his vocation as a journalist.

REV. S. D. RUSSELL, EDITOR TORCHLIGHT APPEAL.

The motto, "Find a way or make one," seems to have been the principle instilled into Rev. S. D. Russell, the brilliant young editor of the only religious paper published at present in Texas. Born in the city of Natchez., Miss., August 3, 1862, of pious parents, he was early imbued with the idea of doing work for the Master. After his conversion he identified himself with the A. M. E. church, in which connection he grew up well educated, and is at present a minister of high standing in that denomination.

But we are to speak of him more particularly as a journalist. In this sphere he is making rapid headway. He believes, as do most Afro-Americans in like positions, that he cannot afford simply to labor in the pulpit for his race but must be an editorial agitator, also; which is well, since in this capacity he is an acknowledged power.

He began a career as journalist in 1885, when he published a "red hot" semi-monthly paper, called *The Herald of Truth.* This he edited with untiring zeal for two years. As editor of this paper, he never wavered in contending for the truth and right, which are priceless to his people. Having been promoted to the presiding-eldership of his church, the name of the paper was changed and became *The College Journal of Paul Quinn College.*

The editorship of *The Southern Guide*, a progressive and live sheet, in Texas, has been tendered Mr. Russell, at a fair salary. Whether he has accepted the position the author is unable at this writing to say. He is now editor of *The Torchlight Appeal*, which is the only paper published in the state by an Afro-American, with Confederate sympathies. It was started in 1888 a very minute sheet, but under the journalistic management of Mr. Russell, it is now a four-column, eight-page quarto, being one of the popular religious journals published by an Afro-American.

Mr. Russell is a journalist whose plans are all original, and when set into action they take well. As a writer, he can hold his own by the side of the best. He has published a treatise on Infant Baptism and has a lecture,—Why the negro is black; which are highly commended by his people. The journalistic fraternity is proud of him as a fearless editorial writer, and an energetic paper-man who is determined to further the cause, and at the same time contend for the rights of his people. His ready courage in seeking to do this endears him to all.

N. B. Since the above was written, Rev. Mr. Russell has removed to Denison, Texas, where he now edits *The Texas Reformer.*

REV. S. D. RUSSELL.

W. C. Smith, Editor Charlotte Messenger.

William Caswell Smith was born in Cumberland County, N. C., February 12, 1856, his parents being Alexander and Violet Smith, both slaves of unmixed negro blood. Alexander, or Sandy, as he was called, was coachman for a wealthy family, and thereby had more privileges, and saw more of the world, than the ordinary slave. He was also known as the neighborhood fiddler. He was very proud, and was popular with the females.

William was the youngest of three children. He entered a public school in 1866, and learned very rapidly, standing at the head in nearly all of his classes. His school training was limited to about five years,—a part of this time being spent in school and a part on the farm. Nevertheless, what opportunities he had to learn were so well improved, he was afterward able to teach, and was thus employed in the public schools of his own and adjoining counties.

In 1873 he entered the printing-office of *The Statesman*, where he learned to set type. He learned the trade rapidly, and at the end of the first year he took charge of the office, having learned to "make up forms" and do any other work about the office.

He was one of the founders of *The Fayetteville Educator*, the first newspaper edited and published by colored men in North Carolina. This paper was published by Waddell & Smith one year, they doing their own type-setting, writing, and everything about the office, Smith acting foreman. After publishing this paper fifty-two consecutive weeks, it was suspended, and Mr. Smith was employed on *The Memphis* (Tenn.) *Planet* several months, but disliking the West he returned to Washington City, where he was employed as compositor on *The People's Advocate*. In 1879, he returned to North Carolina and was put in charge of *The Star of Zion*

W. C. SMITH.

printing-office, the second in the state run by one of our race. He did the mechanical work on this paper in Charlotte, N. C., under the editorship of Rev. J. A. Tyler; also in Concord, under A. S. Richardson, Esq.

In 1882 he established in Charlotte, N. C., *The Charlotte Messenger*, which has met with fair success, though by hard fighting against intemperance, immorality, and all other evils coming in its way. *The Messenger* is very popular with the better class of our people and a terror to evil doers. It has experienced some very heavy tilts with contemporaries, preachers and others, but has carried off the palm in every instance.

Among the most prominent of the controversies in which its editor has been engaged was one with the late Prof. Robert Harris of Fayetteville on Sunday excursions, which he condemned. Another was on secret societies, which he condemned also, and engaged in a lengthy and bitter controversy with Rev. C. S. Brown of the Good Samaritan order. Brown was driven to the wall, also. Another was the fight he made for a college for the colored youth, supported by the state. Another was the strong and memorable fight he made, and is still making, for a female seminary for his church. In this fight he completely demolished the brilliant Dancy and all others who dared oppose it. The heaviest fight, and the most signal victory this editor boasts of, was the controversy between Bishop S. T. Jones and himself. He dared to criticise certain remarks in a sermon delivered by the Bishop, which he regarded as calculated to injure his race and church. The Bishop called him to account, at some length, in his usual sarcastic way; but after this he will inform himself as to the size of the game before he makes another attack on a Smith.

Mr. Smith is a conscientious man, and means to be honest in all things. He tries to take the right side of every

question, no matter how unpopular it is. He is strictly
temporate, having signed a pledge in his youth against the
use of intoxicating drinks and tobacco, and has kept it to
this day. He is always on the side of temperance, and an
advocate of prohibition, local option, or anything that aims
at the destruction of the rum traffic.

He has used the columns of his paper against the practice
of Sunday excursions, and the holding of camp-meetings and
festivals, and endeavors to impress upon his people the
importance of improving their morals, educating their children, and of the ownership of land.

Mr. Smith is a member of the Methodist church, and while
not much of a society man, he has held prominent offices in
the State Grand Lodge of Odd Fellows and Good Templars.
He took an active part in politics in 1888, and represented
his county in the district and state Republican conventions.
He was elected by acclamation in the state convention as
alternate delegate-at-large to the Republican National Convention at Chicago, in 1888.

For several years Mr. Smith was the only negro printer
in the state, during which time he started many colored boys
in the trade he was following. In 1880, he adopted Charlotte, N. C., as his home, after having spent a few years in
traveling.

At the beginning of 1890 he gave up *The Charlotte
Messenger* he was then publishing, and accepted a position in
the government printing-office at Washington, where he is
now employed.

Mr. Smith may be regarded as a pioneer journalist of the
'' Tar Heel '' state, and is certain to do credit to himself and
to his race in any position he may assume, for, once taken,
he will work conscientiously and diligently to discharge
acceptably the duties of his office. He is a man to be
depended on, at all times and in all places.

18

Hon. Richard Nelson, Editor Freeman's Journal.

The above gentleman, who is editor of the most influential paper published in Texas, was born at Key West, Fla., June 16, 1842. He obtained his education in the schools of Key West, Fla. He moved to Atlanta in 1850, and to Texas in 1859, where he has since resided.

Settling in Galveston in 1866, he went into business, and here it was that his active mind and great energy soon brought him conspicuously before his own people, and the public generally, on the question of Reconstruction. His life has been one of prominence in politics, as a speaker and writer.

Mr. Nelson has held important positions in political life, such as justice of peace and notary public for Galveston; postmaster at Highland Station, in Galveston County; and inspector of customs for the district of Galveston. He was prominently mentioned as a Republican candidate for Congress in 1871, and ran on an independent ticket for Congress in 1884.

Mr. Nelson is a public speaker of wide reputation, and a writer of well-earned repute. He is a race man every inch. Concerning his life in this respect, Flake's Bulletin says of him: "His highest ambition is the elevation of his race from their former despondency and degradation, to high attainments in education and the proper discharge of their duties of citizenship in this great and free republic." He was several times delegate to the state and national conventions of his party.

His experience in journalism has been long and effective. In 1873, he began the publication of *The Weekly Spectator*, being sole proprietor and editor. *The Spectator* must have wielded considerable influence. Ex-Gov. E. J. Dana speaks of it as a leading Republican paper in the state.

HON. RICHARD NELSON.

The Freeman's Journal took the place of *The Spectator*, March 19, 1887. It is recognized as the leading Republican newspaper in the state. Mr. Edwin Smith, a reputable citizen of Texas, writes about *The Journal* as follows: "Temperate in tone and conservative in politics, it has gained for the colored people of this state a consideration for their wants and a recognition of their rights, on the part of their white fellow-citizens, that were never before accorded." Trained by experience, he is enabled to make such a wise use of his abilities as to render his paper a recognized power for good among all classes.

His editorial writings, as possibly may be the case with a few other Afro-American editors, are commented on frequently by the leading white organs of the state. There appeared in *The Journal*, shortly after the beginning of the present administration, an editorial on—"The Administration and the Colored Man. Merit and Worth before Political Jugglery." This editorial created a stir all over the country, both white and black papers commenting and criticising the editor, favorably or unfavorably. A portion of the editorial we publish below, which was freely commented on, as the reader will see, by *The San Antonio Express, San Antonio Light*, and *The Fort Worth Gazette*, all white papers of Texas. Editor Nelson writes thus: "The negro must learn one great fundamental truth and act upon it, that his color or previous condition is not a recommendation to office; that when the great Republican party knocked the shackles from his limbs, raised him to citizenship and made him the equal of the white man under the Constitution, and threw around him the full protection of law, its functions ceased, because it could do no more; and it expected him to work out his own salvation the same as the white man, and to expect no special legislation or favors to his race that were not accorded the white race."

Concerning the editorial in full, *The Fort Worth Gazette* says: "The utterance of *The Freeman's Journal* of Galveston on the relation of the negro to the Federal offices, as telegraphed *The Gazette* of yesterday, is worthy the hearty approval of those who sincerely wish for a solution of the negro problem. *The Journal*, as its name indicates, is an organ of the colored people. Coming from such a publication, the following is full of significance:" (Here *The Gazette* inserts the editorial we have alluded to.)

The San Antonio Light says: "An amendment to the Constitution emancipated the negroes from physical bondage, but left them in a condition of social and political tutelage and dependence, where they will remain until they emancipate themselves by accepting the truth and acting upon the wise suggestion contained in the following sentences from *The Journal's* editorial:" Here *The Light* introduces the editorial and comments further by saying: "These words are words of wisdom, by whomsoever uttered. It were well for white and colored alike to heed them. The colored man is made the political equal of the white man under the law; his place as an office-holder he must make good for himself."

The San Antonio Express says: "The telegraphic columns of *The Express* yesterday contained the text of an editorial which appears to-day in *The Freeman's Journal*. This paper is published in Galveston and is regarded as one of the most influential journals of the state, devoted to the interests of the negro race." Then *The Express* quotes the editorial, and wisely adds the following words of approval: "The only political or social recognition which the negro deserves, or will ever get, is that to which his own worth as a man entitles him."

Other prominent papers have commented on Editor Nelson's writings, notably *The St. Louis Globe-Democrat*; which, for lack of space, we cannot publish. If we say no more, the editorial and its valuable comments will suffice to prove our subject a terse, able, and thoughtful writer.   He is an honored member of the journalistic corps.

Rev. F. M. Hamilton, Editor Christian Index.

The most prominent man, exclusive of the bishops of the C. M. E. church, is Rev. Mr. Hamilton.   He was born near Washington, Arkansas, September 3, 1858.   He attended the schools of his state, private and public, and afterwards spent sixteen months in the Theological Institute at Tuscaloosa, Alabama.

He was licensed to preach Nov. 9, 1878.   He has served in several of the most prominent positions in his denomination, among which has been that of Presiding Elder of the Washington district.   He had contemplated the practice of medicine, and to this end devoted two years' study to fit himself for it, but gave it up to accept the positions he now holds,—editor of *The Christian Index* and agent of the book department of his church.   To these he was elected in May, 1886, at the General Conference, which met at Augusta, Ga. His prominence in church circles has been the cause of his being its representative in many of its conspicuous gatherings. *The Index*, of which he is now editor, was the origin of the C. M. E. Church.   He has issued two books, with reference to the church of which he is a member, viz.:   "Conversations on the C. M. E. Church," and, "A Plain Account of the C. M. E. Church."

When he took charge of *The Index*, it was issued monthly, while the outfit for its publication was very limited, the entire material being worth but seventy-five dollars.   Since assuming control, and managing the business for three years or more, he has put in one thousand dollars' worth of material, and established a job department, in which the entire work is done by Afro-Americans.

REV. F. M. HAMILTON.

Mr. Hamilton uses *The Index* office in fitting young men to become printers. At this writing he has five apprentices, whose work is very neatly done. His paper has the reputation of being one of the best edited and neatly printed of our religious journals. It contends for the religious rights of its people, while forgetting not their civil and political rights.

Mr. Hamilton possesses great aptitude for business; and being a quick thinker and a ready writer, he always expresses himself in a style that has drawn to *The Index* a large number of readers.

H. C. SMITH, EDITOR CLEVELAND GAZETTE.

One of the best Afro-American papers published in Ohio, and one of the best edited in the United States, is *The Cleveland Gazette*, whose success has been achieved by the persistent efforts of the subject of this sketch, whom we are proud to record as its editor and proprietor.

Mr. Smith was born at Clarksburg, West Va., January 28, 1863, and is therefore now a very young man. He was taken to Cleveland in 1865, where he attended the schools, finishing his course successfully in 1882.

The next year he devoted his efforts to the study of band and orchestral music. His diligent efforts in the direction of journalism and music have gained for him the place he occupies to-day, "facile princeps" (as a writer says) among the first colored citizens of Ohio. He is now leader and musical director of the Excelsior cornet band. His musical compositions have found ready sale, especially his song and chorus—"Be True, Bright Eyes."

His life since 1880 has been spent mostly in journalism. In connection with three others he launched *The Cleveland Gazette*, in August, 1883,—and afterward became sole proprietor. Few Afro-American journals have proved absolutely

H. C. SMITH.

281

a success, but it can be said that this one has been so from its very beginning, until now its power and influence are recognized by all.

This success is not so much due to the abundance of news-matter in the paper, as to the vigorous and able editorial writings of Mr. Smith. He is known among the white and black press as a fearless and brilliant writer. His paper, Republican to the core, always defends Republican principles.

To impress our readers as we desire in regard to Mr. Smith's editorial career in politics, we will insert what the Hon. Fred Douglass wrote to him in commendation of his course. Said Mr. Douglass: "In the midst of hurried preparations for a long tour in Europe, I snatch my pen, and spend a few moments in telling you how completely I sympathize with you in your political attitude. I do exhort your readers to stand by you in your effort to lead the colored citizens of Ohio to wise political action."

About our subject's course in politics and other matters, another representative scholar and thinker, Prof. W. S. Scarborough, says: "Though at times Mr. Smith has been severely criticised, he has never varied from what he considered his duty. He believes that the Republican party conserves best the interests of the negro, and thereupon he becomes its able and active defender. He believes that mixed schools are the best for all concerned, and especially for the negro—as separate schools imply race prejudice and race inferiority—and therefore he becomes the relentless enemy to the color line in schools. His articles are read with both pleasure and profit, to which fact is largely due the increased and increasing circulation of *The Gazette*."

Judge J. B. Foraker, it is said, owed his first election as governor of Ohio more to *The Gazette* than to any other newspaper, white or colored. As evidence of the governor's recognition of Mr. Smith's work, he secured him an appointment as deputy state oil inspector, the first case of the kind North. A bond of $5000 being required, this was quickly furnished, three colored men signing it. He has discharged with credit the functions of this office for four years,—two terms.

One of the youngest editors of the country, he is probably the only Afro-American who has been a member of a white press association. All the Afro-American members of the Ohio Legislature have been his ardent supporters, and rely absolutely upon *The Gazette* for information on matters of special import to them.

In January, 1888, when Hon. Mr. McGregor, Democratic representative in the Ohio Legislature from Muskingum County, introduced a bill to re-enact Section 4008, which replaced upon the Ohio statutes a portion of the "black laws," Hon. Jere A. Brown wrote Mr. Smith as follows: A bill was introduced this forenoon by McGregor, of Muskingum county, a Democrat, to re-enact Section 4008. Sound the alarm! Let the friends of equality for all, know that again the enemy seeks to re-enact obnoxious, discriminating and unjust laws. When the time comes, I propose, with the aid of our friends, to oppose it to the death. I write hastily, so that our friends may be aroused through our race advocate, *The Gazette*."

Editor Smith *sounded* the alarm, which rang out all over the "Buck-eye State." Said he, commenting on the letter: " The above was received as we were going to press. It tells every race-loving colored man his duty. Let every Afro-American in the state of Ohio who values his rights as an American citizen, write the Senator and Representatives of his county, if he cannot see them personally, and importune them to fight this McGregor bill to the death. We cannot afford to lose a particle of the ground gained by the wiping out of Ohio's infernal 'black laws.' Let us fight as a unit

the effort of this Democrat to re-enact any portion of the
infamous laws wiped from the statute books by the last
Assembly. Now is the time, and here is *the* opportunity, for
every colored man (and woman) in Ohio to show his loyalty
to the race and himself. Eternal vigilance, and good hard
work, is to be the price of our liberty and freedom as
American citizens."

The Virginia Lancet, edited by Hon. W. W. Evans of
Petersburg, Va., pays a glowing tribute to Mr. Smith, which
we cannot fail to insert: " *The Washington Bee* of last week
contained the portrait of Mr. H. C. Smith, the very able
editor of *The Cleveland Gazette.* Mr. Smith has shown
himself to be an unselfish leader of his people. His editorials
are among the brightest and most sensible that come to our
sanctum. If he desires anything under the present administration he should have it."

The author remembers having received a copy of *The
Gazette* shortly after the first issue, and having noticed its
progress, is prepared to say that it is highly deserving of the
continued support of the Afro-American.

We cannot better close this article upon Editor Smith and
The Gazette than by quoting what Rev. J. W. Gazaway,
D. D., pastor of Allen Temple, Cincinnati, O., says about
them: " The most healthful signs of life and a highly useful
career are indicated in the existence of *The Cleveland Gazette.*
That it is a paper of brain and culture can not be doubted,
when the fact is remembered that in its columns are found
communications from the wisest and best minds of our race.
It is a paper for the people it represents, and can be relied
upon as a friend of every colored man, though his face may
be of ebony hue. *The Gazette* is a practical demonstration
of what can be done by the young men of our race. The
editor is a young man who, by dint of industry and economy
and fair dealing, has succeeded in giving to the colored

HON. CHAS. HENDLEY.

people of Ohio and the country a paper worthy the patronage of all. Having been a reader of *The Gazette* since its first appearance, and having watched its course, I feel that in justice to the paper, the editor, and the race, I should urge upon the people generally to support the paper that is practically identified with the colored people, and is in harmony with the interests and success of all, without regard to complexion."

HON. CHAS. HENDLEY, EDITOR HUNTSVILLE GAZETTE.

The subject of this sketch is among the foremost gentlemen who are now engaged in the editorial work; and in various ways has labored untiringly for the intellectual and moral good of his people.

Born in December, 1855, the youngest child of Charles and Polly Hendley, his education was derived in the schools about Huntsville and at the Rust Institute. He began to teach in the common schools, and finally became principal of the graded school in Huntsville, where he remained until President Harrison appointed him receiver of public moneys. He is a mason, and occupies a high position in that fraternal order.

As a journalist, he enjoys the reputation of being the editor of the oldest journal now published in the South. In 1879 the Huntsville newspaper company was organized, and Charles Hendley selected as editor and manager of *The Huntsville Gazette*, a weekly Republican newspaper, established by the company. It has been a successful venture from the first, its continued success being due to Mr. Hendley's able management and editorial skill. *The Gazette* has a rapidly increasing circulation. It has no hot-headed editorials. The editor is a vivid and soul-stirring writer, and is among the few stars on the journalistic stage.

WILLIAM CALVIN CHASE, ESQ., EDITOR WASHINGTON BEE.

"What is there in a name," one asks. Observing the matter closely, we are sometimes compelled to say there is something, after all, in a name. *The Bee* and its editor, in that respect, are fair illustrations. Nothing stings Washington City, and in fact, the Bourbons of the South, as *The Bee.*

William Calvin Chase, the alert, progressive editor of *The Bee* was born in the city of Washington, February 2, 1854. His father, William H. Chase, having died when he was quite young, the burden of his mother's support partly fell upon the son, who took, as means to aid her, the selling of newspapers. This he continued to do successfully, until he came to be a popular crier of the news. From this he seems to have got a journalistic inspiration; for it was not long after, before we find him upon the editorial stool. His educational privileges were furnished him by the private school of John F. Cook and by Howard University of Washington City.

During his youth he was a resident of Methuen, Mass., for a while, where he learned the printer's trade. Mr. Chase, at this early age, was strongly inclined to the use of the quill. He became very proficient in the printing business, and was accordingly appointed to a position in the government printing-office at Washington, just about the time he was to enter the college department of Howard University.

He has held other important positions in the public service, in office of recorder of deeds, under Hon. Fred Douglass, resigning the position to accept a better place in the War Department, at the instance of Ex-Senator B. K. Bruce. Mr. Chase is a prominent lawyer, having been admitted to the bar of Virginia to practice, July 23, 1889.

His life-work, which appears to be that of a literary character, begins with the position of reporter and society editor of *The Washington Plaindealer*, published by Dr. King. In this position he was considered a valuable acquisition. He resigned, however, not being satisfied with the policy of the paper.

His next journalistic move was his acceptance of the editorship of *The Argus*, at Washington, to succeed Mr. Charles N. Otey. About Mr. Chase's course in this new field, a writer says: "He changed the name of the paper to *The Free Lance*. This change of name excited great feeling among the people, as they knew of the vindictiveness and determination of Mr. Chase to expose a fraud, and get even with those whom he considered enemies."

Nor did he disappoint them. His first attack was made on Senator John Sherman, then Secretary of the Treasury. The schools and the police force received attention from his pen, as did also the National Republican committee for taking so little notice of colored men in the presidential campaign. So great was the feeling of the Republicans against him, that the board of directors, who were all office-holders, not daring to remove him, sold out the paper to L. H. Douglass, H. Johnson, M. M. Holland and others, who were likewise office-holders, and regarded by Mr. Chase as his enemies.

He next assumed the publication of *The Washington Bee*, of which he is the present editor and proprietor. Many of Mr. Chase's friends have regarded him as occasionally being very indiscreet; but as Burns says, "for a' that" he has never failed to expose, in the most condemnatory manner, any fraud, unjust attack or evil, that caught his vigilant eye.

Men are not all alike, and whether we approve or disapprove of Mr. Chase's idea of the mission of the Afro-American editor, we commend and admire him for his boldness of thought and fearlessness of speech.

The Bee is read by all, and can be found in nearly every house in Washington, from the Executive Mansion to the

WILLIAM CALVIN CHASE.

most humble hut. It is related, that on one occasion when Mr. Chase called on President Cleveland, he showed him a copy of *The Bee*, in which he (Chase) had said that in consideration of the number of outrages perpetrated in the South upon the Afro-Americans by the whites, it would cost the lives of millions to inaugurate Grover Cleveland, *if elected.* Mr. Chase did not deny being the author of the article. Although Cleveland was elected and inaugurated without any bloodshed, and Chase supported in a measure his administration, yet he received his discharge a few weeks afterward, at the instance of the president and Secretary of War Endicott, from the position he held in the government printing-office.

He has since given his whole time to *The Bee*, which stings in no uncertain manner. His fearless statements have more than once brought him into the courts of justice, having been five times indicted for libel, and acquitted in every case except one, in which he was fined fifty dollars. In these experiences he has a record not held by any one else of the fraternity.

Mr. Chase delights in newspaper controversies, and seldom, if ever, comes out of one worsted. His *Bee* is known by every Afro-American editor, correspondent, or writer, and while many do not agree with him, they all admire the steadfastness with which he holds to what *he* thinks is right. One has said of Mr. Chase: " He will never give up, as long as there is a fighting chance."

He has read several papers at the various press conventions, the most noted of which was the one on Southern Outrages, which was favorably commented upon by the Philadelphia Press. He is now historian of the National Press Convention,

It is our hope that *The Bee* will live long, and its editor continue to be honored as a true specimen of the Afro-American journalist.

AUGUSTUS M. HODGES.

AUGUSTUS M. HODGES, EDITOR BROOKLYN SENTINEL.

Augustus M. Hodges is the son of Willis A. Hodges, one of the early pioneer Afro-American journalists, and evidently inherits his father's journalistic taste. He was born in Williamsburg, Va., March 18, 1854, and attended the Hampton Normal and Agricultural Institute, from which he graduated in 1874.

Mr. Hodges is one of the prominent young men of the race. He has few superiors in the journalistic field. He was a trusted and ready writer on *The New York Globe*, and, more recently, on *The Indianapolis Freeman*. Lately, he has issued a journal of his own, called *The Brooklyn Sentinel*, which is meeting with much favor. *The New York Press* of September 15, 1889, pays him this tribute: "He was elected to the Virginia House of Delegates in 1876, but was counted out by the Democrats. He was connected with *The New York Globe* a few years later, and is at present upon the staff of *The Indianapolis Freeman*, the leading colored paper of the United States. He was a candidate for the position of minister to Hayti, receiving the indorsement of 509 leading Republicans of the United States. He is a French student, a poet, and writer. He stands head and shoulders above many colored men who have received more reward. As a political leader, he has few equals; as a colored journalist, none."

R. A. JONES, EDITOR AND PROPRIETOR CLEVELAND GLOBE.

Richard A. Jones was born July 16, 1847, in Randolph County, Georgia. At the age of twelve he was taken to Rochester, Minnesota, and being very apt with books, was sent to the public school at Rochester, where he received a

R. A. Jones

good, thorough training. While at Rochester, he was taken into the family of Hon. O. P. Whitcomb and wife, who cared for him until he was able to provide for himself. He came to Cleveland in 1873, after having traveled extensively through the South and West.

Mr. Jones is a thoroughly self-made man, and exact and shrewd in his business relations. The thoughtful precision and self-reliance with which he is possessed, indicate that perseverance and push were his chief instructors.

He figures prominently, not only in political but in the social and literary circles of Cleveland, and is well known throughout the state of Ohio as an earnest and intelligent advocate of race principles. He became a mason in Pioneer Lodge, No. 5, St. Paul, Minn.; was made a royal arch mason in 1877, in Cleveland, by St. John's Chapter; and in the same year was dubbed and created a knight templar in the Ezekial Commandery. He afterward withdrew from the Ezekial Commandery and entered the Red Cross, where he has proved a faithful member, giving good counsel on all questions of material interest in the lodge. He has held nearly all the important positions in these bodies, with which he has been connected, and is now a member of the Grand Lodge and Grand Chapter of Ohio, in which he has been very active and prominent.

Mr. Jones was tendered by President Cleveland the office of minister to Liberia, but owing to his urgent duties at home, he was forced to decline the honor. Some time afterward he was appointed United States deputy marshal for the Northern District of Ohio, which position he filled with much ability and credit.

Mr. Jones is a self-made man, possessed of a strong determination to pursue to the very end anything he undertakes in the interest of his race. He is the father of the Forest City Afro-American League of Cleveland, O., which has a membership of abont one hundred, and which he represented in State League Convention at Columbus, O., in 1890. He is now vice-president of Ohio State League, and is one of the organizers for the state, and acknowledged to be one of the most prominent negroes in Ohio; and before him lies a brilliant career.

He was one of the founders of the St. Andrews Episcopal church of Cleveland, O., and has made faithful effort through the columns of *The Globe*, of which he is editor and sole proprietor, to further the cause of Christian principles and right. He now publishes *The Cleveland Globe*, and has, by his pen, done much to bring about the civil and political rights of the negro in Ohio. He has made for *The Globe* an everlasting reputation as a strong defender of law, rights, and Christianity.

JOHN T. MORRIS, M. A., ASSOCIATE EDITOR CLEVELAND GLOBE.

The subject of this sketch, born at Marietta, Ohio, January 19, 1863, was the son of Thomas J. and Susan Morris, whose parents were among the earlier settlers of Ohio.

Young Morris attended the public school of Marietta, and becoming possessed of a desire for a liberal education, at the age of twelve he entered Marietta College, the oldest and most thorough college in the state. His studies were soon somewhat impeded by the sudden death of his father, which threw much of the care of the family upon his shoulders. He was about to give up the idea of continuing his collegiate course, when the corporation came to his aid and furnished him with a scholarship, which did away with many obstacles. By the aid of his mother, and by his own efforts, he was reinstated in his class, and completed the whole collegiate course, graduating with the class of 1883, with honor to his mother, himself, and to his race. He was the only negro student in the college at that time, and the third negro graduate. After graduation, he went to Washington, D. C., and at once secured a position in the office of the register of wills, remaining there until a change of administration. He always exhibited a fondness for literary work, especially for newspapers. Besides contributing frequently to his home papers, he was Washington correspondent for *The Kentucky Republican*, of L:xington, Ky. His articles were much sought after by the n:groes of the South.

Leaving Washington he 'vent to Alabama, where he taught for several sessions until his health became impaired. He went to Cleveland in 1887, and was immediately given a position on the editorial staff of *The Cleveland Globe*. Finding his duties on *The Globe* could be properly attended to without the expenditure of much time, he secured a good position in the office of The Brightman Furnace Company of Cleveland as draughtsman and stenographer, which he now holds with great credit to himself and his race.

Young Morris has contributed much to the daily papers of Cleveland and elsewhere, and has written for several magazines. As a reward for his earnest efforts in behalf of himself and race, his alma mater has conferred upon him the degree of Master of Arts. He is one of Ohio's successful young men, and is very popular throughout the state. He represented the Cleveland constituency in the National Afro-American Convention, held at Chicago, January, 1890, and filled the position satisfactorily.

Aside from his other duties, he still holds his relations as associate editor of *The Cleveland Globe*, and is now corresponding secretary of the Ohio State Afro-American League. He is also corresponding secretary and executive committeeman of the local Forest City Afro-American League, Cleveland, O., and has figured prominently as one of the founders of the

St. Andrews Episcopalian church in the city of Cleveland. Mr. Morris may well be regarded as one of the most popular men of Ohio.

THE CLEVELAND GLOBE.

The Cleveland Globe came into existence April 4, 1884, with R. A. Jones as editor and proprietor. During the political controversies that were going on in Ohio over the mixed schools and other questions of great importance to the negro, *The Globe* was always for the highest interests of the race, and as a firm defender of right and justice has been successful throughout its whole career.

The Globe has never been pledged to any particular party, and has never sacrificed any of the principles with which it so boldly began its career. Nothing could induce it to divert from the path of usefulness and right and go blindly into issues for mere financial gain. It has stood firmly for the race; has waged bitter warfare against Southern outrages, murders, and bulldozing, and has done this in a strictly non-partisan manner.

During the short interval in which Mr. Jones withdrew from *The Globe*, owing to the severe illness of his wife who subsequently died, its management fell into the hands of ten different parties who made complete failures, when he again assumed charge of it. He now became its editor and sole proprietor, and it has ever since been under his supervision.

It has been the advocate of everything that looked to the success and prosperity of the race. It is well known in Ohio for its non-partisan cast, it always placing race before party. It is the official organ of the Forest City Afro-American League of Cleveland, and also of the State League, which numbers about twenty thousand members. It is the only paper in Cleveland that is thoroughly identified with the various negro churches, and in good standing with them. It supports all literary and social organizations, and does what it can to aid the efforts of the young people. It is a general referee in matters pertaining to race interests.

The Globe is the oldest negro journal in Ohio, and has worked itself into popularity by its own diligent efforts, fair dealing and generosity. It has a larger circulation in Cleveland than any race paper published. It advocates the principles it has set forth, and is heartily supported by such men of the race as Bruce, Douglass, Langston, Alexander Clark, McCabe, John P. Green, Fortune, Price, C. H. J. Taylor, Geo. Fields, C. A. Cottrill, H. A. Clark and a host of others. The Globe goes to Europe, Asia, Africa, and Italy, as well as all over the United States. It was one of the first to favor the formation of a National Afro-American League, and has ever since been pushing its cause.

REV. D. J. SAUNDERS, EDITOR AFRO-AMERICAN PRESBY-TERIAN.

The Afro-American Presbyterian is a weekly religious sheet published at Wilmington, N. C., with Rev. D. J. Saunders as its editor. The subscription list reaches nearly two thousand, with a daily increasing patronage.

Mr. Saunders was born in Winnsboro, S. C., February 15, 1847, and educated in the Brainerd Institute at Chester, S. C., and in the Western Theological Seminary, Allegheny City, Pa., graduating therefrom April 24, 1874.

From May, 1877, to January, 1879, he was the associate editor of The Southern Evangelist. He founded The Afro-American Presbyterian, January 1, 1879. It has been published weekly since, and steadily grown in favor. The editor is a bright, cool, and level-headed writer.

Upon the race question he very wisely says: "We are *w* that number who don't believe that God will permit the Negro Question in this country to be settled wrong. The great majority of the Christian and right-thinking people will soon see clearly what is now beginning to dawn upon many minds, namely: that anything short of Christian education, in the broadest and best sense of the term, and the exercise of justice and loving-mercy, only tends to increase the evil which it would destroy. Let this policy be substituted for that of repression, now so generally resorted to, and the era of brighter days will begin, and the race question, now so universally annoying, will be shorn of many of its harassing features, and its final solution will soon be reached."

REV. A. N. McEWEN, EDITOR BAPTIST LEADER.

Rev. A. N. McEwen, editor of *The Baptist Leader*, the official organ of the colored Baptists of Alabama, was born in LaFayette County, Miss., April 29, 1849. Although he has no alma mater, having picked up his education here and there, he is an acknowledged leader of his race.

He is a Baptist missionary preacher. He left Mississippi in the fall of 1866, and went to Nashville, Tenn., where he met Miss Lizzie Harvel, to whom he was married in November, 1869. In 1870, while attending a revival at Mt. Zion church, he was brought to feel the need of a Savior. After his conversion he united with the Mt. Zion church, and was baptized by Rev. J. Bransford. Feeling that he was called to preach the gospel, he petitioned his church for the privilege to labor among the common people of the city. This he did with such success, he finally received a license to preach, and was called to the charge of a church at Tullahoma, Tenn. It was during his pastorate here that his ability as a minister began to manifest itself.

REV. A. N. McEWEN.

He was a lover of books, and an earnest student. He has preached several annual sermons before school associations, state conventions, and various societies. He is a natural orator, and never fails to capture his audience. He is witty and humorous, almost to a fault. It is his aim in speaking to tell the truth, and thereby touch the hearts of his hearers. Although a busy journalist, he is now pastor of the Dexter Avenue Baptist church, whose members are among the most refined people of the state, his congregation being largely composed of the business men of the city, as well as of lawyers, doctors, school teachers, and merchants. The church edifice, one of the finest in the South, was four years in building, and cost over $50,000.

Mr. McEwen is a member of the board of trustees of Selma University, and chairman of the state mission board. In politics, he is a Republican, and is a member of the state executive board of the Republican party.

As a journalist, he stands well with both the white and the colored people. In 1886, he began editing *The Montgomery Herald*, after the Duke trouble, and restored peace between the whites and the blacks. At the request of his friends, he resigned the editorial control of *The Herald*, and in the latter part of 1887 took charge of *The Baptist Leader*, in the interest of 150,000 Baptists of the state. This paper has a wide circulation, and ranks among the best journals of the day.

Editor McEwen is distinguished as a peace-making journalist, and did excellent service when the whites were so excited over articles regarded as incendiary, published by Mr. Duke, then editor of *The Montgomery Herald*. There is nothing of a fiery nature about his writings. He is always cool and deliberate, and a firm defender of race rights and race principles. *The Baptist Leader*, of which he is now editor, in make-up and appearance shows progress upon the

part of the Baptists of Alabama; while the editorial columns
tell the world that a man learned in the editorial art graces
the chair.

Rev. Mr. McEwen's ability and deliberate judgment as an
editor are fully illustrated in his comment on *The Montgomery Advertiser's* account of Senator Morgan's address
before the Howard College students. It is found in *The
Leader* of May 2, 1889. We reproduce for the reader the
squib from *The Advertiser*, and Mr. McEwen's comment upon
it: "'If language means anything, then the concluding
sentences of Senator Morgan's address to the Howard College
students last Tuesday are tantamonnt to a declaration that,
sooner or later, the 15th amendment will be eliminated from
the Federal Constitution. Speed the day when it is so.'

"We clip the above from *The Montgomery Advertiser* of
May. In the same issue is a comment on a harangue
delivered by Senator Morgan before the students of Howard
College. The senator should not forget to tell the students
that it will cost the same to eliminate the 15th amendment
that it cost to make it, and the negro will be there with
every foot up.

" *The Advertiser* again, in a complimentary way, endorsed
the ideas of ex-Senator Alcorn of Mississippi, who says that
the negro is incapacitated to govern. That idea is absolute,
and no sensible man doubts the negro's ability to rule; for
to rule well, means to rule right. We believe that if the
intelligent negro were in power and had the administering
of the law in his hands, he would see that every negro who
killed a white or colored man unlawfully, was brought to
justice and punished according to law. He would also see
that every man's vote was counted as voted, and that the
man elected held the office."

Editor McEwen, still fired by the article appearing in
The Advertiser, and urged on by a question asked by *The*

Independent—"Should the negro be disfranchised?" takes
up the Afro-American and his relation to this country, in
the issue of May 9, and discusses him thus:

"*The Independent* came to us this week, asking the question
'Should the negro be disfranchised?' There is as much
absurdity in thinking of his disfranchisement, as there is in
thinking of placing the United States in the center of
Africa. There have been some curious exaggerations
prevailing concerning the negro, and many have been the
controversies relating to him; but if he is examined with the
view of discovering his noble qualities, he will be found a
being made in the image of God, placed in the United States
there to stay. This is a very broad assertion, but nevertheless true, and will be fully demonstrated by his not
leaving. The negro is not confined to one locality, but his
home or resting-place will be wherever the white man is
found. The South is the place for the negro. It is his
home; and as long as one grain of corn is found there, so
long will the negro be found.

"The charge brought against the negro that he has not
property, and can be gobbled up by the lower class of whites,
is true of a very few. There are as true, noble-hearted men
in the negro race as can be found in the white. There is no
disfranchisement for the negro. He, as the white man, or
one of any nation, has his aim in life, and he intends to
reach it. If honesty is equally practiced by the white race,
as well as by the negro, there will be no need to disfranchise
either party. But bear in mind, that if the white man
doesn't tire of the South, the negro will not. He is going
to stay, and ere long the many wrongs done him will be
turned into justice. The negro (the upper class I speak of,
for the lower class of her sister race has never done anything,
and, I think, never will) is not waiting for his power to
bring it. Justice is what the negro calls for. Give him that,

and he will prove as true a citizen as anybody. Wealth has nothing to do with a man's voting. If he can't buy a resting-place in the grave-yard, if he is a citizen of the United States he has as much right to vote as a millionaire."

We reproduce these deliberate and well-chosen comments to prove Mr. McEwen's journalistic ability. We class him— "A bright star in the journalistic crown."

REV. CALVIN S. BROWN, EDITOR BAPTIST PILOT.

At Salisbury, N. C., was born Editor Brown, March 23, 1859, his parents being Henry and Flora Brown. He was put into school at the age of five years, remaining there without intermission until he was seventeen, when his father died, which necessitated his beginning to work for the maintenance of a widowed mother, three sisters, and one brother. This he did by teaching school.

Some time afterward, he entered Shaw University, with the view of fitting himself for the ministry. Entering the college department of that University, he graduated from that and the theological department as valedictorian of his class. After graduation, he was called to the pastorate of a large country church at Winton. Since then he has been called to three others, making him pastor of four churches with a total membership exceeding fifteen hundred. These churches he has ministered to with signal ability. He is now secretary of several of the prominent Baptist Associations of his state.

His work as a journalist began as editor of *The Samaritan Journal*, organ of the Samaritan Society of North Carolina. From this, he entered into journalistic work in the interest of his church, in which he has done credit to himself and denomination. When he assumed his charge in Eastern Carolina—the pastorate of four churches—he was induced to

20

undertake the erection of an institution of learning at Winton, it being a most desirable locality for such an enterprise. To enlist the sympathy and help of the people, he began to issue monthly a paper known as *The Chowan Pilot*, by aid of which, within less than eighteen months, a two-story school-building, 60 by 30, was completed and paid for.

So brilliant was this brief record of his as a journalist, that in the summer of 1887, at the time of the establishment of *The Pilot* by the North Carolina Ministerial Union, he was unanimously chosen editor-in-chief of the paper. After some solicitation, he accepted this responsibility, and consented to consolidate *The Chowan Pilot* with this new enterprise. He then took immediate steps toward purchasing a printing-press, and to open an office under his own supervision. In less than a month everything was in readiness for operation.

Remarkable to say, he began to issue a bi-weekly paper, according to agreement, without any previous training in the art of type-setting. He not only filled the position of editor, but also compositor. Since its establishment, *The Pilot* has appeared regularly, and has rapidly grown in public favor. It is the only paper published in the town of Winton, and it is read by a majority of the white citizens, such being *bona fide* subscribers. It is a neatly printed, twenty-column paper, devoted chiefly to the denomination from which it derives its name; but in almost every issue are to be found strong articles affecting the race problem of America. The editor believes that the press, in the hands of the negro, may be made greatly instrumental in his advancement.

The success of *The Pilot* is better told by those who have visited the office, than by the author. Prof. S. M. Vass of Shaw University, upon a visit to *The Pilot* office at Winton, writes thus to *The North Carolina Baptist:* "It is my pleasant privilege to be able to sit in the office of *The Baptist Pilot* and write this short article for the Baptists of North

REV. CALVIN S. BROWN.

Carolina to read. I had long cherished a desire to visit the printing department of *The Pilot* to learn how Bro. Brown could send out such an excellent paper, at such a small subscription price—only seventy-five cents a year. Now I understand. Of course, the Ministerial Union owns the press. That much is safe. Bro. Brown just raises enough money to buy the paper. He does all the type-setting himself, assisted by a noble and talented young lady, about fifteen or sixteen years old, Miss Annie W. Walden, to whom he taught the art. And, by the way, who taught him? No one. He purchased the press, without the least knowledge of how to use it; but by bringing to bear his inborn talent for such work, and his iron will, he mastered the effort in a few days. It is, to say the least, a tedious work to sit and handle type. But the toughest part of all is the process of carrying the paper through the press. It makes a man sweat and show his strength, and ruins all his clothes with the ink and grease and—what not. It takes two persons one whole day to do the printing after the type is all set, which consumes quite a while,—several days.

Well, who edits the paper? Brother Brown; he is the man. Several brethren promised to assist him; but the whole work falls upon him."

As to the support that has been gathered to *The Pilot*, it is interesting to read what its editor has to say about it: "It is gratifying to observe the tide which is sweeping the state in favor of *The Pilot*. From every quarter, from hundreds of staunch Baptists whose hearts long for the prosperity of the denomination, come strong and enthusiastic expressions assuring us that the enterprise shall be sustained."

With Editor Brown's continued persistence in the work, we are forced to believe that the future prospects for *The Pilot* are bright for a race organ, which will prove to be of great benefit to it.

REV. GEORGE W. CLINTON, EDITOR AFRO-AMERICAN SPOKESMAN.

Rev. Mr. Clinton, who holds the editorial reins of *The Afro-American Spokesman*, was born in Cedar Creek township, Lancaster County, S. C., March 28, 1859, with, as it has proved, many days before him for journalistic usefulness, as well as that of a dispenser of divine truths.

Mr. Clinton had a little knowledge of letters before the war closed, his father having been his tutor. A desire upon the part of his mother to have her boy fitted for the gospel ministry, induced her to keep him in school, which she did by hard labor. He prepared himself for college, entering the State University in 1874, and remained until it was closed against the black man in 1877. He then began to teach school, with a first-grade certificate, continuing in that work for twelve years.

While teaching, he read law in the office of Allison & Connors for six months. During this time he followed the advice of Blackstone, and read the Bible in connection with his law books. This resulted in a deeper interest in the Bible than for law, and accordingly, after assisting in one case (the papers of which were prepared by himself) he began a diligent study of Scriptural truth. He was licensed as a local preacher in the A. M. E. Zion church in 1879, and admitted to the Travelling Association, November 21, 1881.

He has had some of the best appointments in the Conference, and held some of the most honorable positions in the Conference. He was fraternal delegate from the South Carolina Conference to the New England Conference, Hartford, Conn.; was delegate to the General Conference, at New York City, and one of its trusted secretaries; was also a ministerial delegate to the General Conference at New Berne, N. C., and general secretary of the same, Bishop Charles C.

Petty being absent a while after the Conference had convened. He has served in other prominent positions in church councils. He was transferred, in November, 1888, from the S. C. Conference to the Allegheny Conference, and is now serving as pastor of the John Wesley A. M. E. Zion church in Pittsburg, Pa.

His career as a public writer began in 1877. Among his first contributions to *The Star of Zion* was a poem, entitled "In Memoriam of C. D. Stewart," who was a fellow collegemate. The poem was dedicated to Miss Julia Eagles, the young lady to whom Mr. Stewart was affianced.

His active career as an editor began with his service of seven years upon the editorial staff of *The Star of Zion*. He has written for such Anglo-Saxon journals as *The New York Weekly Witness, The Centenary, The Charleston Sun, News and Courier*, and others equally prominent. His article to *The A. M. E. Review* on "The Pulpit and School-room" was very highly commended.

The Afro-American Spokesman, of which he is now editor, is the only paper published among the Afro-Americans of Pittsburg and Allegheny City. It is supported by a stock company, composed principally of the ministers of the city. It began operations on the 30th of May without a subscriber or helper, except those of the stock company with their capital shares.

Mr. Clinton, as a writer, is clean, with great simplicity of style. He uses his descriptive powers to much advantage. If he continues in journalism, he is destined to be one of the foremost writers of his race. In entering upon his work as editor of *The Spokesman*, Mr. Clinton says: "While we shall devote adequate space to the religious doings of our people and give church work its due recognition, we shall consider ourselves at liberty, and to be in keeping with the aim and purpose of the paper, to give a reason of the faith

REV. GEORGE W. CLINTON.

we acknowledge, and express our opinion upon all questions that pertain to our people and country. We promise the public a paper worthy of their patronage, and our people one that will be ever vigilant in their defence when their rights, privileges and opportunities are trammelled. We shall be no less active in speaking our opinion concerning any faults, short-comings, and indiscretions of our own people. What we desire is to represent the race before the public as it is, and see that it has fair play; and by counsel and encouragement stimulate it to move forward till it has attained the highest possibilities of American citizenship."

The Spokesman, keeping to the line indicated above, will ever conserve the best interests of the race, as it understands them.

WILLIAM BOLDEN TOWNSEND, EDITOR AND PUBLISHER LEAVENWORTH ADVOCATE.

William B. Townsend first saw the light near Huntsville, Ala., about the year 1854. Samuel, the grandfather, as well as master of the subject of this sketch, was originally a Virginian, but returned to Alabama in the early days of the slavery agitation, and became a prominent citizen of that state. Young Townsend having been sold several times was finally bought by his grandfather, and he and his mother were emancipated during the year 1857.

After remaining in Alabama some three years, they went to Kansas in the spring of 1860. Here he was given a chance for schooling, and he applied himself so diligently that in a few years he developed those traits of character which have since distinguished him as one of the foremost advocates of the rights of his race.

After finishing a course of study in the common schools of his adopted state, he went to Mississippi as a teacher, but

WILLIAM BOLDEN TOWNSEND.

finding the treatment of his people so inhuman, and himself meeting many hardships, he again sought the fair and fertile fields of Kansas, where he entered upon a career of usefulness which has been almost phenomenal.

In 1876 he became correspondent for *The Colored Citizen*, a paper published at Fort Scott, Kansas. In 1878 we find him an associate editor of *The Radical*, which, as well as *The Colored Citizen*, was published in the interest of his race.

He has held several appointive offices, both in the county and state in which he lives, and always with credit to himself and honor to his race. At the Republican convention in 1882 he made the nominating speech, and succeeded in having the Hon. E. P. McCable selected as candidate for auditor. At the recent convention of colored men held at Salina, and composed of two hundred delegates, he was elected chairman, and through his influence the Hon. J. L. Waller was made the choice of the convention as the candidate of the colored people for auditor on the Republican ticket.

He was employed for ten consecutive years as letter-carrier in Leavenworth, and only resigned the position for the purpose of studying law. He has been one year at the State University, and hopes to graduate in 1892.

Always devoted to the interests of his people, Mr. Townsend is destined to take rank as one of the foremost leaders of his race in this country.

HENRY FITZBUTLER, M. D.

The following extract from a pamphlet published in Louisville, Ky., containing sketches of colored men in that state, will introduce Dr. H. Fitzbutler:

" Perhaps the most remarkable man identified with the

HENRY FITZBUTLER, M. D.

colored race, who has been added to the citizenship of Louisville, is Dr. Henry Fitzbutler. Born December 22, 1842, he graduated at the Michigan University, in March, 1872, from the department of medicine and surgery, and came to Louisville in July of the same year. Dr. Fitzbutler attracted much attention at once, he being the first regular physician of the colored race to enter upon the practice of medicine in the state of Kentucky.

"At that time the colored people of Louisville were peculiarly under the influences which followed the ante-bellum prejudices. There was an admitted guardianship, comprising perhaps eight or ten men, who dictated public affairs for the colored people in a manner agreeable to the prejudices of the white people, and but few colored people sought business or notable positions without consulting these 'intermediators.'

"The subject of this sketch was recognized by the medical profession in Louisville, and commended as being scientific and proficient in medicine and surgery; but having neglected to consult the colored 'intermediators,' they prophesied a short stay for him, and went to work to fulfill the words of their divination. However, as Providence and progress would have it, eight years have elapsed, and this independent business man and philanthropist is still here, and with many admirers is beholding the dying prejudices that would bar the progress of colored citizenship.

"Dr. Fitzbutler has not lived a selfish life, but of his means from his medical business has contributed largely to the literary and political necessities of the colored race. When a state convention was called in Louisville, about February, 1873, to consider the educational interests of the colored people of Kentucky, many of the old citizens stood aghast, seeming to fear extermination if found participating; therefore, no one aspired to the chairmanship of such a convention, yet, by request, and to meet the unpopular emergency, Dr. Fitzbutler accepted and filled the position fearlessly in the Louisville circuit court room.

"The resolutions passed in this convention demanded equal school privileges for colored school children in Kentucky, and became the basis of the agitation in and out of the legislature, which resulted in greatly improving the educational facilities in this state. Subsequently, he was the chief opponent to a resolution advocating separate schools as the will of the colored people, and the best course for all. This convention was in Covington, Ky., about 1874. And he was a notable member of the State Educational Convention, which met in the State House, at Frankfort, in 1883, taking such a part in the work as to attract the attention of all classes of citizens throughout the state. Here, too, he was not ashamed to advocate the cause of his race, being appointed on permanent organization. He succeeded in getting an able colored man appointed as one of the secretaries, and another well-qualified colored man a member of an important committee. And through all incidental work Dr. Fitzbutler has been an active and reliable physician, receiving a revenue which he has never failed to use to the honor of the colored race, being himself the chief support of *The Ohio Falls Express*, which has been published regularly for nearly ten years, known and felt as one of the most fearless advocates of equal human rights. But his ambition has long been the establishment of a medical school, with doors open to colored medical students as well as white; and many now rejoice to see that design consummated. The legislature of Kentucky, at the session of 1888, granted a charter to Doctors H. Fitzbutler, W. A. Burney and R. Conrad to conduct, in Kentucky, the Louisville National Medical College, and that charter was signed by the governor, April 22, 1888. The school is now in operation, with some of the best talent to be found in the country as students."

Dr. Fitzbutler began journalistic work in the publication of *The Planet*, of which he was editor, and, at the same time, the chief financial manager,—Alfred Froman being its originator, it having been published in Louisville about three years, the first copy appearing in December, 1842. *The Planet* was a fearless advocate of equal rights, and was devoted to the educational interests of the colored people as well.

The publication of *The Ohio Falls Express* has been his chief journalistic effort, and has, at all times, and under all circumstances, exhibited an intrepidity and discretion, indicated in the prospectus :

"*The Ohio Falls Express* will make its *debut* Saturday, September 20, 1879; and although the country may seem flooded with newspapers and other literary periodicals, yet we have no other apology to offer than that there is not sufficient space found within their numberless columns for unprejudiced representation of all races of men; and in the opinion of humble thinkers, the cause of the less favored will faster gain respect 'by a continuous, honest, earnest and amicable effort on their part.

"*The Express* does not presume to be a leader nor a dictator, and is not one of those who regard public sentiment and established prejudices as light things that can be changed in a moment, yet realizes the importance of unswerving advocacy in the establishment of justice and true moral worth; but does presume to avoid the Æolian encomiums sounding in the wake of success, regardless of right or wrong.

" The editorial staff will lead off neither as a *coup de grace* nor *coup de main*, nor open with one grand *fusilade* upon whatever is not in accord with their embryonic judgment; but hope, by adhering to fixed data of reasoning, to have some effective artillery at command and bring it to bear in accord with times and events.

"*The Express* has no selfish battles to fight, no unmerited commendation to bestow; but will be an advocate in the acquisition of wealth, learning, and moral principles."

The Ohio Falls Express is the first successful newspaper effort under the management of colored men in Kentucky, all other previous efforts having failed. *The Express*, though Republican in sentiment, has not depended upon political vicissitudes for existence, but advocating the same principles through different administrations of government has relied upon its own resources in a business-like manner. It has been published weekly, without intermission and without change of editor, since September 20, 1879.

The following are editorial clippings from the successful pioneer of colored papers in Kentucky: "The speculation concerning the danger of imbibing the elements contributory to disease from the Johnstown bodies in the Ohio River water, is not a matter to bring much terror to thinking people. The vastness of the body of water renders the contamination insignificant. Then the changes are very brief; the greater portion of man being water, when free from the body of which it was a constituent, is again as good to form part of another animal body, as any other water. Then the other elements composing the tissues of an animal body, when free in water, soon become what they were originally in relation to the earth. Thus the chloride of sodium, phosphate of lime, carbon in man, when freed in water that has ample connection with the earth, soon become inoffensive, and exist in matter-form as compatible to re-construct a new body as when originally taken into the bodies of Adam and Eve."

Vital statistics furnish interesting problems, not only to the political economist, but to the philanthropist and the Christian. In Nashville careful and fairly accurate reports for the last thirteen years have been kept. The death-rate among the colored people has ranged from about 50 per thousand in 1875 to 23.50 per thousand during the past year, while the death-rate among the whites for the same period has been only a little more than one-half as great. During the past three years, out of a colored population estimated at twenty-three thousand, 951 births and 1,758 deaths have been reported. Among the white population, which is about twice as great, there have been 1,478 births and 1,600 deaths. It is possible that all of the births among the colored people have not been reported. If they have, it would indicate that while the birth-rates are about equal, the death-rate is twice as great.

The causes are numerous, and may be classified under four general heads,—poverty, ignorance of the laws of health, superstition, and lack of proper medical attention.

ROBERT CHARLES O'HARRA BENJAMIN, EDITOR SAN FRANCISCO SENTINEL.

R. C. O. Benjamin was born in the Island of St. Kitts, West Indies, March 31, 1855. He was educated at Oxford University, England, and after graduation he traveled extensively in Sumatra, Java, and other islands in the East Indies. Upon returning to England, he took passage on a ship going to the West Indies, and visited Jamaica, Antigua, and Barbadoes, coming to America by way of Venezuela, Curacoa, and Demerara.

Soon after his arrival in New York he began taking an active part in public affairs, which brought him in close association with such prominent men as Dr. Henry Highland Garnett, Cornelius Van Cott, and Joe Howard, Jr. The latter, then editor of *The New York Star*, employed him as a soliciting agent, and when not at this work he was assigned to office duty. In the course of a few months, business led

R. C. O. BENJAMIN.

him to the acquaintanceship of John J. Freeman, editor of *The Progressive American*, who made him city editor of his paper. Since then Mr. Benjamin has owned and edited several newspapers: *The Colored Citizen*, in Pittsburg, Penn; *The Chronicle*, at Evansville, Ind.; and *The Negro American.* At Birmingham, Ala., he is now editing *The San Francisco* (California) *Sentinel.* The following clippings will give an idea of the esteem in which Mr. Benjamin is held by the press of the country:

"Among the most brilliant exchanges that come to our sanctum is *The* (California) *Sentinel*, edited by our old friend, Hon. R. C. O. Benjamin. This paper is taking the Pacific Coast like wild-fire, and rapidly gaining a national reputation. But this could not be otherwise, because Mr. Benjamin is one of the most able of the negro writers, lecturers and orators in this country. Others may have a bigger name, but when it comes to real talent, versatility, and innate ability, Benjamin can swallow the majority of them at a gulp."

"R. C. O. Benjamin, Esq., editor of *The San Francisco Sentinel*, is getting out one of the liveliest and best negro journals in the country. We wish Mr. Benjamin all possible success financially with his *Sentinel.—Pine Bluff* (Ark.) *Echo.*"

"R. C. O. Benjamin is running a great paper in San Francisco. R. C. O. will be remembered as the editor of *The Negro-American* in this city about four years ago. Benjamin is a born journalist.—*Birmingham* (Ala.) *Bulletin.*"

"R. C. O. Benjamin, the colored lawyer, author and politician, is now editor of *The San Francisco Sentinel.* Brother Benjamin wields a vigorous pen, and is making a good paper. —*So. Cal. Informant, San Diego.*"

"Mr. Benjamin is a ready newspaper man, and we doubt not that *The Sentinel* will thrive under his editorial management.—*New Orleans* (La.) *Pelican.*"

"We welcome to our desk *The San Francisco Sentinel.* This is one of the brightest papers published in the West. We are glad, always, to receive such exchanges. There is plenty of room for good papers. We wish *The Sentinel* a long and prosperous voyage, for we recognize in it a strong and fearless defender of the race. May *The Sentinel* be a power on the Coast, and always the sentry of the race rights." —*The Advocate*, Leavenworth, Kan.

"This week our table holds *The San Francisco Sentinel,* Vol. I, No. 1, with the gifted R. C. O. Benjamin, formerly at the head of *The Negro American* of Birmingham, as editor.

The editor of *Fair Play*, and many others of this city, are well acquainted with Mr. Benjamin and rejoice to know that he again drives the quill. Long live *The Sentinel* to help in the great work of obtaining equal rights and fair play in the race of life for every American citizen, without regard to race or color."—*Fair Play*, Meridian, Miss.

As a newspaper man. Mr. Benjamin has been a marked success. He is fearless in his editorial expression; and the fact that he is a negro does not lead him to withhold his opinions upon the live issues of the day, but to give them in a courageous manner. His motto is: "My race first, and my best friends next." Any one reading his paper will find that his race has an able champion in him, and one who will never fail them. His strictures on the murders and outrages of his race in the South, and his demand for an equal chance in the race of life for his people, show true manliness.

Mr. Benjamin is widely known to the newspaper fraternity by the *nom de plume* of "Cicero," a cognomen he adopted while corresponding editor of *The Nashville* (Tenn.) *Free Lance.* He was for some time the local editor of *The Daily Sun*, a prominent white paper, published at Los Angeles, Cal. and is the first colored man to hold such a position on a white journal.

In the midst of his journalistic work he has found time to write several very interesting books, among the most prominent of which are "The Boy Doctor," "History of the British West Indies," "Future of the American Negro," "The Southland," "Africa, the Hope of the Negro," "Life of Toussaint L' Overture;" besides publishing "An Historical Chart of the Colored Race," and a volume of poems which has passed through several editions.

He is a fluent conversationalist, in both the French and Spanish languages. He has the credit of being one of the finest platform orators of his race in America, and takes an active part on the stump in state and national campaigns. In 1886 he made a tour through the principal cities of Canada, and lectured to large white audiences.

Mr. Benjamin is also a lawyer, having been admitted to the bar in Memphis, Tenn., in January, 1880. His experience as a practitioner has been varied, and the territory over which his legal services have been extended aggregate twelve different states.

In California he is very highly esteemed by both whites and blacks. The California Conference of the A. M. E. church, has elected him Presiding Elder, his jurisdiction comprising the states of California, Oregon, Washington, and Nevada. He is also General Financial Agent and Superintendent of the Connection's Sabbath-school on the Coast.

At the same time, the bench, the bar, the county and city officials of San Francisco, Los Angeles and all Southern California recommended him to the Congressional delegation, who, in turn, did so to President Harrison, for the position of consul to Antigua, West Indies. It being impossible to give him this particular appointment, the president offered him the consulship to Aux Cayes, Hayti, which he declined, preferring to remain at the editorial helm of his paper, *The Sentinel*.

E. A. WILLIAMS.

Dr. E. A. Williams, Editor Journal of the Lodge.

The Journal of the Lodge is the official organ of the (colored) Supreme Lodge of the Knights of Pythias of North America, South America, Europe, Asia, and Africa, and has been adopted as the official organ of the Grand Lodge of Masons of the state of Louisiana. It is edited by Dr. E. A. Williams, the Supreme Chancellor of the order, and Grand Secretary and Grand Recorder of Masonry and Knights Templar of Louisiana. Its columns are devoted exclusively to secret societies, and it is especially the organ for which it was founded. Its circulation is now over three thousand. Its first issue by Dr. Williams was under adverse circumstances. It has just entered upon its third volume, and is now upon a solid basis, with sufficient capital to make it a permanent journal.

Prof. Daniel Webster Davis, Editor Young Men's Friend.

When the history of the country and the present achievements of the Afro-American are written, it will be seen that the young men identified with this race have not been inactive. It will be observed that they have performed the part assigned them in the race of life with courage and fidelity. Upon the shoulders of the young Afro-American, man or woman, devolves the solving of the question, commonly called the Negro (Afro-American) Problem. In any walk of life, the young man or woman striving to do his part in making the race a respected one, must necessarily meet with trials and discouragements. It will be the man or woman who surmounts them and contends for intellectual, moral, and social preferment, that must be great. Are there any thus contending? if so, let history record his name and

D. Webster Davis

work. Prof. Davis is of this number. His life is one that must meet the general recommendation of men. He was born in Caroline county, Va., March 25, 1862. Going to Richmond, Va., he was educated in her public schools, receiving medals from his instructors on two occasions, for proficiency in his studies. He served as an apprentice in a shoe shop, and became a first-class workman there. He was elected to teach in the city schools of Richmond in 1880, where he has been since, having attained a good record as an instructor of youth. He was selected as professor of mathematics and civil government in the summer institutes of Lynchburg, Staunton, and Lexington, Va., by the state superintendent of public instruction. His ability manifested in these institutes, combined with his genial and lovable qualities, did much to hold intact the many teachers who attended them.

Mr. Davis has held many honorary positions. He was president of the Y. M. C. A., of Richmond, Va., and is now associate to the general secretary. For years he was president of the Richmond normal school alumni, and the Garrison and Langston lyceum. He is at present chairman of the executive board of the Virginia teachers' reading circle; also of the executive board of the Virginia Baptist Sunday-school Convention, and is otherwise very prominent in the church and Sunday-school circles of his city. He is also conspicuous in masonic circles, serving at one time as Most Worshipful Master of Social Lodge, No. 6, A. F. & A. Masons. He was Grand Representative of the Grand Lodge of Alabama, with rank of Past Grand Senior Warden, and was also Special Deputy of Grand Lodge of Virginia. He is likewise prominent among the Odd Fellows, as well as in other societies. He was a director of the Building and Loan Association of Richmond City, and a member of the executive committee of the late national emancipation celebration.

Prof. Davis is a great musician, playing on four different

instruments. He appears to be a natural poet. His poems have been published in the newspapers, and read on various occasions. Among the most important of these productions is—" De Nigger 's Got to Go,"—written for *The Planet* of Richmond, Va., and another for the late emancipation celebration, which was very pleasantly commented on by *The Richmond Dispatch*. Mr. Davis has delivered more choice orations on great occasions than any other young man, within the recollection of the author. This of itself bespeaks volumes for his oratorical ability. Upon the following occasions he has delivered orations, which drew from his auditors rapturous applause and laudatory comments : At the memorial exercises of Gen. Grant; graduating class of Richmond high school; alumni association, Lynchburg, Va.; Y. M. C. A. of Petersburg, Va., of Lynchburg, Va., and of Norfolk, Va.; the laying of the corner stone of the Gloucester high school; the unveiling of Capt. Emmett Scott's monument; the soldiers' re-union at Richmond; and before the masonic fraternity of Richmond.

Mr. Davis is a live, vigorous and happy speaker, full of eloquence and oratory. He is daily called upon to speak on an occasion of some interest; for which he is always ready, especially if he sees in the movement a rising purpose on the part of his race.

Few of our young men have done much more in the journalistic calling than has Mr. Davis. He began this work as correspondent for *The Baptist Companion*, the organ of the Afro-American Baptists of Virginia; also, for *The Boston* (Mass.) *Advocate*. In like capacity, he has served admirably *The Richmond Planet*, *The Lynchburg*, (Va.) *Laborer*, *The Masonic Herald* of Philadelphia, *The Masonic Visitor* of Petersburg, Va.; and also *The Young Men's Friend*, before he assumed the editorship.

The Young Men's Friend is the organ of the colored

Young Men's Christian Association of Richmond City. The purpose of this periodical is to supplement the work of the association in promoting the educational, moral, and religious endeavor of the young men. Its motto—"Young Men for Christ," is indicative of its aim and purpose. To edit this organ, no young man better fitted as a Christian and an educated gentleman could have been selected out of the association than Mr. Davis. He is a quiet, God-fearing young man, who is of the opinion that all our success comes from God, and for the ultimate salvation of the race we must rely upon Him. Such a man we must all concede to be the proper editorial director of the young men.

Mr. Davis is a man of brilliant thought and correct judgment, and what he thinks he says in choice, expressive English. His career promises great things for the Afro-American press. Believing as he does in the enlightenment of his country and the salvation of his race, coupled with the entire Christianization of the masses, he will wield a facile and vigorous pen for its accomplishment.

The subscription of *The Friend* has already increased under the editorial management of Mr. Davis, and a bright future is predicted for it. Long may it live for God and humanity.

REV. MATTHEW WESLEY CLAIR, EDITOR METHODIST BANNER.

This gentleman is one of the young men connected with the Washington Conference of the Methodist Episcopal church, whose outlook is for a profitable life in the ministry and as an editorial dispenser of religious, moral, and social truths.

He began life in Monroe county, W. Va., where he was born of humble parentage October 21, 1865. He secured what rudimentary knowledge he could possibly attain in the schools of his county.   He was converted in 1880, and joined the M. E. church, which marked a turning epoch in his life. Having been moved by the Spirit to begin the work of a teacher of divine truth, he applied for an exhorter's license and received it at the hands of Rev. S. A. Lewis, and subsequently was the recipient of orders as a local preacher from Presiding Elder Samuel G. Griffin.

Having the good sense to know that a man, in these days, who enters the ministry, must be trained for the position, he applied for admission at Morgan College, one of the schools controlled by the Freedman's Aid and Southern Evangelical Society, located at Baltimore, Md., and was received there. His attendance at this institution was under some great sacrifices, and therefore he could spare no time for idleness. He at once took a prominent place among the bright students with whom he was associated, and won the G. V. Leech prize for excellence in theology in 1884, and received the Baldwin prize for English oratory in 1887.   He is a graduate of the normal, classical, and theological departments of that college.   He was examined and admitted to the Traveling Connection of the Washington Conference of the M. E. church, in March, 1889, and was stationed at Harpers' Ferry, W. Va., and was sent back in March, 1890.   He is one of the best pulpit orators among the young men of that Conference.   He is winning in his manner, and at the same time he impresses upon his hearers the divine teachings of the Master with force and power.

For some time before Mr. Clair entered the Washington Annual Conference, it was a great question with the members whether a local organ could not be established and maintained by that portion of Methodism.   Several attempts to do this were made, among which were *The Conference Journal* and *The Central Methodist*, noted in other chapters.   *The Banner* is only a resurrection of *The Central Methodist*, after a year's suspension. It is published as a local religious paper by the members of the Conference, who are known as a typographical association. It is officered as follows: Rev. W. T. Harris, president; Rev. W. P. Ryder, vice-president; Rev. S. A. Lewis, secretary; Rev. I. L. Thomas, treasurer.

At a meeting of the association in Frederick City, Md., in March, 1890, Rev. M. W. Clair was elected editor, and C. L. Harris business manager of *The Banner*. The present is the third volume of *The Banner*, and though yet in its infancy it is a newsy and well-edited paper. The aim of its projectors is best understood as they have expressed it. Says the editor: " *The Banner* is now in its infancy, but it is hoped that it may be waved in every home and its news cheer the hearts of thousands."

Mr. Clair is a good practical writer. His editorials are read for the good advice and sound common sense to be found in them. Much can be done for the race, if *The Banner* continues to wave on the present pinnacle. of moral and religious endeavor.

Mrs. F. M. W. Clair, the beloved wife of Rev. Mr. Clair, does much to assist him in his editorial labors. Her contributions to the editorial columns share alike with his the commendation of a reading public. She was born, and reared mostly in Baltimore, Md., being the youngest living daughter of Rev. Perry G., and Mrs. Mary E. Walker. She was educated at Morgan College, and is a graduate of its normal department. Until she assumed the duties of a wife, she was a teacher in the schools of Maryland, and, lastly, an instructor in the Baltimore City Academy. She is well known as an essayist, and as an associate upon the editorial staff of *The Banner*. She has the following to say of the press: " The object of the press is to elevate humanity. It is one of the greatest means of bringing our people to the level of those who have had centuries of privileges."

Mrs. M.W. Clair

Rev. M.W. Clair

CHAPTER XIX.

ILLUSTRATED AFRO-AMERICAN JOURNALISM.

THE illustrated paper, among all classes and conditions, has met the most cordial reception. To read of an occurrence, or about a fixed thing, and to observe the same illustrated, tends to fix in the mind of the reader the facts more impressively; it also better enables him to grasp the situation as intended. He also is enabled to see the purpose sought; and he sees without effort the picture the article intends to have the imagination form. The necessity of such a phase of journalism among any people admits of no argument. With this idea in view, Edward Elder Cooper of Indianapolis, Ind., issued *The Indianapolis Freeman*, (the first and only illustrated journal of the Afro-American race,) consisting of eight pages, July 14, 1888. To say that this was a most commendable step upon the part of Mr. Cooper, is to say the least of it. While the Afro-American seems hardly prepared for a very high plane of journalism, from a money or intellectual consideration, and certainly not from experience, yet in this, as in other phases of the work, he has shown his possibilities, and maintains his stand. The journalist of color finds it a matter of some thought when he first launches his

EDWARD ELDER COOPER.

paper as to whether such support will gather about it as the enterprise deserves.

This may have been so with *The Freeman*, yet it was sent forth in the belief that the race would accept a good, worthy, ideal paper, when presented to it; and there was no disappointment in this case, for *The Freeman* at once drew for itself a hearty, enthusiastic, and lasting support.

The race owes a debt to the man whose experience, money, self-sacrifice, brain and brawn, keep alive this sheet, which is one of the brightest stars in the unrecorded history of Afro-American freedom. A world of thinkers and readers concede its relative superiority. Success with it has been simply phenomenal. The meed of authority as a newspaper has been freely accorded it by its contemporaries and individuals, all over the Union. The white journals of the country, without hesitation, term it the leading paper of the race. In proof of this fact it has upon its exchange list a class of papers and periodicals that no other colored paper has. Among the many can be found the leading white papers of Chicago, Baltimore, New York, Boston, Indianapolis, St. Louis, and Cincinnati.

Besides this honor accorded to *The Freeman* because of its worth and ability, it has also been the recipient of flattering notices from acknowledged white organs, as well as from its race contemporaries. *The Indianapolis Journal,* the most popular Anglo-Saxon journal of Indianapolis, says: "So far as we are acquainted with colored journalism, the best paper published in the interests of the colored people is *The Freeman* of this city. No other paper is doing as good work in the special field indicated. Its advocacy of the interests of the colored people is able and dignified, and its illustrated sketches of the colored literary men and women are exceedingly well conceived and executed." *The Cincinnati Commercial Gazette,* Murat Halstead, editor, says: "*The*

Freeman is by far the best and ablest newspaper the colored people have ever had." *The Advocate* of Leavenworth, Kan., contributes the following to *The Freeman's* glory: "The illustrated *Freeman* of Indianapolis, Ind., is to the colored people what Frank Leslie is to the whites." *The National Leader* remarks: " *The Freeman* of Indianapolis, Ind., E. E. Cooper, manager, is the only colored pictorial published in the country. Though in its infancy, it has taken front rank in illustrated newspaperdom. We consider it the *Harper's Weekly* of the colored race." Admitting the advance of the Afro-American in this great pursuit of life, another says: "It is a credit, too, and shows the progress the colored race is making in journalism."

It will be interesting for one to note the particular characteristics of this journal in question : As a news paper, it gives a complete review of the doings of the Afro-Americans everywhere. As a political paper, it is independent, commending the good and condemning the bad in both parties. As an historical paper, it devotes unceasing research to the hitherto unpublished history of the Afro-American, and from time to time it prints and illustrates the legends and romances of the Afro-American, written by Afro-American authors. As a literary paper, it keeps pace with the educational and literary progress of the race. As an illustrated paper, it portrays the Afro-American as he is, and not as so often represented by many of our white journals. As a general newspaper, it is the peer of any in the land.

Where he came from; how he has reached his present eminent position in life; what he has done for his race and how he is honored by them; his future service to his people; are the points to which we shall be pleased to call the attention of the reader, in dealing with the life of Mr. Cooper. This done, without exaggeration or embellishment, we shall stop, feeling that then there is much more to be said.

22

As is true of the great majority of our really eminent Afro-Americans, Mr. Cooper is a southern product; but early in life, without money or friends, yet full of pluck and ambition, he selected the North for his future home and field of operations. From the South, he went to Philadelphia; and from thence he turned his attention to the setting sun, selecting Indianapolis, the Hoosier metropolis, as his permanent home. Here he entered school and graduated first in a class of sixty-five, all being white, save himself.

In 1882 we find him in the United States railway mail service, soon becoming one of the most efficient men in that difficult and exacting branch of government work, having gone from class 5 to 1, at the time of his retirement from the service. In 1886 he had full charge of his car, being the only Afro-American that ever had a corps of white clerks under him.

In the spring of 1883, though still in the government service, he, in connection with Edwin F. Horn and others, began the publication of *The Colored World*, issued at Indianapolis. The venture was a success from the beginning, but owing to a change of "runs," Mr. Cooper was compelled to sever his connection with the paper, and a stock-company then took hold and ran it.

Leaving the government service in 1886, he once more connected himself with *The World*, then, as now, known as *The Indianapolis World*, and from a puny weakling, head over heels in debt, run without system or method, with a half-paid circulation of less than five hundred, within six months he booked a *bona fide* circulation of two thousand, on a solid and paying basis. One year later, selling out his interest, he left it one of the best equipped, best paying, more widely read and clipped newspaper, than any other that had been published in the Union by colored men up to this time. He then began the publication of *The Freeman*.

As an all-around newspaper man,—that is, in all that pertains to the conducting, preparing, printing, and publishing of a newspaper, we pronounce him America's greatest Afro-American journalist. There are men, perhaps, who, in certain specific fields, may equal or surpass him; but there is not one who has begun to get near him in the possession of all the forces that go to make up the newspaper man of the very first class.

Mr. Cooper is a remarkable and striking character. One is taken with his affableness in a short time after meeting him, for he is always pleasant and agreeable. He believes in system and order, and transacts business with a dispatch, known only of the shrewdest business characters. A glance at his editorial desk reveals the kind of man who sits upon the bench. He has been, and is to-day, a great but careful reader. A profound classical student, he is also a master of the English language, and perhaps the best grammarian of the negro press. As a writer, he is pointed, terse, clear. As a talker, he draws from a well-stored mind, and is always interesting and instructive. In politics, he is independent; as some one has put it, a negrowump, placing his race above his party.

In closing a sketch of our subject in *The New York Age*, W. Allison Sweeney, his friend and neighbor, very eloquently says: "For my part, I am glad that Edward Elder Cooper belongs to the negro race. His glory shall be my glory; his achievements, my achievements. A personal friend that is forgotten now. Such as he, belongs to the whole race, not to the clique, or to the few. He is not coming; he is here. Let us arise and go to him."

CHAPTER XX.

PROMINENT AFRO-AMERICAN CORRESPONDENTS, CONTRIBUTORS AND REPORTERS.

PROF. DANIEL BARCLAY WILLIAMS, A. M.

" ALL is the gift of industry; whate'er exalts, embellishes and renders life delightful."

Prof. Williams, by far one of the most polished and ready writers of which the race can boast, was born in Richmond, Va., November 22, 1861. His mother, a woman of marked industry, early recognizing the capabilities of her son, gave him the advantage of the public school training to be had in that city. He graduated from the Richmond Normal School in 1877; then entered the Worcester Academy, Worcester, Mass., in the fall of 1877, through the influence of Prof. R. H. Manly, and Miss M. E. Knowles. He graduated from this school in 1880, and in the same year matriculated in Brown University. He was, however, unable to remain there to finish, but subsequently pursued, and privately completed, the course. He then began the life of an educator, filling the most responsible and creditable positions of that nature in his native city and county, until, in 1885, he was elected to the chair of Ancient Languages and Instructor in

Daniel B Williams.

methods of teaching and school management in the Virginia
Normal and Collegiate Institute at Petersburg, Va., which
position he still holds.

The professor has had ten years' experience as an educator,
and few can be found who equal him. He possesses executive
ability of a high order, and his decisions may be generally
relied upon. He is a popular linguist, reading with ease
German, French, Hebrew, Latin and Greek. Our subject has
a wide reputation as a brilliant orator and conversationalist.
His services in this respect have been constantly in demand
for ten years. He is one of the best known men in his state,
and has a national reputation as well, and has been frequently
honored as a distinguished leader of his people. *The New
York Sun* of May 15, 1887, presented an excellent cut and
sketch of him, with those of Frederick Douglass, Dr. A.
Straker and others. The same adorned the columns of *The
Cleveland Gazette;* and his is given in Dr. William J. Simmons'
book as that of "a man of mark."

One of Virginia's noblest sons, we have given but the
briefest record of his life thus far. We now point the reader
to a brilliant picture of his literary and journalistic career.
The writer regards this as the brightest part of his record.
His career in this respect began in 1883 and 1884, when he
contributed a series of articles to *The Industrial Herald* and
Richmond Planet on "The Latin Language," and "The
Education of the Negro." In 1884 he contributed another
series to *The Baptist Companion*, on "Why we are Baptists."
Their range of history and philosophy, and pleasing and
attractive style, added much to the popularity of the paper.

He has, at different times, contributed to different papers
on miscellaneous subjects. He now corresponds with *The
National Pilot, The Home Mission Monthly, The Freeman,*
and *The A. M. E. Church Review.* He is also editor of the
department of Theory and Practice of Teaching in *The*

Progressive Educator, of Raleigh, N. C. He is one of our few successful Afro-American authors. In 1883 he published his "Negro Race, a Pioneer in Civilization." In 1885 he sent from the press his "Life and Times of Capt. R. A. Paul," and "Why we are Baptists." These works had a good circulation. In 1886 he wrote "The Theory of Rev. John Jasper concerning the Sun," in "The Life of Jasper."

We here quote the following words of Prof. R. W. Whiting, in regard to his "Science, Art, and Methods of Teaching," published in 1887: "The crowning act of his life, and the brightest star of hope for the future negro author, is the success of his work, 'Science, Art, and Methods of Teaching.' This work is the rose of English literature and the standard work on the subject among our people." Another of his works "Freedom and Progress," is now in press.

Prof. Williams is a strong, versatile writer. Having a massive brain, from which thought after thought freely emanates, he is enabled so to attract a reader as to receive from him the palm of being a brilliant author. He has a style wholly his own, easy and mellifluous. Then his thoughts are original, and are expressed with clearness and force, and in language rich and mellow. Nothing in the least objectionable to the most refined mind can be seen in his writings.

Articles from Prof. Williams are eagerly sought. *The Progressive Educator* has been made a most popular publication among pedagogues by Prof. Williams' contribution on "Theory and Practice of Teaching." If he should espouse the calling of an active journalist, the race would have in him an advocate not surpassed by any other people. In our years of friendship with him, we have watched his upward flight, have read his pithy and convincing writings, have heard his eloquence, and listened to his instructive utterances, and now, in amazement, we pause for words to express our admiration of one who has overcome such apparently insurmountable obstacles, and attained to the eminence he occupies. In conclusion, we are led to exclaim: "His life is gentle, and the elements so mixed in him, that Nature might stand up and say to all the world—' This was a man!' "

JOHN EDWARD BRUCE, (*Bruce Grit*).

February 22, 1855, in the town of Piscataway, Md., the above all-around newspaper man was born of slave parents. When but four years old, he moved with his mother to Washington, his present residence, where he attended the private school of Miss Smith, and also the Free Library school. In 1872, while Gen. O. O. Howard was president of Howard University, he took a course of three months at that institution, and, after this, some private instruction from Mrs. B. A. Lockwood, once the female candidate for president, on the equal rights ticket.

At an early age, he developed a taste for journalism, receiving his first lessons in 1874, in the office of L. L. Crouse, an associate editor of *The New York Times.* In the same year he became special correspondent for *The Progressive American*, published by John J. Freeman, a pioneer journalist. His first contribution to *The American*, was under the caption, "Distillation of Coal Tar," which evoked many complimentary expressions.

From this he began a career as a general news-man, which has hardly been surpassed by any of his race. Under the *nom de plume* of "The Rising Sun," he wrote Washington letters for *The Richmond* (Va.) *Star*, and over his own signature sent letters to *The Freeman's Journal* of St. Louis, *The World* of Indianapolis, and *The St. Louis Tribune.* To these papers he wrote from 1877 to 1880. Having now gotten fully into the work, young Bruce became special

JOHN EDWARD BRUCE.

Washington correspondent of *The Chicago* (Ill.) *Conservator*, *The North Carolina Republican*. *The Enterprise*, of Fayetteville, N. C., *The New York Freeman*, *The Reed City Clarion*, (white), *The Detroit Plaindealer*, *The Christian Index*, and *The Cherokee Advocate*; the latter being published in English and Cherokee, by the Cherokee nation.

Mr. Bruce may be called, with due propriety, the prince of Afro-American correspondents. He is not only sought for by our race journals as a news-gatherer, but by those of the Anglo-Saxon, also. He has, at times, contributed special articles to *The New York Herald, Times, World, Mail and Express.*

Not only has he been a correspondent for other journals, but has actually established several journals himself, whose editorial management was brilliant. He published *The Argus*, at Washington City in 1879, with C. M. Otey, A. M., editor, which he published nearly two years, when it was turned over to a stock-company, and finally died. *The Sunday Item*, established in 1880 by J. E. Bruce and S. S. Lacy, was the first Sunday paper ever published by Afro-Americans, and was fairly successful as a newspaper venture. It, like many other of our journals, lacked capital to put it properly on its feet, and hence had to " die the death of the righteous.''

The Washington Grit was founded by Mr. Bruce, in 1884, as a campaign sheet, he being the editor and proprietor. This sheet, like all others established by him, was a staunch Republican paper, not hesitating to speak out in advocacy of Republican principles. It was quietly gathered unto its projector's arms in the latter part of 1884, conscious of the fact that it had done all it could for the election of the Republican ticket. He also established, at Baltimore, *The Commonwealth*, which survived six months; but the principles for which it contended triumphed, viz., the obliteration of the word "white" from the constitution of the state, the repeal of the Bastardy law, and the modification of the odious distraint law.

Our subject, at various times, has been upon the editorial staffs of *The Exodus* of Washington, (in 1880), *The Maryland Director*, and *The Bee and Leader*, of Washington, D. C. He now writes for *The Gazette* of Cleveland, and *The New York Age*, as "Bruce Grit." He is a successful gatherer of whatever news is afloat; more so than most of the Afro-American reporters, in that he can more readily get an interview with noted men, such as senators and representatives at Washington.

He distinguished himself, some time since, by an expression he got from Senator Hoar, relative to an assertion accredited to him. It was heralded through the country in many papers, complimenting Mr. Bruce on his shrewdness in getting the sentiment from Senator Hoar. One describes him as "vigilant, shrewd, active, progressive, and always on the alert for the messenger news." His expression in *The Bee*, relative to the Payne and Derrick controversy, was full of suggestive thoughts. He is always square upon a matter at issue. "Bruce Grit" never flinches from what he regards a just and frank opinion.

REV. W. H. FRANKLIN, SPECIAL CONTRIBUTOR TO THE NEW YORK AGE AND KNOXVILLE (TENN.) NEGRO WORLD.

In our efforts to give the history of a work so wide and comprehensive as that of Afro-American journalism, the special correspondent of *The New York Age* and *Negro World* comes in for a place. His letters have been racy and of interest to the many readers of those papers. This gentle man, whose writings measure well, in every respect, with the Afro-American editor, was born at Knoxville, April 16, 1852.

His father died in 1868, or when he was but 16 years of age, but his mother is still living.

His education was received in the schools of Knoxville and at Maryville College, he being the first Afro-American to graduate from that institution, which event occurred in 1880. His theological training was had at the Lane Theological Seminary, Cincinnati, from which he graduated in 1883. *The Cincinnati Commercial Gazette* and *The Afro-American*, edited by Prof. Peter H. Clark, paid high tributes to the scholarship and oratory of young Franklin. He is at present pastor of the Presbyterian church at Rogersville, Tenn., and principal of the Swift Memorial Seminary, a school of high grade.

Beginning to write for newspapers when quite young, his experience and ever-increasing knowledge made him prominent as a correspondent, and his articles are read by all. He began his newspaper work in 1878, when he became correspondent of *The Knoxville Examiner*, W. F. Yardley, Esq., editor. He has also given articles to *The Star*, of Tennessee, *Herald Presbyter*, *Critic*, and other papers. He now writes for *The New York Age*, and *The Knoxville Negro World*, two representative Afro-American journals.

Rev. Mr. Franklin is one of the most conversant correspondents that now write for the press. His articles are always fresh and well received, and demand careful thought. He is logical, argumentative and free from abrupt phrases. We wish to reproduce a few extracts from articles of his, which have appeared in various issues of *The Age* and *World*. In one in *The Age*, Mr. Franklin fears that the present administration will mistake the difference in the Afro-American of four years past and the Afro-American of to-day. He very fittingly writes: "If the present administration thinks that it has returned to power, and found us where it left us when it went out of power, it makes a great mistake.

REV. W. H. FRANKLIN.

If it thinks that we have been at a stand-still, it errs. The negro, fresh, anxious and ambitious, has been exerting himself, wherever opportunity has offered, to improve his mind and to prepare himself for the complicated duties imposed upon him in consequence of his citizenship. The great mass, it is true, have not made very much progress. It will require a long period, under the most favorable circumstances, for light, intelligence, and culture to leaven the whole mass. Education and intelligence have not reached every individual in the most favored parts of our Union. But it can be truthfully said that even the mass of negroes are not what they were four years ago. They have learned something and made some progress. Much more can be said of individuals in every community. These individuals may be divided into two classes: One consists of the politicians and leaders who were active in former times; the other consists of young men who had reached their majority and who had been, and have been, qualifying themselves for usefulness and leadership. The Reconstruction period, the sudden enfranchisement of the negro, the pressing demand for persons to fill responsible positions, developed many incompetent and unworthy leaders; a very natural thing, and one which has happened many times before. The incompetent and the unworthy were not acceptable to the more respectable and thoughtful of the race. Many of them were as creditable and capable as their neighbors. In view of all the circumstances they did well, notwithstanding the strong indictment of Mr. Hampton to the contrary." He then reaches the main and vital point, which every one will admit is a serious matter for consideration. Says he: "There are also a number of deserving young men. Some of them were born just before the struggle; some of them in the midst of the struggle; and some of them just after the struggle, which gave birth to their freedom. They found their way early into the school-room, provided by generous friends of the North and finally by the states. They studied hard in school and out of school. They have been forced to be students of public affairs and public men. Their opportunities, their studies, and their training, have given them both character and position in their respective communities. They are universally recognized as men of ability and worth. They are editing our newspapers, teaching our schools, filling our pulpits, pleading our causes, healing our diseases, advocating our rights, handing us out goods, building our houses; indeed, filling every vocation in our busy and complicated life. They have sprung up everywhere, and are capable, energetic, and aspiring. I am writing from knowledge and observation. I see about me what I have written. I have traveled in other sections, and seen and noted the same. If our party and our friends are to know what we are and where we are, they cannot afford to ignore these facts. If they are to deal with us justly and fairly, they must neither shut their eyes to the truth nor suffer themselves to be deceived by a perversion of the truth. I have often been surprised at the ignorance which prevails at the North, in regard to the political, material, social, and religious condition of the negro. It does not seem possible for people who live so near us to have such mistaken views, and yet it is true. Our condition is bad enough, without exaggeration. We have burdens enough to bear, without suffering from the mistaken views of those who ought to help and encourage us."

Mr. Franklin discusses the famous Dortch bill, introduced in the Tennessee Legislature, and does it from the most encouraging stand-point, claiming that the bill will redound to the intellectual benefit of the race. In another issue he comments in a vigorous way upon the opinions in *The New York Independent* on Dr. A. G. Haygood's answer to Senator Eutice's letter in *The Forum*, expressing himself in this wise

on the matter of social equality: "We are not troubled
about social equality, but we are concerned about a fair vote,
an impartial trial, equal public accommodations and courteous
treatment. Our inalienable rights must not be denied,
suppressed or abridged. We shall insist upon being treated
as friends, not as aliens; as brothers, not as strangers."
Shortly after this we find him advising the Afro-American as
to the best way he can survive in this country. "We ought
to cultivate business principles and business matters. They
will help us to retain what we have, and aid us in accumu-
lating a great deal more. The success of our well-to-do and
wealthy men is due to the careful observance of the principles
and methods enumerated above. If we adopt their principles
and follow their methods, we shall not lose anything, and the
probability is that we shall gain something." Mr. Franklin,
while doing able service as a correspondent, would make a
wise advocate in the editorial chair.

MR. J. GORDON STREET, REPORTER BOSTON HERALD, AND GENERAL CORRESPONDENT AFRO-AMERICAN PRESS.

"J. Gordon Street," said T. Thomas Fortune to Dan A.
Rudd of *The American Catholic Tribune,* in a conversation the
two had, some time ago, in Boston, Mass., "is one of the
best newspaper correspondents in the country."

Mr. Street is a West Indian by birth, and first saw the
light May 25, 1856, in Kingston, Jamaica. His journalistic
career began in the fall of 1884, as the Boston correspondent
of *The Detroit Plaindealer.* At the time of his taking charge
of that paper it was little known in Boston. He did his
best to push it, and very soon it was found in the homes of
the leading colored people of Boston. The most prominent
white Republicans in Massachusetts had the paper placed in
their hands. He kept with *The Plaindealer* several months.

J. GORDON STREET.

In November of the same year a very excellent offer was made him by the proprietor of *The New York Globe* to take the Boston correspondence of that paper, which was accepted. Shortly after, *The New York Globe* suspended publication, and when T. Thomas Fortune established *The New York Freeman*, Mr. Street was requested by him to act in the same capacity for *The Freeman* in Boston as he had done for *The Globe*, and he did so from November, 1884, to March, 1888, when he gave it up to go to Zion Wesley College, Salisbury, N. C., to take charge of the agricultural department, which the faculty had decided to institute.

Returning to Boston in the summer of 1885, he was engaged by the editor of *The Boston Beacon*, the leading white society paper, to furnish it matter. The proprietors, on finding that a black man was employed in such a position, objected to it, and of course he had to go.

Though feeling keenly the prejudice with which he had to contend, he was not disheartened, but rather resolved not to give up the contest for a fair and equal chance in the race of life. Accordingly, in about five or six weeks, he went to *The Boston Evening Record* and asked if they would like to buy whatever news he might have. The city editor said " Yes," and the colored news-gatherer went to work to collect the matter. Every man in the office was white; in fact, it might be said right here that there was not a colored man on any of the Boston dailies, at that time, and it was supposed by all that he was connected with *The Boston Record.* Item after item was brought in, accepted and published.

One day Street went to the Boston museum of fine arts to possess himself of some news which none of the other papers had learned of. In making inquiries about it, one of the authorities of the institution asked him for what paper he sought the information; the reply was, *The Boston Record,* and the official cheerfully furnished the facts, so that a valuable item was obtained. It was learned by the city editor that Street had used *The Record's* name in securing this bit of news, and so he was summoned to appear before that gentleman. He went, and the following is the colloquy that ensued : City Editor—"Did you go to the museum of fine arts and represent that you were connected with *The Record?*" Street—"I did, Sir. I supposed I had a right to say, when questioned by persons for what journal I desired any information I might ask for, that it was for *The Record.*" City editor—"You had no right to state you were connected with *The Record.* We do not consider you are; and, further-more, we do not care to have you here any longer." Very well, Sir," was the answer made by Mr. Street. About three months after, he secured a position on *The Boston Herald's* reportorial staff, where he has remained until the present time.

In October, 1885, he again became the Boston correspondent of *The Freeman,* and continued as such until the paper changed hands and name, in 1887. In May, 1888, he took hold of *The Philadelphia Sentinel,* then almost unknown to Boston people. How well he has done with that journal, the circulation of the paper at the present time tells more conclu-sively than anything that could be said here. Mr. Street is also the Boston correspondent of *The Indianapolis Freeman* the great colored illustrated weekly. That he is a man of unusual push is made evident by his ceaseless activity. Not content with the accomplishment of what most men would feel satisfied with, he is ever on the alert for other openings for the exercise of his hand and brain. It was this sleepless desire to be doing something for the good of his fellow-man, especially for the advancement of his Afro-American brother, that led him to establish *The Boston Courant,* of which he is both editor and proprietor. It needs no prophetic eye to state, that if Mr. Street's days are prolonged he will win for

himself a name not soon to be forgotten; and those of his race
who are anxious to see their people attain soon to that
position they believe their Creator has designed for them,
must feel that he is to be an honored instrument in bringing
it about.

BISHOP HENRY MCNEAL TURNER, D. D., LL. D., EX-
EDITOR SOUTHERN RECORDER, AND WELL-KNOWN
CONTRIBUTOR TO THE AFRO-AMERICAN
PRESS.

For us to give an elaborate history of this Afro-American
in all of his connections in life, would be to devote an entire
volume to him. Assuming that the public generally know
of his fidelity to the race, and his labors in the church and
state for their welfare, we will devote the most of our sketch
to his work for the Afro-American press.

Mr. Turner was born near Newberry Court House, S. C.,
February 1, 1833, being the oldest child of Howard and
Sarah Turner. As one says: "His life is full of most
important events. He is a man of great nerve, strong
character and deep convictions. He was admitted to the
Missouri Conference of the A. M. E. church in 1858, having
been licensed to preach by Rev. Dr. Boyd in 1853, and has
served, in his course, from the humble circuit rider to the
bench of bishops, to which he was elected May 30, 1880. In
1872 the University of Pennsylvania conferred the honorary
title of LL. D., upon him, and Wilberforce that of D. D., in
1873.

He has held, all along, most responsible positions in his
church, as well as under the various Republican administrations. In 1876, he was elected by the General Conference of
the A. M. E. church as manager of the publication department,
located in Philadelphia, Penn. While at the head of that

BISHOP HENRY McNEAL TURNER, D. D., LL. D.

department, he wrote much for *The Christian Recorder*, and became noted for his forcible and weighty sentences. But few men in the United States have ever equaled him in that capacity.

Being a man of great nerve and strong character, the missiles he would throw from his pen would rarely ever fail of their mark, and through his wisdom he directed and wrote much Sabbath-school literature, which was circulated all through the United States and fell into the hands of many indolent persons, acting upon them as an incentive for future endeavors, which demonstrated the fact that the press, in the hands of the Afro-American, was, and will ever be, a mighty power.

After serving the time allotted him by the Convention, he compiled a hymn book for the A. M. E. church. He also wrote a standard work, entitled "The Methodist Policy," defining the duties of the officers of the Conference and the functionaries of the church. This work he has revised recently, and it will soon re-appear, more instructive than when it was first introduced.

In 1886, he became convinced that the church needed an organ in the Southland, through which its ardent laborers could express themselves that many might be edified, which could not otherwise be accomplished. Consequently, he caused to appear on the 25th day of September, 1886, a neat sheet, known as *The Southern Recorder*. This paper, from the time of its appearance to that of its becoming a church organ proper, he so managed as to quicken the dormant faculties of many, which resulted in so great a demand for space that he was compelled to enlarge his sheet, long before it was a year old. Daily its subscription list increased, until, at the expiration of a year, thousands were blessed with the privilege of its columns—its editorial columns especially—in which could be found witty and wise expressions, coming

W. ALLISON SWEENEY.

from the pens of learned divines. Never tiring of his task, he continued to cause *The Recorder* to appear until May, 1888, at which time, the General Conference made it an official organ.

Through the whole course of his life Bishop Turner has proved a success, ever and anon giving something to the world to inspire those who were willing to make something of themselves to an effort to do so; and this he has done by untiring industry, ever remembering that

> " Height, by great men reached and kept,
> Were not attained by single flight;
> But they, while their companions slept,
> Were toiling upward in the night."

MR. ROBERT T. TEAMOH, REPORTER BOSTON GLOBE.

Among the rising young journalists is one who, for the past year and a half, has been engaged in work upon one of the leading dailies in Boston,—Mr. Robert T. Teamoh, whose experience in newspaper work has been wide and varied. He was born and educated in Boston, having been a pupil in the Boston Latin school. In 1879 he took a diploma from the industrial drawing school of that city, after which he entered the photographic profession, and, later on, went into photo engraving. He opened up a business in this craft in New London, Ct., and met with much success, applying himself to his work steadily for four years. A special feature was the making of instantaneous pictures of sailing vessels and steam craft, which plied Long Island Sound as far as New London. Just before going to Connecticut he began newspaper work in Boston upon *The Observer*, a paper which was run in the interests of the colored people by a few of the young men of the city. Its existence, however, was of short duration. Soon after, *The Boston Leader* came out with Mr. Howard L. Smith managing editor, and Mr.

Teamoh, city editor, which thrived for some time longer than its predecessor. While in New London Mr. Teamoh was an occasional contributor to *The Boston Advocate,* and under the *nom de plume* of "Scribbler," contributed some excellent letters to that journal. He wrote a number of pamphlets upon tariff reform, during the Cleveland-Harrison campaign, that were widely read and discussed. He has contributed to several Connecticut papers, and also several articles to *The New York Age.*

At the close of the political campaign, Mr. Teamoh accepted an offer upon the reportorial staff of *The Boston Daily Globe,* where he has been working steadily ever since. He is, what is known by newspaper people, a "hustler," and has made for himself, since his connection with that paper, an enviable reputation as a news-gatherer and writer, and has turned out many important readable articles. His style is terse and crisp, and his stories are well written and interesting. Many of his articles have been accompanied by illustrations, some of which have been photographed by him for cuts. These photographs were developed in a dark room, which has been assigned him for this purpose in the Globe building.

There is no distinction made between him and the other "boys" on *The Globe.* He is not only a member but a director of the Globe Athletic Club, having been re-elected twice. He is also one of the trustees of the Tremont Co-operative Investment Association, and is the only colored member of the organization.

Mr. Teamoh is considered an all-around good fellow, and takes an active part and lively interest in all the questions of the day. He is the corresponding secretary of the Colored National League, and was one of the delegates from Boston to the Colored Men's National Citizens' Convention, held in Washington, February 4, 1880. Personally, he is a fine-looking young man. He is tall and well-built, and is affable

JOHN DURHAM.

R. W. ROSE.

and agreeable in conversation and manner.   There is a bright
outlook for him in the future, should he continue the course
he is now pursuing.

MR. W. ALLISON SWEENEY, EX-EDITOR AND PROMINENT AFRO-AMERICAN WRITER.

This gentleman is among the most polished writers of our
age.   He was born in Indiana, and has devoted the greater
portion of his time to journalism, in which he has been
productive of much good.   He has edited several papers,
notably among them the one published at Wheeling, W. Va.,
which is spoken of as having been one of the most brilliant
sheets ever edited by an Afro-American.   We do not question
it, for from what we have seen of Mr. Sweeney's writings we
can readily class him as an able quill-man.   His articles in
The Indianapolis Freeman on the "Religious Press, Men of
Letters, and Noted Black Men," etc., were precious to the
reader who delighted in chaste language and a logical
arrangement of sentences.   About him let us say, as he said
of a friend: "For my part, I am glad he is a member of the
race."   To aspiring journalists we would say: "Behold your
model.   Study him."

These correspondents and reporters upon our various papers
are as numerous as the leaves on the trees.   They are by no
means all capable as writers.   It is a part of the ambition of
the race to see themselves in print, and for that reason many
fondly imagine themselves able to write when totally
incapable of it.   We would mention among the efficient correspondents, Mr. John Durham of Philadelphia, Pa., and Mr.
A. H. Grincke.   Mr. Durham holds a prominent place on
The Evening Bulletin of Philadelphia, Pa., while Mr. Grincke
is a special writer on *The Boston Beacon.*

Mr. R. H. Hamilton of New York, and his brother William

JOHN G. WHITING.

(See Page 366.)

Hamilton, are two excellent writers. They are the sons of the veteran journalist of Abolition times, Mr. Robert Hamilton, Sr., and were brought up in the editorial and composing rooms, so to speak. Mr. William Hamilton is with *The Evening Post*, and Mr. Robert Hamilton is a general gatherer of news for the New York papers. He (Robert) was upon the staff of *The Elevator*, at San Francisco, and *The Progressive American* in New York. Of late, he has been upon the staff of one of the Brooklyn daily papers. He is a terse and ready writer.

R. H. HAMILTON.

We must not omit to mention a Virginia lawyer, R. W. Rose, of Lynchburg, Va., a brilliant writer, lately associated with *The Industrial Day* as corresponding editor. Mr. Rose was an associate of the author on *The Lynchburg* (Va.) *Laborer*, and is a mellifluous writer. He was, for a short time, owner of that journal. Mr. Rose brings to bear upon his contributions vast experience and practical judgment.

Augustus Broussard is a fair writer on *The New Orleans Crusader*. If he continues in the profession he may yet attain to some eminence, editorially.

John G. Whiting of Fort Smith, Ark., is a coming writer of some fame. He was, for a while, associate editor on *The People's Protector*, an interesting paper at the place where he resides.

There are many able writers whose articles appear over *noms de plume* which we could not begin to mention. Suffice it to say, the force is efficient, and is destined to be more so in the future.

CHAPTER XXI.

AFRO-AMERICAN WOMEN IN JOURNALISM.

Prof. Mary V. Cook, A. B., (*Grace Ermine*).

REWARDS to the just always find a grateful heart. God has so ordered, that nothing but God can prevent their bestowment where due; and even he, the God of justice, would have to reverse his character to do this. There is divine poetry in a life garlanded by the fragrant roses of triumph. Aye, this is the more so, when there lies within an earnest heart of an obscure woman a towering ambition to do something and be something for the purpose of enriching the coronet that bedecks the race; and it enhances the laurels it wins in the domain of mental, moral and social conquest. There is romance, rich and rare, in the life of such an one.

It attracts, too, like the needle to the Pole, and it charms one to know such a case. The phenomenal rise of Prof. Mary Virginia Cook to her present position of usefulness and honor is an example to those who still lie in the shadows of obscurity. Let the reader do his part well, remembering that

> " Honor and shame from no condition rise.
> Act well your part; there all the honor lies."

Born of a loving mother, Ellen Buckner, Prof. Cook partook of her gentle and mild manners. Her birth-place, Bowling Green, Ky., like most Southern towns, had nothing exciting or of special character that would impress a child of her refined nature. There was much to give pain and wound a tender heart, in such a hard life as was hers. The unsettled state of affairs at the time had much to occasion alarm. The war was in progress, and with beating heart the mother awaited the settlement of those great questions that had been appealed to the sword, the rifle, and the cannon. On the decision depended the question whether little Mary should rise to the splendid heights in the power of the free, or sink to the insignificance of a fettered slave, with crushed powers.

To one familiar with history, it need not be recounted that she had little chance for learning; she had the appetite, but the food was not at hand. Little by little, she advanced in the inferior schools of the place, till, by her winning manners and perfect lessons, she was acknowledged to be the best scholar in the city. She won signal honor in the small private schools, which is as grand a thing among the home folks, as larger prizes among strangers. Three schools were in a spelling contest for a silver cup which was offered by Rev. Allen Allensworth, a gentleman who did much to encourage her; and being last on the floor she was proclaimed victor. Again, in a teachers' institute, September 30, 1881, a book was offered by a Mr. Clark, a white gentleman, who was stationer in the city, for the best reader; and amid the crowd gathered from near and far the book was awarded to her. The jury was a mixed one, of white and colored citizens. The judges selected the piece to be read, after they assembled. She repeated these triumphs in the State University.

When the Rev. C. C. Stumm, pastor of the State Street Baptist church, of which she is a member, started an academy, he called her to assist him. The pay was small, and she

PROF. MARY V. COOK, A. B.

had the largest number to teach; and one day, as she stood at her work, with tears in her eyes, occasioned by some misunderstanding about her share of the monthly receipts, she said: "The sun will yet shine in at my door." A few hours later the pastor put in her hands a letter from Dr. William J. Simmons, president of the State University, Louisville, Ky., offering to defray her expenses through the American Baptist Woman's Home Society of Boston. This was October 15, 1881. He had seen her before, while on a trip securing students, and said to her: "Would you like to go to Boston to school?" She replied: "Yes, so much." He was impressed with her amiable, meek, Christian spirit, coupled with her reputation for goodness, of which he had heard from various citizens.

She entered the State University November 28, 1881, and became a member of the third normal class. Her decorum was such, that the president testified, on the night of her graduation from the normal course, in a class of thirteen, as he gave her the Albert Mack valedictorian's medal, that she had never been spoken to once, by way of discipline, during her entire course. He afterwards, in writing of his graduates, said of her; "As a student, she was prompt to obey and always ready to recite. She has a good intellect and well developed moral faculties, and is very refined, sensitive, benevolent and sympathetic in her nature, and well adapted to the work of a Christian missionary."

On entering the University, she was almost immediately chosen by the president as student-teacher and dining-room matron, and during the year of her graduation she taught five classes a day. The students honored her with the presidency of the Athenæum and the Young Men and Women's Christian Association. Though she worked all the time, yet in her graduating year she entered the examination and gained the highest mark, 95 per cent, and obtained the valedictorian honor of her class. This same year, Dr. E. S. Portor offered a gold medal to the best speller in the school. Accordingly a contest was held. The work was written, and a large uumber of picked students entered, and again Miss Cook triumphed. Immediately after, she took a silver medal, offered by Dr. D. A. Gaddie, for oral spelling. When the judges made the reports, the students were loud with applause, and made her the center of many demonstrations of rejoicing in her honor. But this was not all. During the same week she took a silver medal, offered by Mr. William H. Steward, for neatness and accuracy in penmanship. She was never beaten in a contest.

On her graduation, May 17, 1883, she was elected permanent teacher, and made principal of the normal department and professor of Latin and of mathematics. This position she still holds, embracing the largest department of the University. By special vote of the trustees she was permitted to keep up her studies in the college department, and at the end of four years she completed them. She was examined, and took the degree of A. B., May, 1887, with her class.

Miss Cook is a bright-faced, intelligent little woman,— what the French would call petite, and until recently did not weigh 100 pounds; but intellectually she weighs 1000. She is quite studious, and is deep in many subjects. She is especially fond of Latin, biography, and mental and moral philosophy. She has a wonderful influence over her pupils, and is much respected by her teachers. She gives heart and hand to every good cause. Her sympathies are quickly touched by the tale of want, and her pocket ever opens to the needs of her pupils. Every public charity gains her ear.

While not a member of the Berean Baptist church, she has labored with it, and in their University society she has been elected president, consecutively, from 1884 until the present writing. The Baptist Women's Educational Convention saw in her the fit material for a worker, and elected her second vice-president in 1884, and a member of the board of managers. In 1885 she was elected assistant secretary of the Convention, and continued on the board. In 1886 she was made secretary of the board, and in 1887 the Convention made her its corresponding secretary and its executive officer for the work of the board of managers.

Her position is one of vast influence among the women of her state. She has appeared on the Convention platform several times, and did so at the jubilee meeting, January 18, 1889. At that time *The American Baptist* said of her: "The history of the Convention, by Prof. Mary V. Cook, their corresponding secretary, was a concise and comprehensive paper. She left the well-beaten tracks of most of the lady speakers, and dealt entirely with facts, and without sentiment traced the Convention from its incipiency until the present time. It was an interesting paper, brimful of information, and was well received. Miss Cook is never more in earnest than when saying a word for the women's work."

She has appeared on the public platform often; notably, before the American Baptist National Convention at Mobile, Friday night, August 27, 1887, when her subject was "Woman's work in the denomination." The article received the warmest praise. And again, she read before the American Baptist Home Mission Society, in its special meeting, September 25, 1888, at Nashville, her subject being "Female Education." Before the National Press Convention, which held its session at Louisville, she read a paper,—"Is juvenile literature demanded on the part of colored children?" This was in 1887. She was again appointed to read a paper at their session at Nashville in 1888, but could not attend. She read a very strong paper on "Woman, a potent factor in Public Reform," before the Kentucky State Teachers'

Association in 1887. On this subject she is not a loud clamorer for "Rights," but, nevertheless, she quietly and tenaciously demands all that is due her.

Her newspaper work began in 1886, and she was then introduced to journalism and the fellowship of the fraternity. Her contribution, "Nothing but Leaves," in *The American Baptist*, is indeed one of her ablest efforts. The following strong sentences are worthy of note: "We are pointed to great men who have made themselves famous in this world. Some are praised for their oratory, some for their fine learning, some for their benevolence and various other qualities, which are all good enough; but they, within themselves, are nothing but leaves, which fall to the ground in their autumnal days and return to dust. True fruit is holiness of heart, and clusters, ripened by the grace of God, be they found in persons ever so lowly, hang higher than all the growth of the intellectual powers. Fruit is the evidence of culture. Leaves grow with little care, and they, with all their beauty, are not the essential part of the plant; but the chief aim of a plant, and the object for which it spends its whole life, is to bear fruit. So the highest aim of God's creation is our fruit-bearing."

Having been converted in 1876, she herein shows the character of a developed spirituality. She is a noble-hearted woman, full of blessings and love; a woman with a soul deeply divine.

In 1887 she edited a column of *The South Carolina Tribune*. At the same time she controlled a column in *The American Baptist*. She writes under the name of Grace Ermine. She is a strong, graceful, vigorous writer, and tends to the argumentative, pointed, terse style. One understands what she means when she speaks. When writing concerning the outrages in the South, she said: "White faces seem to think it their heaven-born right to practice civil war on negroes, to the extent of blood-shed and death. They look upon the life of their brother in black as a bubble to be blown away at their pleasure. The same spirit that existed in the South twenty-four years ago, is still recognized in its posterity. The negro is still clothed in swarthy skin, and he is still robbed of his rights as a citizen, made dear and fairly won to him by the death of those who fell in the late Rebellion. This outrage cannot endure. God still lives, and that which has been sown shall be reaped."

Speaking of our people once, she wrote: "As a people we are not easily led, and we often slaughter the one who attempts it. There is always fault to be found, which thing should be left to our enemies, while we, like faithful Aarons, should uphold the arms of those who have dared to strike for us. There is a natural antipathy against our leaders. If they act as gentlemen, dress decently, and have ability, we call them stuck-up and big-headed; and often a majority will join hands with the Irish, or some other nationality, to get them defeated."

Her position as editor of the educational department of *Our Women and Children*, published in Louisville, gives her wide scope for editorial work. She is gifted with the pen, and in the near future will become an author. She is ascending slowly the ladder of fame, as the morning sun climbs the heavens to the zenith to shine for all. She is a vast reader of the best works, and keeps abreast of the times. She is making herself efficient in short-hand and type-writing, and has many accomplishments that mark her a cultured lady. She is molding the lives of many, and, as the sun, gives light to them. May heaven bless her. Let those who read be encouraged that poor girls can rise, and gain the good opinion of their elders who will help them. The close of a life like hers must be grand and will bless the world.

MRS. W. E. MATHEWS, (*Victoria Earle*,) GENERAL NEWS-
PAPER REPORTER AND NOVEL WRITER.

While journalism among the Afro-Americans has been
and is honored with many lady writers, none are more
popular than Victoria Earle. She was born May 27, 1861, at
Fort Valley, Ga. Her mother, Caroline Smith, being a
Virginian, was a slave, and subjected to the most cruel
treatment by her master. Several times she attempted to
escape, and at last succeeded in reaching New York, leaving
her children in Georgia, in the care of an old nurse until
she returned. For eight years she toiled, hoping to amass
enough money to go back to Georgia for her children. When
at last enabled to do so, she found only four living, Victoria
being among them. After considerable legal trouble, she
succeeded in gaining possession of her children, and returned
with them to New York, stopping on the way at Richmond
and Norfolk.

Victoria had no chance for an education until her arrival
in New York, when she attended the grammar school, 48.
Later, her circumstances were of such an embarrassing nature,
she was forced to leave school and go to work. Though
compelled to launch out into the world for her support, she
was ever a diligent student. Her newspaper labors began
on a larger scale than that of most female writers. She was
first a "sub" for reporters upon the large daily papers of
New York, such as *The Times, Herald, Mail and Express,
Sunday Mercury, The Earth,* and *The Phonographic World.*
This kind of work being her forte, she continued it, in
addition to being New York correspondent to *The National
Leader, Detroit Plaindealer,* and *The Southern Christian
Recorder.* She has also contributed to *The A. M. E. Church
Review,* and has written for various papers at different times.
The Afro-American journals are always anxious to get a

letter from Victoria Earle. Some even dispense with their editorials to make room for her letters. She has written for our brightest and best papers, such as *The Boston Advocate, Washington Bee, Richmond Planet, Catholic Tribune, Cleveland Gazette, New York Globe, New York Age,* and *The New York Enterprise.* No other Afro-American woman has been so eagerly importuned for stories and articles of a general news character, by the magazines and papers of the whites, as has Victoria Earle.

She has met with marked success in story writing, and tales written by her expressly for *The Waverly Magazine, The New York Weekly,* and *The Family Story Paper,* have readily found place in the columns of those publications. She is indeed entitled to the highest honor from her race by her efforts to dignify her work, and eminently prove Afro-American journalism to be the peer of any.

In closing the life of this honored lady journalist, we could not say more of her than *The New York Journal* does in the following: "Victoria Earle has written much; her dialect tid-bits for the Associated Press are much in demand. She has ready several stories which will appear in one volume, and is also preparing a series of historical text-books which will aim to develop a race pride in our youth. She is a member of the Women's National Press Association, and no writer of the race is kept busier."

MISS LUCY WILMOT SMITH, EDITOR WOMAN'S DEPARTMENT OUR WOMEN AND CHILDREN MAGAZINE.

The enthusiast who writes the history of a life of modern times is too apt to paint the virtues of his subject in such glowing colors, that, on becoming acquainted with the party, we hardly recognize the person as the one described. With this in view, we wish to state the points of Miss

MRS. W. E. MATHEWS.

Smith's career in journalism, in the light of truth and justice to herself. She is the daughter of Margaret Smith, who welcomed this child upon the arena of life November 16, 1861, at Lexington, Ky.

Her education was obtained with much difficulty, owing to the fact that she had nothing upon which to lean for support, save her hard-working mother. She was forced to teach when quite young, in 1877, serving under the Lexington, Ky., school board. However, she graduated from the normal department of the State University in 1887. She was, for a long time, private secretary to Dr. William J. Simmons, by whose aid she was introduced to the world of thinkers and writers in newspaper life. Dr. Simmons himself testifies of her that she is careful, painstaking, and thoughtfully helpful.

She is a prominent member and officer of many of the female societies, looking to the advancement of religious truth and action in her denomination, the Baptist. She is now one of the faculty of the State University. Several papers which she has read before national bodies show carefulness of thought, as well as logical arrangement of her subject-matter.

We have referred to the fact that it was through Dr. Simmons she began, in 1884, what has resulted so successfully, her newspaper work, when she controlled the children's column in *The American Baptist* of Louisville, Ky. She was for quite a while on the staff of *The Baptist Journal*, of which Rev. R. H. Coles of St. Louis was the editor. She recently furnished sketches of some newspaper writers among the Afro-American women for *The Journalist*, a paper published in New York in the interest of authors, artists, and publishers. These articles were highly complimented by the editor, and were copied, and the cuts reproduced, in *The Boston Advocate*, *The Freeman* of Indianapolis, and other papers.

MISS LUCY WILMOT SMITH.

Miss Smith is a writer of good English, and produces sensible reading matter. She tends to the grave, quiet and dignified style. Her best efforts have been for *Our Women and Children* Magazine, published in Louisville, Ky. The department of "Women and Women's Work" receives the benefit of her cultured hand regularly. She is deeply interested in the elevation of her sex, and is a strong advocate of suffrage for women. Upon this subject she wrote these strong words: "It is said by many that women do not want the ballot. We are not sure that the 15,000,000 women of voting age would say this; and if they did, majorities do not always establish the right of a thing. Our position is, that women should have the ballot, not as a matter of expediency, but as a matter of pure justice." It cannot be denied that the women have done great and lasting work, that needs our encouragement. Miss Smith is a member of the Afro-American Press Convention.

Our assertions as to her editorial ability are backed by some of the prominent writers of the country. The editor of *The American Baptist* says: "She frequently writes for the press, and wields a trenchant pen. Is ambitious to excel, and will yet make her mark." Mrs. N. F. Mossell says: "Miss Smith writes compactly, is acute, clean and crisp in her acquirements, and has good descriptive powers. Of strong convictions, she is not slow in proving their soundness by a logical course of reasoning. Her style is transparent, lucid, and in many respects few of her race can surpass her."

To show the reader Miss Smith's idea of the women in the field, we clip the following from her " Women as Journalists:" "The educated negro woman occupies vantage ground over the Caucasian woman of America, in that the former has had to contest with her brother every inch of the ground for recognition; the negro man, having had his sister by his side on plantations and in rice swamps, keeps her there, now that

he moves in other spheres.   As she wins laurels, he accords
her the royal crown.   This is especially true of journalism.
Doors are opened before we knock, and as well-equipped
young women emerge from the class-room, the brotherhood of
the race, men whose energies have been repressed and
distorted by the interposition of circumstances, give them
opportunities to prove themselves; and right well are they
doing this, by voice and pen."

MISS LILLIAN A. LEWIS, (*Bert Islew*,) BOSTON CORRE-SPONDENT OF OUR WOMEN AND CHILDREN AND EX-EDITRESS OF THE ADVOCATE.

Miss Lillian Lewis is among the youngest and brightest of
the Afro-American women writers, and her career in
journalism, although a comparatively short one, has been
exceptionally brilliant.   Naturally of a literary bent, and an
excellent scholar in literature and composition, she showed
marked talent in this direction in her earlier days.

During her successful school life, she wrote, besides essays,
a number of lectures upon various topics.   There was a vein
of humor running through each, but under it all was a deal
of practical thought.   Her first effort in the lecture field was
upon temperance, she, on several occasions, addressing temperance societies.   She also wrote and delivered lectures
upon "Man's Weal and Woman's Woe,"—and "Dead Heads
and Live Beats;"and was eminently successful with the one
under the caption: "The Mantle of the Church covereth a
Multitude of Humbugs."   This discourse, with dashes of pertinent witticism, struck at the root of a good deal of pious
hypocrisy which is constantly practiced.   This was delivered
by the young writer four or five times in Boston, and two or
three times in small towns in the suburbs.   The innate love
of composition alone tempted Miss Lewis to enter the lecture

domain, where her career was brief, lasting but one short season.

All this time she was attending the girls' high school, and additional and more difficult studies claiming her undivided time and attention, she was obliged to close her lecture career. She could not be induced to give up her studies in music and elocution, but pursued them for a year or more.

Upon graduating from the high school she immediately turned her attention to literary work, and the next winter was spent in the preparation of a novel, " Idalene Van Therse," which is not yet published. Shortly after, she began newspaper work, and contributed special articles to *The Boston Advocate*. *The Advocate*, at that time, was the victim of much adverse criticism, and was rapidly losing ground with its Boston readers. Miss Lewis at once perceived the cause, and immediately set about to meet the exigency, if possible. Her aim was to edit a column of matter that would take with all classes and all ages, and the result was the " They say" column, which has for about two years become proverbial with readers of *The Advocate*. At first the paragraphs were short, crisp, and breezy; but later on Miss Lewis began to add comments and criticisms on what "they say," which was a happy thought, and made the column more attractive than before. *The Advocate* soon began to regain its former popularity, and subscribers increased, until to-day there is scarcely a colored family of intelligence in Boston that does not read *The Advocate* and *Bert Islew's* gossip.

A short while ago, Mr. Powell, the proprietor and editor of *The Advocate*, offered Miss Lewis the society editorship, which she accepted, and which position she now fills; and what was generally known as " They say" column, is now virtually the society department of the paper. While writing for *The Advocate*, Miss Lewis contributed to *The Richmond*

MISS LILLIAN A. LEWIS.

Planet; but pressing and urgent duties soon forced her to discontinue the work in that direction.

About two years ago, Miss Lewis took up stenography, and after much diligent study and careful instruction under an excellent teacher, succeeded in mastering Graham's system. It was then that she obtained the position of stenographer and private secretary to the widely-known *Max Eliet*, of *The Boston Herald*, who is one of the cleverest woman writers and critics in the country, and who occupies an important editorial position on the staff of *The Herald*.

Finding that her duties as a private secretary called for a knowledge of type-writing, she set herself to the acquisition of that art, and is now able to write from dictation with ease and rapidity. In fact, her record for taking copy verbatim ranks among the highest in New England. Miss Lewis also does good reportorial and special work, as well as work in the society department of *The Herald*, upon the staff of which paper she is a regular salaried employee. Miss Lewis is peculiarly fitted for the position she holds.

MRS. LUCRETIA NEWMAN COLEMAN, GENERAL NEWSPAPER CORRESPONDENT AND WRITER.

The truth is expressed in the sentence which says: "Mrs. Lucretia Newman Coleman is a writer of rare ability." Discriminating and scholarly, she possesses, to a high degree, the poetic temperament, and has acquired great facility in verse. She was born in Dresden, Ontario, being the fourth child of William and Nancy Newman. Her father died when she was quite a child, and her mother soon after the death of her husband became an invalid, and died after thirteen months' suffering. The household duties then fell upon this "petted child."

Inspired by the words of her dying father and mother, she

withstood temptations, patiently bearing the burdens laid upon her, and led a pure, Christian life. She obtained her education in the common and high schools, and graduated from the scientific department of Lawrence University. She began to teach soon afterward, and continued to for some time.

During her life she has filled many good positions, which came without her seeking them. She has been successful as a teacher in high schools, a teacher of music, and as a clerk in dry goods stores. In 1883, she was assistant secretary and book-keeper in the financial department of the A. M. E. church. While at this work she began to sail upon the journalistic ship, which has been one of continued progress. *The American Baptist*, then edited by Rev. William J. Simmons, contained an account of her career in one of its issues of September, 1884, which gives her standing at that time: " As a writer, her fame is fast spreading, not only in one or two states, but throughout the United States. Should she continue with the same success in the future as she has had in the past, she will be equal to Harriet Ward Beecher Stowe, if not her superior.

Since then she has steadily progressed, until now she may be looked upon as indeed our " Harriet Ward Beecher Stowe." As a poetic writer, there is possibly no female Afro-American of her age that can surpass her. Concerning her poetic and scientific writings, we can say no more than a well-known writer has in the *The Indianapolis Freeman:* " Her last poem, 'Lucille of Montana,' ran through several numbers of the magazine *Our Women and Children*, and is full of ardor, eloquence and noble thought. Mrs. Coleman has contributed special scientific articles to *The A. M. E. Review* and other journals, which were rich in minute comparisons, philosophic terms, and scientific principles. She is a writer more for scholars than for the people. A novel entitled 'Poor Ben,'

25

which is the epitome of the life of a prominent A. M. E. bishop, is pronounced an excellent production. Mrs. Coleman is an accomplished woman and well prepared for a literary life."

Afro-American journalism among our women has been brought to a grander and nobler standard, by the lofty tone our subject has given it. Mrs. Coleman continues to devote her time to literary pursuits, and ranks among the most painstaking writers.

GEORGIA MABEL DE BAPTISTE, CONTRIBUTOR TO OUR WOMEN AND CHILDREN.

This young lady, with more than ordinary accomplishments as a writer, was born in the city of Chicago, November 24, 1867, her parents being Rev. Richard and Georgia De Baptiste. Her father (who appears in this work) was a prominent writer and preacher, from whom Georgia seems to have inherited a love for literature. Her mother having died when she was only six years of age, she grew up to womanhood sadly feeling the need of a mother's care and devotion. True to the promptings of a good child, she learned early the need of a Savior's love and protection, and when only twelve years old was converted to God, baptized by her father, and received as a regular member of Olivet Baptist church, Chicago.

Having a desire to obtain a good education, both literary and musical, in order that she might lift the burden of her support from her father and be able to cope with the brighter intellects of the land, she began the public school course. Graduating from the grammar school and receiving a diploma, she entered the high school. Her stay here was brought to a close by her removal to Evanston. She, however, took a modern language course in the high school. While

GEORGIA MABEL DE BAPTISTE.

in Chicago she took music in connection with her school duties, and by continual study has become very proficient in that line.

Her life as a writer began in Evanston, being inspired thereto by an article she read from the pen of a lady friend. So well received was her first production, she became a regular correspondent to *The Baptist Herald*, for which she wrote two years, or until its suspension. Since then she has written for *The Baptist Headlight*, and *The African Mission Herald*, and is, at the present, a regular contributor to *Our Women and Children*, an excellent magazine published at Louisville, Ky.

Miss De Baptiste is fully alive to the needs and necessities of the race, and will yet make a brighter life for herself in this field. She is regarded as one of the most gifted writers on the staff of *Our Women and Children.*

Concerning her bent and purpose in life, she writes to a friend as follows: "I am fond of literary work, and I hope to become a writer of real power of mind and character,— with true dignity of soul, and kindly bearing toward all among whom I may be thrown; not for mere social attainments, but that such may be the outward expression of inward grace and courtesy." We predict for Miss De Baptiste continued success in her literary efforts.

MISS KATE D. CHAPMAN, NEWSPAPER CORRESPONDENT AND POETICAL WRITER.

The future of no female writer is prospectively brighter than that of Miss Kate D. Chapman of Yankton, Dakota. First seeing the light February 19, 1870, at Mound City, Ill., she now, at the age of nineteen, enjoys the reputation of being above the average lady correspondents and writers of poetry. Born of poor parents, Charles and Laura Chapman, she had

MISS KATE D. CHAPMAN.

no educational facilities until her twelfth year, though then able to read. Upon moving to Yankton she entered school, and is now the leading member of her class in the Yankton high school.

During her continuance in school she has been an incessant reader, and as such is familiar with all questions of interest, and able to write so as to please those who may perchance read her articles. Her first poem, "A Dying Child's Fancy," was written at the age of fourteen. It is said to have been good, all things considered, but it was never published. Beginning her correspondence to papers and periodicals in the summer of 1888, she made herself prominent at once by her lively and interesting articles, which appeared mostly in *The Christian Recorder* and *American Baptist.* She is now a regular contributor to *Our Women and Children* magazine, and we occasionally find articles from her pen in *The Indianapolis Freeman.* One styles her as being bright in thought and unique in expression.

As a poetical writer, there are few among the young Afro-American women who can excel her. She is given to the lively and vivacious, rather than the pathetic and humorous. We reproduce one of her poems, published in *The Indianapolis Freeman,* in which she depicts the condition of the Afro-American, and questions its continuance. It is entitled

"A QUESTION OF TO-DAY."

" And shall our people, long oppressed
  By fierce, inhuman foe,
Not seek to have their wrongs redressed?
  No ! by their manhood, no !

" You men do call us women weak.
  By Him who ruleth all,
For what was ours we'd dare to speak,
  Menaced by cannon ball.

" Human we are, of blood as good;
As rich the crimson stream ;
God-planned, ere creation stood,
However it may seem.

" Oh ! sit not tamely by and see
Thy brother bleeding sore ;
For is there not much work for thee,
While they for help implore?

" From Wahalak came the news,
Our men are lying dead.
Did it not hatred rank infuse
When word like this was read?

" And now White Caps, with hearts as black
As hell,—of Ku-Klux fame,
Still ply the lash on freedman's back;
And must he bear the same?"

Thus said a woman, old and gray,
To me, while at her door,
Speaking of what so heavy lay
And made her heart so sore.

" What, woman ! dost thou speak of war,
The weaker, 'gainst the strong?
That, surely, would our future mar,
Nor stop the tide of wrong.

" We must be patient, longer wait.
We'll get our cherished rights.—"
" Yes, when within the pearly gate,
And done with earthly sights,—"

Replied the woman, with a sneer
Upon her countenance.
" You men do hold your lives too dear
To risk with spear or lance."

" Naomi, at Fort Pillow fell
Three hundred blacks one day ;
The cannon's roar their only knell,
In one deep grave they lay.

" Our men have bravely fought, and will,
Whene'er the time shall come;
But now we hear His ' Peace, be still !'
And stay within our home.

"Let but our people once unite,
  Stand firmly as a race,
Prejudice, error, strong to fight,
  Each hero in his place,—

"And not a favored few demand
  Bribes of gold, position,
While many freemen in our land
  Bewail their hard condition,—

"Liberty, truly, ours will be,
  And error pass away;
And then no longer shall we see
  Injustice hold her sway.

"As Americans we shall stand,
  Respected by all men;
An honored race in this fair land,
  So praised by word and pen.

"And those to come will never know
  The pain we suffered here;
In peace shall vow, in peace shall plow,
  With naught to stay or fear."

Said Naomi: "You may be right;
  God grant it as you say.
I've often heard the darkest night
  Gives way to brightest day."

This young lady, as will be seen from an extract of a letter to the author which we take the liberty to produce, is fully alive to the work of the press and the demand for active laborers. She writes: "Allow me to say, that I think my work as a writer but barely begun, for, God helping me, I mean to become one of no mean caliber. I regard the press as one of the mightiest factors that move this universe of ours. So great is its influence, so powerful its results, I verily believe that if we, through any unseen force, should lose our free press, our republic would be shattered. It is my aim to become an authoress, because, chiefly, having been strengthened by good books myself, I would like to give to my country and people a like pleasure."

Would that all Afro-American women were inspired with the same zeal and determination found in this young lady. Journalism will be brightened by the poetical and prose writings of Kate D. Chapman; for, as Miss L. W. Smith says of her—"She has read much, and will write much."

MRS. JOSEPHINE TURPIN WASHINGTON, PROMINENT NEWSPAPER CONTRIBUTOR.

Mrs. Washington first saw the dawn of day in Goochland county, of the Old Dominion state, July 31, 1861. Her parents were Augustus A., and Maria V. Turpin. She was taught to read by a lady who was employed in the family. Subsequently moving to Richmond, she graduated from the normal and high schools and the Richmond Institute, now the Richmond Theological Seminary. From there she entered Howard University, graduating from the college department in the class of 1886. She has held positions in both of her alma maters, having resigned the one in the latter to marry Dr. Samuel H. H. Washington, now a practising physician in Birmingham, Ala.

She is a scholarly woman, and has acquitted herself most creditably in many walks of life, which have necessitated a highly intellectual brain and a pureness of heart. She has held a position as teacher in Selma University, Ala., and also as copyist under Hon. Fred Douglass, when Recorder of Deeds for the District of Columbia, to whom she owes a debt of gratitude for kind acts and personal friendship.

Mrs. Washington gained her literary reputation while Miss Turpin. Just where she began her work is not definitely known, but it seems as though she were born with an inclination to write, so early did she manifest a disposition to do so. Her first publication appeared in *The Virginia Star*, in 1877, regarding which a writer says: "About this time her first contribution to the public press was made to *The Virginia Star*, then the only colored organ in the state. This article was entitled 'A Talk About Church Fairs,' and was a protest against selling wine at entertainments given by church members for the benefit of the church. It elicited much favorable comment; and from that time on, Miss Turpin continued to write at intervals for the newspapers, always finding ready welcome and generous encouragement from the press and people."

With an irrepressible desire to continue her literary work, she has written for *The Virginia Star, Industrial Herald, Planet, New York Globe, New York Freeman, Christian Recorder,* and also for *The A. M. E. Church Review,* and is still a contributor to some of them and other journals.

Concerning some of her best contributions to the press, Mrs. Mossell, the gifted writer, says : "Her subjects have been various,—educational, moral, social, racial, and purely literary. Among her most popular productions are probably the following : A series of descriptive papers written to *The Industrial Herald,* of Richmond, during a six-weeks' stay in New York and Boston, in the summer of 1883; "Paul's Trade and the Use he Made of it," read before the Baptist Sunday-school Union of Washington, D. C., and afterwards published in *The Christian Recorder;* "Notes to Girls," a series of letters in *The People's Advocate;* "Higher Education for Women," an oration before the Young Ladies' Literary Society of Howard University, at their public meeting in 1885, and subsequently printed in *The People's Advocate;* "The Hero of Harper's Ferry," delivered at the junior exhibition of the class of 1886 of Howard University, of which she was a member; a reply in *The New York Freeman* to Annie Porter, who had published in *The Independent* a vigorous onslaught against the negroes; "The Remedy for War,"—her graduating oration, since given to the public in

MRS. JOSEPHINE TURPIN WASHINGTON.

395

The A. M. E. Church Review; and " Teaching as a Profession," published in the October number of *The Review.* Mrs. Washington continues to write, and productions from her pen are welcomed alike by publishers and the public.

MISS ALICE E. McEWEN, ASSOCIATE EDITOR BAPTIST LEADER.

On Hardings street, in the city of Nashville, July 29, 1870, was born the above-named young lady, whose work in the literary sphere has been marked with that success which would attend many a person's life whose aim is right, and whose dependence is God.

Of Christian parents, Rev. and Mrs. A. N. McEwen, she grew up a God-fearing child, receiving a religious as well as an intellectual training. She acquired the rudiments of an education in the Nashville public schools, and subsequently attended Fisk University, (1881) and, after the death of her mother, Roger Williams University, (1884.) She did not, however, finish the prescribed course here, as her father, knowing the care a motherless girl requires, and feeling that a ladies' institute would best supply the need, sent her to Spelman Seminary, at Atlanta, Ga. This was in 1885, which also dates the preparation and publication of her first article for the press, which was printed in *The Montgomery Herald,* under the caption of " The Progress of the Negro.

During her school life at Spelman, she wrote various articles for the newspapers, until her graduation, May 24, 1888, at the age of eighteen. She was then engaged as associate editor to her father, Rev. A. N. McEwen, who was editor of *The Baptist Leader,* a five-column, four-page journal, neatly printed, and presenting as attractive an appearance as the average race journal.

Miss McEwen is a journalist under the guidance of her

MISS ALICE E. McEWEN.

father, and her fame is extending all over the land. She is widely known by her having appeared before several national bodies to read some of her productions. She read a paper before the last National Press Convention, at Washington, D. C., upon " Women in Journalism ;" also a paper before the Women's Baptist State Convention, at Greenville, Ala., the same year. The paper before the Press Convention was afterward published in *The Leader*. It is indeed a fine presentation of the subject, showing thought and careful preparation. She opens with a statement of the success which has attended the efforts of our women; then, in speaking of the field which this work offers to women, she says: " There is no work which women can engage in that its influence will be brought to bear upon the public more than this. It is here that their utterances will commend themselves to the mind of the young. America has furnished her share of noble women in this work, and they have done much in molding the national life. Their words found, and are still finding, an echo in the life of the nation. They were thrilled with the forces and vitality of their age, and by their noble words helped to mold the destinies of coming generations." She then discusses at length the women whose work has been glorious, and closes with an eager appeal to our women to engage in this work, as the following lines will show: " While we appreciate the work that has been done by these women, yet we must not think the work completed, This century opened with as broad a field as did the other."

" Let us not merely speak of the praise due, but show our heartiest thanks by taking up the work where they left it and carrying it forward, even to a higher standpoint. If we will nourish the seed sown by them, I believe we, in the near future, shall garner a glorious harvest, while women advance to high moral and intellectual development. Let

MRS. C. C. STUMM.

us not undervalue the work of these noble women. The wisdom of the philosopher, the eloquence of the historian, the sagacity of the statesman, the capacity of the general, may produce more lasting effects upon human minds, but they are incomparably less rapid in their influence than the gentle yet wise words of these women."

"All praise to these noble women. May their names ever live upon the lips of all true Americans."

MRS. C. C. STUMM, BUSINESS MANAGER AND CORRE-SPONDENT NATIONAL MONITOR AND OUR WOMEN AND CHILDREN.

Mrs. Stumm, daughter of Thomas and Eliza Penman, and wife of Rev. Mr. Stumm of Philadelphia, Pa., was born in Boyle county, Ky., March 25, 1857. Her father died when she was quite young, yet the inflexible zeal of her mother insured a good schooling for her child. She remained in Berea College for two terms, gaining a fair amount of knowledge, which has been added to since by her personal efforts. She has taught in private institutions and public schools, having been employed in Hearn academy, Texas, and Bowling Green academy of Kentucky.

Mrs. Stumm's journalistic work began in 1879, at Elizabethtown, Ky., in a newspaper discussion with a preacher upon a certain question, which resulted in a victory to her. She contributed occasional articles to *The Bowling Green Watchman*, (Ky.) and while she was in Boston, she worked as agent and contributor for *The Hub and Advocate*, and other Afro-American journals published in that city. She has since resided in Philadelphia, and has energetically acted as Philadelphia agent for *The National Monitor*, Brooklyn, N. Y., and for *Our Women and Children* magazine, at Louisville, Ky.

Mrs. Stumm is a good thinker and a florid writer, and from what her pen has already produced, it is safe to predict she is destined to accomplish much for her race.

MISS A. L. TILGHMAN, EDITOR MUSICAL MESSENGER.

Miss A. L. Tilghman was born in Washington, D. C., her parents, Henry II., and Margaret A. Tilghman, being among the oldest and most highly respected citizens of that city. Miss Tilghman was a student at Howard University, and graduated with high honors from the normal department in 1871. For fourteen years she was a teacher in the public schools in Washington, and was considered one of the finest teachers and most successful disciplinarians in the corps, so much so, that when pupils were sent out from the Miner normal school to visit other schools and receive ideas on teaching and governing, the superintendent almost invariably selected her school as one among the number to be visited.

She has been regarded for several years one of Washington's finest vocalists.. In December, 1881, she was engaged to sing in New York; and the New York press spoke of her as "The bursting forth of a musical star, whose singing completely captivated the praise and admiration of the critics of the metropolis, and elicited their concession to her richly earned title of 'Queen of Song.'" In 1881 she was engaged to lead the Saengerfest, at Louisville, Ky.; and in 1883 she traveled as leading sopranist for the Washington Harmonic company. It was while she was with this company that she was severely hurt, in walking up a street in Saratoga, N. Y., by the falling of a brick from a structure in process of building. Her skull was much fractured, and it was some time before she could resume her duties. This accident impaired her chances in life, since she had to abandon the stage, and give up teaching. Upon resigning her position as

26

teacher in the Washington public schools, she was highly complimented by both trustees and superintendent.

As a musician, she is of the highest order. Her training was received at the famous Boston Conservatory of music, with private instruction under Prof. Jameson of Boston. Upon leaving that city she was engaged to teach a large class of pupils in Montgomery, Ala., which she did with remarkable credit to herself and class. While in Montgomery she was constantly engaged in devising some new step for the further development of her race. The greatest musical entertainment ever known in Montgomery, namely, the cantata of Queen Esther, was presented by Miss Tilghman, with a chorus of sixty singers, all in full stage costume. The following is the press comment upon Miss Tilghman as "Queen" and as manager: "Miss Tilghman represented the beautiful queen, and she manifested that solemn, pathetic, and dramatic force throughout the play, which gave it life-like appearance, as one would picture it as he reads it in the Bible. The highest praise is due her for the presentation of this cantata. She was the sole organizer, and deserves the thanks of the citizens generally for her interest in everything which tends to the improvement and elevation of our race."

It was while in Montgomery that Miss Tilghman first published *The Musical Messenger*. In December, 1887, she was invited by the faculty of Howe Institute, New Iberia, La., to take charge of the musical department of said school. After receiving many urgent letters, she concluded to accept the position, and amid the regret of the entire community, she left Montgomery and went to New Iberia, where she was much needed. After remaining there one school year, she was induced to return home on account of the continued illness of her mother, and now resides there, teaching music and publishing *The Musical Messenger*.

MISS A. L. TILGHMAN,

The Messenger is one of the spheres in which our lady writers who are musicians can make themselves known. It is greatly to the credit of Miss Tilghman that she assumed the management of such a magazine. She is the only Afro-American woman who edits a paper devoted to the musical elevation of our race. Her knowledge of music and musical people enables her to treat in an intellectual way all subjects pertaining to the musician's welfare. Not only does *The Messenger* give light to the musical world, but its editor often turns the light on our moral actions, and advises the Afro-Americans in a most practical way. She says to them: "Stand fairly and squarely for the race to which you belong, and whenever there comes a moment when principle and money clash, then stick to principle and let the money go; and in the end you will reap a rich reward." *The Richmond Critic* pays her this tribute: "We have received a copy of *The Musical Messenger*, edited by Miss A. L. Tilghman. It is a perfect sheet, of good form, and we congratulate the editor, and hope our people will take advantage of this opportunity to learn something of music." Miss Tilghman can accomplish much in her sphere. She is a woman of great energy, and it naturally follows that *The Messenger* must and will be supported.

She has for an associate in her editorial work, the well-known Lucinda Bragg Adams. Whatever may or may not be the success of *The Messenger*, its associate editor is a valuable acquisition to the staff. Born of Mr. and Mrs. George F. Bragg in the city of Petersburg, she early began and continued the study of music until she became highly proficient.

She is a woman of indomitable will. and a writer of superior ability. She has contributed to the leading magazines of our race during her life, upon various newspaper topics. An article upon music was published in *The A. M. E.*

Review, which drew much attention and many compliments. Her composition, "Old Blandford Church," which was dedicated to Hon. John Mercor Langston, had a profitable sale. *The Messenger,* with Mrs. Adams' aid, will be a paper of commanding influence in Afro-American journalism.

MRS. N. F. MOSSELL, CORRESPONDENT INDIANAPOLIS FREEMAN, AND OUR WOMEN AND CHILDREN.

To every reader of Afro-American journals the above name is familiar. Beginning as a journalist when quite young, Mrs. Mossell has, for sixteen years, continually written for our race journals, and reported for the foremost white papers in Philadelphia. Her first article, an essay on Influence, was published by Bishop B. T. Tanner in *The Christian Recorder* when she was a mere school girl; and up to the present day she has written essays, poems, short stories, and race sketches, which have been published far and near.

She was especially sought for, and assumed the position of editor of the woman's department of *The New York Freeman* and *The Philadelphia Echo.* While engaged upon these papers she also reported for *The Philadelphia Press* and *The Times,* two of the most widely circulated papers in the country. She is now upon the staff of correspondents of *The Indianapolis Freeman, The Richmond Rankin Institute,* and *Our Women and Children.* Though a regular contributor to these papers, she nevertheless writes for other race journals, from the great *A. M. E. Review* to the smallest paper published.

Mrs. Mossell has selected journalism as her profession, believing, as she expressed herself once, that the future of women, especially of Afro-American women, is on this line of literary work. In her writings she deals particularly with the women and the Afro-American race as a whole. She hopes to write a book of some value to our literary world. She is alive to all the interests of our race; and since journalism is her mission, she is ever on the alert to ascertain some way in which to make it a success. As a writer, the reader may readily learn how Mrs. Mossell ranks, by her very pleasing and interesting articles, "Power of the Press" and "Women in Journalism."

In writing to *The New York Age* concerning the means by which success may come to us in journalistic work, she says: "I hold that no colored journal yet has done all it could do for itself, or has had all done for it that might have been by its friends. Now I have some suggestions to make, which I believe would help our papers to succeed. I have never yet seen a colored newspaper sold on the streets by a newsboy. We sell at the newsdealers; we get subscriptions; we sell through agents; but the main means why white papers succeed, we do not use at all. Sunday morning I am awakened by the white boys shouting their papers. *The Sunday Mercury*, with its colored column, 'Items on the wing,' is sold all through the street. Now we live in sections; our boys would not have to walk their legs off. See to it that boys are put on the streets Sunday morning, and on Saturday night where colored people market. Call out the name of the paper and what it contains of interest. Hundreds of papers would be sold.

"Next, the papers could contain more valuable articles. Let *The Age, The Indianapolis Freeman, Detroit Plaindealer, Washington People's Advocate,* and *Philadelphia Sentinel,* or others in widely separated sections, form a syndicate and pay the best colored writers to write on a given subject. Each could pay three or five dollars, and good articles could be written. Very few people take all these papers; so even if they do not appear on the same date, it would be of little matter, if only it came the same week. The most successful articles could be put in tract form, and kept for sale by an open letter agency of the syndicate."

Mrs. Mossell is a telling writer, her thoughts being clear and clean-cut, in the main. We append the following tribute to her from *The Indianapolis Freeman:* "Mrs. Mossell is one of the most gifted as well as versatile women writers in the country, and rightly does the race honor and appreciate her genius."

MISS IDA B. WELLS, (*Iola,*) GENERAL NEWSPAPER CORRESPONDENT AND ASSOCIATE EDITRESS.

That "perseverance overcomes all obstacles," is fully verified in the life and character of Miss I. B. Wells, who was born at Holly Springs, Ark., and reared and educated there. Her parents died while she was attending Rust University, which compelled her to leave school in order that she might support her five brothers and sisters, all being younger than herself.

She taught her first school at the age of fourteen, and with this work and journalism she has been an incessant laborer. She has taught in the schools of Arkansas and Tennessee, and has at various times been offered like positions elsewhere; but preferring to teach her people in the South, she has continued to labor there. For six years she has followed her vocation as teacher, in the city of Memphis.

During this time she began to write for the press. Her first article was a "write-up," at the request of the editor, of a suit for damages, in which she was the complainant. This paper was *The Living Way*, which she contributed to for the space of two years. This engagement introduced her to the newspaper fraternity as a writer of superb ability, and therefore demands for her services began to come in.

T. Thomas Fortune, after meeting her, wrote as follows: "She has become famous as one of the few of our women who handle a goose-quill, with diamond point, as easily as any man in the newspaper work. If Iola were a man, she would be a humming independent in politics. She has plenty of nerve, and is as sharp as a steel trap."

She is now the regular correspondent of *The Detroit Plaindealer*, *Christian Index*, and *The People's Choice*. She is also part owner and editor of *The Memphis Free Speech* and *Head Light*, and editress of the "Home" department of *Our Women and Children*, of which Dr. William J. Simmons is publisher. Decidedly, "Iola" is a great success in journalism, and we can but feel proud of a woman whose ability and energy serves to make her so. She is popular with all the journalists of Afro-American connection, as will be seen by her election as assistant secretary of the National Afro-American Press Convention, at Louisville, two years ago, and her unanimous election as secretary of the recent Press Convention, which met at Washington, D. C., March 4, 1889. Miss Lucy W. Smith gives an account of the many papers to which "Iola" has contributed.

In summing up her character as a writer, we can but say "Amen" to what Miss Smith says of her: "Miss Ida B. Wells, "Iola," has been called the "Princess of the Press," and she has well earned the title. No writer, the male fraternity not excepted, has been more extensively quoted; none struck harder blows at the wrongs and weaknesses of the race.

"Miss Wells' readers are equally divided between the sexes. She reaches the men by dealing with the political aspect of the race question, and the women she meets around the fireside. She is an inspiration to the young writers, and her success has lent an impetus to their ambition. When the National Press Convention, of which she was assistant

IDA B. WELLS.

secretary, met in Louisville, she read a splendidly written paper on "Women in Journalism; or, How I would Edit." "By the way, it is her ambition to edit a paper. She believes that there is no agency so potent as the press, in reaching and elevating a people. Her contributions are distributed among the leading race journals. She made her debut with *The Living Way*, Memphis, Tenn., and has since written for *The New York Age, Detroit Plaindealer, Indianapolis World, Gate City Press*, Mo., *Little Rock Sun, American Baptist*, Ky., *Memphis Watchman, Chattanooga Justice, Christian Index, Fisk University Herald*, Tenn., *Our Women and Children Magazine*, Ky., and the Memphis papers, weeklies and dailies. Miss Wells has attained much success as a teacher in the public schools of the last-named place." All in all, we are proud to own Miss Wells as our "Mrs. Frank Leslie."

Miss Ione E. Wood, Editress Temperance Department
Our Women and Children.

Among the young writers of to-day, few have gained a wider celebrity and a more deep-rooted recognition in the popular mind than Ione E. Wood. Being only about twenty years old, and hence with but a brief experience in journalism, the rank attained by her exhibits her ability in a wonderful degree.

She was born in New Jersey. At an early age she attended the public schools in Burlington, and afterward the mixed high school in Atlantic City. After the establishment of the State University, Louisville, Ky., by her uncle, Dr. William J. Simmons, she was enrolled as a student of that institution for the purpose of pursuing a liberal education. So diligently did she prosecute her studies that the institution, in seeking an assistant teacher, found in her the material for that position. Filling the appointment with such general

MISS IONE E. WOOD.

satisfaction, she was, later on, appointed permanently as instructor in Greek, During all this time her studies were kept up in the college department, of which she considered herself a member. In 1888 she received her degree of A. B. Since the organization of the B. W. E. C. of Kentucky, she has held important offices therein, and is now a member of the board of that body.

At first, Miss Wood was an occasional contributor to newspapers and magazines. From the start, her publications have gained popularity. As a writer, she is clear, terse and vigorous. Her subject is always well understood and well managed. Her language is free from catchy phrases and by-words, and is smooth, agreeable and earnest. It is free and natural, devoid of all jerkiness and splash. Her sentences drop like the oar of the sturdy sailor. With a turn of mind little imaginative and poetical, there is not much use for tropes and figures; yet she has attained such remarkable clearness of expression as to resemble the crystal lake. From the first, one can see the point at which the writer aims. She pursues it with unerring approach, swerving to neither side, and has learned the happy faculty to leave a point when made. The many excellencies of this writer are clearness, force, simplicity, perspicacity, smoothness and agreeableness.

Miss Wood is now a stock-holder of *Our Women and Children*, as well as a regular contributor to it. The work assigned her is the promotion of temperance. As its advocate, she lacks much of the ardor and aggression common to those who are engaged in furthering this cause; but her deep-seated earnestness and a consciousness of the correctness of her position leads her to give frank and emphatic expression to her views.

There is danger in the utterance of unwholesome thought. In an age rankly luxuriant with pomp and pride, a thirst for

uiiginality and novelty tends to make us victims of cruel
deception. Language is often used to give color and attract-
iveness to vice and heartless fashion. In view of this, it is
no small compliment to say of this young writer she has the
Christian ingenuity to intermingle much practical piety with
what she writes. Herself a staunch Christian, her writings
in no respect belie her good profession of faith.

MRS. LAVINIA B. SNEED, CONTRIBUTOR AFRO-AMERICAN PRESS.

This lady, a regular and excellent writer, was born near
New Orleans, La., May 15, 1867. Upon moving to Louisville
she entered the public schools, and afterward attended the
State University which was established in 1881. Being a
new institution its students encountered many obstacles
common to such enterprises in their incipiency. Mrs. Sneed,
desiring to enhance its prosperity, was one of the first to
travel with a concert troupe for the purpose of raising funds
for the furtherance of the work. She labored zealously for
the institution; and is one of the few women who have
received the title of A. B., having graduated from the college
department of this university as valedictorian of the class of
1887. She is a singer of merit, as well as an elocutionist of
superior ability.

While her journalistic life has not been as great as others,
yet she has written much for our magazines and papers.
Her contributions are always looked upon as choice English,
while the thought is pure, clear, and easy to catch. She is
indeed a writer for the populace, in that she writes so that
the meagerly educated may understand the purport of her
articles. In most of her writings her decided ability has
been made apparent.

In the summer of 1888 she married the highly intellectual

MRS. LAVINIA B. SNEED.

Prof. Sneed, by whose side she stands with unswerving fidelity. Her journalistic future is bright and promising, and the idea that she will do much for her race, through the medium of her pen, is the thought of many.

MISS MARY E. BRITTON, (*Meb*,) EX-EDITOR AND CONTRIBUTOR AFRO-AMERICAN PRESS.

Miss Britton was born in Lexington, Ky., thirty-three years ago, and still resides there. She was educated in its schools, and at present is a teacher in one of the public schools of that city.

Her first literary publication was an address delivered at the close of her school. It was published in *The American Citizen*, a Lexington weekly, now extinct. One who knows, says: "It was a strong paper, showing the relation of parent, teacher and pupil." Her next publications were in the interest of the Afro-American cause, and were published in *The Cincinnati Commercial*, in 1877. Mrs. Amelia E. Johnson says: "She has an excellent talent for comparing, explaining, expounding and criticising, and has made no small stir among the city officials and others for their unjust discriminations against worthy citizens." Articles of such nature were published often in *The Daily Transcript*, a Lexington paper.

She wrote regularly for the women's column in *The Lexington Herald*. Through the columns of this paper she agitated a reformation in society, total abstinence from alcoholic liquors and tobacco, and the importance of active work and the influence of example upon the part of teachers and preachers. She wrote for *The Herald* under the *nom de plume* of "Meb."

She has contributed literary productions and discussions to *The Courant*, an educational journal published in Louisville,

Ky.; to *The Cleveland Gazette*, Ohio; and to *The Indianapolis World*, Ind. She wrote for *The Ivy*, a paper edited and puplished at Baltimore, Md., in the interest of children and youth. Her *nom de plume* while writing for *The Ivy* was "Aunt Peggy." Her contributions to this journal were chiefly philosophical, and written in a simple, pleasing and instructive manner; and many were the compliments they received from the young folks, who thoroughly enjoyed her articles. In 1887, a paper on "Woman's Suffrage as an important factor in Public Reforms," was published in *The American Catholic Tribune*, at Cincinnati, O. She writes now for *Our Women and Children*, and for *The Courant*.

Miss Britton claims to be neither a poet nor a fiction writer; but she is a prolific writer on many subjects of a solid, practical, forcible character. Teaching is her forte, and she prefers to perfect herself in both the science and art of the profession. As a teacher, she is greatly respected and esteemed. A writer to *The Indianapolis World*, Ind., refers to her and her work in the following appreciative terms: "The city (Lexington) officials are building the colored people a school-house on the corner of 4th and Campbell streets; and Miss Mary E. Britton, the "Meb" of our literature, smiles even more pleasantly than usual. She has done a great deal to educate the youth here, under the most vexing circumstances; and none can appreciate or rejoice more in better facilities than she."

Miss Britton is a specialist. Recognizing the fact that one can not satisfactorily take in the whole field, she wisely concludes to pursue and perfect herself in such branches of it as she feels confident are hers by adaptation. Such a course can not fail to give success to the one pursuing it. She is an ardent student of metaphysics, and a firm believer in phrenology, and had her phrenological character written out by Prof. O. S. Fowler. He describes her predominant

MISS MARY E. BRITTON.

characteristic as "ambitious to do her level best." He speaks of her as "thoroughly conscientious, and actuated by the highest possible sense of right and duty; as frugal and industrious and adapted to business." This description, added to her natural force, resolution and vim, can be fully corroborated by those who are intimately acquainted with Miss Britton.

When connected with *The Lexington Herald* as editor of its women's column, she was an indefatigable worker, and rendered efficient aid. She was spoken of by that journal as follows: "The journalistic work seems to be the calling of Miss Britton. No other field would suit her so well. In manner and style, her composition is equal to any of her sex, white or black. As an elocutionist, she stands next in rank to the accomplished Hallie Q. Brown. No literary programme gotten up by the Lexingtonians is complete without the rendition of some choice selection by her,—Miss Britton. She is a hard student, a great reader, and a lover of poetry. Miss Britton is an acknowledged teacher, of high intellectual attainments."

The above speaks well indeed of this energetic young woman, while, with reference to her ability as a writer, *The American Catholic Tribune* (Cincinnati), has this to say: "It is with pleasure that we call the attention of our readers to a paper read by that talented young woman and rising journalist, Miss Mary E. Britton, at the State Teachers' Institute, held in Danville, Ky., last week. Without comment on the terms it proposes, we give it to the public for careful perusal."

The Christian Soldier (Lexington), says: "Miss Mary E. Britton is one of the brightest stars which shine in Dr. Simmons' great magazine, *Our Women and Children*; and the magnitude of those stars is national. Lexington never gets left, when it comes to pure, good and sensible women."

Who can say that the perusal of this sketch can fail to benefit and inspire our young girls. Does it not show what can be done by them, if they will? Miss Britton is not an isolated case of hardships surmounted,—an honorable place gained among the world's busy workers; for the colored race possesses many women of brain, nerve, and energy, who, when left to wage a hand-to-hand combat with adversity, fight along bravely and well; and in the end come off victorious.

MISS META E. PELHAM, REPORTER FOR DETROIT PLAIN-
DEALER.

This lady, a writer of much culture, was born in Virginia. Her parents, when she was quite young, moved to Detroit, and Meta found her way into the mixed schools of that city, where she graduated as valedictorian of a class of fifty-three pupils, only four of whom were Afro-Americans. She afterward took a normal course at Fenton College of Central Michigan. She began to teach school, but owing to declining health she had to return home, when she entered *The Plaindealer* office, and began a most successful career as a writer for newspapers.

She is a woman of most excellent traits of character, and has a prolific and productive brain. In her newspaper experience she has written for other publications, but her work on *The Plaindealer* has been marked with the most fruitful results.

Miss Pelham is not so well known as many lady writers of less ability,—because, in her entire writings, she has used no *nom de plume*, or signature. It is thought that she will soon edit a particular part of *The Plaindealer*. As it now is, she is a general writer upon the editorial staff.

The Plaindealer, in its anniversary issue of May, 1888,

speaks at length concerning the achievements of the Afro-American woman in newspaper life. It has the following in regard to Miss Pelham and her connection with the paper: "Since the inception of *The Plaindealer*, the influence of woman has sustained it in adversity; the product of her mind has given lustre to its columns; and now, more than ever, much of its success in the character of its productions is due her. To Miss Meta Pelham is due the credit of this aid, who has always taken an active interest in the paper, and often contributed to its columns. For the past two years she has become one of its essentials in the office, and she devotes her whole time to the work. She was among the first Afro-American graduates from our high school, and subsequently took a normal course at the Fenton normal school. She also spent several years teaching in the South, until newspaper allurements became more tempting. Her idea of a newspaper is, that it should be metropolitan in character, deal in live issues, and be reliable."

Her idea of newspapers makes her a live and indispensable factor in the fruitful field of Afro-American journalism, and she is surely destined to be brought prominently before the public by the aid of her pen.

Mrs. Frances E. W. Harper, Time-honored Contributor to the Afro-American Press.

The name of this lady naturally brings to the mind of the reader the heroic efforts she made in the dark slavery days for the freedom of those in bondage, and she labors now for the removal of those things that she considers most harmful to her race. Her endeavors to promote the "Prohibition Movement" will have their place in history, as well as her writings which have inspired the youth in the past, as they will in the future.

MRS. FRANCES E. W. HARPER.

Mrs. Harper was born in Maryland in 1825, and grew up there, leaving school at the age of fourteen. As a lecturer, she has few equals, and possibly none among her own race. Mr. Still has given a record of her energetic labors in his *Under-ground Railroad*, as has also William Wells Brown, in his *Rising Sun.* She has even been a promoter of Afro-American journalism, and a regular contributor thereto. *The New York Independent, The Christian Recorder, The A. M. E. Review,* and *The Anglo-African,* have been made the more attractive by her productions. Her poems and prose writings have been found in other papers; but those mentioned are the most prominent. Her poetical and prose writings are excellent, and have been extensively read by white people, as well as by the blacks. The Afro-American press would suffer a great loss by the withdrawal of her intellectual and cheering aid. She has been the journalistic mother, so to speak, of many brilliant young women who have entered upon her line of work so recently.

MRS. A. E. JOHNSON.

The subject of this sketch was born in 1858. Her parents were both natives of Maryland. She was educated in Montreal, Canada, and came to Baltimore, Md., in 1874, where she has made her home ever since. She was married to Rev. Harvey Johnson, D. D., in 1877.

Mrs. Johnson began literary work by writing short poems, etc., for various race periodicals. In 1887 she was strongly impressed with the idea that there ought to be a journal in which the writers among our people, especially females, could publish stories, poetry, and matter of a purely literary character, for the perusal of young people; so, in the year above mentioned, she launched upon the uncertain waves of journalism *The Joy*, an eight-page, monthly paper, containing

MRS. A. E. JOHNSON.

original stories and poems, and interesting items from a number of exchanges, solicited for the purpose; also, pithy and inspiring paragraphs from the writings of people of our race.

The contributors to *The Joy* were faithful, and the paper kept up in interest while it lived; in proof of which we quote the following extracts from *The Baltimore Baptist*, the widely-read weekly journal of the white Baptists of Baltimore: "The contents were original, and the general tone very creditable to the editor. . . . . . So far as it has gone, the editor must be conscious of having done a good work, and shown the way for some other to follow." Mrs. Johnson has a large collection of letters and newspaper clippings, further testifying to the appreciation in which her little journal was held.

Her stories, etc, have always been favorably commented upon. *The National Baptist* of Philadelphia reproduces one of her stories, entitled "Nettie Ray's Thanksgiving-day," in its "Family Page" for Thanksgiving week; and has also, at different times, short poems from *The Joy*. *The National Baptist* is one of the largest circulated white denominational journals in the country.

Mrs. Johnson has, in the past year, conducted a "Children's Corner" in *The Sower and Reaper* of Baltimore, for which she wrote "The Animal Convention," "The Mignonette's Mission," and other original contributions.

But in 1889-90 she reached the place for which she had been aiming and preparing herself. She wrote for publication a manuscript, which was purchased by the American Baptist Publication Society, one of the largest publishing houses in America. *The American Baptist* of Louisville, Ky., in alluding to this, said: "Mrs. Johnson has the deserved distinction of being the first lady author whose manuscript has been accepted by this society." *The Indianapolis*

Daily Journal referred to her as having been engaged upon a book "which is now in hand by the Publication Society, she being the first colored woman to be thus honored;" and *The Baltimore Baptist* said: "Mrs. Johnson is a fine writer." Thus was given to the public "Clarence and Corinne; or, God's Way." (12 mo. 187 pp.) Of this little book the press speak as follows: "This, we believe, is our first Sunday-school library book written by a colored author. Mrs. Johnson is the wife of a noted and successful Baltimore pastor, and in this book shows talent worthy of her husband. . . . . The tale is healthy in tone, holds the attention, and is well adapted to the intermediate classes of Sunday-school readers." (*The Missionary Visitor*, Toulon, Ill.) "It is a pathetic little story." (*National Baptist*, Philadelphia, Pa.) "The interest of the reader is early excited, and held steadily to the close." (*Baltimore Baptist*.) "One feature of this book makes it of special interest,—it is the first Sunday-school book published from the pen of a colored writer." (*The Baptist Teacher*).

Rev. Dr. J. B. Simmons of New York, speaks of the "purity of style, and the delightful character of the story;" and a lady whom we do not feel at liberty to name, but who is well fitted to judge, and has been denominated as "scholarly, gifted, and a wide traveler," in a private letter to Mrs. Johnson says: "I hope you will still keep on, and let us have other books as graceful, as earnest, and as encouraging to young people, and, indeed, to all folks, young and old, as this first fledgling of your pen."

All of the foregoing expressions are from members of the white race, and have been thus quoted because they were unexpected tributes. The book was written from affection for the race, and loyalty to it, the author desiring to help demonstrate the fact that the colored people have thoughts of their own, and only need suitable opportunities to give them utterance. Others may be led through her to develop a gift for writing, unconsciously possessed hitherto.

Our own journals have also been ready with a hearty reception of this product of the pen of a fellow-laborer. *The Baptist Messenger* of Baltimore says that "the fact of its being published by the American Baptist Publication Society, speaks volumes of praise for the book;" and again,—"This is one of the silent, yet powerful agents at work to break down unreasonable prejudice, which is a hindrance to both races." *The Home Protector* of Baltimore says: "It ought to be in every home; and parents should secure it for their children, and see that they read and re-read it, until they make the principles set forth by the writer the rule of their life." *The National Monitor*, Brooklyn, N. Y., says: "The story is carried on in a natural, graphic, pathetic, and deeply interesting way, through nineteen chapters." *The Sower and Reaper* says: "As a literary production, it is a most excellent book, a model of perspecuity, energy and elegance."

The author of "Clarence and Corinne" feels confident that there are those among the race who needed only to know that there is a way where there is a will, to follow her example, and no doubt far surpass this, her first experience in book-making; and she is happy in knowing that come what may, she has helped her people.

These are by no means all of our women in journalism who have made themselves felt in that sphere of life. A host of them are doing local work upon newspapers and magazines. Some quite prominent ones have not as yet been mentioned.

Virginia scored a noble record for Afro-American women in journalism through Miss Caroline W. Bragg's editorial connection with *The Virginia Lancet*. Miss Bragg proved herself a writer of much ability, and met in a commendable way the shots hurled at her from male journalists.

Mrs. M. E. Lambert of Detroit, Mich., edited for some time *St. Matthew's Lyceum Gazette.* Mrs. Lambert is a clever gatherer of news and a pleasing writer.

Mrs. M. S. Crary was, for a long time, editor of *The Provincial Freeman* of Canada, which was considered a good journal.

Miss Clanton of Chattanooga, Miss Lewis of Philadelphia, Mrs. F. J. Coppin of Philadelphia, Miss Mason and Mrs. Frank Grimcke of Washington, D. C., in common with others, have done good work in journalism, either as reporter, contributor or regular correspondent.

There are at present distinctive departments for women in *The Afro-American Budget* and *The Southland,* the former being edited by Adah M. Taylor, and the latter by Mrs. A. G. Cooper. These ladies are showing remarkable activity and adaptiveness to the work. *The A. M. E. Review* always contains articles from various of our lady writers, while the newspapers are constantly presenting to their readers some contributions from our women whose talent is being recognized. With them, there is nothing in the past that warrants any reason for discouragement for a profitable and useful life in this department of labor.

CHAPTER XXII.

OPINIONS OF EMINENT MEN ON THE AFRO-AMERI-CAN PRESS.

AUTHOR'S INTRODUCTION TO OPINIONS.

TO the unthoughtful the following opinions which we have solicited would seem a matter of poor judgment upon our part. In fact, some have doubted our propriety in propounding such questions to those who have so kindly given us their views. This, of course, has arisen from the lack of knowledge as to our aim and purpose. All cannot see alike, and it is not expected that the reader will accurately see our purpose until it shall have been explained. However, the one who will take the time to give our questions mature thought, will see, without an explanation, that our purpose, in a nutshell, is to get the expression of the race as to whether, in their judgment, our press has been fruitful to them, and, as such, whether it has been a success, with the disadvantages encumbering it; and what they conceive to be the achievements that compose such a success. We claim, with all the right thinking people, that the press, an expressor of the popular will, is an indispensable part of the nation's freedom. We claim that since it purports to work for a race's benefit;

since it purports to express a race's thought upon all questions
affecting their material, moral, religious, social and intellectual
welfare, their civil and political rights, the race for which it
labors is entitled to a free expression as to its success and
achievements. The question is liable to arise: Do the
gentlemen expressing opinions herein represent the race for
which the Press is laboring? The answer to such question is
evident from the fact that those who here offer their opinions
are among the recognized leaders of the race, in the various
vocations of life. We are fully confident the race will
recognize the sentiment here expressed as theirs, free and
unbiased. We claim that it is not for the Press to say that
it has been successful, or what its achievements have been.
The Afro-American Press has guided a race of freemen who
have been watching its course with unabated interest.
These are the people whose province it is to declare what
the Press has accomplished and what has been its success.
Our Press continually claims a lack of support upon the part
of the race, for whose interest its labors are especially directed.
For this reason we, as well as the toiling Afro-American
editor, desire to know the cause. If the reason for non-
support be traceable to the editor, he should know it; if to
the people, they should know it. It will assuredly satisfy
the editor to learn that the cause, in a measure, lies at his
door, and also at the door of his people. With such a
conclusion accepted, the remedy can be readily applied.
The future of the Afro-American is bright, in the majority
of instances, while deplorably dark in others. The object of
the question is to learn the general sentiment as to the
future course of the race, if it be possible. The fact is
prominent that the answers will give a unity of purpose in
the future efforts of the Press. While these opinions are for
the editor to ponder upon, yet it must be conceded that it is
his prerogative, after giving them the thoughtful consideration

to which they are entitled, to accept or reject them, as in his judgment, he deems best; and then direct his course accordingly. They will assuredly tend to his enlightenment, and may aid him materially. We say: Accept the good and reject the bad.

The following circular was addressed to the Hons. Frederick Douglass, John R. Lynch, Rev. J. C. Price, D. D., Rt. Rev. Benjamin W. Arnett, and others, to which replies have been received:

LYNCHBURG, VA.

DEAR SIR:

I am impressed with the idea that the Afro-American Press has been a great success, and that it has wrought many achievements, and has been a great benefit in promoting race progress among our people. I also think that before both the religious and secular press lies a vast field for doing good among our people.

Since this is a fact, I have assumed the laborious task of compiling the history of Afro-American journalism and its editors, which will be published in book form, to be known as "The Afro-American Press and its Editors." This work is expected to be very comprehensive and highly illustrated. An introductory sketch of the compiler's life and work will be prepared by Prof. Daniel B. Williams, professor of Greek and Latin in the Virginia Normal and Collegiate Institute. Mr. Williams is the author of "Science, Methods and Art of Teaching," "Life of Capt. R. A. Paul," etc., and has the well-earned reputation of being one of the ablest and most eloquent writers among the Afro-Americans of Virginia. I shall also have the opinions of our ablest men, lawyers, ministers, doctors and teachers, as to the success, achievements and the future prospects of the Afro-American Press.

If you, as a foremost lawyer, minister, doctor, teacher or politician, whose opinion carries with it power and influence,

will consent to allow your opinion to be published in the
work, as coming from you, kindly answer the following
questions, carefully and concisely, and forward to me by
mail within thirty days:

Do you think the Press in the hands of the negro has been
a success?

In your judgment, what achievements have been the result
of the work of the Afro-American editor?

Do you think the Press has the proper support on the part
of the Afro-American?   If not, to what do you attribute the
cause?

What future course do you think the Press might take in
promoting good among our people?

If you will furnish the opinion in thirty days, address me
a postal card stating the same.

Yours for the Race,
I. GARLAND PENN.

OPINION OF W. S. SCARBOROUGH, A. M., LL. D.

1st. I believe that the Press in the hands of the negro
has fully demonstrated the possibilities of the race, in all the
routine of journalism. The success of the negro journalist
has been phenomenal, notwithstanding the lack of encouragement and the indifference on the part of those who ought
to rally to his support. The fact that the negro Press has
succeeded, despite adverse circumstances, is conclusive proof,
in my mind, that its future is assured.

2d. Among the achievements of the Afro-American
editors, the first and foremost has been the establishment of a
closer bond of union among us, by which we have been
enabled to present a solid front, make a stronger fight for
our rights, and thereby demand fair play in the race of life.
The negro editor, by virtue of his position, has not only

become a live factor in our American body-politic as a dictator and molder of public opinion, in common with the white man, but he is the spokesman of the race, and the guardian of its best interests. When he falters, when he becomes derelict in regard to duty, there will be a perceptible dereliction among those whose cause he represents. Seven millions of American people are speaking through the negro Press, or are supposed to, at least. These journals have become a part of the race,—an inseparable part, and as such, we are accustomed to turn to them to plead our cause. This, too, is an invaluable achievement, well worth the money and time it has cost.

3d. The Press has not had the proper support on the part of the race. If it had been otherwise, the humblest journal among us, would have not less than ten thousand annual subscribers,—which is not the case. Leading journals, such as *The Age, Gazette, Plaindealer, World, Planet, Sentinel, Conservator, Star of Zion, Louisiana Pelican,* and others, would surely have not less than thirty thousand subscribers, with the bulk of negro advertisements and job printing, etc, etc. "Charity begins at home," is an old saying; but it is nevertheless true. The negro, like other people, must look out for No. 1. If he fails to do so, he is very likely not to succeed. This trite maxim may be studied with profit by all of us. If the negro could be led to see the force of it, and could be induced to act accordingly, we should very soon build up permanent enterprises of our own that would add materially to the solution of the so-called "Negro Problem." I attribute the cause of the apathy on the part of the negro, at this time, to the jealousy among the non-intelligent and to the ignorance of the masses. Time will evidently bring about a change, and the negro editor will doubtless see better days. Further, the editor himself is not always a representative man; a man in whom the people have

W. S. SCARBOROUGH, A. M., LL. D.

implicit confidence; a man of much learning and wide experience, whose character is above reproach; and, as a result, the people are not drawn to him as they should be. This is the exception, however, and not the rule.

4th. Above all, avoid printing slanderous talk and statements against one's character, unless its evidence is so conclusive that there is no doubt as to the guilt of the party in question. I would advise as little publication of this kind as possible. Further, I would suggest more general news of a racial character, gleaned by agents located throughout the country, who make it a specialty to gather everything pertaining to the moral, intellectual, social, religious, political, and commercial relations of the race. Editorials and reviews of a comprehensive nature on all phases of the race's progress should be an indispensable part of the journals of our people. No compromise should be allowed at the expense of sound morals. Economy should be advocated, on all lines where extravagance now reigns among us, and the recognition of the negro, in all that the term implies, or, in other words, manhood's rights. There should be a vigorous policy and an aggressive movement, whenever the exigencies of the times demand it. The race first, and the individual second, should be the editor's motto.

If the Press should take this proper course, it will be more largely instrumental in promoting good among our people.

OPINION OF HON. JOHN MERCER LANGSTON.

Whatever appertains to the freedom, the rights, the advancement, the elevation, the prosperity, the happiness, the welfare, of the newly emancipated classes of our country, dwelling especially in the Southern section thereof, are subjects for our thoughts, our readings, our pens, our journals, and our papers. We do not live alone in this great nation.

HON. JOHN MERCER LANGSTON.

We are not isolated, neither indeed can we be. We compose a part of the indivisible natural body. So, while it is a fact that our previous condition presents some special wants and racial peculiarities, and we may therefore, in some sense, be considered a distinct branch of the national population, yet we require no special appellation or peculiar definition to make known our legal and political status as American citizens. Hence, we perceive at once that while the mission of our editors and journalists may more especially pertain to our class and its interests, we may not limit their work to it. Whatever concerns the general welfare must find in them a judicious and proper advocacy, if they would perform their whole duty with wisdom and efficiency. Finally, then, that which pertains to the common and general welfare of the whole people of our common government, a united, happy, and prosperous people, dwelling together in peace and harmony, their education cared for and fostered, their industry wisely maintained and promoted, impartial justice and right duly supported in their behalf, with their general welfare conserved, alone should constitute the crowning consummation of our editors. May God speed this consummation, and may their efforts contribute not a little to this end. Such is the duty of the Afro-American editor; but the object sought can not be attained unless the editor insists upon these things in his journals and papers: First, considering the fact we are Americans by nativity, the measure of our rights, of every sort and kind; the measure of our privileges and immunities, of every sort and kind; the measure of our opportunities and duties, of every sort and kind, is that which is common to every one who is entitled to the name and status of American; and we claim such appellation by reason of our nativity alone. No surrender should be made. Upon this point the journalists and editors must insist with all their power.

HON. JOHN R. LYNCH.

Secondly, if Americans by nativity, we are citizens, according to the opinion of the late Attorney-General Bates, which is able and exhaustive on this matter of citizenship; and in the light of what he says, if the law be enforced, every white citizen will be accorded his rights, and every colored one will be protected in his. The editor should say whether this be practicable, for he is the wielder of the pen from which should come such information, either original or quoted, as shall give the mode and manner of procedure that shall accomplish the purpose sought.

Our editors should see to it that our race and cause suffer no detriment. If ability be required, the editor should have it; if learning, he should gain it; if sacrifice, he should cultivate its spirit, and make it; and in the end he shall gain the fruition of a glorious, crowning success.

There is to be no compromise connected with the manly and fearless advocacy of all that pertains to the rights, the elevation, the advancement, the general and equal good of our race. No mutual repellency, sometimes called prejudice, at others' hatred, whether claimed to grow out of previous social condition or complexional and race peculiarities, must be allowed to weigh even an atom against our first demand for immediate emancipation from every sort of evil,—social, political, or official thraldom. The editor is to march boldly forward in the discharge of his duty. He should see that our interests, especially so far as our freedom and rights are concerned, are in no wise abridged, circumscribed, or destroyed.

OPINION OF JOHN R. LYNCH.

Your circular received. In answer to the question, "Do you think the Press in the hands of the negro has been a success?" I must say, financially, No; but the Afro-American editor has accomplished some good in shaping public opinion in the right direction. A majority of the papers receive, perhaps, as much support as their merit deserves. Some, however, do not receive what they merit. This, in my opinion, is due to two causes: First, the poverty and illiteracy prevailing among the blacks, and, secondly, the inferiority of the papers published as mediums of news.

To the question, "What future course do you think the Press might take in promoting good among our people?" I would say, the publication at some important point, the the national capital, for instance, of an ably edited daily newspaper which shall be the equal of other daily metropolitan papers published in different parts of the country. One such paper, with capital at its back, and brains, integrity, and principles at its head, would do more good in the direction spoken of than all the other colored papers in the United States combined. With suitable effort on the part of reputable persons, I think such a paper can be established, and would be a success.

Why can not a number of those now engaged in the publication of unimportant local papers unite their means and efforts, and undertake the publication of such a paper?

OPINION OF DR. WILLIAM H. JOHNSON.

I do most decidedly think that the Afro-American Press has been a success, and is to-day doing a Herculean work for the up-building, the development, and the broadening of the true and manly character of the Afro-American. I thank God for it. Were it not for the intelligent and aggressive Afro-American editor of these states, the Afro-American would be in a deplorable condition.

I remember vividly, with profound satisfaction, the grand pioneer work iu the anti-slavery crusade performed by snch publications as *The Ram's Horn*, *The North Star*, and a paper edited by Stephen Myers and his gifted wife Harriet, in this city, away back in the "forties." It was from the teachings and precepts of these advanced journalists, that I received my first inspiration for public work.

The achievements of the Afro-American editor have resulted in the unification of the Afro-American people and the development of race pride, as well as the proper diffusion of knowledge; and, above all, in the far-reaching publication of the educational, moral, business, agricultural, and mechanical resources and capabilities of the race.

The Afro-American Press has not been properly supported by the race. There are a hundred and one reasons that might be assigned for this state of affairs. It will suffice for me to say that all these reasons, whatever they are, are fast giving way, and a substantial and healthy sentiment is crystalizing in favor of race papers. This is hopeful in the extreme.

Not being a journalist myself, I will not venture an opinion as to the fourth question. However, I believe that the Afro-American Press is essential to race development as men and citizens, as are the genial rays of the sun and the warm rains to an abundant harvest. The Afro-American Press has done much, but there is room to do more. It can and ought, withont fear or favor, to point out to our brethren in the South the line of policy that alone will conserve to our best and lasting interest. The Press can do much in molding public sentiment, since experience has demonstrated beyond the possibility of a doubt that laws, be they ever so just and proper, can not be enforced successfully against public opinion.

The sentiment of the old South is to-day against a free ballot. By forbearance, discretion, and judicious deportment, the new South may be enlisted in the cause of a free, untrammeled ballot. No people, once oppressed, ever succeeded in reaching the goal of their ambition, none ever

WILLIAM H. JOHNSON. M D.

demonstrated their claims to pre-eminence and distinction, except through trials and much suffering. The Afro-American is no exception to this rule. The guarantees in the amended Constitution are all right; so, also, are the enforcement laws on the statute books. The legacy is ours. Our cause is in the courts of public opinion, and if our advocates are strong, learned, zealous and untiring, the verdict in the end will justify our dearest hopes.

Opinion of Prof. Frank Trigg.

I think there can be no doubt that the negro press has been a success. My opinion is, that the Press voices the feelings of the public toward the negro, and puts him upon a more amicable plane with respect to all nations, both abroad and in America; and it has presented the true status of our race, so that a fair mind could not be mistaken in its comprehension of the great questions relative to the negro.

Were it not for the negro Press, the country would be in comparatively total darkness as to the negro's real condition, on all the lines of human treatment and improvement; and his freedom might as well be taken from him, as to deprive him of his journalistic privileges. In my opinion, the greatest boon of our American citizenship is the free Press; quench it, and we shall begin to wane.

Many of our papers are shamefully neglected. We should ascertain which of them deserve to live and which should die; and that as early as possible. I fear that the poor support of our Press is largely due to the lack of a proper conception the majority of the race have of the importance of its unity, and of its concert of action in all matters pertaining to the race's weal or woe. Our daily papers should be more liberally patronized by our people. The negro Press has no specific lines upon which to move, other than the presentation

Prof. FRANK TRIGG.

of those facts which look to the up-building of the race. It is certain that the future negro Press will be more liberally supported, because each succeeding generation will perceive its duty more clearly with respect to its newspapers, and thereby enable them to be improved, year by year.

OPINION OF PROF. D. AUGUSTUS STRAKER.

To the question, Do you think the Press in the hands of the negro has been a success? which is a very general inquiry, I answer generally, Yes. Whatever may have been the failures in the management of journalism by the negro, however poor the financial profit has been to one and all engaged in this pursuit, yet the net result shows success, and not failure. To-day we have newspapers published by the negro, which demand and receive the recognition of competent journalists, who once stood as uncompromising critics, and non-believers in the capacity of the negro for intellectual advancement. The Press, in the hands of the negro, has been a success in the work of the education of white Americans respecting the manhood and capacity for advancement of the negro.

The second question is so intimately connected with the former, that the answer to it must be regarded as a continuation of that to the first. The achievements of the Press in the hands of the negro have been numerous. After the schools, the Press has done more for the intellectual advancement of the negro than anything else; and in his moral advancement it has been the efficient handmaid of the church. Before the publication of newspapers by the Afro-American, little or nothing was known of the true status of the negro in America. Prejudice and blind unbelief of others placed him on the lowest round of the ladder. We were unknown in history, in art, in science and in industry. Through the

PROF. D. AUGUSTUS STRAKER, LL. D.

work of the Afro-American editor, the public to-day understands to what extent the negro is a tax-payer. In regard to his millions of dollars in property, his school-houses, churches, private dwellings and his bank deposits, the country is now well informed. His place and achievements in the schools and universities are known. If his rights are violated, the fact is proclaimed and his oppressor denounced. His writings are published. Indeed, to my mind, the Press, in the hands of the Afro-American editor, is doing the work of reviving the lost arts among us, and pointing us to the way to success on the one hand and the achievements of the race on the other.

Unquestionably, I answer No to the third question. I attribute the cause, first, to our financial weakness as a race, and, secondly, because our journals are too much African, instead of American, thus keeping our minds, as a race, isolated from the great mass of American citizens, instead of making us a part of the great whole.

To the fourth question, I would say to the Afro-American Press go ahead in the course you are pursuing. Let justice be your guide, integrity your sword of defense, and virtue your pedestal. Teach the people that rights which are worthy of being received should be protected, even at the cost of their lives. We must die to rise again. This should be the motto of our journals.

Opinion of Prof. B. T. Washington.

Few agencies for the uplifting of the colored people have accomplished more good than the negro newspapers. These papers have served to create race confidence, in that they have taught the colored people that the colored man could manage a business requiring the out-lay of money, brains and push that a newspaper enterprise demands. The colored

PROF. B. T. WASHINGTON.

editors have rendered most valuable service to the cause of education by constantly stimulating and encouraging our people to educate themselves and their children.

The papers have served as educators to the white race, in matters that pertain to the progress of the negro. The white press readily sees our dark side, but is not disposed, as a rule, to go far out of its way to let the world know of the negro's advancement.

The work of the colored newspapers has thus far been one of love and self-sacrifice, few if any of them paying in dollars and cents; but there has been evident growth, both in the make-up of the papers and in the paid circulation, and I apprehend that the day is not far distant when they will bring in an encouraging revenue. Already Mr. B. T. Harvey is publishing in Colnmbus, Ga., a colored daily, and he seems to be supported in his efforts to an encouraging degree.

OPINION OF HON. FREDERICK DOUGLASS.

1st. Yes, but only as a beginning.

2d. It has demonstrated, in large measure, the mental and literary possibilities of the colored race.

3d. I do not think that the Press has been properly supported, and I find the cause in the fact that the reading public, among colored people, as among all other people, will spend its money for what seems to them best and cheapest. Colored papers, from their antecedents and surroundings, cost more, and give their readers less, than papers and publications by white men.

4th. I think that the course to be pursued by the colored Press is to say less about race and claims to race recognition, and more about the principles of justice, liberty, and patriotism. It should say more of what we ought to do for ourselves,

HON, FREDERICK DOUGLASS.

and less about what the Government ought to do for us; more in the interest of morality and economy, and less in the interest of office-getting; more in commending the faithful and inflexible men who stand up for our rights, and less for the celebration of balls, parties, and brilliant entertainments; more in respect to the duty of the Government to protect and defend the colored man's rights in the South, and less in puffing individual men for office; less of arrogant assumption for the colored man, and more of appreciation of his disadvantages, in comparison with those of other varieties of men whose opportunities have been broader and better than his.

OPINION OF REV. A. A. BURLEIGH.

I am of the opinion, 1st., That if we judge journalistic pursuits in the light of the vicissitudes common to it as a business, Afro-American journalism will compare favorably with that of any other class in our country.

2d. I am of the opinion that, as a lucrative business, it has been largely a failure; but viewed from the higher standpoint of worth and usefulness, its success and achievements are as unique and unprecedented as has been the progress of our race in other respects, because (a) it has largely furnished a causeway and outlet for our stifled public sentiment, and given public expression to the under-current of thought among our people, the *sine qua non* of freedom and happiness; (b) it has greatly assisted in the unifying and centralizing of this thought, thus infusing a spirit of ambition and activity in the hearts of our people.

3d. I am of the opinion, that our Press has had neither a fair and adequate support nor recognition from our race. The causes are far-reaching and varied. Among them may be noticed: (a) Lack of confidence and appreciation among the masses; a spirit inoculated by the subtile influence of

REV. A. A. BURLEIGH, A. M.

slavery; (*b*) unequal competition with established current
literature; (*c*) intellectual and financial inability, as manifested
in collecting, selecting, classifying, and arranging matter; (I
have reference here, not to appearance on the printed page
but to its fitness, force and character,) also, a failure to get
into the markets and homes.

4th. The future course of our Press. This, doubtless,
would appear to be suggested from what has been said. Let
me add, that, as a fact, the colored man's success in every
avocation will depend, not so much at being at "par" with
the white man, but the circumstances force it, and the future
demands, that he should be par-excellent to the average white
man; not that he must know more, or be more wealthy, but
his standard must be higher. Loyalty to the eternal
principles which alone can secure human success and
happiness, must be his constant and single aim.

OPINION OF JAMES T. STILL, M. D.

I think from my limited acquaintance with negro journalism, I am not able to give unqualified, positive or negative
answers to the questions in regard to the Press in the hands
of the negro. If a statement of my opinions may be of any
value, they are as follows: I think the negro has, upon the
whole, done an immense amount of good, not for his race
only but for the American people also, by the part he has
taken in journalism. Within a few years, his participation in
this, to him, new occupation, has, by the fascinating, conta-
gious fever of imitation, rivalry, and emulation, caused
hundreds of our people, young and old, male and female, to
bring forward their thoughts, ideas, and desires before the
public; it is true, too generally, in rude garb, chirographically,
typographically, grammatically, and rhetorically; yet, upon
the whole, the volumes of these compositions have been of

JAMES T. STILL, M. D.

great value, and a better understanding has been established between the two races that might never have existed otherwise. Hence, I think the Press in the hands of the negro has been a great success. It has been supported as well, probably, as could have been reasonably expected. Remembering our position and condition when this new vocation was first eagerly entered into,—so much ignorance and want of general culture existing among us, it seems but natural that envy, jealousy and strifes, the children of this ignorance on the one side, and possibly a consciousness of superiority, imaginary or real, on the other, has caused much less support to be given to negro journals than ambitious or verdant editors anticipated. I think the future of the negro press will be bright, if conducted upon wise and business-like principles. Its motto should be one adapted to all ventures that hope for life and progress, viz: Excelsior. In order to advance under this noble banner, our editors should adopt some such general rules as these, which must be surely winning ones: Originality, accuracy, truthfulness,. promptness, manly independence. Thus conducted, I believe we should soon have one of the greatest and grandest forces for the promotion of invaluable good among the Afro-American people.

Opinion of Ex-Gov. P. B. S. Pinchback.

I think that the Afro-American Press has done good, but has fallen far short of being a success. It is not half supported. This is owing to several causes, viz: Illiteracy of the Afro-American masses, and the abundance of other and much better publications, etc., etc., If the Afro-American Press will assail more vigorously the enemies of the people it represents, adhere strictly to principles, be lenient in criticising the Afro-Americans, and elevate their moral tone, it will accomplish much good. I advise leniency

EX-GOV. P. B. S. PINCHBACK.

in criticising the faults of the Afro-American, because their enemies never fail to criticise them without stint.

OPINION OF BISHOP BENJAMIN W. ARNETT, D. D.

There is but one answer to the first question, no matter from what standpoint I look at it, whether as to number, circulation, or editorial ability displayed in the columns of the Afro-American newspaper. As regards number, I can remember when we had only one journal in the country, *The Mystery*, published by that grand hero and pioneer, Dr. Martin R. Delaney, in 1847. In 1848, the A. M. E. church started *The Christian Herald*, the first religious paper controlled by colored men. Rev. A. R. Green was manager and editor.

Frederick Douglass entered the journalistic world and pleaded the cause of his race, on two continents, with both tongue and pen. Others followed, until to-day over two hundred intelligent colored men are engaged in speaking for the race by their journals, in almost every state of the Union.

Some think that there is no necessity for colored newspapers; that papers owned and controlled by white men would answer all purposes; but I think that it is as essential to have a newspaper to speak for us as a race, as it is for each individual to have a mouth and a tongue to speak his own sentiments. It is impossible for a white man to enter into the aspirations of another race, as one who, when he expresses his own aspirations, expresses theirs also. We must have some one who can understand our position from within and without, and present it to the world in the strongest light.

Now, whether the Afro-American newspapers are supported as well as they ought to be: They are not receiving the

BISHOP BENJAMIN W. ARNETT, D. D.

support I would like them to have. But there are several things to be considered in explanation. We have had only twenty-five years of training, in the matter of a taste for reading newspapers. Previous to that time we were not allowed to read the Bible, much less a newspaper. It is a very hard thing to overcome in manhood and old age, the habits of youth; so we have had to acquire the ability to read, and create a taste for it, within the short space of twenty years. It is marvelous, therefore, to perceive that we have done so well. There is no historical parallel to it. The people need to be congratulated rather than censured, for the manner in which they support newspapers.

Many of our people buy other than Afro-American newspapers; therefore we must not take the list of subscribers to Afro-American journals as the full representation of their support of newspapers. There is no class of persons who take as many newspapers and buy as many books as the Afro-American, North and South, according to population and wealth. There is a large number of agents for books and periodicals, entirely snpported by the Afro-American. The Afro-American Press ought to utilize these men and make them contribute to the success of black as well as white enterprises. These people will take papers printed by white men, if they are brought to their door; but if the Afro-American newspaper was brought to the door in competition, nine times out of ten the Afro-American paper would be taken.

As to the fourth question, I say,—First: Let those who write do so from beneath the shadow of the Cross, and teach the people that the Gospel is more potential than dynamite; that men can do much, but God can do more; that it is better to trust in the Lord and their own individual efforts, than it is to trust in any political organization.

Secondly: The next good thing the Press can do, is to

organize the moral and religious forces and set them in motion to bring the pulpit, printing-press, school-room, college, board of trade, and farm, in communication with each other, and fight against sin, crime, intemperance, ignorance and poverty; to cultivate in every man a personal pride, in every home a family pride, in every individual a race pride; to encourage charitable and benevolent societies and the organization of co-operative associations; to support each other in business, encourage young men to learn trades, and to start some in business.

Thirdly: By encouraging the formation of organizations for the care of the living, instead of burying the dead; to buy clothes, instead of shrouds; to buy houses, instead of coffins; to buy lots in the city of the living, instead of in the city of the dead; and to teach our people that money, education, religion, morality and integrity, are the powers of race elevation; that the spelling book, Bible, and blank book are as potential as the ballot, and that one of the greatest needs of the race is "commercial power." We cannot enjoy, to its fullest extent, our social, civil, political and religious rights, without the aid of it.

OPINION OF REV. J. C. PRICE, D. D.

Yes, I think the Press in the hands of the negro has been a decided success, especially if we take into consideration the great disadvantages under which the negro has labored. The Afro-American editor has been instrumental in demonstrating the intellectual capability of the race and its eminent fitness for literary work. He has been the means of informing the public as to the negro's development, achievements and progress. I do not think that the Press has received a proper support on the part of the Afro-American. This is attributable to more than one cause. In the first place, the masses are uneducated, and, as a matter of course, they do not take to literary enterprises. We are permitted, however, to hope for more encouragement in the near and distant future.

Secondly: Some of the Press are a little to blame for this lack of support. A great many newspapers have been of the mushroom order; they spring up in a day and die equally as soon. Subscriptions are often paid, and one or two copies of the paper received, and then it is reported dead. On account of such experiences the confidence of the people and the Press is greatly shaken.

Thirdly: The Press has not always made itself attractive. Some papers contain a few locals, but real food for thought and instruction has not always been given the reader. I am glad to know there are notable exceptions. There are Afro-American editors who expect the people to take their journals, simply from the fact they are published by colored men, and not because they give an equivalent for value received, in the make-up of their paper.

As to the future course of the Press in promoting good among our people, I think it well first to inspire confidence as to its stability and devotion to the interests of the race; and at all times to take an uncompromising stand against those who outrage, oppress and malign the negro. I now, and always, hope to be the friend of the Press, and shall be glad to do all I can to advance its interests.

OPINION OF PROF. GEORGE E. STEPHENS.

1st. The negro Press has been a success, relatively speaking. I do not understand the question to have an absolute sweep. There are many milestones between it and its goal to be reached yet. In my opinion, paradoxical as it may seem, its true success will have been reached when our Press ceases to depend entirely upon the negro for support,

PROF. GEORGE E. STEPHENS.

and shall have assimilated fully with the white Press, and be considered a component part of the news-bearing instruments of our country, and, I might add, of the world.

2d. The achievements of the Afro-American editor have been of a twofold character, and they presage the final triumph, if he adjust his views to the advancement of the public thought; or if he keep pace with the progressive ideas appertaining to a wide-awake country and age like ours. His constituents, when he first began to mold public sentiment among them, had small conception of the power of the Press. In the years that have elapsed a change has been going on, and the negro has given tangible proof of it in the increased patronage he has given his own Press.

3d. It is hardly necessary to state that the efficiency of the negro Press is the measure of its support. I have already intimated that our newspapers must be cosmopolitan. An intelligent man wishes to know the doings of all the people of his own country and of the civilized world. The negro is but a fractional part of it. A paper that purports to contain the news must be a medium of it all. In looking at the negro Press from this standard, it is clearly seen that it lacks proper support from those for whom it is especially published.

4th. While party fealty, according to the shibboleth of very modern politics, deserves recognition, it may be safe to assert that the great masses of all parties are far more interested in good government than in political preferment. The negro's attention should never be divorced from an intelligent appreciation of and interest in the affairs and principles of good government; but he needs to be told plainly, positively, and continually, that neither parties nor office can, in themselves, bring him place, unchanging power, and unfailing consideration in this country.

Far greater attention, now and for a long time to come,

needs to be given to the principles of political economy and to their practical exemplification among us. The money men of the race should invest in enterprises calculated to give us a standing in the great mining, manufacturing, and commercial pursuits of the land.

The negro must be taught thorough race pride and confidence. He should be urged to combine in various kinds of business enterprises, and pay less attention to petty organizations, limited largely to ministrations to the sick and the burial of the dead. If the papers will discuss the welfare of the race along these lines, a reformation and revolution will take place, that must bring the negro and his Press in thorough assimilation with his country and age. This may not come in the memory of the youngest child now living; still it must come, and if the acquisition of this power rests upon good character, nothing beneath the sun can displace the negro.

OPINION OF HON. JOSIAH T. SETTLE, LL. B.

Considering the many difficulties which the negro has encountered in journalism, the Press in his hands, has been as great a success as thoughtful men could have anticipated. When his opportunities to prepare himself for journalism, and the length of time he has been actively engaged in it, and the field to which his opportunities are principally confined are considered, there can be no question as to the success of the Press in the hands of the negro. No other race, laboring under the same difficulties, has, in the same time, done as well.

The Afro-American editor has demonstrated the capacity of his race to win success and distinction in every department of life in which he finds his white brother a competitor. He has, by his capacity for his work, both natural and acquired, demonstrated to the world that he does not represent a race of mere imitators, but a race, which, under the same conditions, is capable of doing all the Anglo-Saxon race can accomplish. No agency has been more potent in compelling a just recognition of the negro, as a man and a citizen, than the Press in his hands. Through this agency he shows what the race is doing in the world of letters and in all the other departments of life, with a minuteness which would otherwise be impossible; thereby inspiring an earnestness and enthusiasm in his own race, and compelling the respect and admiration of all others. Through his paper, the editor stamps his individuality upon the public opinion of the day, and this individuality permeates the entire field of his circulation, making him a part of the body politic, and gives him a power for good or evil, which no other agency possibly can. The editor is a daily teacher and the reading public are his pupils, and with a well-filled mind and a trenchant pen, his capacity for good is only limited by his ability and his industry.

The Afro-American editor has done more, probably, than any other to acquaint the world with the exact condition of his race, and to him, more than any other, belongs the credit and honor of opening the way through which the negro is able to make his just demands upon those in high places, to whom is intrusted the guardianship of every right that belongs to him as a man and a citizen, as well as a member of a political party. He has made it impossible to oppress his race in secrecy and silence, and has established a sure and permanent medium through which the doings for and against his race are given to the world. He has done all this and more; he has exploded the doctrine of race inferiority, and established the moral and intellectual equality of his race, as well as his ability to win success and distinction, whenever and wherever the opportunity is given.

HON. JOSIAH T. SETTLE, LL. B.

Not being connected with the Press, but actively engaged in the practice of the law, I can not say to what extent the Press is supported by the Afro-American. That it should receive, at his hands, all the support necessary to insure its success, should not for a moment be questioned. If the proper support is withheld, the cause may rest with both the members of the Press and the people. The editor should strive to make his paper the equal of any of its kind, giving his readers as much, both in quantity and quality, as any other paper of a similar size and character. The negro has passed the point in life when mere printed matter satisfies his reader's appetite; he wants food for thought.

He should have current news of the day. The scissors can not always supply the place of brains in the editorial chair, and while we may not, and do not, expect the associate press news to be contained in all of our journals, we do expect such news as will inform us upon all the important issues of the day, and such editorials as will educate the readers upon questions of public import. Less society news, and more general information, would impart a healthier tone to most of our race journals. In fact, business, and not sentiment, is what the masses want.

When our race journals present the best medium of reaching the masses of our people, the business men of a community will not be slow to avail themselves of their use. Sentiment and prejudice can not weigh against business principles and business interests, and the more business our journals represent, the more readers they will reach. We can not expect support and patronage for an inferior journal because it happens to come from our race; nor can the reading public expect an inferior article at superior prices and with indifferent support. The annual conventions held by the Afro-American members of the Press, are doing a great work in extending its usefulness.

My opinion as to what future course the Press should take to promote the good of our people, may be expressed in u very fow words: Huvu ull of our puuplu, us far as possiblu, read our papers, and then make our papers just what they should be. The Press must devise its own means of extending its field of operation, and our people must open their hearts and purses. The direct benefits resulting will be reciprocal, and as a result the highest and best interest of our oppressed race will be promoted.

OPINION OF HON. JERE A. BROWN.

Allow me to say, first, that I know the Press in the hands of the negro has been a success, when and wherever it has been conducted in the interest of the race and not for self-aggrandizement or mercenary motives. In arriving at this conclusion my mind reverts to the events of the past forty years, when I read, for the first time, a newspaper, owned and edited and controlled by the late Major M. R. Delaney, known as *The Mystery*, and published at Pittsburgh, Pa. Short-lived as it was, it clearly demonstrated its worth and the necessity for a race paper.

Coming down through the dark days of our history, here and there, throughout the northern states, newspapers edited by colored men sprang into existence. Their specific work and object was the overthrow of slavery. and well did they perform their work. Here was a channel through which we could advocate our cause, without the fear of having it misrepresented, smoothed over, or in any manner shorn of the truth; for, as a general thing, the Press was subsidized largely by the influences created through our enforced servitude. Thus it was that we brought our woes, burdens, and grievances before the enlightened world, pressing our own way against the monster, as the ax does its work for the pioneer of the forest. Therefore, I regard the Press, in the hands of the negro, as one of the most potent levers in assisting in the total destruction of American slavery, that existed in the ante-bellum days, which is the greatest achievement, to my mind, accomplished in the history of our country, and fully answers the second question.

At present, I do not think the Press has the proper support that it should have from our people. This is a question that has many attributable causes, if one is allowed to judge from the environments of special sections of the country where such periodicals are issued. Of course we must speak of this matter in a general or national sense. As a rule, our people are poor, earning a precarious livelihood, which demands the last penny to meet the necessities of their families. We are not yet educated to that spirit of appreciation we should possess for those who are struggling to perfect themselves in journalism. The great mass of our people do not look upon our Press as educators, or even truthful reporters or delineators of the live issues of the day. Most of our papers are issued weekly, generally containing news read in the daily Press, and many things are found in them foreign to a well-conducted newspaper, which some denominate gossip; and again, there is a demand for light reading matter to the exclusion of all other. How much foundation there is for these reasons, all of which I have heard mentioned, I leave for others to decide. My opinion is this, and it is given frankly, without reference to any particular person or paper:

First: We do not yet possess a paper that we can call a national organ; if we did, it would demand national support.

Secondly: Most of our editors are comparatively young men, who have lately entered the field of journalism, often without the experience demanded, which, before they gain, their efforts are of that kind that alienate rather than draw. Although doing their best, they find themselves in debt, and

HON. JERE A. BROWN.

their subscription list reduced to such an extent that their venture perishes.

Again: The absence from the field of such a veteran in journalism as Frederick Douglass, is to me another cause; for such as he could demand, nay, command the support from our people of any paper he should edit. It is true, that, in time, these causes I have just mentioned will be removed, as our young men advance in age and become thoroughly familiarized with journalism. Having carefully watched the rise and progress of many of our Western papers, notably *The Cleveland Gazette, Detroit Plaindealer, Indianapolis World, Chicago Conservator* and others, the improvement has been so marked, both in style, perspicuity, terseness, tone and vigor, that it appears to be a transformation, although so gradual as to be almost imperceptible to the casual reader. Hence it is, I say, that we are gradually arriving at that stage of proficiency so essential for success in this particular field.

The future course of our Press, to promote good among our people, (I only speak of the secular Press,) is the teachiug of good morals; the education of our youth; the necessity of possessing refinement and culture, which stamp the true lady and gentleman; to teach every colored man, woman and child that he is an American, in all that the word implies, until this idea permeates the whole race; to teach that "the cause of one is the cause of all;" that, as we are equal in the sight of God as men, we must be equal in all things that pertain to the happiness of all men; that we were men before man made any law that detracted or abridged any of our inherent rights; to teach patience, forbearance, kindness and love towards those who are our enemies, and not seek to convince them of their injustice by saying hard words or writing threats against them; to teach our youth that, although our race was enslaved, in the history of this now proud, arrogant and haughty race which so persistently domineers over us, they can read and learn of the conquest and subjugation to slavery of the Anglo-Saxon; that he did not, in one hundred years after emerging from the Norman yoke, show as much advancement as the American negro has in twenty-five.

Last, but not least, teach an implicit faith in Him who created all men; and although his ways may appear inscrutable to us, He is still the God of our Fathers who led us from the dark, pernicious, and baneful effects of an enforced servitude.

Let me add as words of encouragement to the men and women of our race, the future of our youth depends largely upon our teachings, as it depended upon those who preceded us. We have a great work to perform, and, so far, it has been nobly done, and I am confident we shall yet do grander work. But beware of strifes against each other, bickering, jealousies, and sentimental effusions; for we need the undivided support of each other to gain that of which we have been robbed. Let us take courage from the lessons of the past; girding on our armor with renewed vigor and energy still advance, working out our own destiny, and we shall soon solve that great question, which only exists in prejudiced minds, "the Negro Problem."

OPINION OF REV. T. G. STEWART, D. D.

Twenty-five years ago, when Emancipation became a fact, and the enfranchisement of the colored people of the South became a political necessity, many reasons combined to urge the adoption of the most comprehensive and most effective measures to secure their rapid education. Christianity, humanity, and patriotism, all said these people must be taught to read at once, in order that the important lessons relating to conduct, in all its bearings, might be successfully imparted to them. Under these influences, schools were opened in all parts of the South; and the good work begun by the Northern people has, to some extent, been supplemented by the people of the South, and by the colored people themselves, in opening and maintaining such schools as Morris Brown College at Atlanta, Allen University at Columbia, and Paul Quinn College at Waco, with others of equal or lower grade. As a result of all this educational work, it is now quite certain that one-third of all the colored people of the South, over ten years of age, can read; and while we must not forget the other two-thirds who can not read, yet in locating the field for the colored man's paper, the one-third who can read must be given the chief place. From these must come, in the main, the subscribers; and without subscribers the publisher of a paper can not hope to command advertisements.

The reading population, among whom the colored man must circulate his paper, is probably about equal to the city of New York. I am now speaking with reference to the South alone. Two things will at once present themselves to our view, as we attempt to survey this field. First, we will notice that the literary appetite is quite weak, and the taste undeveloped; and, second, we will observe that the field is very poorly supplied. In regard to the appetite, I make one remark to point out its weakness. It is a recognized fact that colored readers in the South care almost exclusively for local news. Indeed, they simply desire to see their own locality written up. The news of the great, wide world, or even the news of the great, wide country, or the news even narrowed down to the experiences and doings of their own race, as they are scattered abroad throughout our land, is not desired to any great extent by them. They have but little appetite for it, and so are not willing to pay for it. This localism can not be disregarded at present.

REV. T. G. STEWART, D. D.

473

A word as to the taste: It must be remembered that these people have not been reading long, and consequently have not read much. The colored editor can not mold his weekly after the literary weekly of the country, nor after the daily of the city. His model must be, rather, the average country weekly; and he must afford such reading matter as will suit his customers. The great colored newspaper must begin at the bottom and grow up with the advancing race. So far as I am able to judge, neither the great newspaper, nor the great editor, has yet appeared; but I have no doubt that the editor will come, and come from the ranks of those who are passing through the experience common to those who have been enslaved.

Many things in politics, religion, and philosophy seem to combine to point out for the American negro an important and commanding future. The great poets, orators, and literary men of the nation ought to, and I believe will, come from this race. Compelled to come up fresh from first principles, they will throw a glow of warmth and originality over American literature, which the world will not fail to recognize. To assist in shaping the course of the writers and bringing out this literature, is the mission of the colored man's paper. Up to the present, he has been presenting crude and cheap thoughts, and dealing with unimportant, petty facts, and reeling off much jargon. He is running off the froth of an effervescent race; but the good wine will come after a while, and these rich, fresh minds will give out their brilliant, sparkling thoughts in charming melody, and the colored man's newspaper, purged of its dross, will be as pure gold.

I do not leave out of account, in marking out the field for the colored man's journal, the thousands of colored people scattered throughout the North. These are the Old Guard. They have shown their faith, over and over again, by their works. But it must be remembered that, to a large extent, through the public schools and other methods, they have become amalgamated with the general citizenship, and a race paper does not appeal to them with the force which it did a quarter of a century ago.

The great field for journalism to be represented by the Afro-American Press must be in the late slave states; and it is a field which promises an abundant harvest, in both literary and pecuniary results. To mold and solidify this race in the South-land, to inspire and direct the Afro-American, I conceive to be, in conjunction with other forces, the mission of the Afro-American Press.

OPINION OF PROF. J. H. LAWSON.

To the 1st and 2d questions, I answer, I do. I use the term success as commonly understood. The negro Press is part of the American Press. It is a vital part. It has done much in elevating a favorable sentiment in regard to the negro question. This I consider a positive gain. It has done much in vindicating local rights of negroes. It has been the chief source of knowledge as to how the machinery of government is operated. It has demonstrated negro capacity. It is the mouth-piece of negroes in legislative halls, where they can not speak. In fine, whatever claim is set up for the great American Press, a proportional part is due to the negro. As the body is not whole if deprived of any of its members, so the American Press is shorn of its full praise, if the negro's contribution to it goes unnoted and for naught.

To the third question I must say: I think it does. Colored papers are too costly. I can buy *The New York Tribune* for three cents, but I can not buy a negro paper for less than five cents. I have yet to see the colored paper,

PROF. J. H. LAWSON.

with texture and quality equal to *The Tribune.* It seems to me, now, that an intelligent man, or one simply desiring information, would see what benefit he is getting for his money, in taking a paper. It is the principle in all other matters. I can see no reason why it should not apply here. As a rule, both editorial and news-matter are of higher quality in white papers. The news-matter in colored papers is absolutely worthless. Whatever news there is of public or special interest, is first procured by white papers, which, for the most part, have agents on the spot. For news, the colored paper falls back upon the white paper. Sympathy, on the ground of race pride, is an unjust and unmanly demand. It is dangerous as well, since unworthy papers might feed upon public patronage and usurp the field of meritorious ones.

To the fourth question I answer:

1st. To consolidate in dailies.

2d. To employ good editors, managers and correspondents.

3d. To use the same means employed by the best papers of the country.

CHAPTER XXIII.

THE AFRO-AMERICAN EDITOR'S MISSION, BY EMINENT JOURNALISTS.

THE AUTHOR'S INTRODUCTORY.

IN the light of the opinions here rendered regarding Afro-American journalism, the purpose and aim of the author is to have actual assertions from three of the prominent personages in the field as to their idea of the great work intrusted to their keeping. The press, the most potent factor for good on the one hand, or for evil on the other, must be piloted in the light of the knowledge as to how it will subserve the best interests of the nation. It must of all forces be pure, and free from any contaminating influence, be it in the religious or secular field, it being far from our aim to insert here articles from these personages merely to "fill up," but to give an interested public the information as to what we are striving for in our exercise of the freedom of the press. At the instance of the foregoing letters, Hon. T. Thomas Fortune, representing the secular press, Rev. L. J. Coppin, D. D., the religious press, and Mrs. N. F. Mossell, our women, give us the benefit of what they conceive to be the telling work at their command. The following is a copy of the communication sent them: The Afro-American editor should, most assuredly, know for what he is striving, and the public, in whose welfare he is interested, should know, through this medium, in what way he is using his freedom in their behalf. Will you, as an Afro-American editor, kindly consent to give me your purpose in journalism, and your views as to the mission of Afro-American newspapers?

Dr. Coppin was requested to give his views upon "Our Work as Journalists;" while Mrs. Mossell was asked to give hers upon "The Power of the Press," and "Our Women in Journalism." How near the views of these writers meet the expressions of the many whose opinions will be found in the preceding chapter of this book, can be readily seen by the editor and reader. As Mr. Fortune says in his letter: "Editors are servants of the people, more than any other class of servants," and, as such, the people's right to understand in what way their servants are striving for their total freedom, is a right of theirs which in no way can be denied.

Opinion of T. Thomas Fortune.

If the institution of slavery hung for four years upon a doubtful contingency, and was overthrown at last by the proclamation of President Lincoln and the obstinacy of President Davis, it will readily be perceived that the final adjustment of the questions arising from the conditions of negro citizenship offers as many snares for the wary feet of statesmen of the present and the future, as did the questions growing out of the conditions of the negro as a slave to statesmen of the past, many of whom beat themselves to death against those questions, and carried with them to the grave their shattered hopes and tarnished fame.

If the negro did not carry with him in his face a proclamation of his race and previous condition of servitude, as lepers in Oriental countries are compelled to cry aloud upon the approach of strangers their accursed isolation from the rest of mankind, a half-century would have sufficed to obliterate from the minds of men the facts that slavery once prevailed in the Republic, and that the slaves were now free men and citizens, equal under the Constitution and before the laws and the other citizens of the country; but the mark of color remains and makes its possessor a social pariah, to be robbed, beaten and lynched,—and a political nondescript, who has got his own salvation to work out, of equality before the laws, with almost the entire white population of the country arrayed against him.

Surely, no race of people ever had a larger job on their hands than have the colored citizens of the United States. The older they grow, the larger the job will become; so that fifty years hence, it will be to this government all that the Irish question is to-day to the government of Great Britain, and perhaps more. Read by the light of history, the signs of the times, since the close of the Civil War, all point unerringly to the conclusion here reached. There are those, I am mindful, learned in the wisdom of age and experience, who regard this view of the situation as that of an alarmist; but, as Patrick Henry declared, "I have but one lamp by which my feet are guided," and that is the history of the vicissitudes of other races, whose condition was not unlike, in many respects, the condition of the colored citizens of this Republic. Already we are in the fury and heat of the conflict, but thousands of us do not know it, or, knowing, take no heed of the awful fact, and will continue to nurse the ignorance Alexander Pope declared to be bliss, until aroused by some shock which shall destroy, once for all, the citadel where we have harbored our sublime confidence.

It is here that the relations the negro Press sustains to the negro problem, are thrown out as clearly as the sun in the heavens, against the mountainous wall of observation. The newspaper has become, in every country where modern civilization exists, the oracle of the people. More than that, it has become the defender of the just rights of the people against the encroachments of the ambitious and the covetous few; so that it may of a truth be said that error and wrong can not long prevail where the Press is left free to combat them. The editors of the great newspapers are more absolutely the servants of the people than any of the servants placed in positions of trust and profit and power by their votes. They are more faithful to the people's interest, they are more inaccessible to the allurements of corruptionists, they have generally a clearer and more thorough understanding of the rights of the people, and voice their demands with greater accuracy and force, than any other class of men in the Republic, simply because they live nearer to the people and are, in many respects, the servants, in a more general sense, of the public opinion to which they give voice. The people are true to the editors only just as long as the editors are true to the people. An editor, with no readers of his paper, is in a much more pitiable plight than a lawyer without briefs, or a preacher without a charge.

Only those who understand thoroughly the serious nature of the contention of colored citizens for the cession to them of their full rights under the Constitution, and the magnitude and power of those who are now withholding those rights, and who also correctly estimate the commanding influence of the modern newspaper in creating, as well as giving, voice to public opinion, can have a correct idea of the great work reserved to the colored newspapers of the country. Even the colored people themselves do not understand it. Some of them even declare that colored newspapers are a nuisance; and so they are, in a measure, just as the colored people are a nuisance, in so far as they have a grievance which they

31

persistently obtrude upon the notice of others, who either have no such grievance themselves, or do not wish to be reminded of the fact that they have one. As long, however, as men are struck, they will cry out in protest or indignation until the wrongs are avenged.

A sufficient answer to all those who do not understand why we have colored newspapers, would seem to be the fact that white men have newspapers; that they are published by white men for white men; give, in the main, news about white men, and pitch their editorial opinions entirely in the interest of white men. I know that there are many papers in the country whose editors make great profession of love for colored citizens; but they are partisan advocates, striving for partisan advantage, and have no more real, practical love for the negro than the editors of newspapers, avowedly their enemies. I have more respect for the latter than for the former. An open enemy is an easier man to handle than a hypocritical friend. A man who preaches one thing and practices another, is beneath contempt. Is there one paper published by white men in any one of the eleven Southern states to-day, in which colored men receive the same news and editorial treatment that white men receive? Let those ignorant negroes, who pretend that they can not understand why colored newspapers are published, answer this question; and if they can not, let them slink away out of the sight of honest men who understand the serious nature of the negro problem, and are honestly endeavoring to solve it in the right way. I confess that I have small patience with this sort of negro Jonah. I would throw him overboard in short order, and with no thought or care that he find a haven from death in some vagrant whale's belly.

As a regrettable fact, the white Press of the South is leagued against the negro and his rights, and it is re-enforced by quite two-thirds of the Press of the North and West.

How are we to overcome this tremendous influence? Are we to prevail against our enemies *not* as other men prevail against theirs? Can we reasonably expect other men to use their lungs to cry out for us when we are wronged and outraged and robbed and murdered? If we do, let us look at the white papers of the South and learn from them the necessary lesson, that the only way we can hope ever to win our fight is to arm ourselves as our opponents do, support those newspapers alone that support us, and support those men alone who support us. In following this rule, white men's newspapers, and white men's schemes of ambition or profit, will, very generally, be weighed in the balance and found wanting.

The colored newspapers of the United States, some one hundred and twenty-five, are the only papers that are making a square, honest fight for the rights of our race. Not one of them receives the support it deserves; and, mainly on that account, not one is doing the work it could and should do. A colored newspaper, with one hundred thousand subscribers, would be a greater power for good than any other agency colored men could create,—than even fifty black members of Congress would be; and until we have newspapers equal in circulation to those controlled by our enemies, the contest for our just rights under the Constitution will remain pitiably unequal. We must realize this fact before we can expect to cope with the enemy.

OPINION OF REV. L. J. COPPIN, D. D.

The subject, "Our Work as Journalists," is as important as it is comprehensive. The journalist has the largest audience of all the public speakers. The Pulpit and the Rostrum address themselves to the hundreds who come within hearing distance; but their utterances are taken up by the Press and

given to the multiplied millions who read. Such an opportunity to be heard is accompanied with grave responsibilities;
therefore, to faithfully echo the voice of others is among the
first and most important duties of the journalist.

The journal that simply seeks to attract, without a due
regard for truth, justice and fair play, dishonors itself and
the journalistic fraternity; is unworthy of public support, and
will eventually be crowded out by more worthy contemporaries. The columns of a public journal should never be
used as a sewerage for that which is harmful and degrading.
Such matter may tickle the ear of the gossip-seeker, and by
attracting a large class of such readers, enable its editor to
boast of "the largest circulation;" but it is the prostitution
of a high office, which, in the end, will meet its just deserts.
In these days, when sensational and degenerate literature
is doing so much to corrupt our youth, I say to every
journal in the land, "Keep thyself pure."

The journalist is the people's attorney. He has every
man's case, and can rightfully have but one purpose, which
is, justice to all. It is no fault of his, if justice itself makes
against his client; his only business is to be a faithful
recorder of the *facts in the case.* As a public recorder of
facts, then, our work as journalists is to make faithful entries,
in all cases, and we are not at liberty at any time to so change
things as to make them suit our fancy.

The journalist is a molder of sentiment; or, as it is, perhaps,
more frequently called, "public opinion." It is a mistaken
idea for a journalist to suppose that it is his business to take
the "public pulse" and then adapt himself to whatever
condition he finds to exist. It is his business to educate and
to elevate public opinion; and if he is true to his trust, he
will find himself equal to the task. Public opinion is an
organism, and must have something to feed upon, in order to
live. True to nature, its development will be after the

manner of the food it eats. Sometimes a false growth is
made, and then it is the business of the journalist to use
corrective measures.

For many years, it was the prevailing opinion in this
country that a man had a perfect right to own men and
women, and to deal in them as marketable property. Had
there not been among those who were in the minority brave,
wise, and good men to protest against such an evil, slavery
might have remained until to-day. This minority was weak
at first, but possessing the elements of right, it possessed also
the elements of power. And so with all moral reforms; they
are brought about finally in answer to a public demand; but
a demand upon the public had first to be made, in order to
bring it into the right way of thinking, and to induce it to
act according to duty. While we should hesitate to make
any one agency responsible for the course that public opinion
finally takes, we venture the assertion that no agency is so
fruitful in this direction as that of the public Press.

There was a time when the public speaker had almost sole
charge of this business. But the printer's ink has largely
taken his place; that is, it multiplies his words a thousand
fold. Give us wise, judicious, reliable and high-toned newspapers, and we are most likely to have a public opinion that
is safe, and worthy to be consulted.

But "Our Work as Journalists," as we take it, has special
reference to colored journalists. We have purposely first
called attention to those general rules which govern journalism,
because they are applicable to all. This is a comparatively
new field for colored men, and their work is specially
important because it is two-fold. Besides representing the
public in a general way, as we have already remarked, they
stand in a particular sense for their people. It is folly for
any one to shut his eyes to the fact, that the war for human
rights in this country is not closed. When the agitation for

freedom began, the colored man was not in the position to speak for himself; so the work had to be done almost entirely by his friends. But in his new condition, he must be the principal actor in securing the rights and privileges yet denied him. We must have leaders, just as all people have; and this fact brings the colored people to the front. Our newspapers must be a reliable source of thought and direction for the masses of our people. Here their grievances must be recorded, with suggestions as to how they may be redressed.

Another department of work among us as journalists, is to guide the masses into the best way of living. No people can be legislated into greatness. All we ask, all we can ask, all that any people can ask, of the Government is, that a fair chance in the race of life shall be guaranteed. We must do the running ourselves. There are certain things that tend to the elevation of a people, and without these no substantial progress can be made. First of all, we should say a good, solid character must be built up and maintained. History unites with reason in recording the fact, that no people of weak and corrupt morals has been able to endure. Slavery left us an abundant heritage of moral weakness which must be overcome. The fact that it is inherited can be no excuse for its continued existence. In rising to positions of responsibility and trust, the same demand for virtue will be made upon us that is made upon others; and less than this would not be for our good.

The accumulation of wealth is also a necessary factor in the elevation of a people. Poverty is weakness. Especially is this true when predicated of a people situated as we are, in the midst of a strong nation. Weakness can not dictate terms to strength. To remain *en masse* in the position of servants, is to be handicapped and kept down. With great odds against us, great sacrifices must be made in order to materially change our present condition. Industry and economy must go hand in hand; for it is not so much what men earn that makes them rich, as what they save.

Great stress has been laid upon the work of education among us. We should not feel free to recommend an abatement of this work; but it is already apparent that an industrial education must form no little part of it. Unskilled labor demands small revenue, compared with skilled; and, besides, for that kind of work the supply is greater than the demand. As yet we are largely of the laboring class, and in order to make any headway, must make our labor valuable. It behooves the journalists among us to consider well such questions as these and to give no uncertain sound in bringing them before the public.

OPINION OF MRS. N. F. MOSSELL.

Every few months we find some amateur literary association discussing the question of the comparative power of the Press and the Pulpit. It used to be a standing subject for discussion and amusement, but the laugh, in the opinion of the religious world, has completely died out.

That the Press is intrenching on the power of the Pulpit is growing more evident daily. People are coming to prefer to sit by their own cosy firesides and read sermons at their leisure, to traveling in inclement weather to the house of worship; and the poor feel they are thus on a level with the rich, or, at least, are not pained by the contrast in their conditions, as they often are when assembled in the house of God.

What world of meaning in the phrase, "The Power of the Press!" Our colored men are realizing its latent force. Through this medium they are rapidly pushing their way, strengthening race pride, and making their wants and oppressions known. Every corporation or large business house now has its own journals, advertising its goods, and delighting its patrons with its literary feast. The Press is a sleeping lion, which men are just waking into life. We should estimate rightly the great obligation that is upon us to use this immense power rightly. We, of all people, can ill afford to make blunders. We must teach wisely and lead aright, that the generation to come may bless us, as we bless those who have passed before us. Our Press association is well organized, and we should be able, at its meetings, to give each other wise counsel.

The study of other journals, from every point of view, has its benefits: their circulation and where they circulate; the editorials, the news letters, the personals; every department; reading articles on journalism; noting our own experiences from day to day; and getting the advice of those who have grown gray, and perhaps lost fortunes in the cause.

We should study the field from which our support must come. One New York publisher knows every county in every state and the literary caliber of its inhabitants, and is therefore able to put each book he has for sale on the market, at the best advantage to himself and the author. How many of our editors have thus studied the colored constituency of the various states?

We must watch the signs of the times and show business tact. I am forcibly reminded that the white race, even the ignorant portion, possesses this faculty largely beyond our own people, even the intelligent ones among us. A white man, knowing it was a season for negro revivals, furnished himself with a goodly-size bundle of spiritual hymns, and went shouting them up and down the street, and the colored people flocked to him with their pennies. Not a single white face did I see among them but that of the singer, who was gathering in the dimes and nickels from our poor. It was fit tribute to his business tact.

MRS. N. F. MOSSELL.

Our journals should improve greatly in this decade upon which we are now entering,—this bright opening of the New Year and century. Let the work and field be studied, a policy marked out; and the greatest good to the greatest number be the aim of each. Get the intelligent sympathy and advice of all connected with publications. Form syndicates and pay for good articles on selected subjects from our best writers and authors. Secure the assistance of some wise, helpful, intelligent, and enthusiastic woman. Do your best, and success will surely crown your effort.

Before closing, we must speak of "Our Women in Journalism." They are admitted to the Press' association and are in sympathy with the male editors; but few have become independent workers in this noble field of effort, being yet satellites, revolving round the sun of masculine journalism. They still remain willing captives, chained to the chariot wheels of the sterner element, and deem it well, if 'united they stand.'

Let us have a few more years of co-operative work. Our women have a great field in literary work. Sex nor color does not bar, for neither need be known. As reporters, women are treated with the courtesy due their sex. We have tact, quick perception, and can readily gain access to both sexes. Again, we are "lookers on in Venice." We are not in the thick of the battle. We have time to think, frame our purposes, and carry them into effect, unlike the editor harassed with both literary and business work and other great responsibilties incident to such an enterprise.

Women can do much to purify and strengthen life through the columns of the daily press, or the weekly, or monthly journals. Right well do they seem to appreciate their opportunities; and a broad view of life and its purposes will come to them through this source. Let one who desires journalism as her life-work, study to acquire a good knowledge of the English language, and of others, if she desires; but the English language she must. Be alive to obtain what is news, what will interest. Let the woman select her *nom do plume*, or take her own name, if she prefers, and use it always, unless for some special purpose it is changed. Write oftenest for one journal and on one subject; or on one line, at least, until a reputation has been established. Work conscientiously, follow the natural bent, and the future will not fail to bring its own reward.

I shall close this article by a note on our late advancement in journalistic effort. We have one daily, published in Georgia; an illustrated paper, published in Indianapolis; (*The Freeman*, E. E. Cooper editor and proprietor ; one paper published as the only journal in the town ; one colored editor, H. O. Flipper, editing, temporarily, a white journal, in the absence of its editor; and several women editors of various publications and departments.

Hoping that these few scattered, irregular thoughts on "The Power of the Press" and "Our Women in Journalism" may serve as seed-thoughts to lead to more serious thinking, I bid my readers adieu, believing that no brighter path opens before us, as a race, than that of the journalism of the present age.

CHAPTER XXIV.

THE ANGLO-SAXON AND THE AFRO-AMERICAN PRESS.

TO the reader of our current literature, and to the slightest observer of our literary efforts, the positions of the Anglo-Saxon and the Afro-American newspaper seems curious and interesting, as well as important. The former, through its many years of existence, has been backed and supported by an intellectual and reading people, whose love for the sublime and beautiful in literature, as well as a thirst for an actual knowledge of the affairs of the world, has been transmitted from generation to generation. In the exercise of its power it has known no opposition, save the little friction occurring between the North and South. Its resources are manifold; while its ability to create sentiment among the people for whom it is especially published is readily conceded. The latter has not been backed and supported by a reading people; the masses of its readers now have only been allowed the privilege of reading within the last twenty-five years; therefore, with respect to support upon the part of its people there is no comparison. Then allowing for the great lack of editorial ability upon the part of many white and black journals, all things considered from a comprehensive standpoint, there is no equality between the Anglo-Saxon and Afro-American Press. The reader, with but little reflection, can produce ten able and competent Anglo-Saxon editors to one of our people; to say more than ten, would be a questionable matter, since "the solution of the race problem" would most likely render some editor barren of editorial food.

There is a wide distribution of the Anglo-Saxon papers, while the readers of such are easily impressed with good or bad by their ready ability to understand properly what they read. The white papers have for their field of readers both the Anglo-Saxon and Afro-American; in fact, the entire world. It knows no rejection; it seeks the uttermost parts of the globe to deliver its news.

From a recent calculation, it seems that 100,000 (perhaps more, certainly not less) Afro-Americans are regular subscribers to the white journals, not including the vast number, who, while traveling, or in public places, etc., incidentally purchase the products of their more favored brother's brains. The writer is under the impression that two-thirds of the reading Afro-Americans support the white dailies and weeklies, at a cost of from one to six dollars per annum, while many of them fail to support the black papers, even at the lower cost of from seventy-five cents to two dollars per annum.

There is much argument put forth by those who support white journals in preference to our black ones, which is plausible, and which we shall not refute or affirm; neither are these thoughts penned as a denunciation of those who support white journals; nor is an attempt made to injure the patronage of the above-named papers.

There are other vast differences that go to make up the relative inequality of the two presses. Enough has been said, however, to show their relation, and the reader, in a concluding thought on this point, must be compelled to concede the superior power of the Anglo-Saxon press. The Afro-American is also left to see that his press will never be able to overcome the arguments he makes against it, in his support of the white journals, until his big heart causes him to correspondingly support his race papers.

We can now see the relation of the two presses to each other, and that not only is there no equality between them, but a vast inequality; hence, an organized effort of one against the other admits of no argument, and the suppression of one by the other of no commendation. Let us ascertain the duty of the two, and let us examine the claim which a country has upon the Press, unmindful of its color, its size or circulation, the previous condition of its editors, or what not. Let us at once admit the fact, that for the welfare of the country, its development and its progress, the safety of its people and its institutions, the perpetuity of its government, something is demanded of the Press, which has been termed in another chapter of this volume a bulwark of the nation.

For convenience and brevity, we will consider in order the various demands made upon the Press of a common country:

1st. It pleads for a recognition of the fact, that in the Press rests the ability to cause the development of a country.

2d. Equality of citizenship, and constant entreaty for law and order in the community and respect for the eternal principles of law, which make up a good government.

3d. An advancement of every measure for the protection of life, property and the pursuit of happiness, which has been handed down from Jeffersonian times, and which will remain sacred and true for all generations.

These, with hundreds of other demands, the Press should work for. There should be no friction in contending for these cardinal principles, only when there is a legitimate and reasonable difference of opinion in the advocacy of them.

Certainly, no friction ought to arise on account of the fact that a white man or a black man edits the journal. Are we not all here to stay, both white and black? Are we not all black or white citizens? Are we not all expected to respect the majesty of the law? Is not an editorial, written in the interest of the country's development, an article in favor of the black man, as well as the white?

We feel assured that the reader has already arrived at the conclusion that a suitable response to the above questions is Yes. We wonder why every man, as well as every editor, does not see that God created all men equal, and that He is recorded in His Holy Word as a non-respecter of persons. We wonder why the Afro-American yet suffers for a lack of protection; why it is that the argument brought forth is "their condition," since there are men and women, with Ethiopian blackness, acknowledged to be great orators, editors, teachers, etc.; yet these persons, though well behaved, neatly dressed, and with plenty of money, can not be admitted to first-class accommodations upon the trains, in the hotels, and many places of public amusements. But amid our wonderings, we come to the conclusion that this is not the state of affairs in all the land; that there is yet a phalanx of our more favored brothers, North and South, who recognize the "Fatherhood of God and the brotherhood of man."

We have been noticing the duty of the Anglo-Saxon and Afro-American press in a common country. Now let us lift the curtain and behold the Anglo-Saxon press, North and South, its views of our race, and its manly fight for and against us. We shall also beg indulgence while we give expression to some views of eminent white men, North and South, on the race question, which so decidedly divides the press. With regard to the commendatory opinions of Afro-Americans, great stress has been laid upon the statement, (which is generally admitted among us as a fact) that the entire North has been our friend and the entire South our enemy. This the author considers a very erroneous view of the matter! Let us consider it in the light of past and present circumstances, and see if we can not find men, both in the North and South, who take a friendly view of the Afro-American. We do not propose, however, to question the belief that the majority of the Afro-Americans' strongest friends are in the North; but in both the North and South we assert that the Anglo-Saxon newspapers and individuals may be divided into three distinct classes,—the friendly, the semi-friendly, and the unfriendly. The majority of the white citizens, North and South, thank God, are friendly to us. The friendly class of editors are of that humane and Christian sect that recognize the Afro-American as a man, created in the image of God, susceptible to the same improvement as any other race, and entitled to a fair chance with others in the ways of life, especially, in the necessary educational advantages of which he was so recently unlawfully deprived; and also to a filial consideration from those for whom they labored so long, without even a kind word or a pleasant look for a reward,—whose families they protected from harm or danger, while "Master" was unable to protect them himself. They are those editors who encourage the education of the black man, justice and equality to him as a citizen, with a fair chance for the exercise of suffrage, upon the plea that he is a man, a brother, and a citizen, regardless of the educational ability, *en masse*, for such exercise. The friendly editors waste not their time and talents in advocating the disfranchisement of the black man, when he is daily increasing in literary ability, wealth, and social importance. They are those who have the good sense to know that twenty years after such rights have been granted the Afro-Americans, it is positively foolish to advocate their nullification

The friendly men who do not, as the editor, wield their pens in the black man's defense, liberally respond to his call for help. They glory in the advancoment of the Afro-American; and accord him intellectual, moral, and religious position. They are those who, from the sacred desk, the hustings, the marts of trade, plead for the elevation of the Afro-American from the depth of ignorance and superstition. They are those who do not argue that the condition of the black man is the cause of his rejection and non-recognition, and offer no remedy for his elevation; but they heed the black man's continued cries for assistance, in his efforts to advance; those who give a listening ear as he cries—"Save me, or I perish." This friendly class knows that we are seeking for educational, moral and religious improvement, not social equality; and when others demand the expulsion of the race from America, though we have been here three hundred years, they, in accents loud and strong, proclaim our freedom. They say: "Educate him; make him a man; let him stay." Oh, for a phalanx of such friends! Who knows but that God has entrusted this home mission to this phalanx? While, as has been noted, these friends are found in the South, as well as the North, yet when it comes to this mission work, they know no South, no North, but the broad United States, where the Afro-American is to stay, and where he is to be prepared for the duties of citizenship.

For the benefit of the reader, and to support the assertions here made by actual expressions of some of the editors, let us behold their testimony. *The Indianapolis Journal* says: "From present indications, the colored race in this country will not much longer be lacking in numerous examples of men who have earned recognition by their ability, education and force of character. The election of a colored student as class-orator at Harvard University, has already been

32

mentioned in *The Journal.* The same thing came near happening last week at Cornell. Prof. Langston, of Virginia, who is now making speeches in Ohio, surprises the people of that State by his cultivated oratory and eloquence. Prof. W. S. Scarborough, a negro of unmixed blood, who fills the chair of Greek and Latin in Wilberforce University, is one of the finest Greek scholars in this country, the author of a Greek text-book now used in Harvard, Yale, and other colleges, the translator of many Greek classics, and, though less than forty years old, a recognized authority in Greek literature. He ranks high as an essayist and lecturer, and has published papers which have attracted attention, on " Andocides and the Andocidean orations," the " Eclogues of Virgil," the " Greek Verb" and " Fatalism in Homer and Virgil." Prof. Scarborough was born a slave in Georgia in 1852, and is a graduate of Oberlin College, Ohio. He has pursued the right course to obtain recognition for his race and himself, and nobody can make him believe that the negro is incapable of progress, or that the way is not open for him if he has the qualities to win."

On the question of Afro-American emigration, *The Journal* further remarks: " *The Journal* sees no reason why colored people should desire to emigrate from the United States to Mexico. This is a better country than Mexico, in every way, —better to be born in, to live in, and to die in. It is better for the black man, as well as the white man. Circumstances have made it the black man's home, as much as the white man's. The colored people have done their share towards contributing to the prosperity of the country, and have a right to stay here. There is work for them here, as well as in Mexico. There is abundance of room for them here, and more avenues of usefulness and happiness open to them than they would find in Mexico."

In various editorial articles on this subject, *The Hartford*

(Conn.) *Courant* and *The St. Paul* (Minn.) *Pioneer Press* indorse *The Journal* by taking the same view of the question. *The Chicago* (Ill.) *Inter-Ocean*, one of the largest and most widely circulated papers of the Northwest, gives the following opinion of Afro-American progress: "In the entire history of mankind, no race has ever made such rapid progress against tremendous odds as the colored people of this country have since the chains of slavery were stricken off, less than a generation ago. Nor did emancipation, followed as it was by enfranchisement, remove their disabilities. The negro color has remained, with all its disadvantages."

Commenting on the election of Mr. C. G. Morgan to the class oratorship of Harvard College. it says; "Such a star as Clement Gerrett Morgan relieving the darkness, is a star of hope for the entire race. By doing him justice, his college associates performed a high duty, which can not fail to exert a most wholesome general influence upon the public sentiment of the country, and prepare the way for the enforcement, South as well as North, of the last and crowning amendment to our national Constitution. It will not long be possible to deny, and with impunity trample under foot, the political rights of a race that has, in this centennial year of the Constitution, borne off what may fairly rank as the highest of collegiate honors."

These are only a few of the comments on the progress of the race from Northern journals. We will name a few of the hundreds that declare for his development incessantly: *The New York Independent, New York Press, Philadelphia Press, New York Tribune, Springfield Republican, Boston Herald, Philadelphia Evening Bulletin, Rochester Democrat and Chronicle, The Baltimore American, The Minneapolis Tribune,* and *The Journalist.*

Let us examine the views of the Southern press, and ascertain its opinion of the Afro-American and his condition, etc.: The view of *The San Antonio* (Tex.) *Express*, far in the sunny South, is the first whose testimony sounds friendly. Says *The Express*: "All schemes for the removal of the Afro-American are schemes and nothing more. He has lived in America long enough to become part and parcel of it. He will not be taken to Africa, South America or Mexico, or anywhere else. If the promoters of these attempts to get rid of a very valuable and necessary class of citizens could revisit the earth 100 years from now and see the man and brother in his perfected state of development, they would return to their graves with a feeling of weariness over the fact that they could have been so foolish in life."

The Natchez (Miss.) *Democrat* is awakening to a sense of its duty, as the following clipping will show: "The negro is here to stay, and it is the part of wisdom and humanity to make his condition as prosperous and contented under just laws as circumstances will permit and the higher civilization of the dominant whites demands it should be."

To our mind this argument is good. Higher Christian civilization will not suffer itself to oppress the weak and ignorant; it rather seeks to lift them up.

The Chattanooga Times, another Southern contemporary, says: "That the negro has acquired twenty millions worth of taxable property in Texas and two hundred millions in the late slave states,—these things go for naught with the crusaders who would hustle them off the continent as aggregated nuisances. These attacks on the race by a section of the press have undoubtedly encouraged attacks on quiet negroes and a wanton abuse of them in many instances."

A most commendable and sensible view of the race question is also taken by *The Raleigh* (N. C.) *News and Observer* in the following language, which can not fail of appreciation and interest. Speaking of the race, the editor says: "We wish to see them all elevated and brought to a full realization of the duties of citizenship, and all enlightened as to society, to the state, and to the community in which they live and of which they form a part. Notwithstanding the white race has been the most progressive known in history, notwithstanding they have been entirely free since their original settlement in the wilderness of this new world, we find among our white people here in North Carolina much poverty, much illiteracy, much backwardness in the progressive ways of the world."

There are other Anglo-Saxon newspapers in the South which take a kindly and sympathetic view of the race as is done in the North. The most prominent are the following: The *Knoxville* (Tenn) *Journal*, *The Petersburg* (Va.) *Index Appeal*, *The Memphis Commercial*, *The Charleston* (*S. C.*) *News and Courier*, *The Atlanta* (Ga.) *Constitution*, *The Charlotte* (N. C.) *Chronicle*, *The New Orleans* (La.) *Picayune*, and *The St. Louis Republican*.

The progress of the race, however, has called forth louder and more friendly expressions from whites in the North and South, than from editors of newspapers. We can not fail to call attention to some of these views from our friends. At the suggestion of Ex-President Rutherford B. Hayes, Mr. A. K. Smiley, proprietor of the Mohonk Lake House, one of the New York summer resorts, invited a conference of leading men, North and South, recently, to assemble at his hotel for a discussion on the "race question." Addresses were made by distinguished white men of the country favorable to the Afro-American, prominent among whom were Gen. S. C. Armstrong of the H. M. and Agr. Inst., Dr. Allen of the Presbyterian Board of Missions, Dr. A. F. Beard of the American Missionary Society, President Gill of the Swarthmore College, Judge Tourgee, President Woodworth of Tougaloo University, and Andrew D. White.

One of the greatest and most telling speeches made during the conference was by Rev. Joseph E. Roy, whose effort on ·"The Higher Education of the Negro,—No Mistake," was a high compliment to the race and an exhaustive account of our situation in the South. In the course of his speech he introduced the following expression from Col. J. S. L. Preston of Lexington, Va., which speaks well for our situation in that state: "I speak advisedly when I say that the negro population in this locality has made surprising progress in material, intellectual, moral and religious departments, since their emancipation."

Upon the question of higher education, or the danger of over-education on the part of the Afro-American, Mr. Roy quotes Prof. A. K. Spence as follows: "None; the danger is just the opposite, that of under-education. A smattering of knowledge may work conceit, while thorough study makes men modest. The black man is a *man;* apply to him all the rules of humanity. Good for white, good for black."

This conference, familiarly termed The Lake Mohonk Negro Conference, passed resolutions as a result of their deliberations, commending the Afro-American as educators, students, land owners, etc., and urged better home life among them as a mass, industrial training in connection with the education of the head, and the formation of enlightened Christian · sentiment on the race question and an unselfish service on the part of the whites, in helping the Afro-American to help himself. The fact of Ex-President Hayes having been elected president of the conference, brings to mind his Fourth of July oration in 1888, at Woodstock, Conn., on which occasion he said:

"The colored people were held in bondage, and therefore in ignorance, under the Constitution of the nation. They were set free and made citizens and voters by the most solemn expression of the nation's will; and now, therefore, the duty to fit them by education for citizenship is devolved upon the whole people."

The sentiment of Bishop Fowler of the M. E. church is one ringing with truth and encouragement. Says he : "One hundred and thirty years hence, and the Stars and Stripes will float over a thousand million citizens,—almost as many as the entire population of the earth to-day. What a privilege to have a hand in forming and developing the institutions of to-day ! The six million colored people will be grown to one hundred and fifty million, with great universities and renowned scholars, with statesmen and rulers, with honors second to none known to the race. It can not be a vain thing to purify the fountain, out of which such a vast stream shall flow, Brothers, be patient. With one hundred and fifty millions back of you, nothing shall be impossible to you."

Bishop Whipple, in delivering the opening address at the Episcopal convention in New York City, October, 1889, said: " We have some problems peculiar to ourselves. Twenty-five years ago, four million slaves received American citizenship. The nation owes them a debt of gratitude. During all the horrors of our civil war, they were protectors of Southern women and children. Knowing the failure of their masters would be the guarantee of their freedom, there was not one act that master or slave might wish to blot out. We ought not, and God will not forget it. To-day there are eight millions of negroes. They are here to stay. They will not be disfranchised. Through them Africa can be redeemed. They ought to be our fellow citizens in the kingdom of God."

The Rev. Michael Burnham, D. D., of Springfield, Mass., is quoted as having said to the students of Livingstone College, in an address, May 22, 1889, the following cheerful words: " As a people, you have had on you the eyes of the world,—all this nation. As a people, you have manifested the spirit and deeds of heroism, which can never be forgotten.

. . . .

From four millions, in a quarter of a century you have become eight millions, with schools established at many points; and the necessity is laid upon the hearts of the people of God in America, to educate and make Christians of eight millions of people."

At a recent meeting of Afro-Americans in Rochester, N. Y., Mayor William Carroll delivered the welcome address. To them he said: "Since my youth, I have aspired to see a race which was down-trodden come up and receive recognition as fellow-citizens. Forty years ago I was in St. Louis and saw how badly the escaped slaves were used. How awful it was for men to sell human beings! We are all descendants of Adam and Eve, and yet some people had the privilege of selling and buying others. Wicked act though it was, it was sanctioned by the law of the land. How much Providence has done for the colored man since 1850! He has been freed and made the equal, as to rights of citizenship, of the white man. The war of the Rebellion did this when the people of the nation declared in favor of freedom for all."

Hon. Geo. Raines uttered the following sensible words, at the same gathering: "This city has a record for kindness and liberality toward your race for many years, even extending back to the days when it was dangerous to advocate any rights for the colored men. In Rochester, the colored people have been people of character and ability. They have enjoyed with us all the benefits of living in this city, and have taken a fair share in the work and responsibility. It is therefore most proper that the delegates to the Afro-American league should be welcomed to this city. We are one with you in sympathy for the objects of your organization. We rejoiced with you when the barriers that held you down in former years were removed. We are glad to see you join the great mass of laboring people, working for the commercial greatness of the country. In your efforts to widen the field of your race, in diversifying the industries in which to participate, you will assist the material progress of the state." The reader will pardon us for not further indulging in these cheering expressions from our Northern friends. We wish to turn your face Southward and consider the men's view of us with whom the mass of us live. What our former masters have to say complimentary to us will be read with interest. We are satisfied that the Sumner, Garrison and Phillips spirit still pervades the North.

In the South, there is a considerable portion of the white population who are friendly to the Afro-Americans, and they are people of wealth and of the best blood. They are too intellectual and aristocratic to be so silly as to worry themselves about a people who are two hundred and fifty years behind them in the race of life. They believe in helping the Afro-Americans to a higher civilization and letting them climb the ladder if they will. Among these is the Hon. Joseph E. Brown, U. S. Senator from Georgia. In an address before the Senate, in advocacy of the Blair bill, the senator uttered these words: "A grave problem arises here for solution. They must be educated; but we are not able to educate them.

. . . .

During the period of slavery it was not our policy to educate them; it was incompatible, as we thought, with the relation existing between the two races. Now that they are citizens, we all agree that it is policy to educate them. As they are citizens, let us make them the best citizens we can. I am glad to see that they show a strong disposition to do every thing in their power for the education of their children.

. . . .

I confess I have better hopes of the race for the future

than I had when Emancipation took place. They have shown capacity to receive education and a disposition to elevate themselves, which is exceedingly gratifying, not only to me but to every right thinking Southern man."

The Hon. Gustavus J. Orr, LL. D., once School Commissioner of Georgia, gave a manly expression on the progress of the race, in an address before the Chautauqua Association, some summers ago, his subject being, " The Education of the Negro; his Rise, Progress and Present Status." Dr. Orr asserts—" They have been declared free; to this we most heartily consent. They have been admitted to all the rights of citizenship; in this we acquiesce. Our state constitutions and our laws have declared that they shall be educated. To bring about this result we will do all that in us lies."

We quote this to show the expressed will of the better class of white citizens to aid us in our education. Let us state here for the commendation of the South, that forty millions of dollars have been spent by the states in Afro-American education. Half of this amount has been donated by the North.

Bishop A. G. Haygood, decidedly the best friend to the black man in the South, says these laudable words in regard to his progress :

" The most unique and altogether wonderful chapter in the history of education is that which tells the story of the education of the negroes of the South since 1865. No people were ever helped so much in twenty-five years, and no illiterate people ever learned so fast." This tribute Bishop Haygood paid the Afro-American in Harpers' Magazine of July, 1889.

Mr. Lewis H. Blair, a wealthy and influential merchant of Richmond City, has written a work entitled " The Prosperity of the Sonth dependent upon the Elevation of the Negro." In this he speaks gloriously of the Afro-American and his development. He remarks: "When on Sundays we enter negro churches and behold large, well-dressed, and well behaved audiences, presided over by pastors of good standing and ability; when we observe their numerous benevolent societies conducted; when we enter their schools and see large numbers of obedient pupils diligently studying their books, and when in their high schools we see exhibitions of scholarship that would be creditable to the whites, with all their present and antecedent advantages, we must confess that here is an immense advance."

There are dozens, yea, hundreds, whose views are similar to these that have been quoted. These people behold every day, by contact and observation, the progress of the race, and they are always ready to commend us and bid us "go on."

(We will now deviate a bit from our stated topic, but the reader will indulge us in so doing, we trust, since he may be benefited by a knowledge of the facts we are about to state,—having briefly given which we shall return to the subject proper.)

The greatest progress made by us has been in the professions of teaching and preaching. This has been a sensible and manly step; since the education of the children depends upon good Christian teachers and divine instruction from competent preachers. A devout and well-trained preacher is necessary to a moral and virtuous people. The foundation for a legal or medical education must be laid by the pious and God-fearing teacher.

In 1889, there were 16,000 common schools in the South, taught by Afro-American teachers, and 1,000,000 Afro-American children attending such schools. There are now in the South 2,000,000 freemen who can read and write. The ministry is receiving many additions of brilliant and competent young men. The Conferences, Conventions, Associations, Presbyteries and Councils, will not admit men who are not trained for pastoral labors. In other words, they have severely shut down on ignorance in the pulpit. We have never seen an estimate of the value of our church property, but it is safe to say it would run up iuto the millions. In Lynchburg alone, Afro-Americans own church property valued at $75,000 or $100,000.

In almost every city of the South there are Afro-American physicians, from one to three or four in number. There are also many of them practicing in the North and West. These physicians are getting much of the practice of the race and also much of the white practice, where they show superior fitness. Many are growing wealthy, possessing property estimated at ranging from $20,000 to $95,000.

The Baltimore American states that there are two hundred and fifty lawyers in the United States, some of whom have a practice worth from $1000 to $3500 per annum.

The Afro-American's personal property in the United States is placed, at a close calculation, at $263,000,000: Texas, $20,000,000; Louisiana, $18,100,528; New York, $17,400,750; Pennsylvania, $15,300,648; Mississippi, $13,-400,213; South Carolina, $12,500,000; North Carolina, $11,010,652; Georgia, $10,415,330; Tennessee, $10,400,211; Alabama, $9,200,125. The other states range among the millions. *The New South*, alluding to these figures, states very confidently: "These speak volumes in themselves and show very plainly that this race problem is not such a difficult one after all. It needs only a little patience and forbearance on the part of those who come in contact with the question, coupled with fidelity to duty, and it will soon settle itself. Indeed, there would be no problem to settle. What constitutes the problem is the lack of these very things in so many of those who have to deal with the question, in one way or another."

The race has also furnished from two hundred and fifty

to three hundred authors of creditable volumes. If the authors of pamphlets were included, the list would be surprisingly large.

The reader is to understand that the number of teachers named heretofore does not include the many Afro-Americans who are now instructors, professors, and presidents, in our seminaries, colleges and universities.

We have feebly attempted to discuss that kind and lovable class of friendly white editors and individuals, from Maine to the Gulf. The next class which we wish to look at is the one which may be termed the unfriendly. To a certain extent, it is our impression that conscience would lead every being to a sensible and manly view of the race question; in other words, to a view of equality as to creation and susceptibilities. Especially is this the case with the class we are considering. In short, they recognize all that the first class does, only their prejudiced thoughts will not be guided by their consciences, on the one hand, and the fear of ostracism and non-support forbids an expression of what their consciences teach, on the other.

This half-friendly class of newspapers are supported by what they conclude to be a prejudiced community; and while the editor may be conscientious in his views, he is bound to meet the popular demand. He says a word, now and then, in favor of the black man, because his conscience is so greatly moved upon by a sense of right that he can not do otherwise.

This editor, again, is passingly polite to the gentleman of ebony hue in the office, and, to all intents and purposes, he possesses friendly feelings for the race; yet in his next paper you may see an editorial, in which he sends the Afro-American to the very courts of destruction. He will declare the Afro-American an inferior in the editorial; while in his sanctum, a while ago, he treated him as a gentleman and an equal. Personally, he knows the difference between a brute of the race and a gentleman, but editorially we are all alike, with not a particle of difference among us. This class of editors always carry, stamped upon their consciences, an editorial with the caption, "Consistency, thou art a jewel." Editors, with the above characteristics, prevail in the South.

There is a class of semi-friendly editors and individuals that inhabit the North. They profess friendship for the race, yet are always eager to injure us in the eyes of our Northern friends. They talk about "liberalizing sentiment." Some of the editors prate about the Afro-American being able to maintain himself unaided now; others that he is doing nothing with what the North has given him. They publish dispatches from the South, which always put the Afro-American in a bad light. In short, they are those who are ever anxious to parade the faults and fallacies of the race. If they demand equal justice for the Afro-American, it is in the hope of reaping a political harvest in the future. They parade an harmonious and mellifluous speech, like that of the immortal Grady in Boston, in 1889, in the hope of injuring the kindly relation of the Northern friend to the Afro-American.

The semi-friendly individual is he who accepts the teachings of the semi-friendly journal. There is a great number of such people, and they represent the average wealth and intelligence.

Let us now briefly pay our respects to the class of unfriendly editors and individuals. Let us see who they are, whence cometh their hatred to us, and what effect their unfriendliness has upon their brother in black.

This class is to be found prevailing in the South to an alarming extent, while the second class will be found in the majority, North. The third class of editors have only the race question to subsist upon. The editorial columns of their papers are forever filled with articles on some phase of the race question. They are more or less of an abusive and disturbing nature. They delight in advocating race emigration, mob violence at the polls, and the supremacy of one people over another; forgetting that wealth and intelligence will rule. The Afro-American knows he can't rule as yet, and does not desire to; so it is a waste of precious time to discuss the matter. These editors would be without a subject to write upon, if they were to let their hobby alone. Their littleness can be seen at once. It is the same class of "scribblers" whom *The Chattanooga Times* so completely condemns in the following editorial paragraph: "We believe these scribblers are responsible, in a great measure, for the existing discontent and defiant mood of the negroes, and we do not wonder that discontent exists. The negro is an impressionable creature, whose emotions, rather than perceptions and judgment, determine his moods and actions. It is not to be supposed that he will be content under the rude clamor raised in favor of his exclusion, first, from all rights and privileges heretofore granted him, and, finally, from the country where he was born and reared, and which his labor has enriched and is still enriching."

These editors also glory in encouraging lynch law, by publishing the press dispatches, under such bold captions as "SERVED HIM RIGHT," "THE GOOD WORK OF JUDGE LYNCH." The person lynched may deserve speedy punishment in that way, yet the better element of the press should encourage a respect for justice and the eternal principles of law.

It has been estimated that of the illiterate people of the South, at least a million are poor whites. Ignorance being a dangerous element in the white man, as well as the black, it is a wonder that they have not come together with a greater crash.

It is our impression that those who compose the ku-klux gangs, the regulators, and mobs for lynching, are, in the main, of this illiterate class, urged on by a few intelligent and prejudiced persons, who stand to see their fiendish work well done. The author is in possession of a private letter from the "Sunny South," that warrants this belief. Our informant exalts the better and liberty-loving whites in his section, and states that he was ordered to leave a district in which he was assigned to teach, by the chief of the regulators for that district who did not know the first letter of the alphabet.

There is much danger in this illiteracy among the whites and blacks, and serious conflicts may be looked for until each receives a Christian education. The great and good Bishop John P. Newman is very explicit on this point. He says: "The race problem is to find its solution in Christian education. In this is the defense of the rights of the manhood of the uneducated whites and the emancipated blacks. Their intelligence will disarm prejudice, and commend them to the respectful attention of all fair minded men. The preacher and the teacher will make the new South a glorious realization."

Bishop Andrews says: "The poor white man and the colored man are here to stay and to increase. If permitted to remain ignorant, they will prove the blind Samsons to pull down the pillars of our temple, and involve all classes in a common destruction."

Dr. J. C. Hartzell indorses the same idea, in an address before a white conference of North Tennessee. He offered as a solution of the race problem the education of the whites and blacks.

Summing up the whole matter as to the white man's view of our race, we think it safe to say that it is, in the main, of a commendable and sympathizing nature. Great work is being done in the North for us, while the South does not forget its duty. Virginia, alone, appropriates $300,000 a year to our common school education, beside $30,000 for our higher education.

Let us remember that we are not to win the victory on flowery beds of ease, or be swift in running the race. Let us be patient until we shall *en masse* win the prize of education, morality, complete freedom, and citizenship.

CHAPTER XXV.

RECOGNITION OF THE AFRO-AMERICAN AS A CONTRIBUTOR TO ANGLO-SAXON JOURNALS.

H AVING noticed the relation of the Anglo-Saxon and Afro-American newspapers, and the views of the different classes of Anglo-Saxon editors and individuals, we shall be pleased if the reader will go with us while we briefly consider the recognition which we receive at the hands of the Anglo-Saxon press as contributors and reporters. The recognition which is paid the Afro-American by the leading journals goes far to show what estimate is placed upon our ability as journalists. The white papers, as a general thing, will accept a contribution showing any thought, or that is an interesting item of news, provided the consent of the editor is diligently sought for on the part of the contributor. This surely can not be considered a recognition of the writer's ability, in a broad sense. Technically, it is, for the matter would not be published if it were not good; and so, in a measure, it is a recognition of the writer's ability. In this instance the old adage relating to the "cart before the mule," is very applicable; the effort seeks the newspaper, instead of the newspaper seeking the effort. The seeking of our efforts by newspapers is the recognition we desire to bring to notice.

"The greatest characteristic of a true-born journalist," says a writer, "is the aptness with which he can distinguish news, and the ability to clothe that news into appropriate and readable language." It need not be adorned with flowers and rhetorical flourishes, but the facts should be presented in a clear, easy style, so that there can be no danger of a misunderstanding on the part of any reader. It is our impression that we have many able to do this among our Afro-American people; yes, many endowed with that journalistic power, which, if cultivated by continual use and strengthened by constant reading and studying, will make them members of one of the greatest professions we have knowledge of.

In newspaper work, the Afro-American may regard it an honor to have any of his productions published in a white journal; he may regard it a favor, a compliment to himself and to his race; but how much more credit it would be to the race and to himself, were he employed upon the editorial staff of a metropolitan daily, or as a reporter for a large and widely-circulated white journal; or to be held in such estimate as to be asked by the leading magazines and dailies of the country for a letter, or a contribution on some stated subject. This we conceive to be the recognition which the ability of many of our journalists demands, but which only a few have received.

In what section of our country this recognition is accorded us, the reader will readily conjecture. There can be no dispute as to whether it comes from the North or the South, since it is so apparent it is from the North. We do not, however, receive full recognition in the North; for many young men, educated at Harvard or Yale, too lazy to work and afraid to come South, are employes of the hotels; whereas, in the South, if we are educated, we can get, at least, a country school to teach.

The fact that we are not accorded proportional recognition may be due to the relative difference in numbers and to so much competition. This, however, is not the issue confronting us. Grant that there is a difference of opinion as to the proportional recognition, we have the consciousness of knowing that we are recognized as journalists, and as contributors to Northern magazines, dailies, and weeklies. We have no such recognition in the South.

We have made an assertion which it becomes us to support. The reader of this volume has already learned that Mr. T. T. Fortune was upon the editorial staff of *The New York Sun.* He has furnished articles to the various metropolitan journals. In fact, he is accorded a place among the first journalists of New York. John S. Durham, lately appointed consul-general to the Republic of San Domingo, was associate editor of *The Philadelphia Evening Bulletin.* Robert Teamoh is on the editorial staff of *The Boston Globe.* J. Gordon Street and Miss Lillian Lewis are on *The Boston Herald.* Prof. W. S. Scarborough has time and again contributed to *The Forum, Harper's Magazine,* etc.

The American Baptist Publication Society has made a step in advance by recognizing the Afro-American Baptists as editorial writers upon *The Teacher.* Rev. W. J. Simmons, D. D., Rev. Walter H. Brooks, D. D., and Rev. E. K. Love, are among those thus complimented. The Methodist Book Concern has also recognized Afro-American ability upon *The Journal.* Rev. A. E. P. Albert, D. D., is one thus recognized. The press clubs and associations in the North have admitted Afro-Americans to membership. The white journals. from the Mason-and-Dixon line to the far North, are cognizant of the Afro-American's talent, in this direction.

In the South, some of the white journals have had Afro-American reporters. This has been the case with some of the papers of Baltimore, which have given us positions as space writers. Other cities have done likewise, among them Lynchburg and Petersburg.   But none of the large, influential Southern papers, such as *The Constitution* and *The News and Courier*, have as yet accepted us as contributors. It is true, that news items relating to some demonstration, such as a commencement, etc., are received occasionally.

It is for this reason, as much as any other, that the white man in the South does not really understand our true development. He does not read our race papers, and thus learn of our advancement, nor does he get the information from his own papers. He never goes into an Afro-American church or attends our literary entertainments, nor does he witness our home-life; therefore, he is left to conclude that all black people are like those he sees frequently arraigned before the magistrates and mayors of the town.

In many of the papers nothing is seen about the Afro-American, save his record in some court. Such is not the case in all cities, but it is in the majority of them. The Afro-American certainly knows more about his race than any one else, and for the more conservative Southern papers to give them recognition would go a long way in producing a just and fair opinion of us as a race.

After discussing the position of the white press, both as to section and its attitude toward the Afro-American press and people, it seems as though it must be very generally admitted that the greatness of America, and her continued development depend upon the unity of the press and the pulpit. In this fight, the cardinal points must certainly be unity of purpose and design. Our prejudiced friends should remember that the Afro-American is surely an important part of the nation, and that so long as the desire to keep him back gets the better of their desire for the country's progress, so long will the country, especially the South, be kept back. "In union there is strength;" therefore, a concerted action of the whole press is bound to bring progress, as well as "liberty and union, now and forever, one and inseparable."

CHAPTER XXVI.

THE FREEDOM OF THE PRESS.

NATURALLY, with all people, the freedom of speech and thought are cardinal principles to be devoutly wished for, and sought. Whether this freedom of thought is expressed through the instrumentality of the press, or by our vocal organs on the stump, pulpit or rostrum, it is nevertheless a dear and precious privilege that we cannot afford to abuse, but one that we should use in the maintenance of good and wise principles.

To no country is the freedom of expression by means of printed characters, or what is popularly known as the freedom of the press, more fully guaranteed and protected by the powers that be, than in our own United States and in England.

However, before discussing it in this wise we may be profited by a proper understanding of what we mean by the freedom of the press. Chambers' Encyclopedia defines it as the absence of any authorized official restraint on publication.

In other words, there is no law defining the direction of the press, or any expression of its opinion, so long as it conforms to right. The Britannica Encyclopedia on the freedom of the press gives this definition: "The free communication of thoughts and opinions is one of the invaluable rights of every man; and every citizen may freely speak, write, and print on any subject, being responsible for the abuse of that liberty."

It may be of interest here for us to still further consider the opinions on the freedom of the press. Lord Wynford says: "My opinion on the liberty of the press is, that every man may fearlessly advance any new doctrine, providing he does so with proper respect to religion and the government of the country, that he may point out errors in the measures of public men; but he must not impute conduct to them. The liberty of the press can not be carried to this extent without violating another equally sacred right, the right of character. This right can only be attacked in a court of justice, where the party assailed has a fair opportunity of defending himself. Where vituperation begins, the liberty of the people ends."

To the thoughtful reader, the entire measure of the freedom of the press can be readily comprehended from these opinions; but if not yet clearly understood, a consultation of the views of our martyred President, James A. Garfield, will probably serve the purpose. It was on account of this freedom that the Earl of Beaconsfield was proud of his identity with the press.

We have fully considered the freedom of this force; we may now observe the official protection the various countries offer it and whether the same liberty exists in all countries alike.

Long before the discovery of America the press was in operation; not, however, as a free and equal privilege of every one who wished to express himself through this medium. Certain authorities took hold of this way of expressing thought freely and held it within their grasp, and no one was allowed to publish or print on paper, without their consent. It also soon became subject to the censorship of the religion of England, especially on matters pertaining to Christianity.

After this the press passed into the hands of the crown, by mutual consent upon the part of the religious and secular powers who were the censors. There was a certain license to be paid for the publication of papers now, and only certain people were allowed to publish them. Those who did so unlawfully, were punishable by law. If caught, the presses were levied upon by an officer, who was known as "press messenger." In 1693 the censorship of the English press ceased to exist, and there has been perfect freedom of the press, with certain restrictions on publishers of libelous or criminal matter. That this freedom, in all respects, is the same as in the United States, the author is unprepared to assert.

The freedom of the press in our country is guaranteed by the Constitution, with a few restrictions, as every one conversant with our laws is aware. Article I of the amended Constitution says: "Congress shall make no law abridging the freedom of speech or of the press." The restrictions that are imposed upon persons, matter, etc., in the various phases of law, such as libel, copyright, and rights of a private character, are presumably imposed for the public good.

It is safe for us to say that in our own country the press has unlimited freedom. The restrictions put upon it do not limit its freedom, since they are imposed principally to suppress censure and abuse, and, as Lord Wynford says: "Where vituperation begins, the liberty of the press ends."

It goes without saying, that since the press is allowed perfect freedom in its expression of opinion, and since the Constitution licenses it by asserting that no law shall abridge its freedom, and since its editors have often large abilities, the greatest power imaginable attends its utterances.

The increased popularity of the English press, and its retention within the grasp of a few men for so long a time, was due to the discovery of its power as a political engine and in various other directions.

A high authority defines the power of the press in this language: "The press is an instrument well adapted for disturbing the functions of government, and committing injuries against reputation."

In the creation of sentiment there is not a force in all the land with sufficient power to array itself as an equal of the press. This is the whole power of the press in a nutshell. In what direction, for what cause, for and against whom is this sentiment created, are the various phases of its power. The press can elect a president of the United States; it can sink a public measure into oblivion; it can create wars; it can cause the destruction of a nation by creating public sentiment.

The ability and fitness of the press is the measure of a country's progress and of its power. It causes the country to develop, by publishing its resources. A unanimous suggestion of the press is followed by an equally unanimous action of the people. It can rear up and pull down; it can create and it can destroy. In fact, there is no speech or language in which we may express ourselves forcibly enough, to depict accurately the Herculean power of the press. It is a nation's great stronghold and defense. It is the popular teacher of every individual. In some way, it reaches into every household.

These last thoughts, coupled with the opinion of Lord Wynford on the liberty of the press, call to mind the fact that in our country, where all men are recognized as one people, the cannon mouth of the press, in many instances, is turned as a formidable enemy against a certain portion of this people. Remember the opinion of Lord Wynford, an Englishman of high culture, with much wealth and of royal blood, an editorial sire. Again, remember that principles and doctrines may be advocated, so long as there is proper respect for the government and religion. The inference is, that outside of this, there is no freedom of the press, but an abuse of the right extended to it.

Notice again that a creation of sentiment against the right of character is another abuse of its freedom and power, and that where censure, abuse, creation of strife, and the indorsement of unlawful measures begin, there the liberty of the press ends. Are all of our newspapers free from this abuse of their liberty? In the light of Lord Wynford's opinion, is any part of the press of our country responsible for the maltreatment of one people by the other, and a continued existence of prejudice? If "where vituperation begins, the liberty of the press ends," is there more vituperation than liberty exercised by a part of our press? Is the press accountable for any disregard of the law? Is it in its power to cause peace in every nook of our commonwealth? These questions, with many others that will naturally arise in one's mind, are presented for consideration.

Milton in his Areopagitica gives the true scope of the press, so far as every individual is concerned, when he said: "Give me the liberty to know, to utter, and to argue freely according to conscience, above all other liberties."

The press standing as one of the great safeguards of the nation should carry out the mission which the following lines so plainly portray:

> " Here shall the press the PEOPLE'S RIGHTS maintain,
> Unawed by influence, and unbribed by gain.
> Here patriot truth her glorious precepts draw,
> Pledged to religion, liberty and law."

CHAPTER XXVII.

THE AFRO-AMERICAN LEAGUE.

THE condition of the Afro-American in the Union, particularly in the South, as to protection of life and property, the lack of enjoyment of equal rights and privileges in every instance previous to and since 1887, made the demand for an organized effort of some character upon the part of the Afro-American to maintain and defend his rights a necessity. "What shall we do to save ourselves, and our people?" was a question of pressing importance to every one of the emancipated freedmen. The decision of Chief Justice Taney, which is remembered by the blacks with regret, and by many of the whites with pleasure, and the Southern policy of President Hayes, with the repeated declarations of Chief Executives and Congress to Afro-American delegations that they could not interfere with State rights, hence could do them no good, made the demand for race concentration greater and greater every day. The race leaders were put to their wits' end to devise some means which would lead to the accomplishment of their desire. From the first sitting of an Afro-American convention in Syracuse, N. Y., October 4th, 1864, to the present day, these grave questions confronting the race have been soberly and wisely considered. The question assumed prominence in the Syracuse convention by the attacks and jeers of some evil designing white men It was in thin convention that Hon. Frederick Douglass answered with telling effect some whites, who, after noticing the Afro-Americans passing to and from the hall, sarcastically asked— " Where are those d——d niggers going?"

At this convention the business committee, through its chairman, Rev. Henry Highland Garnett, D. D., reported " A Declaration of Wrongs and Rights;" these were nothing more than a parcel of resolutions introduced and passed. This precedent, once established, was devoutly clung to until 1887, when something tangible was laid before the Afro-Americans all over the country for their consideration and sanction.

Heretofore, resolutions had been introduced in convention after convention, and passed several national and state conventions, setting forth our needs, etc. These resolutions introduced and passed were delivered by delegation to the president and members of Congress, who gave them the following words of assurance : " Gentlemen, we appreciate your position; your case shall have proper consideration." This said, we heard no more.

This state of affairs the black newspaper fraternity decided could not longer exist; accordingly they began to think profoundly, and soon one of the number, Editor T. Thomas Fortune, aroused from his revery and brought from its depths the Afro-American League.

In *The New York Freeman* of August and September, 1887, Mr. Fortune published a series of articles, stating the cause for organization, the manner of organization, and the results sure to attend its efforts, if properly managed. These articles were considered the ablest treatise on the condition and remedy for race recognition ever published by a black man. The issue of September 10, 1887, contained the plan of organization. Several leagues were immediately organized, the first being that of Richmond, Va.

The author, having been forcibly impressed with the expediency of such an organization, read a paper in its interest (August 15, 1887,) before the New Era Literary society of Lynchburg, Va. The Afro-American citizens of the Union, though under oppression and desirous of relief, did not take to the organization, presumably on account of the lack of proper knowledge of it, as succeeding action proved. Thus it was not until Mr. William E. Matthews, LL. B., a prominent Afro-American banker of Washington, having been deeply impressed with the courtesy extended him while on a trip to Europe, and noticing the lack of such courtesies and the race restriction and discrimination on his return to America, addressed a letter to Hon. John M. Langston, M. C., in which he urged the organization of the Afro-American league; hence, the credit for the revival of the same belongs to Mr. Matthews, and accordingly *The Plaindealer* pays him the following tribute: " When the concentrated efforts of the whole race, acting through the agency of the Afro-American league, shall have secured to every man and woman of African descent the protection and justice enjoyed by all other classes of citizens, the name of William E. Matthews will be intimately associated with the history of this great movement."

The institution of the league was at once taken hold of with renewed strength by individuals of the race and by all of the Afro-American journalists, with a vim and a power known only to the newspaper man of firm and unflinching convictions. Every Afro-American editor, with quill in hand, took a decided stand for the league, proclaiming to the world—" Upon this rock I stand; all other is sinking sand."

The New York Age began a lively crusade, while *The*

Plaindealer of Detroit, Mich., issued a circular to the leading men, calling on them for aid. The response from these circulars was both satisfactory and encouraging. The *Plaindealer* publishes them under the caption—"Let us reason together."

Judge A. W. Tourgee, in his answer to *The Plaindealer*, said: "If Irishmen may organize, to aid in improving the condition of Ireland; or other nationalities among our citizenship, to perpetuate the tradition of the land of their nativity, I can not see why it is not only the privilege but the bounden duty of the only class of our citizens whom any one has ever proposed to deprive of the rights so readily conferred upon the alien, to organize for consultation and harmony of action in the maintenance of their lawful rights, in a lawful manner."

Prof. B. T. Washington said: "An organization of this kind, I am sure, can be made to serve a good end, if it can, in some way, be made to reach the masses of the colored people. Most of our conferences, conventions, etc., have reached only the mountain peaks, leaving the great Alpine range of humanity and activity below."

Other views were received from Hons. John R. Lynch, J. M. Townsend, Rev. J. C. Price, D. D., and a host of others. Suffice to say, the consensus of opinion was so satisfactory to *The Plaindealer*, it was led, editorially, to ask for a call, as follows: The success of the proposed national Afro-American League is almost assured; there remains but one preliminary arrangement to be perfected, and that is the call with the number of delegates to which each state is entitled. This should be made before new state organizations are effected, to save the expense of two state conventions. The consensus of opinion, as gathered from *The Plaindealer* from those in a position to represent the sentiment of their localities, is almost unanimous as to the need of such an

organization to exhaust every legal remedy to secure rights
which the Constitution guarantees. There is no question
that if the league be non-political, that we shall have
thousands of white men who will aid us in every material
way. The sense of justice, both North and South, among the
intelligent people is greater than a casual observer would
suppose. The agitation pushed so far has been productive of
rich, yet unexpected fruit already."

The New York Age said: "Interest in the Afro-American
league constantly augments. From all sections of the
country letters are received, asking for information upon
which the league should be organized. Leagues are springing
up at points so far apart as to indicate unmistakably how
extensively diffused and deep rooted the idea has become in
the minds of the people.

.   .   .   .

Let us have a national meeting. We submit in another
column the plan of organization published by us September
10, 1887, for the guidance of those who desire now to move
in the matter of organization, and we do so because the
correspondence from all parts of the country for information
as to plan of organization has grown so enormous as to be a
drain upon our time."

The following constitution was then offered by Mr. Fortune:

Sec. 1. Any person of the age of eighteen and upward
(without regard to race, color or sex) can become a member
of this league by subscribing to its constitution and by-laws,
and by the payment of the entrance fee and monthly
assessment of————.

Sec. 2. The objects of this league are to protest against
taxation without representation; to secure a more equitable
distribution of school funds; to insist upon fair and impartial
trial by judge and jury of peers, in all cases at law wherein
we may be a party; to resist by all legal and reasonable

means mob and lynch law, whereof we are made the victims, and to insist upon the arrest and punishment of all such offenders against our legal rights; to resist the tyrannical usage of railroad and steamboat and other corporations, and the violent and insulting conduct of their employes in all instances where we are concerned, by prosecution of such corporations and their employes in state and federal courts; to labor for the reformation of our penal institutions, where barbarous, cruel, and unchristian treatment of convicts is practiced, and to insist on healthy emigration from terror-ridden sections to other and more law-abiding sections.

Sec. 3. A general tax of $1. per annum on all members of this branch league shall be levied and conserved by the treasurer into the treasury of the national league, to carry out the objects set forth in Section 2.

Sec. 4. The objects of this league shall be conserved by the creation of a healthy public opinion, through the medium of public meetings and addresses, and by appealing to the courts of law for redress of all denial of legal and constitutional rights; the purpose of this league being to secure the ends desired by peaceable and lawful methods.

Sec. 5. This league is in no sense a partisan body, and no man shall be debarred from membership therein because of his political opinions.

BY-LAWS.

1. The name of this organization shall be the Afro-American League of—No.—

2. The officers of this league shall be one president, two vice-presidents, one secretary and two assistant secretaries, one treasurer, two chaplains, two serjeants-at-arms, and an executive committee of five, the officers to be elected (as the league shall determine.)

3. This branch league shall meet at—the first Tuesday in each month (or oftener, at the discretion of the league,) at

34

8 o'clock p. m., with open or secret meetings at the discretion of the league.

4. This branch league shall be subject to the laws hereafter made by the national Afro-American league.

With this published, and the rapid formation of branch leagues in many states, the desire for a national call grew greater and greater. The newspapers were loud in their demands, in response to which the following call was issued November 4, 1890:

To the Colored Citizens of the Republic: Being convinced that the time is ripe for the organization of the National Afro-American League, proposed by me two years ago, to successfully combat the denial of our Constitutional and inherent rights, so generally denied or abridged throughout the Republic, and being urged to do so by members of branch leagues all over the country, I, by these presents, issue a call to all the branches of the Afro-American League, and invite all clubs and societies organized to secure the rights of the race, to meet by their representatives in National Convention at Chicago, Ill., Wednesday, January 15, 1890, for the purpose of organizing a National Afro-American League; *the basis of Representation to be four delegates for every one hundred members, or one delegate for every twenty-five members*, constituting the branch league, club or society, desiring to co-operate in the movement for National organization.

Correspondence from all organizations desiring to join in this movement is requested.

Very respectfully,

T. THOMAS FORTUNE.

New York, November 4, 1889.

Concurring in this call:

ALEXANDER WALTERS of New York,

J. GORDON STREET of Massachusetts,

W. A. PLEDGER of Georgia,
ROBERT PELHAM, JR., of Michigan,
EDWARD E. COOPER of Indiana,
H. C. SMITH of Ohio,
JOHN MITCHELL, JR., of Virginia,
MAGNUS L. ROBINSON of Virginia,
J. C. PRICE of North Carolina,
JOHN C. DANCY of North Carolina,
THOMAS T. SYMMONS of the District of Columbia,
F. L. BARNETT of Illinois,
Z. T. CLINE of New Jersey,
VAN N. WILLIAMS of Alabama,
B. PRILLERMAN of West Virginia,
WILLIAM H. HEARD of Pennsylvania,
R. K. SAMPSON of Tennessee,
H. M. MORRIS of South Carolina,
JAMES G. MCPHERSON of Mississippi,
and others.

The reader will notice that this call is signed, in the main, by the young and progressive newspaper element.

The local leagues having been organized in various sections, delegates were elected to the national convention according to the direction of the call. The call for the convention was indorsed by *The A. M. E. Church Review*, in the following forcible language: "The interest and enthusiasm with which the call for a meeting of the Afro-American leagues in the several states to convene at Chicago, January 15, 1890, for the purpose of effecting a national organization, has been received by the race in every section of the country, is one of the most remarkable and significant manifestations of awakened manhood shown by the race since or before the war. The unanimity with which the people have responded to the call for national organization effectually disposes of the belief, long current and firmly rooted, that the Afro-American

was constitutionally incapable of grasping the potentiali-
ties of co-operation and of turning them to advantage. To
be sure, the great work to be done by the league remains
to be subjected to the crucial test of practical demonstration;
but, as a matter of fact, the victory is more than half assured
in all such efforts when large masses of men, widely separated
and differently circumstanced, begin to think in a given
groove, and to declare their readiness to move together as
one man, to accomplish a given result. That the race has
reached this point to-day, and will meet in convention to
perfect a permanent organization which shall put to the test
its capacity for intelligent and uncompromising contention for
absolute justice under the Constitution, marks a tremendous
advance in all the elements of strong, resourceful and
aggressive manhood."

In accordance with the call, the league convened in
Chicago, January 15, 1890, and was an enthusiastic gathering.
There were twenty-one states represented by a convention of
one hundred and forty-one delegates. A national organization
was effected, with Rev. J. C. Price, D. D., of Livingstone
College, president; T. Thomas Fortune, Esq., editor *New
York Age*, secretary; Lawyer E. H. Morris, Chicago, attorney;
and George H. Jackson, Esq., treasurer.

The object of the meeting was clearly and forcibly made
known when Mr. Fortune said: "We have met here to-day
as representatives of 8,000,000 freemen, who know our
rights and have the courage to defend them. We have met
here to-day to impress the fact upon men who have used us
for selfish and unholy purposes, who have murdered and
robbed and outraged us, that our past condition of dependence
and helplessness no longer exists." Thus the key-note was
sounded which united the clansmen.

The work of the league organization is a very thorough
and matured plan. It is divided into three sections, national

THE AFRO-AMERICAN LEAGUE.   533

state and local. The state organizations are subordinate to the national, and the local leagues are subordinate to the state. The object of the national league is the same as that of local and state leagues, only the national is pledged to support the local and state leagues in any way whetever in the carrying out of the principles set forth in Article II of the constitution for local leagues heretofore quoted. The means for accomplishing the ends of Article II is sufficiently provided for in Section 3 of the constitution.

The great and pleasing feature of the whole league is expressed in Sections 4 and 5. "A peaceable and lawful method" is to be pursued in contending for the objects outlined. It was argued by many that the league would be construed as an organized effort among the Afro-Americans for physical warfare. This idea is completely obliterated in the light of Section 4,—so much so, that the evil-designing papers which are always ready to question any thing planned for the good of the Afro-American, have not dared to raise such an issue. It was also argued by many that the purpose was to strengthen this or the other political power. This, Section 5 of the Constitution clearly settles.

Again, this section is strongly supported by the constitution of the national league, Article XIV, Sections 1, 2, and 3, which read thus: "This league is a non-partisan body, and any officer or member of the executive board attempting to use the league for individual purposes shall be expelled."

"Any officer or member of the league being elected to any political office, or appointed to the same, shall resign the office held by him in the league."

"The work of the convention was strongly indorsed by all of the white papers of Chicago, save *The Tribune*, also *The New York Sun* and *Rochester Democrat and Chronicle.* By the Afro-American press the league was indorsed unanimously. We append a few of the comments:

The national Afro-American league called at Chicago, Ill., last week, was well attended and laid the foundation for local leagues for the advancement of the rights and interest of the colored people throughout the country.—*Southwestern Christian Advocate.*

It is a good time for our people to occasionally formulate their grievances and appeal to the judgment and fair play of the American people. If it is possible at this stage of our advancement for our people to keep up a national organization, we are disposed to feel that the league has secured the best men we have for that purpose.—*Augusta (Ga.) Sentinel.*

The earnestness, unity and good will which pervaded the action of the convention, showed that all had come to the conclusion to take united steps in the direction of banding the race together for the purpose of working its own destiny. —*Pittsburg Spokesman.*

One of the grandest and most important organizations ever effected for colored people was completed and sent forth for the ratification of 8,000,000 of America's most industrious, yet most abused and misrepresented citizens.—*Lexington (Ky.) Soldier.*

The young men who assembled at Chicago went there to do their duty by the race. They succeeded admirably, displaying the nicest discrimination in the adoption of resolutions and exercising the most intelligent care in the selection of leaders.—*Philadelphia Tribune.*

The meeting was a representative body of the colored people of the country; and more than that, it was a coming to the front of an entirely new element, with new ideas, larger aims, and higher and nobler aspirations.—*Philadelphia Sentinel.*

These comments cannot fail to impress the reader that the league is meeting with popular favor.

Enthusiastic state organizations have been effected in New York, Ohio, and other states, while local leagues are being set up daily. In Ohio, state organizers have been commissioned by the state league to organize every township and city into a league.

Upon a recent meeting of the New York state league at Rochester, *The Democrat and Chronicle* said, editorially, the following words of commendation:

"The delegates from Afro-American leagues of New York state who have assembled in convention in this city for the purpose of forming a state organization, are a fine-looking, representative set of men, and their proceedings are marked by evidence of intelligent thought and an earnest desire to improve the opportunities which are offered in the commercial and intellectual world. The object of this league, as we understand it, is self-development and the creation of relations which shall be eventually beneficial to the members in the various enterprises in which they may engage. Necessarily, the beginning must be small; but it is a step in the right direction, which will have a strong tendency to stimulate self-respect and honorable ambition."

The national league has already begun its humanitarian work. In the case of Fortune vs. Trainor for ejection from the Trainor hotel of New York and false imprisonment, the league has indorsed Mr. Fortune in the suit for $10,000 damages, instituted in the courts of New York. The following eminent counsel have been retained by the league, through Mr. Fortune: Hon. J. M. Langston, M. C., T. McCauts Stewart, attorney for New York state league, Jacob Simms, Esq., New York City, and E. H. Morris, Esq., of Chicago, attorney for the national league. These able and efficient lawyers will defend Mr. Fortune's rights, which, in a measure, involve the right of every other Afro-American leaguer.

This unity of the race promises to be the best means yet

for securing the legitimate rights of the black man. It means to back resolutions and assertions with financial substance and intellectual power. The effort has been briefly referred to in this volume to prove to the reader that something is being done for the race by the Afro-American press. Is there one who will gainsay that the Afro-American press is not forging us to the front?

Contending for what he knows to be right and for what he believes to be the race's salvation, the Afro-American editor has thus far gained the merited "Well done." There is no one who can dare say that, with thorough aud compact organization, with trusted leaders, this scheme may not prove the salvation and redemption of the black man. The unanimity with which our Afro-American editors took hold of the scheme means more than the average man suspects. The author's impression is, that these editors, with their pens of warfare, mean to press every man of the race into line of battle for a peaceable and aggressive warfare. These gentlemen of the press recognize the fact that the public conscience must be quickened, in the light of human freedom and happiness. We are supported in this assertion by the words of one of our ablest and most experienced editors, probably the oldest man of our race now editing a newspaper, namely, Rev. Mr. White of *The Georgia Baptist*. Says he:

"The time has now come for the colored man to organize effectively in the South for his own protection. Our hope in this respect must be in the creation of a public sentiment by which the better element of white people in the South shall combine to put down lawless treatment of colored people. Still, we have not a word to say against any movement that tends to impress the colored men of the country with the necessity of combined effort for bettering the present condition of the race."

Another one of our ablest contemporaries, *The Indianapolis*

Freeman, gives some pertinent thoughts just on this point: "The organized protest of the representatives of nine millions of people against flagrant, unprovoked bloodshed and wrong must attract attention and arouse the intelligent, humane pulse and conscience of the nation and civilized world. That once aroused, light will begin to break upon the dense wilderness of hate and persecution by which the Afro-American is enveloped, and a way will be blazed for him, which, followed, must land him at the summit of complete American citizenship."

It seems the intention of the press to lay before every Afro-American this effort, which, in their judgment, is the best road to the goal. It is their intention that not an Afro-American shall be ignorant of the league and its purposes. It shall be so simple and plain, that " a way-faring man, though a fool, shall not err therein." This aggressive, yet peaceable manner of agitating is a commendable step, for the best sentiments of the people may be relied on to take the side of the right; and since the side of the right is the complete emancipation of the race from social, moral and political injustice, it is safe to say that the Anglo-Saxon, with whom we live and move, will some day, *en masse*, get on that side.

Then it is the business of the Afro-American to contend, to agitate; and it can be done in no more effectual way than through the league system. The press is determined ; let the people rally.

CHAPTER XXVIII.

THE ASSOCIATED CORRESPONDENTS OF RACE NEWSPAPERS.

IT is a fact not to be denied, that since the Afro-Americans compose a portion of the nation inhabiting the United States, and since what is done to the uttermost of one part affects the well-being of the other part, proper and reliable information from the nation's capital is desired by the Afro-American journals, as well as by any other.

Nearly all of the Afro-American journals prefer the most accurate information from Washington, and so the leading ones have enlisted the services of some very able correspondents. These organized themselves April 23, 1890, under the name of the "Associated Correspondents of Race Newspapers," for the purpose of furnishing data for papers, and to establish a better medium of communication from the capital with all Afro-American journals. The article of organization reads very significantly. It says: "The object of this Association is to form a more perfect union of the correspondents at the national capital, in any way identified with Afro-American journals or journalists, and to promote in every legitimate way the best interests of our race through the medium of the press."

Through the organized effort of this Association the race will, no doubt, be benefited a hundred fold. Already, the encomiums heaped upon the Association from the readers of those newspapers containing letters from its members are many. The Association seeks to come into communication with all journals; and the writer takes the liberty to say, that when all of our newspapers shall have obtained the assistance of the Association, they will add a very important feature to their journalistic pretensions.

The membership at present is forty; the papers represented, ten. The following able and influential gentlemen direct the affairs of the Association: Prof. E. L. Thornton, *New York Age*, president; J. E. Bruce, *Cleveland Gazette*, first vice-president; C. Carroll Stewart, *Indianapolis World*, second vice-president; C. A. Johnson, *Chicago Appeal*, recording secretary; B. C. Whiting, *Indianapolis Freeman*, corresponding secretary; R. J. Raymond, *Chicago Advance*, treasurer; C. E. Lane, *Knoxville Negro World*, manager.

Edward Loften Thornton, of *The New York Age*, the president of the Association, was born in Fayetteville, N. C., in 1863, his parents being A. G. and Elsie Thornton. They were well-to-do people; and it may be said that Edward came of a worthy and good parentage. He is the only boy of five children, and his life has been one of great credit to himself and people.

He began to attend school at the age of five years, and graduated from the state normal school at Fayetteville. Bishops J. W. Hood and C. P. Harris were among his first teachers. From this school he graduated as valedictorian of his class. He matriculated at Howard University in the fall of 1878, and was assigned to the junior preparatory class, and at once took the lead in his classes. He graduated from Howard as Bachelor of Arts in 1885.

Since graduation, he has been principal of Edgecombe

normal school, which position he resigned in 1889 to accept a position in the Census Department at Washington. He now holds a $1200 clerkship in the Record and Pension Division of the War Department.

While an able editor, he also ranks high among the orators of North Carolina,—that state of orators. He has made a splendid record as an orator. He delivered the first annual address before the Garrison Lyceum of Livingston College. He was the orator at the fifth annual fair of the North Carolina Industrial Association, held at Raleigh, N. C. He was the orator at the third annual fair of the Eastern North Carolina Stock and Industrial Association, held at Goldsboro, N. C.

He was president of the Edgecombe County Teachers' Association, and in 1888 was elected president of the Eastern North Carolina Stock and Industrial Association, and in this capacity conducted one of the most successful fairs ever held in North Carolina.

He began his first active newspaper work, as the Washington correspondent of *The Charlotte* (N. C.) *Messenger.* His letters to this journal attracted the widest attention throughout the country, and were generally clipped. During the summer of 1882, he edited that journal with signal ability. He was universally esteemed by his fellow collegians while at Howard University, and as an evidence of their esteem and a compliment to his ability they elected him editor-in-chief of the first and only college paper organized by the students. At the organization of the Associated Correspondents of Race Newspapers at Washington, D. C., he was unanimously elected president, and has filled the office creditably. He is now the regular Washington correspondent of *The New York Age*, a leading Afro-American paper, and his letters from the capital are read with interest and are one of the leading features of that deservedly popular and aggressive journal.

EDWARD LOFTEN THORNTON.

Mr. Thornton is quite a young man, and stands high in the estimation of the journalistic profession as a writer and thinker.

Charles A. Johnson, of *The Chicago Appeal*, the recording secretary of the Association, was born in St. Louis, Mo., April 4, 1865. His parents moved to Ironton, Ohio, when he was only seven years old, presumably for the benefit of better school facilities. He attended school regularly and graduated in 1882 from the high school of Ironton. After this he taught school in Ironton, It will be interesting to note that the admission of young Johnson into the high school of Ironton was the first opening of that school to Afro-American students.

While teaching school he learned the printer's trade, in the office of a white paper, *The Ironton Busy Bee*, and during vacation was city editor, and in winter, during the school term, he had control of the educational column of that paper. For two years he was local correspondent of *The Columbus* (Ohio) *Evening Dispatch*, and at other times the correspondent of *The Sentinel* and *Afro-American* of Cincinnati and of *The Globe* at Cleveland, Ohio.

In 1886, in company with Calvin W. Reynolds, since engrossing clerk of the House of Representatives of Ohio, he started *The Spokesman*, an Afro-American journal at Ironton; but like a rose blighted by frost from too early setting out the attempt failed, and *The Spokesman* became a thing of the past.

Going to Missouri in 1886, he taught school in Webster Groves until 1889, and while there was local correspondent for *The St. Louis Globe-Democrat*, and for *The Clayton Watchman*, both white papers, his work being devoted not to race news alone but to the public. He is now the correspondent of *The Chicago Appeal*, from Washington, where he is a clerk in the War Department.

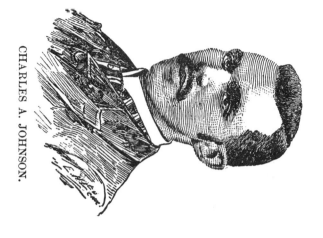

CHARLES A. JOHNSON.

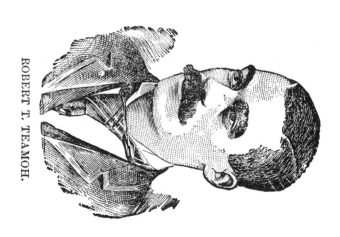

ROBERT T. TEAMOH.

Charles Carroll Stewart, of *The Indianapolis* (Ind.) *World*, second vice-president of the Association, was born at Annapolis, Maryland, February 28, 1859. In 1862 he moved with his parents, who were free-born, to Washington, where his father, Mr. Judson Stewart, engaged in business. He is a descendant of one of the best Afro-American families of Maryland. His grandmother was a Bishop, while his grandfather was a Jackson. These families are well known throughout Maryland and in Washington as large owners of real estate.

Mr. Stewart was educated in the public and private schools of Washington, and there studied dentistry for several years. When but sixteen years old he had a desire to see more of the world, and in 1874 an opportunity to do so presented itself to him. He accepted a position with a party of surveyors that were to go to Panama to survey and lay out the plan for cutting the Panama canal. During this trip he visited Central America and the Southern seaport towns of the United States.

On his return, he was apprenticed at ship-building by Hon. George M. Robeson, then Secretary of the Navy. Serving at this over a year, he resigned. Since then he has traveled extensively in the United States, Europe, and some parts of Africa and Asia. In 1876 he was with the relief party that went to Custer's aid, at the time he was killed in the Black Hills. During the time intervening since his travels.abroad, he has held several government positions at Washington, D. C.

In 1882 he began his work in journalism as business manager and publisher of *The Washington* (D. C.) *Bee*, which, under his astute management, rose to popularity. He severed his connection with *The Bee* in 1884, to take the position of Washington correspondent of *The Baltimore Vindicator*.

In March, 1884, he organized a national news bureau, which was composed of representatives of the Afro-American

CHARLES CARROLL STEWART.

press from nearly every state in the Union. He was made president at its organization, and succeeded himself twice, despite repeated declinations. He has since corresponded for *The Richmond* (Va.) *Planet, Cleveland* (Ohio) *Gazette, The Arkansas Sun, Indianapolis World,* and other papers. His writings are often quoted by leading white and black journals. As a writer, he stands well among the first; as a politician, he is a shrewd and tireless worker.

He was the only Afro-American representative of the press invited to the dedicatory exercises of the Washington monument, in 1885. Great courtesy was shown him in the reporter's gallery of the House, on that occasion, as well as at the exercises at the base of the monument, over which President Arthur presided. He is at present an employee at the government printing office, and has many warm and personal friends among the leading white and black Republicans.

In April, 1890, he was elected second vice-president of the National Associated Correspondents of Race Newspapers, which Mr. Stewart aims, as far as he is concerned, to make a powerful combination.

Benjamin C. Whiting, of the *Indianapolis Freeman*, corresponding secretary of the Association, was born at Frederick City, Md., and received a common school education. He was employed upon a farm, at intervals, until the age of ten. Although too young to assist in the late civil war, it so filled him with patrotism that, at the age of sixteen, he enlisted in Company M, 10th United States cavalry and was sent to Fort Still, Indian Territory. The Company commander, Capt. S. I. Norwood, paid great attention to young Whiting, and it was here that he got a fair knowledge of book-keeping, under Captain Norwood's instructions. During the first year, he was reappointed corporal ; and afterwards he became quartermaster sergeant to the regiment, during the campaign of 1876 against the Comanche Indians, and was engaged in several

BENJAMIN C. WHITING.
(See Page 546.)

DAVID C. CARTER.
(See Page 545.)

547

battles. He was personally mentioned in the company's orders for his gallantry at the battle of Cheyenne.

In 1879, at the expiration of his term of service (five years) he retnrned East and entered the grocery business. Later, he accepted a position as restaurateur, in connection with the United States senate. After three years' service he was appointed to a position in the treasury department. A few years later, he entered the service of the Pullman Palace Car company and remained in their service until receiving an appointment in the United States repair shop, post-office department, at Washington.

He has always been prominent in the organizations for the benefit of his race ; also, in the order of Odd Fellows. He represented his lodge at several general conventions. He is a member of P. G. M. Council, No. 44, Patriarch No. 42, and chairman of the Hall building committee, an advocate for his lodge, a member of the county Republican committee of Washington county, Md., the John Sherman Republican league, the Afro-American league, and many other charitable and benevolent associations. He has been on the staff of *The Washington* (D. C.) *Bee* for five years..

Mr. Whiting is a genial gentleman and has many warm friends among both white and black. As correspondent for *The Freeman*, he has been an exceptionally faithful and successful worker. His letters are newsy and pointed, and his efforts have been the means of introducing *The Freeman* into many new quarters. He was recently elected corresponding secretary of the Associated Correspondents of Race Newspapers, and is filling the office very fittingly.

The sketch of the first vice-president, John E. Bruce, will be found in another chapter of this volume. Messrs. Raymond and C. E. Lane entered the arena of journalism as correspondents, respectively, of *The Indianapolis World*, *St. Louis Advance* and *Knoxville Negro World*. They have filled their places with ability. The letters of each of the A. C. of R. N. are looked for and admired. There is much within the grasp of this Association to make our press a unanimous agitator for the rights and privileges of citizens. The hope is, that the organization will not lose sight of its far-reaching possibilities, but with a keen perceptive faculty may seize every opportunity which will redound to the favor of the race and the perpetuity of our free institutions.

REV. J. ALEXANDER HOLMES.

(See Page 140.)

(NOTE. These portraits inserted have been received too late for insertion in connection with the text concerning them.)

DANIEL A. RUDD.

BISHOP JABEZ PITT CAMPBELL, D. D., L.L.D.

BISHOP JOHN M. BROWN, D. D., D.C.L.

ALEXANDER CRUMMELL.

REV. BENJAMIN F. LEE, D. D., L.L.D.

HON. MIFFLIN W. GIBBS.

INDEX.

APPENDIX.

REV. T. J. SMITH, JOHN M. CLARK, AND A. C. DELPHY, A. B.
OF THE " BROAD AXE," PITTSBURG, PA.

Rev. T. J. Smith, better known as Broad-Axe Smith, was
born at Sandy Lake, Mercer County, Pa., on the 29th, of
December, 1838. He entered the ministry at the age of
seventeen, and was connected with the Underground Rail
Road. He embarked on the sea of Journalism with twenty-
five cents in cash, borrowed money, in 1881. He first
published the " *Colored Citizen* " and as it seemed the *Colored
Citizen* had no rights which its subscribers were pecuniarly
bound to respect, it went to the bottom of the sea. Shortly
afterward he started the daily *Wasp* but got stung so badly
that he had to hew it to death with a Broad-Axe. The
Broad-Axe still lives, hewing to the line, letting the chips
fall where they may.

John M. Clark, one of the proprietors and publishers of the
Broad-Axe, was born at Drummonsville, Ontario, May, 1850.
He started life as a butcher, and afterward went into the
horseshoeing business. He is now a contractor and one of
the editors of the *Broad-Axe*.

J. C. Delphy, A. B. was born in Pittsburgh, Pa., on July
14, 1857. Shortly after graduating from Howard University,
Washington, D. C. in 1881, he became correspondent for the

THE AFRO-AMERICAN PRESS.

Cleveland *Gazette.* In 1882, associated with E. A. Knox, J. A. Strickland and R. Day Jr., he edited the Pittsburgh *Commoner.* Since 1884 he has been associate editor of the *Broad-Axe.*

Rev. C. H. Payne, D. D. of the "Pioneer," Huntington, Va.

Christopher H. Payne was born near the Red Sulphur Springs, Monroe County, Virginia, since West Virginia, September 7, 1848.

His father was free born and mother was set free by her owner. The subject of this sketch was their only child. He was left fatherless when about three years old.

His mother, having received the rudiments of an English education from her master, became the anxious teacher of her little son. He learned rapidly and had read through the New Testament when he was but ten years old.

While quite young, he married Miss Ann Hargo, a lady who has clung to him in adversity as well as honored him in prosperity.

They have born to them two girls and four boys, all of whom they are striving to educate.

They own a comfortable home in Hinton, W. V.

Mr. Payne's first lessons in school were learned in a night school in Charleston, W. V.

From this place, he returned to his home where he engaged in farming. He often plowed with his arithmetic between the plow handles and would commit a rule to memory while his horse was resting. He would sometimes walk two or three miles at night, to get some one to solve a problem for him.

In a short time; he began to teach in the public schools of Mercer, Monroe and Summers counties.

CHRISTOPHER H. PAYNE.

He became a Christian in 1875, was licensed to preach in 1876, and fully ordained to the gospel ministry in 1877.

In September of the same year, he entered the Richmond Institute, now the Richmond Theological Seminary.

Here by dilligent study and Christian deportment, he won the implicit confidence and universal respect of students and teachers. He graduated from this school in 1883.

He belongs to the Baptist denomination and has, more than once, been appointed to address the national assemblies of white Baptists in their annual meetings.

The church at Coal Valley of which he has been pastor six years is one of the most flourishing in the State of W. Va.

In 1885, he established the West Virginia Enterprise, at that time the only weekly negro journal in the state.

While editor of this paper, he did much toward creating a sentiment in favor of negro equality before the law and in arousing in many an ambition to buy land, build homes and educate themselves.

He had been correspondent to the *Virginia Star*, the *Richmond Planet* and to several other negro as well as to white journals.

In 1884, he was alternate to the national republican convention that met at Chicago, and in 1888, he represented the Third Congressional District of West Va. in the convention that nominated Hon, Benjamin Harrison for President of the United States,

He has been tendered the nomination for the state legisla-lature and has been a member of the congressional committee for six years.

He exerted such an influence in the politics of W. Va. in 1888, that Gen. Goff and other leading men in the state, credit him largely with success of the republican party in that year.

The Republican executive committee the entire state ticket and many other prominent men, in the state and out, endorsed him for minister to Liberia in 1889.

In 1890, the State University of Ky. conferred upon him the degree of D. D.

In the same year he was appointed deputy collector of internal revenue, with his office in the custom house, Charleston.

It was solely thought the efforts of Dr. Payne and Prof. Byrd Prillerman that, in 1891, the legislature of W. Va. established the Mechanical and Agricultural College in Kanawha County for the benefit of the negro youth of the state.

It was in this year that he became one of the proprietors of the *Pioneer*, a weekly journal printed in Huntington with Rev. I. V. Bryant editor in chief.

As a preacher and an orator he is dignified and eloquent.

As a writer, he is polemic, his diction pure, and his style graceful.

He is unquestionably, the most representative negro in the state of W. Va., both in religion and politics.

REV. JEREMIAH R. B. SMITH, TIME HONORED AFRO-AMERICAN CONTRIBUTOR.

The subject of our sketch, the Rev. Jeremiah R. B. Smith, was born in Brooklyn, N. Y., on the 19th day of April, 1846. His father, whose name was Francis Smith, was a native of Virginia, and, though born a slave, became a portrait painter and after attaining his freedom practiced his art with credit in New York City. His mother was a native of New Jersey, likewise born a slave: her maiden name was Sarah Jane Van Dorn.

J. R. B. Smith commenced his schooling in his native city, and was a pupil of Professor Wilson who taught what was known as the "Willoughby Street School." At the death of his father he removed to Buffalo, where he attended the Vine Street School. Among his teachers were Professor Pierce and Theodore Hawley, the latter now Bishop of Hayti. He afterward removed to Toronto, and while there studied at the Model Grammar School and the Upper Canada College. At the age of 13 he became noted as a writer on *The Toronto Globe*, then edited by the Hon. George Brown. Later on he became a contributor to *The Anglo-African*, a paper devoted to the interests of the negro race. While in Canada he was actively indentified with all matters pertaining to the amelioration of the condition of fugitives who sought refuge under the British flag.

Though young, he took part in the meetings of, and met with John Brown, the hero of Harper's Ferry.

At the age of 16 he returned to the United States, and settled at Rochester, N. Y. In the same year he entered the army and served for three months in the 54th Massachusetts regiment. Being discharged therefrom in consequence of his being under age, he afterward enlisted in the 27th regiment of the United States colored troops, which was organized at Delaware, Ohio. He became a non-commissioned officer of the same, and was wounded in an engagement in front of Petersburg on July 30, 1864; he was also engaged in the battles of Chapin's Farm, Strawberry Plains, and Cold Harbor, and took part in the battle of Fort Fisher, and in the capture of Wilmington. He was then, with others, detailed by General Terry to organize the first Sunday School among the freedmen of that city.

At the conclusion of the war he was identified for a time with the freedmen's work, and in 1866 resumed his studies

REV. JEREMIAH R. B. SMITH.

at Lima, N. Y. Among his teachers there were the Rev. De Witt Huntley, and William Whiting. He concluded his studies under the directions of the Rev. J. Q. Galpin at Naples, N. Y. While at Naples he became attached to the staff of *The Democrat and Chronicle* of Rochester, N. Y., and was noted as a brilliant writer under the nom de plume of "Neopolitan."

. Mr. Smith subsequently spent some time in the South, and in 1872 became permanently connected with affairs political in the State of New York. He was delegate to the Colored Men's State convention at Troy, N. Y., and was chosen by that party delegate to the Republican State convention which was held at Elmira. He was largely instrumental in having the Rev. William F. Butler sent as a delegate-at-large to the Philadelphia convention which renominated President Grant. Under the direction of the National and State committee he took an active part in the political canvass of that year. In 1873, together with William H. Johnson, a prominent citizen of Albany, he was active in securing the passage of the Civil Rights Bill in New York State. In 1876 he served as first vice-president of the Colored Men's State committee, of which the Rev. Henry Highland Garnett, D. D., was chairman, and spoke largely in New York and other States.

In 1877 he became the editor of *The Western Echo* in Bath, N. Y., which paper was the organ of the colored men of the State. While at Bath he rendered efficient aid in the establishment of the Soldiers' Home in that place. The office of *The Echo* was afterward removed to Utica, N. Y., and in 1881 the paper was located in Brooklyn, with an office in New York City, and did good work in assisting the election of Hon. Seth Low as Mayor of Brooklyn.

In 1882 Mr. Smith joined the conference of the African M. E. Zion's church and is now a prominent member of the same.

In 1887 he was elected, and in 1888 re-elected, chaplain-in-chief of the G. A. R. department of New York, being the first of his race to hold an elective position in that organization. He attained the distinguished honor of being the first of the colored race to offer prayer in the Senate of the State of New York. His re-election to the above chaplaincy in 1888 was by an almost unanimous vote in the face of many competitors.

In the same year at Columbus, O., he was elected president of the association composed of officers and men who served as colored troops, which position he still holds.

He continues to be a writer for the press, being a contributor to *The National Tribune* of Washington, D. C., *The G. A. Journal* of New York State, *The Star of Zion* — the organ of Zion's connection — and other papers and periodicals devoted to the advancement of the race.

Mr. Smith is yet a comparatively young man, enjoying the companionship of a charming family. He married in 1867, at Rochester, Miss Rachel Murphy, a sister to the wife of Charles R. Douglass, son of the race orator, Fred Douglass. He is a talented man, a fluent speaker, and believes in the future of his race with strong faith.

C. E. YARBORO, ESQ., EDITOR THE SOUTHERN APPEAL.

C. E. Yarboro the talented, thrifty and enterprising young editor of *The Southern Appeal*, published in Atlanta, Ga., was born at Louisburg, N. C., October 17, 1863. His father was a blacksmith, his mother a seamstress. He is their only child. He is one among the natural born Afro-American newspaper men of this country. His manly independence, his polished boldness in expression and his deep reasoning on matters commanding public thought have made for him a

C. E. YARBORO.

national reputation both commendable and meritorious. He was educated at Shaw University in Raleigh, N. C., and was for a time private secretary to the president of the university. After five years services as teacher in the public schools of North Carolina and special correspondent for several race papers, he moved to Georgia and established *The Southern Appeal* of which he is editor and proprietor.

The Southern Appeal is a bright newsy weekly and reflects credit upon its sprightly management. Its Democratic advocacy has made it one of the most popular negro journals in the South and Editor Yarboro has made it a paying institution. Though only 28 years of age, he is a power in the cause which he has espoused. Our journalism would be without a prominent personage if he should sever his connection.

FREEDOM'S JOURNAL.

"RIGHTEOUSNESS EXALTETH A NATION."

CORNISH & RUSSWURM, Editors & Proprietors.

NEW-YORK, FRIDAY, MARCH 30, 1827.

[VOL. I. No. 3.

MEMOIRS OF CAPT. PAUL CUFFEE.

Being now master of a small covered boat of about 12 tons burthen, he hired a person to assist as a seaman, and made many advantageous voyages to different parts of the state of Connecticut and when about 25 years old married a native of the country, a descendant of the tribe to which his mother belonged.—For some time after his marriage he attended chiefly to his agricultural concerns, but from an increase of family he at length deemed it necessary to pursue his commercial plans more extensively than he had before done.—He arranged his affairs for a new expedition and hired a small house on West-Port river to which he removed his family. A boat of 18 tons was now procured in which he sailed to the banks of St. George in quest of Cod-fish and returned home with a valuable cargo. This important adventure was the foundation of an extensive & profitable fishing establishment from Westport river, which continued for a considerable time and was the source of an honest and comfortable living to many of the inhabitants of that district.

At this period Paul formed a connexion with his brother-in law Michael Warner, who had several sons well qualified for the sea service, four of whom have since laudably filled responsible situations as Captains and first mates. A vessel of 25 tons was built, and in two voyages to the Straits of Belisle and Newfoundland he met with such success as enabled him, in conjunction with another person, to build another vessel of 41 tons burthen in which he made several profitable voyages. Paul had experienced too many disadvantages of his very limited education, and he resolved, as far as it was practicable, to relieve his children from similar embarrassments. The neighborhood had neither a tutor nor a school-house. Many of the citizens were desirous that a school-house should be erected. About 1797 Paul proposed a meeting of the inhabitants for the purpose of making such arrangements as should accomplish the desired object. The collision of opinion respecting mode and place occasioned the meeting to separate without coming to a conclusion; several meetings of the same nature were held, but all were unsuccessful in their issue. Perceiving that all efforts to procure a union of sentiment were fruitless, Paul set himself to work in earnest and had a suitable house built on his own ground, which he freely gave up to the use of the public, and the school was open to all who pleased to send their children. How gratifying to humanity is this anecdote! and who that justly appreciates the human character would not prefer Paul Cuffee, the offspring of an African slave, to the proudest statesman, that ever dealt out destruction among mankind?—About this time Paul proceeded on a whaling voyage to the straits of Belisle, where he found four other vessels completely equipped with boats and harpoons, for catching whales. Paul discovered that he had not made proper preparations for the business, having only ten hands on board and two boats one of which was old and almost useless. When the masters of the other vessels found his situation they withdrew from the customary practice of such voyages and refused to mate with his crew. In this emergency, Paul resolved to prosecute his undertaking alone till at length two other masters thought it most prudent to accede to the usual practices as they apprehended his crew, by their ignorance might alarm and drive the whales from their reach and thus defeat their voyages. During the season they took seven whales: the circumstances which had taken place roused the ambition of Paul, and his crew: they were diligent and enterprising and had the honor of killing six of the seven whales; two of these fell by Paul's own hands.

(To be Continued.)

PEOPLE OF COLOUR.

I have had three objects in view in thus going into the examination of the nature of slavery as a legal institution. In the first place I wish it to appear that the relation between the master and slave is a proper subject of legislation. It is a conventional right and depends entirely upon the laws.—as the laws create it, they may modify, enlarge, restrain, or destroy it, without any other limitation than is imposed by the general good. It is not so much a right of property, as it is a legal relation; and it ought to be treated as such.

The second object was, to relieve slave-holders from a charge, or an apprehension of criminality, where in fact, there is no offence. There can be no palliation for the conduct of those who first brought the curse of slavery upon poor Africa, and poor America too.—But the body of the present generation are not liable to this charge. Posterity are not answerable for the sins of their fathers, unless they approve their deeds. They found the blacks among them, in a degraded state, incapable either of appreciating or enjoying liberty. They have, therefore, nothing to answer for on this score, because they have no other alternative, *at present*, but to keep them in subjection. There is nothing so de- [illegible] by our principles, to the acknowledgment of guilt, in that which we at the same time believe to be absolutely unavoidable, and in which therefore, it is impossible really to feel self-reproach. Our southern brethren have high ideas of liberty.

There is nothing so calculated to make men restive under command, as a habit and love of commanding others. Upon their own principles, they have been forced to acknowledge even the existence of slavery, in any shape, as criminal. They have therefore concluded that as heavy a curse hung over the present generation for continuing slavery, even when it is plainly unavoidable, as over the last for introducing it. The consequence has been, that those who seriously bewailed the evil, have folded their arms in despair; and those who regarded only their own gratification, expecting to hear the curse at any rate, have taken the desperate resolution, "Let us eat and drink, for to-morrow we die." But the principle is preposterous, and the conclusion incorrect. A Christian *may* hold slaves, and exact their services, without any occasion to feel a pang of self-reproach *merely on account* of his holding slaves.

The third object aimed at, was to fasten the charge of criminality on the very spot where such a charge will be; and where it ought to be felt; and where alone reformation is practicable. There are no duties, without corresponding rights, and no rights without corresponding duties. While it is the duty of the slave to submit himself to his own master, so long as the laws of his country make him a slave, it is his right to be protected, *by the laws*, in the enjoyment of life, health, chastity, good name, and every blessing which he can enjoy consistently with the public welfare.—And on the other hand, masters and legislators should feel, that subjection itself, in the best circumstances, is a sufficient calamity; and that the yoke ought to be made as light as possible. Christianity enforces this dictate of sound reason.* "Thou shalt love thy neighbor as thyself," is as much the law between master and slave, as between any other members of the human family. This is so obvious, as to appear almost like a truism. And yet this is the very thing that has always been lost sight of, among slave-holders. It has been wholly disregarded, in our own nation. Here is the point to be debated, and settled. This is the ground for fastening the charge upon our whole nation. The law of God requires that all the provision should be made *by law* which the public welfare will admit, for the protection and improvement of colored subjects, as well as white subjects. *And this has not been done.* We cannot free ourselves from this charge, by pointing to the comfortable mud or even *brick* cabins, the warm jackets and shoes, and the abundance of corn and salt, with which the slaves are furnished.—We are travelling out of the record, by comparing their situation as regards food and lodging, labour and health, with that of the labouring peasantry in the old despotisms of Europe. We do not answer to this indictment, unless we either plead guilty, or show that our *laws*, our customs our modes of thinking and acting, recognise the humanity of the blacks. We must show that their rights are acknowledged, their protection secured, their welfare promoted; and that, in every particular, excepting that of involuntary servitude and its *necessary* attendants, they stand upon the same ground with their masters.—When this is done we shall feel no guilt on the subject. We shall fear no divine vengeance. We may hope to enjoy the favor of our merciful heavenly Father. But this is not done. I think I may venture to assert, that most of the slave-holding states, neither the laws, nor public opinion, secure to the slaves any of the privileges of humanity. Nothing more is done for them, in *kind*, than is done for the domestic beasts; and nothing more in *degree*, except as they are a more valuable species of property, and are recognised, to some extent, as possessing rational faculties. Let the contrary be shown. I say that of all that kind of provision, which goes to purify and elevate the character, and to create in the subject affection and confidence towards the government, every trace and track is completely excluded. The culture of their minds, the preservation of their morals, their instruction in the only religion which can make them good servants, happy neighbors, and hopeful heirs of eternal life, every thing of the kind is guarded against, by the *laws* at least, even more studiously than the abuse of their persons, and the destruction of their lives. Whatever is attempted for their improvement, is done by individual effort, and in direct violation of the laws. Here is our guilt; our full, dark, unmitigated guilt. It is the guilt of our nation. We in the non-slave holding states, do not feel it as we ought. But we cannot wash our hands, until we can safely declare, that we have done every thing we can, by public and private efforts, to remove the injustice. We have not done this. Comparatively speaking nothing has been done. The Colonization Society has indeed made a beginning, and done as well as could be expected. But I ask how long it will probably be, before that institution can dispose of 30,000 blacks in a year, which is only the *present* annual increase? Until they can do this, the number must be continually increasing. Indeed, I do not believe our southern brethren, in general, intend to do any thing more than to provide a sort of *safety valve*, by this Society, to serve as an outlet for their free blacks and supernumeraries. In our country, acts of the legislature are to be taken as to the expression of the public feeling, on all great subjects.—Towards the blacks, the language of each successive legislature has been, "Our fathers made your yoke heavy, but we will add thereto; our fathers chastised you with whips, but we will chastise you with scorpions." Something must be done, to avert the fearful consequences.

We cannot expect any efficient measures to be adopted spontaneously in the slave-holding states. The natural effects of slavery, upon the morals, industry, population, strength, and elevation of character, of a state, are so destructive, and it produces so much vexation, trouble and danger; the necessity of it is so very questionable; and its advantages are so trifling, compared with its evils, that we should naturally expect that those who are embarrassed with it would be solicitous about nothing else, than how to be delivered from the curse. But it is not so. The people are so wedded to their habits, and so fond of exercising unlimited power, and so many of their comforts seem to depend upon slavery, that we cease to wonder, at not finding any thing done by them towards improvement. I quote the language of Mr. Clarkson, the great friend of the blacks. "Their *prejudices* against the slaves are too great to allow them to become either impartial or willing actors in the case. The term *slave* being synonimous according to their estimation and usage, with the term *brute*, they have fixed a stigma upon their blacks, such as we who live in Europe could not have conceived, unless we had irrefragable evidence upon the point.—What evils has not this cruel association of terms produced? The West Indian master looks down upon his slave with disdain. He hates the sight of his features, and of his color; nay, he marks with distinctive opprobrium the very blood in his veins, attaching different names, of more or less infamy to those who have it in them, according to the quantity which they have of it in consequence of their pedigree, or of their greater or less degree of consanguinity with the whites.—Hence the West Indian feels an unwillingness to elevate the condition of the black, or to do any thing for him as a human being. I have no doubt, that this prejudice has been one of the great causes why the improvement of our slave population *by law* has been so long retarded; and that the same prejudice will continue to have a similar operation, so long as it shall continue to exist. Not that there are wanting men of humanity among our West Indian legislators. Their humanity is discernable enough when it is to be applied to the *whites*; but such is the system of slavery, and the degradation attached to slavery, that their humanity seems to be lost or gone, when it is to be applied to the *blacks*. Not again that there are wanting men of sense among the same body. They are shrewd and clever enough in the affairs of life, where they maintain an intercourse with the *whites*; but in their intercourse with the *blacks* their sense appears to be shrivelled and not of its ordinary size. Look at the laws of their own making, as far as the blacks are concerned, and they are a collection of any thing but—wisdom."† If these remarks are not applicable to the slave laws of our own states, let the contrary be shown.

* See Ep. vi. 5, 9. Col. iii. 22. iv. 1.

† "Thoughts on the necessity of improving the condition of the slaves, &c. with a view to their ultimate emancipation," p. 10, 11.

(To be Continued.)

CURE FOR DRUNKENNESS.

In speaking, on a former occasion, of the remedy for intemperance proposed by Dr. Chambers of this city we expressed ourselves with a considerable degree of caution. As it is a subject of great importance to the community, and one on which they ought to be explicitly and accurately informed, we have within the past week spent more than one whole day in making a personal investigation into cases where the remedy has been applied, and into the nature of the medicine, in the hope of coming to a full and satisfactory conclusion. The result of our enquiries will be seen in the sequel.—*N. Y. Obs.*

The remedy is not the same with that proposed by Dr. Loiseau of New-Orleans: or if it is, the coincidence is unknown to Dr. Chambers. They have had no manner of intercourse on the subject, and are entire strangers to each other. Dr. C. has been in possession of the secret, in its essential principles, for a number of years.

The medicine is taken in liquor:—that of which the patient is most fond, is usually preferred. It is not unpleasant to the taste, as we have ascertained from those who have taken it, and still more accurately, from having tasted it ourselves.

In its operation it is powerful, but not dangerous. It usually operates as a cathartic, and also as an emetic; but not always in both respects. In all cases nausea is produced.

There are three modifications of the medicine; adapted to the peculiar habits of the patient and inveteracy of the disease. Of course it is important, in making application for persons at a distance, to state these particulars as definitely as possible. In the mildest form, we are told by Dr. C. that it fails of curing in about four cases out of twenty. Resort is then had to the other modifications.

In almost every instance, more than one dose is necessary. The greatest number of doses which have been taken in any case which we have examined, is seven or eight. The cure is generally complete in the course of a single week.

Before being mingled with the liquor in which it is to be taken, the medicine subsists in two forms—as a liquid and as a powder. The former is of a red color, the latter of a light brown, in this form it can be forwarded through the PostOffice, in letters containing the proper directions.

Dr. C. has had the generosity to offer it to the poor *of this city* who are unable to make any compensation, gratis. To others the price is not extravagant considering the nature of the remedy, and is varied in some measure according to the circumstances of the individual.

It has already been applied in a large number of cases; in only two of which so far as known to Dr. C. has it failed of effecting a cure, unless prematurely relinquished.

We have conversed with two respectable gentlemen, entirely disinterestedly which have had opportunity to witness its effects on a large number of individuals, and it is their decided opinion that it is a real remedy.

Several persons of good standing in society